04/03
49.40

To Destroy a City

To Destroy a City

Strategic Bombing and Its Human Consequences in World War II

Hermann Knell

DA CAPO PRESS
A Member of the Perseus Books Group

Published by Da Capo Press
A Member of the Perseus Books Group
http://www.dacapopress.com

Copyright © 2003 by Hermann Knell

Typeset and designed by K & P Publishing

Cataloging-in-Publication data for this book is available from the Library of Congress.

ISBN 0-306-81169-3

Da Capo Press books are available at special discounts for bulk purchases in the U.S. by corporations, institutions, and other organizations. For more information, please contact the Special Markets Department at the Perseus Books Group, 11 Cambridge Center, Cambridge, MA 02142, or call (617) 252-5298.

First edition, first printing.

1 2 3 4 5 6 7 8 9—07 06 05 04 03

Printed and Bound in the United States of America.

Contents

Part Three
THE EFFECT AND EFFECTIVENESS OF
STRATEGIC BOMBING

ABBREVIATIONS

ACPS	American Commission for the Protection and Salvation of Artistic and Historic Monuments in War Areas
AFSHRC	Albert F. Simpson Historical Research Centre, Montgomery, Alabama
AWDP	Air War Division Plan
BC	Bomber Command
BA	Bundesarchiv, Koblenz
BBC	British Broadcasting Corporation
BCWD	Bomber Command War Diaries
BEF	British Expeditionary Force
BMA	Bundesmilitärarchiv, Freiburg
HE	High Explosive
HMSO	His/Her Majesty Stationary Office
IAF	Independent Air Force
KAGOHL	Kampfgeschwader Oberste Heeresleitung, bomber squadron German Supreme Command
LC	Library of Congress, Washington, D.C.
LMF	Lack of Moral Fiber
LW	Luftwaffe
MEW	Ministry of Economic Warfare
MP	Member of Parliament
NA	National Archives, College Park, Maryland
NSDAP	Nationalsozialistische Deutsche Arbeiter Partei
NWAAF	North West Army Air Force

ORB	Operational Record Book
PRO	Public Record Office, London
RA	Regia Aeronautica
RAF	Royal Air Force
RFC	Royal Flying Corps
RN	Royal Navy
RNAS	Royal Navy Air Service
SHAEF	Supreme Headquarters Allied Expeditionary Force
SOAG	Strategic Air Offensive against Germany
ToT	Time over Target
USAAF	United States Army Air Force
USTAAF	United States Tactical Army Air Force
VE	Victory in Europe Day
VJ	Victory in Japan Day
WWI	World War I
WWII	World War II

ACKNOWLEDGEMENTS

The writing of this book would not have been possible without the generous and intensive assistance of many people and institutions. It is my pleasure and duty to thank them here.

The collection of information and data started in libraries. The West Vancouver Library with its excellent computer system and its supportive staff was the beginning. In particular I want to thank Mr. Steven Williams who performed miracles in obtaining relevant titles through inter-library loans. From West Vancouver, I moved on to the libraries of Vancouver, the Royal Roads Military College, the University of British Columbia, the New York Public Library, the Bundeswehr Library at Dresden, the Würzburg University Library, and the Air University Library on Maxwell Air Force Base at Montgomery, Alabama. A special thanks goes to Mrs. Silvia Geissler at Dresden who dug up many publications of great value. The staffs of all the libraries supported me and my work and helped me to find my way through the reference and computer systems. My sincere thanks go to them.

Simultaneously, I visited archives, where again the staffs and the reference systems offered enormous help. It started at the Bundes Militär Archiv at Freiburg, Germany, where Mrs. Scholl and Mr. Moritz steered me onto the most efficient path for archival research. There followed many visits and weeks of studies at the Stadtarchiv and Staatsarchiv at Würzburg, the Public Record Office in London, the Bundes Archiv at Koblenz, the Humboldt University Archiv in Berlin, Stadt and Technische Hochschule Archives at Darmstadt, the National Archives of Canada in Ottawa, the Library of Congress in

Washington, D.C., the National Archives at College Park, Maryland, and the Albert F. Simpson Historical Research Centre on Maxwell Air Force Base, Montgomery, Alabama. Of particular help was Mrs. Ann Webb at the AFSHRC. My thanks to her and the staffs of all the archives.

In collecting information I enjoyed the help of relatives and friends as my daughter Eva, my brother Dieter, and Messrs. Klaus Voss and Bruno Walther and Mrs. Helmes and Mrs. Siebert.

Once I had produced the manuscript I had friends review and edit it. I am grateful for the improvments made by Messrs. George Sharp, William McCorquodale, Philip Pinkus, and Patrick Taylor.

Mr. Leon Krawczyk helped me in recording the illustrations.

At times it was hard work but the help of all the people mentioned above made it possible.

— Hermann Knell
October 2002

PREFACE

Many books have been written about aerial warfare since its start in World War I, with authors who are historians, academicians, commanding officers, and airmen. The subjects cover fighter combat, reconnaissance, tactical and strategic bombing. There are accounts of personal experiences, biographies of flying aces, complete histories of campaigns, and in many books an evaluation of the circumstances of the fighting from the technical and historical points of view. The books published on strategic bombing cover its questionable success, its use by the military, and its appalling consequences for civilians. Up to World War II the sufferings of civilians under this method of warfare were acute, but by comparison with what happened after September 1939, relatively small. It was in World War II that bomber raids were flown in ever-increasing numbers causing the deaths of more than 1 million civilians who could not defend themselves.

International literature has many books on the bombings of Hiroshima and Dresden, generally considered the most destructive that ever happened. Little has been written about Nagasaki, or the worst raid in terms of human losses, the Tokyo raid of 9-10 March 1945. Many people think that Dresden and Hamburg were the most destroyed cities in Germany. But the British and U.S. bombing surveys prepared after World War II tell us that Wesel, a city of 25,000 inhabitants, Wuppertal-Elberfeld with over 400,000 inhabitants, and Würzburg with 107,000 inhabitants, were 97 percent, 94 percent, and 89 percent destroyed, respectively. They were the

1

three most ravaged cities in Europe. Yet one has to search intensely beyond the local libraries to find any publications on these particular human tragedies.

The books written about bombing are either strongly pro or strongly con. There are books telling us what happened, why it happened, and how it happened. Few go in their analyses beyond the immediate period treated and the background of this warfare. Few books explain why strategic bombing was often used as response to other forms of warfare, such as naval blockade or as retaliation for perceived enemy transgressions. In the endeavor to trace the political, economic, and military background of strategic bombing and its distasteful offspring, area bombing, one cannot find a conclusive published reasoning. The British historian Geoffrey Best laments the fact and asks how much longer one must wait for an appraisal of the origins and development of strategic bombing.[1]

To come to terms with the subject of strategic and area bombing we need a debate. Books such as Ronald Schaffer's *Wings of Judgment*, which covers the American bombing in World War II, form a partial basis, although the author says his presentations are bound to stir controversy.[2] An international conference was held at the *Militärgeschichtliches Forschungsamt* (Institute of Military History), Freiburg, Germany in 1988 at which many renowned historians presented papers on "The Conduct of the Air War in the Second World War." Strategic and area bombing were extensively covered. The head of the institute expressed hope that the publication of the proceedings would contribute to an objective analysis.[3] One wonders whether it could, because many prominent authors/historians were not present.

There is a psychological need to forget and a moral obligation to remember. There is the human desire to forgive and the ethical necessity to warn of a possible repeat of the disaster. There is above all still great public interest in the subject with the hope that historians can arrive at a verdict. Either condemn it and have the courage to pronounce the perpetrators of it, politicians and military, guilty, or accept it as a fact of modern war, inhuman but unavoidable.

The human suffering of both the bombed on the ground

and the bombers in the air must be brought into focus. Why could it all happen and why was it implemented beyond all humane considerations? Why was Würzburg, a city in southern Germany, destroyed beyond any military necessity and, above all, why is so little known about it?

Based on personal experience and considerable research this book tries in small measure to fill the gap in this literature. It is meant to contribute to a better understanding of strategic and area bombing. It is meant to honor the victims, both the civilians and the air crews, who lost their lives. It is meant to fulfill the same purpose as Hoito Edoin's book *The Night Tokyo Burned* which offers an understanding of the worst air raid and is dedicated to the U.S. airmen and Tokyo citizens killed.[4]

INTRODUCTION

In Europe the Second World War had come to an end. It was May 1945 and for any German citizen living in the devastated, conquered, and politically extinct Third Reich the future looked bleak. Very bleak indeed. The war had ended with a crescendo of fighting, killing, destruction, and the arrival of the victorious Allies. The dictatorial regime of the last twelve years had evaporated and the place was calm, and above all there were no more air-raid sirens howling day and night. During the day you saw no more of the contrails of the high-flying silvery U.S. bombers; nor did you have to watch out for the low-flying, disaster-spewing fighter bombers. At night there was no more droning of British bomber formations, no sky markers, no flak, and above all no more fear during the day or night that your community would be the target area of these aircraft.

Peace had returned and there was no more obligatory black-out at night, but life was far from peaceful. A whole nation was paying for what its government had done to neighboring nations, to the whole world, and to its own people.

For myself, a young man in his late teens, excused from serving in the Wehrmacht (German Armed Forces) because of the aftereffects of polio and, therefore, at the end of the war living in my parent's home, there seemed little hope. It was early April 1945 and we were surviving in a one-room garden shack on the outskirts of my home city of Würzburg. We had been bombed out, or dehoused, as it was euphemistically termed by British Royal Air Force commanders. We had lost the apartment we had lived in with all its contents, except a few pieces we had crammed into the garden shack a few weeks before.

My father's two businesses were ashes and twisted lumps of machinery.

Yet we had to consider ourselves lucky, as compared with other victims of the bombing war, and the stream of refugees expelled from the eastern states of Germany. We had a place to stay, inadequate as it would have been under normal conditions, we had some clothes, and we had put some food supplies into the "Gartenhaus." We each had a bicycle and even more important we had a small hand-pulled cart. All of our immediate family had survived the war and the bombing. Compared with others—Würzburgers, Germans, and Europeans in neighboring countries—we had not been uprooted, we knew where we belonged, and our safety net was still there. But the place had to be rebuilt, which at the time seemed a hopeless task. There were no radio and newspapers. We had no water and no electricity. That Roosevelt had died, that the German Wehrmacht had unconditionally surrendered, and that the war in Japan was still going on, we found out only by word of mouth.

The first few weeks after the raid of 16 March 1945 were occupied with extracting from the basement of our flat and the basements of destroyed houses of friends or the still-intact houses of friends in the suburbs, the goods and chattels we had stored there. Not all the things we had relocated survived the raids. But one was glad to dig out any piece and put it on that most valuable handcart to pull it the many kilometers to our abode. Then there was the drudgery of securing the daily necessities. The water came from a well two kilometers away, where one had to line up about an hour for a pailful. Food was hard to come by and when there was some, many people had no money to pay for it. There were no pay envelopes, as all commerce and industry were disrupted, and there were no banks from which to withdraw savings.

But after a few months the tap outside the shack delivered some murky water, the power returned for a few hours a day, some food became available, and life in general improved marginally. Over the precious small radio we had saved we could now hear our new master's voice and after many more months there appeared even the odd newspaper.

The news was anything but cheerful. It was filled with accounts of German atrocities, news of the war in the Far East, the statements of the Potsdam Conference, and orders from the military governments of the Zone of Occupation one lived in. It was the communiques of the Potsdam Conference that depressed me most. Germany was to be spared the Morgenthau Plan, but the agreements between Truman, Churchill/ Atlee, and Stalin did not bode well for a young German who had his life ahead of him.[1] The government of Germany was to be taken over by the Allied Control Commission, which would act as supervising body of the military governments of the four Zones of Occupation. There were to be reparations, restrictions on all aspects of life from travel to education, and reductions in industry, such as only a few thousand cars per year for all Germany i.e. no hope for the dream of a young man to ever own one. But at least we were not all to be castrated, as Roosevelt and Morgenthau had tried to convince each other was a measure to secure eternal peace.[2] The country was not to be reduced to farming only, although the major German farming areas were to be handed over to Poland; the German inhabitants were to be expelled and resettled in the remaining part of Germany. Even Würzburg, destroyed as it was, and the surrounding areas, overcrowded with dehoused citizens as they were, had to accept a quota of refugees. The arrival of these unfortunate people, who had to leave behind everything, and many of whom had died in transit, caused new and additional hardships.

The months that followed were harsh. There was little food, little fuel to keep warm, and above all there seemed no future. Yet by January 1946 the Würzburg University reopened by the grace of the local military governor. It offered courses to complete high school matriculation. For me that was great until one Sunday afternoon in March while I was walking through the rubble filled streets, an American army truck took aim at me, ran me over deliberately and left me there with a broken leg and other smaller bones broken. The truck never stopped and it was some time before people who had gathered around me stopped a passing U.S. Army jeep, whose driver reluctantly brought me to the Luitpold Krankenhaus in the outskirts of the city. What had happened to me was not unusual as I learned from one of the men with whom I shared the hospital ward. He had been shot in the head by a U.S. trooper and survived. These things happen in war especially under foreign troop occupation. It had happened to a young man in Poland in the early 1940s. He was run down purposely by a Wehrmacht vehicle and left. The man became Pope John Paul II.

My quest for an education was temporarily interrupted. My broken leg healed, though crudely, and by fall 1946 one local high school was allowed to reopen by the military government. I could obtain my matriculation, which I needed to enter a technical university to become an engineer as I had decided on long before.

Conditions improved further and you could start to think that maybe there was a future after all. Food, fuel, clothing, anything down to a pound of common nails was rationed or required a purchase permit from some sort of government agency. But at least with some luck, some bartering, and lots of patience one could acquire most of the necessities of life. Electric power had been restored to the livable houses in the outskirts, even to our "Gartenhaus." A newspaper appeared, irregularly first, but then at least once a week.

From the paper and the radio we were informed that we were all really a bad bunch. Toward the end of the war the Goebbels propaganda had told us that we were bad because we were not sacrificing ourselves enough to win the war the Nazis had brought about. Now we were being told that we had done too much to support that evil Nazi war, and that collectively we were guilty.

The biggest Nazis were brought before the War Crimes Tribunal at Nürnberg. Volumes of books have been written about that event and to this day expert opinions differ about the justification and the legitimacy of it all. The victors had intended to call the Kaiser and other German military commanders into the dock at the end of World War I. The Compiègne Armistice of 11 November 1918 states that. The Versailles Peace Treaty signed in June 1919 did not elaborate about it any further. This time the Allies were not to make the same mistake again. Germany's armed forces had unconditionally surrendered and the very short Reims surrender document of May 1945—compared with the lengthy Compiègne document of November 1918—and the Berlin surrender document of 8 May 1945 made it clear that the Allied Supreme Commander could order any measure.[3] Hitler, the Reich president and chancellor or Führer, as he was called, was dead. Before his suicide he had installed Admiral Dönitz, the famed commander of the U-boats, as president and Joseph Goebbels as chancellor. But the latter had also committed suicide. Legally speaking, based on common international law, there was a German government, theoretically in charge of the country, its people, infrastructure, armed forces, etc. But based on the unconditional surrender the Allies took the political leaders prisoner on 23 May 1945,[4] issued an international declaration that the German government ceased to exist on 5 June 1945 and that the Allied Control Commission had taken over.[5] That was the end of the Third Reich at the federal level. Since at the provincial and local levels the leaders had also been staunch Nazis, they were sent either to the converted Nazi Concentration and POW Camps or went into hiding. From May 1945 the Allied Military Government, as conceived at the Conference of Yalta, was the government of Germany. And what a mess they made of it!

One of the few things they could agree on was to bring all war criminals to trial. There was a need to punish the crimes that had been committed. In the Far East and in Europe, on the high seas and in the air, acts had been committed that called for retribution. The legal basis for prosecuting was and has been there since the Hague, Geneva, and other conventions. I have read many publications on the war crime trials but found little reference to these conventions. It would appear that the legal basis for Nürnberg became an ad hoc undertaking, defined after the fact.

The fallen leaders, irrespective of what they had done to other nations, had forfeited the trust of the German people. They had been constitutionally elected in 1933, but through shams and abuse of constitutional power had established themselves as dictators. They had not only brought disaster to other nations, but to the Germans as well. Their punishment from that standpoint alone was amply deserved.

But by looking at the mass graves and the rubble of my hometown I felt that the leaders responsible for the bombing war should also be made accountable. I decided then and there that I would dig into this bombing. I knew little about it then and all its implications but I was going to study it, and as history is normally written by the victors, I as a vanquished would put down what I thought about it.

I planned to write the facts, that the Luftwaffe had bombed Warsaw, Rotterdam, cities in Britain, Belgrade, Stalingrad, and many other places; that the RAF and the USAAF had flattened my hometown when there was no more military necessity for it. I would dig up the facts and pillorize the planners, leaders, and men who executed it all. These people should have also been in the docks, if not at Nürnberg then at least in The Hague in front of the International Court of Justice.

About twenty-five years before retirement, in the mid-1960s, I picked up again on my original thoughts. My family and I were living in England and on my way to work on the train from Brighton to London I saw grown-over bomb craters next to some of the railway bridges. The area around St. Paul's Cathedral was full of new buildings. I read books such as Arthur Harris's *Bomber Offensive,* and every time I visited my old hometown in Germany it looked more rebuilt and as a matter of fact better than before its destruction. My interest was rekindled and I began to study the subject. The books I read were, of course, all of the type written by the victors. They glorified the raids and in many cases did not even attempt to justify the campaign. The more I read, the more I became convinced that there was room for some writings from the vanquished. But there were constraints. I had to make a living and I was working for years far away from my home base in Canada.

Not until the mid-1980s did books appear, albeit most of them still written by the "victors," that threw a more critical light on the bombing subject. There were books by Germans which castigated the Luftwaffe for what it had done, but in typical German self-flagellation, were easy on the bombing of

Dresden and Hamburg. The worst air raid ever, in March 1945 on Tokyo, I only learned about one year before writing these lines. More books have appeared since 1980, but still there are gaps of knowledge. Some of these gaps can be covered when more closed files at the Public Record Office at Richmond outside of London will be available; others, when scholars have the time and money to study now available Soviet archives.

It became clear to me with the study of available literature that I was facing a number of problems: Despite the multitude of books published in the last fifty years and the masses of documents available in archives, there is still much research needed to gain an objective view; composing something as a "vanquished," as I had thought of in 1945, would be unfair and not objective; many books have been written on the subject, but most seem to be in essence either praising the wisdom and results of area bombing or condemning them; interpretations can be rather biased and many books leave out facts which would not support the biased view (similarly, I found that quoted documents have been interpreted to suit the authors' views which brought me to the conclusion that I may have to look up some documents myself and then arrive at my own interpretation); few authors went into the background of area bombing—the political, economic, and military implications as to why this disaster culminated in World War II; and that I could contribute personal experience and detailed knowledge of one of the worst examples of area bombing.

These thoughts went through my mind and my attitude toward the subject changed. In the more than fifty years since it happened I have come to the conclusion that what is needed is an objective assessment. I have long given up the idea of castigating the perpetrators of bombing on both sides of the two world wars. Or condemning the bomber crews or the civilians who mistreated and often even killed downed flyers. It was war time. People were guided by patriotic fervor and were convinced that they were right, the enemy down to the last citizen wrong, and that even God was on their side.

The bomber leaders were soldiers and all acted in the best tradition of their profession. A soldier's duty is to protect his country and defeat the enemy. There are international agreements and there is a code of ethics, all of which define the conduct of war. Yet war is not merely a matter of fighting. As Clausewitz, the German military philosopher wrote in the early nineteenth century, war is the continuation of diplomacy by other means. In other words, there are political implications for war. War costs money and any responsible soldier leader will attempt to defeat his enemy at the least possible cost.

I came to the conclusion that, if at all possible, I would see both sides of the bombing war—the victor's and the vanquished's. The fact that World War I ended over eighty years ago and World War II over fifty years ago, had to influence my writing. There was no point in regurgitating old hatreds and misunderstandings that mankind cannot possibly be proud of. What happened was bad. Both sides committed acts which history has since condemned. The bombing wars from 1914 to 1945 are now history. Terrible history at that. Whether historians prove that the bombing, killing, maiming, and destructions did not win the wars, or whether respected military leaders in their memoirs prove that the bombers brought victory and above all quick and economic victory, is in my opinion not the point. And mankind must learn from history. Clausewitz may be correct in his theorem, but he does not say what happens when the military have run out of war. Peace is the continuation of war after the military leaders have done their job and have run out of ideas and means to carry on. In the end the enemies have to live with each other again. There will be interactions again, foes become allies and even friends and the best thing for continued peace is to forgive and try to understand the other side. For me it is, therefore, far more important to understand why it all happened than to point a finger and pillorize people and events. It has become history and let us learn from it.

Obviously we have not done that yet. The bombings in the Korean War, the Vietnam War, and the numerous smaller conflicts since 1945 have continued to make the bomber aircraft a weapon well-liked by the military. Worse, the ballistic missiles of the great powers, pointed at large population centers indicate that nothing has been learned from the misery between 1914 and 1945. On the contrary, the killing of masses of people, mostly innocent civilians, has become the envisaged ultimate modern warfare. Fortunately there were enough responsible civilian leaders on both sides of the Cold War to prevent Armageddon. International agreements have been signed providing for the destruction of some of these ultimate weapons. But the technology will always be available.

I do not think that Bomber Harris should be condemned. His decision in the morning hours of 16 March 1945 to send Mosquitos and Lancasters of No. 5 Bomber Group over Würzburg that night has affected me among thousands of others. His decision caused me personal loss and pain. In the years immediately after 1945 I was ready to prove that there was a war criminal who got away. But as the years have passed, so has my pain and the loss has passed into history. So has Air Chief Marshal Sir Arthur Harris. I now want to know why it all happened. What were the reasons behind it? I might wish to judge, but I cannot and do not wish to condemn. The case is too complex. History will be the judge, but the verdict will have to wait, because the jury is still out. My interest in the subject is to show how a controversial weapon affected individuals and what the many reasons and justifications were for putting hundreds of thousands of civilians on both sides of these wars to the sword. What led to the destruction of Würzburg?

Part One

Würzburg

*"Like Phoenix it burned, died and
then rose from its ashes."*

1

WÜRZBURG AS TARGET

Würzburg, a city of just over 100,000 inhabitants halfway between Frankfurt and Nürnberg, was the target of Allied bomber raids a number of times in World War II. The first one happened during the night of 21-22 February 1942, when a seemingly lost RAF bomber dropped its load. The last one occurred on 31 March 1945 when the U.S. Army Air Force flew bombers and fighters over the city for about seven hours.

Yet the raid that caused the overwhelming damage and which as such was one of the more effective ones of the Allied bomber campaign against Germany, occurred during the night of 16-17 March 1945. Mosquitos and Lancasters of the RAF Bomber Command unloaded tons of incendiary and high-explosive bombs that night. The results in pure ice-cold statistics were: 89 percent of the city was destroyed, an estimated 5,000 civilians were dead, 90,000 people had lost their homes, and, last but not least, one center of occidental culture was a pile of rubble.

The disaster of Würzburg and the experiences of its citizens were described in a few books published in small editions after the war. They make bone-chilling reading. None of them have been translated into English. However, books by British authors Martin Middlebrook, David Irving, and Alexander McKee give the English-speaking reader a chance to relive similar tragedies that befell Hamburg and Dresden.[1]

Obviously, Würzburg, a town in the heart of Germany situated on the Main River, had suffered from a well-planned and executed military operation. Why was it necessary to destroy it

Würzburg

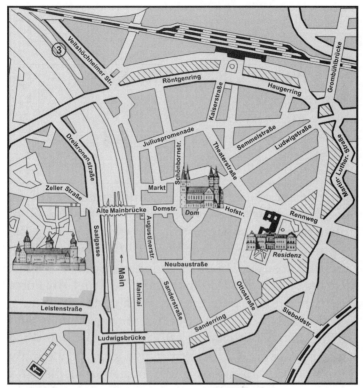

Inner
City

1. Area of marshalling
yard, Koenig & Bauer
factory, transformer
station, new harbor

2. Area of military
barracks

3. Old harbor

Environs

completely in March 1945, less than two months before the fighting of World War II stopped in Europe and only two weeks before the U.S. Army was at its western gates? War is a terrible thing and logic that would satisfy both sides of a conflict rarely enters its course. To me personally, present during all but one raid visited upon the city, there seemed at the end of World War II no logic in the destruction and killing. And today, after years of reading and studies, I still do not understand why Würzburg was destroyed.

STRATEGIC AND NON-STRATEGIC ASSETS
OF WÜRZBURG

Studying a map one cannot escape the observation that Würzburg was and is a city of importance for German infrastructure. Rail lines from east to west cross with lines from northeast to southwest and from northwest to southeast. Long before World War II there also existed a net of first-class roads which intersected at Würzburg.

Also the Main River, on which Würzburg is situated, is an important inland waterway. King Ludwig I of Bavaria had the Main-Donau Canal dug in the nineteenth century to allow small barge traffic from Rotterdam to Bucharest. Between 1933 and 1939 dams with large locks were constructed along the Main upstream as far as Würzburg. These structures with their Rhine barge-size locks allow the transport of mass goods. Today, thanks to a new canal, the Rhine connects to the Donau via the Main.

The dams or *Stauwerke*, as they are called in Germany, also generate electric power. They all have turbines which have been feeding into the superbly laid out and operated German national electric power grid.

In addition to the strategic assets which nature had given Würzburg and which industry, commerce, and government had developed over the years, there were, in World War II, a number of installations which could not be denied a certain war potential. As part of the German national electric grid there was (and still is) a large transformer station in the northwestern outskirts. There also was a small steampower station in the inner city which supplied outmoded DC current at 110 Volt.

Because the city was a rail center there were and are railway installations: A central station for passenger traffic north of the city center; a marshalling yard for freight traffic in the suburb of Zell, northwest just beyond the transformer station; and roundhouses complete with locomotive repair shops adjacent to the passenger station.

Long before World War I an inland harbor had been built, complete with warehouses, cranes, road and rail sidings. It is still in use today. By the mid-1930s it had proven too small and too old. A new harbor, again basically only a quay side like the old one, was built close to the railyard at Zell before World War II.

For industry Würzburg had always been a difficult place to settle. Geographically there is little space in the valley that would allow easy access by rail and road. Any industry that required water for either process or steampower generation had to face the problem of one of the hardest waters in Europe. Yet there were and still are today in and around Würzburg midsize industrial plants. At the end of World War II none of them employed more than five hundred workers. There was the steel fabricator Noell AG, which built railway signal equipment and steel structures. It was located northeast of the city center. From about 1943 onward this shop built sections of U-boat hulls, about one every two months, which were transported on low bed trailers to the Main River for loading onto barges and shipment to assembly wharves in northern Germany. Another factory has been located for well over 150 years near the marshalling yard at Zell. Koenig und Bauer AG is a well-known and respected producer of high-speed printing presses and its products have been sold in the world markets for generations. The machine tool capacity of the factory had been used after every raid on the ball-bearing factories at Schweinfurt, about forty kilometers from Würzburg, to repair the damaged and salvaged ball-bearing production machinery. There may have been production of strategic value, but as the factory was completely destroyed by the USAAF and artillery fire on 31 March 1945, no records survived.[2]

Further smaller industries in and around Würzburg at the time included the chocolate factory Franconia, a plywood and exotic wood sawmill, two breweries, and a small ball-bearing plant relocated from Schweinfurt after the raids on that city.

But certainly of military-strategic importance were the barracks of the 55th Infantry Regiment, the artillery barracks adjacent to it, the barracks housing a communication unit of the army close to the Noell plant and the Hindenburg Kaserne (barracks) near the Koenig und Bauer plant. The Wehrmacht had several big warehouses adjacent to the railway yard. They were crammed with food supplies when the war ended. Then there was the *Fliegerhorst* (airfield) of the Luftwaffe on the hill east of the city. It had been a clandestine military training school during the Weimar Republic. When Hitler started to build up the Luftwaffe from 1933 it was fenced off and a secretive building activity began. By the end of the war it must have been a Luftwaffe experimental station, because I remember the Me-262, the world's first jet fighter, screaming over the city when it took off or landed.

Würzburg, as a functioning city, had water and gas works aside from the above mentioned electric power installations. These works supplied their services to the inhabitants and to the established industry and commerce. There have always been considerable commercial installations not only for the city itself but above all for the large agricultural hinterland. Agriculture is a prominent factor in the life of this area.

Last but not least must be mentioned the administrative offices for the northwestern part of the State of Bavaria. During the Third Reich there were also party headquarters with their subsidiary organizations including a local Gestapo office.

In contrast to installations of value to the German war effort, one must list the many non-military assets of the city. High above the west bank of the Main River is the "Festung," the castle which dates back in its earliest parts to Celtic times of about 1000 B.C. During the Thirty Years War, troops of Swedish King Gustaf Adolf II had besieged and conquered the place. As a result, the prince bishop, the ruler of the bishopric of Würzburg, had an outer ring of fortification added to the fortress. The military value of the castle ceased after the 1864 war during which the Prussian army lobbed a few shells at the occupying Bavarian forces.

The Festung was the residence of the prince bishops until they somehow convinced the population not to rebel at the expense of building one of the finest baroque/rococo palaces in Europe. This has been there in the city center since the middle of the eighteenth century. It contains the world's largest fresco, painted by the Venetian painter Tiepolo, and many other treasures.

There were many churches in the inner and outer city. Some in the center were of particular cultural value because they dated back to the years when Irish monks came to Würzburg to convert the heathen Germanic Franconian tribe to Christianity in the seventh century A.D. The biggest church is the "Kiliansdom," the Kilian Cathedral, named in honor of the principal Irish monk. The "Dom," as it is called, dates back to the eleventh century. It was built in Romanesque style with later additions of gothic and rococo cloisters and chapels. Other churches of all building epochs are connected to religious orders, hospitals, or just to the congregations around them. As the city grew, modern churches of considerable aesthetic value were built outside the inner core. There were also three Lutheran churches and a synagogue.

There were hospitals with thousands of beds. The biggest in the inner city being the "Julius Spital," founded in the seventeenth century. During World War II it was upgraded and modernized to attend to thousands of Wehrmacht casualties. In the outskirts there were and have been the Luitpold Krankenhaus, a large complex of university clinics and the Wehrmacht Hospital. Besides these major hospitals there were numerous smaller ones and many convalescent homes for wounded soldiers. There were so many hospitals in Würzburg at the time that people believed it had been officially declared a hospital city and would be immune to air raids. I remember very well that all these buildings had huge red crosses on white backgrounds painted on their roofs, as stipulated in the Geneva conventions. Copies in my possession of the RAF aerial reconnaissance photographs, taken before Armageddon, are too grainy to show these red crosses, but they were there.

As Würzburg has always been the administrative center for the area, the *Regierungsbezirk*, it also harbored many institutions for the blind, the deaf, and the crippled. There has been a university since 1582 with institutes for all fields of medicine, for law, the arts, chemistry, and physics. In the latter, Roentgen had discovered X-rays in 1896. Further institutions for learning included a teachers' academy and academies for music and agriculture.

The list of significant non-military objects within the city limits of Würzburg in March 1945 would be endless. The city had developed in more than fifteen hundred years from a heathen Germanic settlement to the capital of a dukedom in the Holy Roman Empire, where the secular duke was simultaneously the Roman Catholic bishop. Eventually, after Napoleon had raged through Europe, the Congress of Vienna gave the prince bishopric to the king of Bavaria. And the Würzburgers have since been citizens of Bavaria in whatever form that state has existed by itself and within Germany. The city has a long history of stability. The Peasant Revolt of the fifteenth century affected it only on the outskirts. The Reformation did not touch it, as it had always been stoutly Catholic. The Thirty Years War rolled through it and there are no accounts of sufferings from the Great Plague. The Napoleonic Wars and the French invasions before had left no mark, although Napoleon stayed once at the bishop's palace, the "Residenz," and pronounced it the most beautiful vicarage in Europe. The revolutions of the nineteenth and early twentieth centuries left no visible marks, and even the Nazis could not change the town. Würzburg's rulers, its citizens, and time had formed and transformed the city, developing it over the centuries from a small town to a solid middle-class city of over 100,000 inhabitants. There had been no great political, social, racial, or religious problems. The city lived the life of an unobtrusive, self-supporting central European community, a pleasant and peaceful place.

But disaster struck with catastrophic results on 16 March 1945 between 9:20 and 9:37 P.M., Central European Time.

Possible Reasons for the Raids

How did it come to that? Why would such a city of small strategic value and with few facilities to support the German war effort be the target of a bomber fleet? Rumors had gone around before the big raid—and everybody believed them and passed them on—that Churchill had studied at Würzburg University, and that the city had been declared a "hospital town." It was thought that any one of these facts would save us from being visited by the Allied bombers. Then, after the raid, other rumors were circulating to explain why it had happened after all. The most plausible was that the U.S. Army was advancing eastward and that the Allies had demanded that the Gauleiter of Mainfranken, the party chief and at the same time the president of the government of the *Regierungsbezirk*, declare the city an "open city" in accordance with international conventions. Since the Nazi Party ruled Germany to the last moment with an iron fist and final German victory was still a proclaimed certainty, the Gauleiter would not and could not at the pain of personal death for treason make this declaration. Many historians have since clearly established that the "gauleiter story" was a myth. There were no such communications between the enemies.

In early March 1945 the U.S. Army advanced in western Germany toward the Rhine. It crossed the Rhine by a daring strike which gave it the bridge at Remagen intact on 7 March 1945 and another bridge at Oppenheim, due west of Würzburg, on 21 March. The Rhine is well over one hundred kilometers west of Würzburg. At the time, on clear nights with westerly breezes, one could hear the rumbling of artillery fire on the hills surrounding the city. It was an ominous sign of things to come.

That raises the question whether Würzburg was attacked as a tactical target in advance of the approaching U.S. forces. If the main raid of 16 March and any of the others had been tactical ones, i.e. in support of ground troops, the judgment on these raids and the thousands of similar ones on other cities would have been and would be to this day that they were fully justifiable and legal military operations.

But as the documents at the Public Record Office, the

National Archives at College Park near Washington, D.C., and other archives show, the Royal Air Force Bomber Command and the U.S. Army Eighth and Fifteenth Air Forces operated independently from SHAEF (Supreme Headquarters Allied Expeditionary Force under General Eisenhower).

Shortly after the war we were told that the RAF had orders to destroy all German cities with more than 100,000 inhabitants. Since Würzburg had at the beginning of the war only 107,000 people we were at the end of the list, after such cities as Hamburg and Munich, and, therefore, our moment finally arrived toward the end of the war. But as one can gather from literature and documents in the respective archives there is no truth in that. However, one fact is clear. Arthur Harris, the RAF Bomber Command chief, and Carl Spaatz, commander of the U.S. Army Air Forces stationed in Britain and Italy, had run out of worthwhile targets by early 1945.[3]

Target categories had been worked out in Britain before and during the war by the Ministry of Economic Warfare and in the United States, before it entered the conflict, by the USAAF in AWDP-1 (Air War Defence Plan 1). The detail targets came eventually from the Allied Target Committee. Its recommendations were passed on to the commanders of the respective bomber fleets. Much research went into producing statistics, from numbers of inhabitants to distances from bomber bases, significance for the German war effort, and all intelligence which had an impact on implementing the instructions from the Air Ministry in London and the chief of staff in Washington on the conduct of the bomber offensive.

For each significant German city the information coming to the Target Committee included lists of industrial, commercial, and infrastructure installations. For Würzburg it gave unbelievable details but on the other hand also irrelevant information and missed some very important sites. The list prepared by the Ministry of Economic Warfare (MEW), a section of the Foreign Office, makes no mention of the Star Werke, the small ball-bearing plant relocated from Schweinfurt. It says nothing about the submarine hull sections fabricated by Noell AG, but it lists the Eugen Flurschütz shop, where five ladies in a very restricted location were knitting sweaters. It also lists W.

Stecher, a tin smith of small trade shop proportions.[4] It looks as if someone had consulted a telephone directory and interpreted the listings and the advertising. It mentions that there were flour mills. There were none at that time to the best of my knowledge. Yet the report fails to list the new inland harbor. There was a medium-size paper converting plant and several fair-size car and truck repair shops, which would have qualified for the MEW list. Since the report goes down to mini-enterprises, it left out dozens of them, including one of my father's businesses, a bookbinding and printing shop employing five people (sometimes this number increased to six when I had misbehaved as a boy and as punishment had to work there).

The MEW report classified infrastructure and commercial/industrial targets into fourteen categories. The highest rating was given to transportation targets and the lowest to foodstuffs. For each category the listings were further broken down on a scale of 1+ to 3. A 1+ rating being assigned the highest priority for installations supporting the German war effort and a 3 being the least priority.[5] The report on Würzburg listed targets in the categories of transportation, public utility services, liquid fuels and substitutes, non-ferrous metal manufacture and fabrication, shipbuilding, engineering and armaments, chemicals and explosives, textiles/rayon/pulp and paper, leather, and foodstuffs, in all ten out of the fourteen possible. Nineteen targets out of twenty-seven listed could either not be classified for lack of information, or simply did not rate classification; i.e. 70 percent of the known targets were unknown for their importance. As an example, the biggest industrial plants in Würzburg, Noell, the steel fabricator, and Koenig & Bauer, the printing press factory, were listed under engineering and armaments and qualified only under class 3. At the same time the printing plant of Stürtz, employing about five hundred, was listed under engineering and armaments. The MEW report did mention that there were barracks northwest and northeast of the central area of town. It claimed that they were occupied by armored and motorized divisions. Not that we had ever seen any of the armor, tanks, or similar vehicles. No mention is made that there was a Luftwaffe aerodrome, although the Air Ministry in a communication of 20 May 1944 did list this airfield as a repair facility.[6] Thus the target information was at best incomplete and spotty.

If the raid, as officially termed, was "to burn and destroy an enemy industrial centre"[7] its base of information was limited and the question must be asked was it worth the risks, costs, and effort to send 225 bombers off into the hostile night. Last but not least as seen from the Allied side, was it worth the loss of the one bomber shot down by a Luftwaffe nightfighter during the raid over the city. And worse still, was it worth the loss of its crew of seven. Six killed in action and one shot deliberately two days later by an SS police officer after the RAF man had been flushed out of his hiding place.[8]

When one studies the statistics published by the city administration one can easily see that Würzburg had some strategic importance.[9] But the question remains, of course, was the destruction justified at the time, when the Third Reich was in its last fatal convulsions. The last statistics available for river transport show in a published report for 1943 the following:

> The Old Harbour (Staatshafen): Turn-over of goods: 306,737 t
>   801 barges came in with 153,834 tons
>   861 barges left with 152,903 tons
> The New Harbour (Neuer Hafen): Turn-over of goods: 682,862 t
>   1,214 barges came in with 563,174 tons
>   995 barges left with 119,688 tons

Total turnover in the harbor installations was close to a million metric tons in 1943 and one can assume that in 1944 the tonnage was probably the same. The goods transhipped were coal, ores, grain, building materials, and bulk food. As Würzburg was at the end of the river transport system these goods and materials were loaded onto or from freight trains in the adjacent marshalling yard. There are no records of the *Reichsbahn*, the German state railway, for these periods, but the magnitude of the operation can be assessed when one considers the capacity of the marshalling yard. It was at the time two thousand cars per day. The largest German marshalling yard was at Hamm and had a capacity of ten thousand cars per day. When one transposes the above river transport turnover figures into trains per day by using the information contained in

Alfred C. Mierzejewski's book one arrives at about ten trains of forty wagons each leaving the yard to transport the goods from the barges alone.[10]

Further statistics available at the Stadtarchiv for 1944 show that the public works of the city sold 28 million kilowatt-hours of electricity, 16 million cubic meters of gas, and 6 million cubic meters of water to its citizens and other consumers.

Any researcher looking for strategic targets will find the above numbers significant and recommend that these installations be destroyed. In themselves the numbers are impressive and towards the end of the war they undoubtedly represented a few targets still available for the bombers.

Würzburg never made it on the original list of German cities to be destroyed. The cities recommended at various times at the beginning of the bomber offensive by such people as Churchill's scientific advisor, Lord Cherwell, had far more important industrial installations than Würzburg. The detail planning of the Allied bomber offensive started in late 1941. It was not until April 1942 that Würzburg cropped up in a list of secondary targets.[11] The Ministry of Economic Warfare prepared what was named the "Bomber Baedeker," a reference to the well-known European travel guide. One has to assume the information was distributed and, as regards Würzburg, filed for possible future reference.

The nearby town of Schweinfurt with its ball-bearing factories suffered numerous raids and we saw and heard the armadas flying in and out of this target area. One U.S. bomber even crashed into Würzburg without killing anybody on the ground. But the first signs of change happened in mid-1944. One night, long after the air-raid sirens had howled, there was engine noise in the air and suddenly flares were dropped. The city was bathed in artificial daylight. I remember the details of noise and light, because I was standing, foolishly and ignorant of the possible consequences, in the front door of our building; albeit ready to run down to the air-raid shelter in the basement at the first sign of trouble. What I do not remember is the date. Nothing happened and after a while the flares burned out and the city was in darkness again. Nobody understood what had happened and even today, after much research at the Public

Record Office, I cannot say whether we were photographed or whether the fireworks were one of Bomber Command's spoof exercises to mislead the German defenses. But around that time we *were* photographed as the pictures in the Public Record Office show. The irony of these photographs is that despite all the camouflaging the authorities of Würzburg had gone into, the city was clearly identifiable in every detail. One of the RAF photos even has marked on it the locations of the town hall and the Nazi headquarters. We did not know and could not possibly guess the implications of this visit; but Bomber Command was getting its file updated.

Yet Würzburg was still not a priority target. With the entry of the United States into the war and the posting of a huge bomber fleet to Britain the target selection had been given to the Combined Target Committee. On 31 January 1945 it handed out a revised list based on instructions from the Air Ministry identifying categories of targets.[12] In the third and fourth category one could with some justification include Würzburg, because these categories included transport centers and jet fighter airfields. Jet fighters took off and landed from the Luftwaffe airfield at Würzburg. But by the activities as they were observed by the citizens, there could not have been a large number of these aircraft stationed there. At any rate Würzburg was not identified by name on this list.

That changed on 8 February 1945, when a newly revised list was passed to Bomber Command in which the city is indicated as a secondary target in tenth place in the event that primary targets could not be attacked for meteorological, technical, or other reasons. The list contained seventeen cities ending with Ludwigshafen.[13] This last place had been visited before and therefore obviously needed less attention.

Now we were officially earmarked, albeit in the latter part of a long line-up. Simultaneously there was political pressure in the House of Commons in London. On 7 February 1945 Labour MP Edmund Purbrick asked when Würzburg, which together with a number of other German cities had been spared the experience of major attacks, would be given a lesson.[14] He did not really have to ask. Bomber Command was well on its way to actually planning the attack.

Würzburg - Areas Bombed

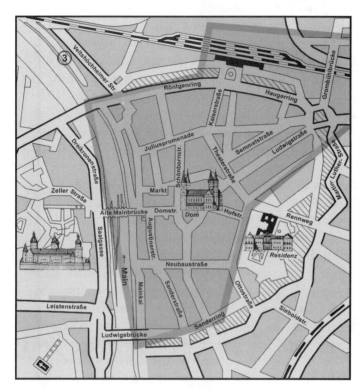

Area designated
by RAF Bomber
Command
Headquarters at
High Wycombe
for destruction

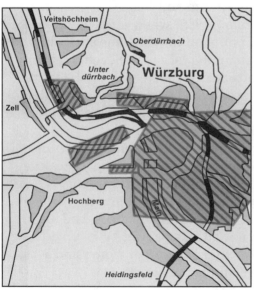

Areas actually
bombed by RAF
and USAAF

 RAF

 USAAF

2

THE RAIDS BEGIN

Würzburg had been bombed for the first time on 21 February 1942. The Bomber Command Operational Records Books indicate that twenty Hampdon bombers of No. 5 Bomber Group were dispatched to attack cities in south and southwestern Germany that night.[1] These were the nuisance raids which the leaders of Bomber Command had initiated to cause general disturbance in Germany. And disturb us they did. We had been sitting for some time in the shelter when there were a number of explosions in the distance. After a while the all-clear was sounded. Next day we learned that two bombs had been dropped in the eastern section of town. Nobody was killed or hurt and damage was light. The only real memory of this raid I have is that a few days later we were told by friends of the reaction of a child in a shelter near the bomb explosions. The child asked its mother: "Do we have to die now?"

From the documents at the Public Record Office it would seem that one bomber was lost and in accordance with instructions dropped its bombs on "any good looking built up area instead of bringing them home."[2] RAF navigational aids at that time were rather inadequate and it is most likely that we were the target of last resort for a bomber crew that wanted to get home.

Würzburg had also been given a lesson in July 1944. On a clear summer day, 21 July, 1,180 USAAF bombers were dispatched from bases in Britain to attack targets in Germany. At noon twenty B-17s of the 1st Air Division suddenly came up over the city from the southeast and dropped twenty tons of high explosive bombs.[3] Whether they were meant for the relocated ball-bearing factory, the Star Werke, or one of the Main bridges, is not clear from the references. But their bombs were loosened a few seconds too late and they all fell on a purely residential area killing forty-two civilians. Most of the dead had not gone to the air-raid shelters because nothing had happened before during the ceaseless alarms to which the population had been exposed and had become accustomed.

From the USAAF files at the Albert F. Simpson Historical Research Centre (AFSHRC) at Maxwell Air Force Base, Montgomery, Alabama, and the National Archives (NA) at College Park, Maryland, it appears that the bridge was the target.[4] The originally assigned target for 305 A Bomber Group of No.1 Bomber Division was elsewhere but bad weather prevented that attack and Würzburg was bombed as a designated secondary target. The USAAF files referring to this raid show that only seven aircrafts attacked dropping 17.5 tons of bombs. The files state that the bombs missed the bridge and fell in a residential area as observed by the departing bomber crews.[5]

On 4 February, three days before Mr. Purbrick asked his question, we had a visit from two Mosquitos of No. 8 Pathfinder Group, Squadron 128. Three were dispatched, but one was lost prior to the raid. The attack is termed an experimental raid in the Bomber Command Intelligence Narratives on Operations.[6] They dropped 3.6 tons of high explosive bombs and stayed about seventeen minutes over the target. The Bomber Command report says that there was 10/10th thin cloud. One has to assume that experimental raid meant what it said. They must have tried out the reception of radio signals emitted from Britain to locate the target, the response to the H2S radar sets carried by many bombers to show the target below, the weather, and whatever was needed to plan a major attack.

I remember the attack very well. It was a Sunday evening at around 8 P.M. We were sitting around the dinner table when suddenly a sound came into the air as if one of the jet fighters stationed at the Luftwaffe base was coming in low for landing. But a split second later there was a loud explosion nearby and, although I had never experienced a bombing, there was no doubt what had happened. We rushed down the stairs to the shelter in the basement. On the way down a second explosion was heard. The Bomber Command report indicates that two bombs of a total weight of 3.6 tons were dropped from a height of seven thousand feet. No previous alarm had been sounded in the city and it is not clear whether somebody was asleep at the switch, or whether no alarm had been given because of only two aircraft in the area, which at that time of the war was not considered a great danger.

The alarm was sounded belatedly, but the local police radio, which had been instituted about a year before to give situation reports, was completely silent. After some time the all-clear was sounded and we went to bed. Next day it became clear that one of the bombs had hit a bridge spanning the Main without destroying it and the other had fallen in one of the outer sections of the town. Nobody ever found out how many people were killed because there was considerable traffic on the bridge and some people had been blown to bits. The estimate ran at twenty killed and fifty wounded.

After the first "experimental raid" by Bomber Command in February 1945 we were beginning to get concerned. From friends and relatives in other cities we had heard that such attacks were the sign of Bomber Command taking the measure of a city. No doubt one of the measures would have been whether the intended target had any flak defenses. It must have been the reason the two Mosquitos stayed seventeen minutes over the city. They must have observed to their great satisfaction that nobody was shooting at them.

The next night, 5 February 1945, No. 8 Group returned with four Mosquitos for another experimental raid. They stayed twenty-seven minutes above us at thirty thousand feet and let us have nine tons of high explosives. This time "small alarm" had been sounded, but just barely before the first bombs exploded. We had just made it into the shelter. A total of four bombs were dropped and the blast of one of them smashed the shop window in my father's store; the first material damage my family suffered in the bombing war. The four bombs were widely scattered over the city and, as with any of the previous raids, their impact locations did not indicate a desire to hit a specific target. Six people were killed.

After a lull of one week, on 12 February No. 8 Group returned with four Mosquitos and carried out another experimental raid. They stayed only five minutes over the target and dropped seven tons of blast bombs over a wide area. The B.C report lists that there were no defenses. The damage was negligible as some of the bombs fell in open fields and nobody was killed or wounded.

Yet, if our measure was being taken, more experimental raids were obviously necessary, because a week later on 19 February at 8:30 P.M. six Mosquitos of No. 8 Group returned and dropped eleven tons of blast bombs. Full alarm had been sounded long before and all the tenants of our building were sitting in the shelter when the first bombs came down. There appeared to be many of them and after the second one I sprawled out on the floor. We could not feel any blasts but the walls of the basement shook and the plaster began falling off. After what seemed like the end of the raid, I went upstairs into our flat and confronted the damage. Windows had been blown out, with glass shards everywhere. Some doors had become unhinged, but otherwise there was little damage. The nearest bomb had fallen about one kilometer away. However that bomb had done considerable damage to my father's store. It had come down about fifty meters away from it and destroyed several buildings. The three-hundred-year-old woodframe house that my grandfather had bought in 1888, in which there was the store and where he lived upstairs, withstood the blast, but in it there was complete chaos. My grandfather and his housekeeper, ever the optimist he was, had not gone to a nearby shelter and when the bomb exploded fifty meters away they were both thrown down a flight of stairs. Unbelievably, they both survived, got up and walked to the shelter up the street— he was eighty and she sixty.

Obviously this had been a bigger raid. Most of the bombs had fallen in the inner city. A total number of 112 people were killed and many injured. Immediate damage was considerable and grew worse during the night when fires caused by thrown over furnaces spread. One of them must have been in my grandfather's place or nearby, because hours later the top floors were on fire. On these floors my father had stores of the stationery business he owned. All the fires were soon brought under control by the city fire department. But the cost to us was high, because what the blast and the fire had not destroyed, the water of the firefighters had soaked completely.

From the events that followed, but not apparent until long after they happened, Würzburg had now obviously been "experimented" with enough and Air Marshal Harris could make the decision to send his forces to attack. The routine for selection of targets for each night started with a morning meeting at High Wycombe, the Bomber Command headquarters west of London. Target lists were consulted and assessed, meteorological reports submitted, and then Harris would make a decision. Air Marshal Saundby, his deputy, would send out telegrams to the Group commanders outlining arming and fueling requirements and indicating the targets. If possible, later in the day a fighter would be sent over to the Continent to gather final meteorological data. After its return the raid instructions would be confirmed by Saundby with coordinates of the area to be attacked and the bomb releasing instructions for each squadron.

But before Bomber Command appeared again in our skies at night we experienced what the U.S. Army Air Force could do. For months the gleaming bomber formations with their vapor trails had passed over us during the days. The Voice of America had told us that American bombers would only attack military targets. We believed them. The BBC broadcasts made no such statements for the British bombers.

There had been "full alarm" for some time and I remember being bored in the shelter. It was Friday, 23 February, a beautifully clear and sunny day. Suddenly at around 11 A.M. there was the howling of falling bombs, explosions, and blasts of air. We were being raided again. This time it was the 1st Air Division of the Eighth U.S. Army Air Force which had sent thirty-seven B-17s to destroy the Würzburg railway station, its surrounding workshops, and the marshalling yard at Zell. They dropped two hundred bombs with a total weight of 111 tons, all high explosives.[7] Most of the ones aimed at the railway station hit their intended target with bulls-eye precision, and we believed even more in the Voice of America; at least until further notice. But some bombs came down outside the station and hit private homes. One destroyed the transformer station that supplied the area we lived in with electricity. From then to the bitter end we had to live without electric power. The death toll was considerable with over 170 people killed. The exact number varies between 171 and 178, depending on the source of information. The damage to our flat was small. The bomb hitting the transformer station exploded about three hundred meters away from our building. We had boarded up the windows destroyed in the previous raid with cardboard and had swept up all the broken glass. Now the cardboard was all blown to bits, more windows were smashed, and some plaster had ended up on the floor.

The attack had ripped up many tracks and the main station building was a pile of rubble. The post office next to it and the workshops around the station were all badly hit. Rail traffic through Würzburg was interrupted for two days. The Germans had learned how to deal with this type of damage. Hundreds of men and their heavy equipment had the wheels rolling again in short order. The damage to the marshalling yard at Zell was minimal. The returning bombers reported that they had hit the southern choke point of the yard. The photos taken by the same bombers show that they missed the yard narrowly.[8]

Würzburg's railway installations were actually not on the target lists of the USAAF and the USTAAF. In September 1944 two hundred German railway centers had been selected for destruction and when the list was reduced to eighty targets in January 1945 Würzburg still was not on it.[9] The thirty-seven aircraft in this raid belonged to Bomber Groups 305 A, B and C and were to attack Bayreuth, but bad visibility prevented that attack and Würzburg, given as a secondary target, was bombed instead.[10]

Next, it was the turn of the RAF again. At around 8:30 P.M. on 3 March 1945, thirty-one Mosquitos appeared over Würzburg, marked the city with skymarkers, and dropped forty-seven tons of high explosives into the defined area. Time over target (ToT) as it is referred to in Bomber Command reports, was fifteen minutes. The bombs came down all over the city, in the center and in outlying areas. One hit the old power station in the inner city and blacked out the area which was supplied with DC power from that source. This was the only target of strategic value. The rest were residential areas, open fields, and the monastery of the Franciscans. That bomb made a complete shambles in the other business my father had, the printing/bookbinding shop. Based on past experience and on the police radio announcements, which had warned of the approaching armada, most people had been in their shelters when the bombs started to fall. Despite these precautions eighty-six civilians were killed. As before, fires started from blown over furnaces and before long the sky over the city turned crimson.

My own experience of the raid was different this time. After the daylight raid on the railway station my father decided that the danger was getting worse and that he and I (my mother had died in 1941) needed sleep. We had spent the nights during the last months mostly either fully dressed in the flat waiting for the noise of approaching bombers or, as often happened, we were in the shelter because there were planes flying over us for hours. During the day it was similar and during the short periods of no alarms we had to work hard to salvage from the businesses what there could be salvaged. We owned a little garden cottage about five kilometers outside of town. It was more like a shack. Cold, damp, with hardly any furniture and no water. The sanitary facilities consisted of an outhouse at the end of the property. Now at the end of each day we mounted our bicycles and rode to the cottage. It was not comfortable, but we could sleep without interruption. We were on the way to our nightly quarters when the raid of 3 March started. No bombs fell in our vicinity, since we were already outside the marked area. Yet we were ready to jump into the ditch along the road any time. We felt the blasts and concussions of the detonating bombs and realised that this was more than just a small raid. Once the bombing stopped we returned to the city and inspected our properties and the places where we had stored, in the basements of friends and relatives, goods and valuables. Streets had become difficult to pass through because there was rubble from bombed houses or glass which would have cut the tires of our bicycles. It was the heaviest raid Würzburg had endured so far, but one could see that the firefighters, civil defense, and police were coping with the situation.

None of the previous raids, not even the last one, had made the daily news bulletins issued by the German Supreme Command. Undoubtedly the reason was that there had been bigger raids on other cities and that raids of the magnitude we suffered were so common that they could not all be listed. Last but not least such a listing would not have made a good "party line" press. On the Allied side the 3 March raid was widely publicized. It was called a raid on a transport center. The transport center, i.e. the railway installation, had already been demolished by the USAAF and the RAF raid was anything but an aimed attack on the railway or the harbor area. It was an "area raid" as it was called in official parlance.

Next followed thirteen days of more continual alarms day and night but no bombing. The news from the battle fronts became worse, the overflights increased, and life was far from normal. We could not even listen to the radio because there was no electric power. The local newspaper was the only source of information and it was full of Nazi propaganda. The equally skewed news from the Voice of America and the BBC could not be received and frankly I did not miss them. We were being clobbered and the question in everybody's mind was how to survive the coming end.

The Big RAF Raid

By March 1945, nobody was under any illusion that Würzburg had now received its measure of bombs. Everybody deposited cartons, suitcases, chests, and whatever one could stuff something into with friends either outside of town or in their basements in town. The idea was to spread the risk, to have at least some essentials if one's home was destroyed.

I attended high school until it closed after the daylight raid on 23 February. The weeks before we had spent most of the school time in the shelter below the schoolhouse. It was a cramped and dingy place and the teachers had a terrible time keeping us there. We were supposed to study, but who could under those conditions. I distinctly remember one morning when we had to go downstairs soon after school started. Our English teacher made us take along our books and we were to memorize Marc Anthony's speech to the Roman citizens from Shakespeare's *Julius Caesar*. I was studying from a beautifully printed and leather-bound volume of Shakespeare's collected works. With so many of our possessions it went up in flames a few weeks later. I have only memories left of this precious tome, one thousand of which were printed in London in 1623.

What was hard to reconcile for some of us was that the Nazi propaganda told us day in and day out how base anything Anglo-American was: Their culture, their political system, and their values. Then just to confirm it all, we civilians were bombed and strafed by their bombers and fighters. Yet here we were studying their literary achievements. It did not add up. I sneaked out of the shelter, got to the front door and saw in between the low clouds formations of U.S. bombers flying north. It was 14 February, the day after the infamous RAF Dresden raid, followed early the next morning by a devastating U.S. raid on that burning city.

My father and I kept working during the day whenever there was no alarm. We salvaged from the businesses what was salvageable. We arranged for a truck to take my grandfather to relatives in a village outside Würzburg. On the way I dropped off a few more possessions in a place we had rented and where a year before we had already stored about 10 percent of the merchandise of the stationery store. The government had ordered all retail businesses to move that much of their goods to what were considered safe places in the country.

At night we became trekkers and slept in the cottage. When the Luftwaffe bombed Britain in 1940-41 many citizens there left the cities. They were called trekkers. Our conditions and fears were probably the same the British people had endured then.

When the big raid came on 16 March 1945 we were already asleep. The alarm had been sounded in the city when we were crawling into our damp beds. After a while there was a roaring noise of aircraft engines and before long we could see through the closed shutters that the sky was red. We dressed, stepped outside and knew at once that the hour had come. The sky was full of markers, Christmas trees as we called them. Our property was southwest of the city, outside of the marked area. The engine noise grew stronger coming from the south and soon the explosions started. We were too far away to feel the blasts, but the noise was deafening. I noticed explosions in the air and thought that Würzburg finally had some flak to defend it. Later I learned this was not flak but bundles of incendiary bombs which were scattered by an explosive device. Obviously this was a major attack and I was scared. There was no place for shelter at the cottage and when a few bombs came down closer to us we just ducked. The stream of aircraft seemed endless. The sky was getting brighter and redder with uncountable flashes of explosions. What seemed an eternity, but in reality was only seventeen minutes, passed and the engine noises subsided. There were still explosions, but we guessed that they came from the dreaded time-delayed bombs. We climbed on our bicycles and pedalled toward the city. In the outskirts we encountered rubble, wires, glass, craters, and uprooted trees which barred our way. We left our bikes in a barn of people we knew and tried to proceed by foot. At one point there was earth spread over the road. My father who had spent part of WWI in the trenches said that there must be a time bomb nearby and we hurried on. He was right, hours later when we passed the same spot there was a deep crater. Further towards the city there was suddenly a big flash ahead of us about one hundred meters away. We both hit the ground, opened our mouths to compensate for the blast and had a few pieces of earth come down on us. Everywhere people were fleeing from the city, there were fires even in the outskirts and an unbelievable roar of wind. We had heard of the firestorms in Hamburg and we knew we were in for something similar. Approaching the city became impossible so we climbed up the western hills. Over the city there was a pall of smoke whipped by the firestorm. The whole town was on fire. Later we found our way down toward the river and crossed over one of the bridges. As we were walking over the bridge the firestorm hit us and we had trouble staying on our feet.

After the bridge we entered the Ringpark. The inner city of Würzburg is surrounded by this park. Until 1871 medieval walls and moats had been there. They were leveled and a beautiful park created in their place. For us and thousands of people this park meant refuge. The inner core of Würzburg had become a cauldron of fire. The roar of the conflagration was deafening and the smoke suffocating. When we arrived at the place where we wanted to leave the park and penetrate into the city to our flat we were driven back by a wall of flames, heat, and smoke. We tried another street further on with the same result. There we met one of our neighbor families. They informed us that when they left the building it was completely in flames. They had tried to fight the incendiary bombs and the fires they had created but they had to flee because the house was about to collapse and they would have been killed. Now we knew that our home was gone and with it all that was in it. We did not even try to reach the businesses, or what was left of them before this raid, because they were located well inside the city. There was no hope of getting there. People who escaped from there were lucky. Many suffocated in the smoke, were hit by falling debris, or worse, never escaped their shelters. There they were killed by the heat or carbon monoxide.

My father and I turned around and hiked over the debris in the streets towards the Frauenland, a subdivision outside the Ringpark. We walked through streets with houses on fire on either side. There were detonations from time-delayed bombs, facades falling into the streets, and we missed by a few seconds being buried under one of them. That was a close call. When we reached our friends' home we found that it had burnt down to the ground floor, but the basement was not yet on fire. There was no sign of our friends and nobody around to tell us whether the occupants of the house had escaped. We crawled into the basement and removed some of the valuables we had stored there. To return to our cottage we had to make a long detour because retracing our steps had become impossible. The conflagrations started by the incendiaries even in the less built-up suburbs were combining into large area fires and impeded our progress. It was 4 A.M. when we finally got to the cottage. It was to be our "home" from now on, inadequate as it might have appeared days before. At least we had a place to go to. The majority of the bombed-out citizens had no such comfort. They were at that moment either in the parks or along the river fleeing the inferno in masses.

To describe what happened in general and to us in particular that night would fill books. A few books have been written and to repeat with more and other words the misery that had been cast upon us would not serve the purpose of this work. But I must continue with what I found out about this raid when I researched the events. For the night of 16-17 March 1945 the Bomber Command War Diaries list as targets for major raids the cities of Nürnberg and Würzburg.[11] Further raids were flown by fifty-six Mosquitos to Berlin and twenty-four Mosquitos to Hanau and a few other places. A total of 717 aircraft left British bases that night. Thirty did not return, a loss rate of 4.2 percent. A loss of 5 percent of the dispatched planes was considered the highest acceptable by Harris. It is surprising that at this stage of the war German defenses were still effective despite the loss of early warning radars in the previously occupied western countries, the efficiency of the British radio war, the lack of fuel for the Luftwaffe planes, and the turmoil caused by the advancing Allied armies.

In the afternoon of 16 March, the headquarters of Bomber Command had instructed No. 5 Bomber Group to attack "Grayling" (the code name for Nürnberg) and "Bleak" (Würzburg) with two hundred-plus aircraft each. The instructions must have originated in the morning meeting and they were routine but very explicit. The teletypes gave routings to and from the targets for the bomber stream, bomb and fuel loads, strategy of marking the target, bomb release for each squadron with timing and altitude over the target, and many more details.[12] The most fateful teletype for us on the ground contained the instructions for the Mosquito Pathfinders of No. 5 Bomber Group to mark the target area.[13] The aiming point was identified as an easily recognizable athletic field along the Main River. From there the Pathfinders had to outline the target area with their marker bombs. The master bomber flying over the city just prior to the raid was to assess the marking and call for corrections with further target indicators of a different color. His instructions were quite explicit and left no doubt that the area foreseen for destruction was properly marked.[14] Four minutes before H-hour, the designated start of the raid, the marking and illumination of the city was to be complete and the bombers were to start coming up. The purpose of the raid was "to burn and destroy an enemy industrial centre."

When one plots the marking coordinates on a city map of Würzburg, one finds, however, that the target area left out the industrial sections, the infrastructure installations, and all military establishments. The only strategic targets in the defined area were the small relocated ball-bearing factory and the area of the main railway station. The latter was already a pile of twisted steel and rubble. The rest of the "industrial centre" as marked was the baroque/rococo town with its treasures and the dwellings of its citizens. The area slated for destruction went beyond the inner city and included residential subdivisions outside the city center.

The H-hour for Würzburg was to be 21:00 Central European Time. But something must have gone wrong because it was not before 21:20 that the bombing started. It lasted seventeen minutes. There are several books that describe what happened in detail.[15] They are based not only on reports of eyewitnesses, but are the results of extensive research in British and German archives. The books make gruesome reading. What they cannot impart are the suffocating and pungent smells of a burning city and the stench of decomposing and seared human and animal flesh. The books show how innocent and also some not so innocent citizens were sucked into the maelstrom of World War II. Many lost their lives, many more were wounded, and the majority lost all their belongings.

The statistics of this raid are in cold figures:

No. 5 Bomber Group dispatched 225 Lancasters and 11 Mosquitos.

13 Lancasters aborted the mission for technical problems.

212 Lancasters and 11 Mosquitos attacked the city.

Six Lancasters were lost en route, one shot down by a German nightfighter during the raid; all Mosquitos returned.

Actual tonnage of bombs dropped was 967 tons, of which 389 tons were high explosives, 573 tons were incendiaries, and 5 tons were marker bombs.

Total number of high explosives was 256, of which 5 weighed
12,000 lbs., the majority weighed 4,000 lbs.

Total number of incendiary bombs was 307,650; they weighed
4 lbs. each.

The area attacked was 422 acres.

The raid lasted 17 minutes.

The number of people killed: estimated at 5,000; exact figures
could never be established; only 1,387 could be identified.

Number of air crew killed or taken prisoners: 49.

Estimated breakdown of victims: 34% male, 66% female,
of the total 14% were children.

50% of the victims died in the inner city.

90,000 citizens were dehoused.

21,000 homes were destroyed, only 6,000 inhabitants could
continue to live in the city limits.

Total volume of debris removed during reconstruction after
the war: 2,250,000 m³.

Relative number of dead: Würzburg: 41.8/1,000 inhabitants
(Hamburg: 36.1/1,000 inhabitants).

Indeed it was a very successful raid considering the relatively small effort involved. After all, this was not one of the one thousand bomber raids, which had started with Cologne in 1942 shortly after Harris had taken command of the bombers. The first one thousand bomber raid on Cologne the night of 30-31 May 1942, cost the lives of 486 people. By 1945 methods had become advanced and the Pforzheim raid, flown by 380 planes the night of 23-24 February 1945, claimed about 17,000 lives.[16] Compared with Dresden, which had happened five weeks earlier, and the Hamburg raids of 1943, the Würzburg raid was of the small category. But the efficiency of it was devastating.

Bomber Command did not waste any time assessing the results. On 18 March we were photographed again, while the city was still burning. On 19 March, High Wycombe issued a preliminary damage report and on 10 April a final one.[17] The reports claim that the city was 90 percent destroyed. They mention that the railway facilities were further damaged, that industrial enterprises such as Noell AG (the steel fabricator), Stürtz (the printing house), Frankonia (the chocolate factory), and others were hit. It is correctly stated that the city hall and other administrative buildings were destroyed. So were the bishop's residence, several hospitals, the Residenz, and many university institutes. Where the reports lose some of their credibility is when under transport targets destroyed they list Alter Bahnhof and Südbahnhof. The Alter Bahnhof (the old railway station) had been decommissioned before the turn of the century. The Südbahnhof (a suburban station) was nothing more than a whistle stop. Military installations are listed as lightly damaged and nothing was said about the Luftwaffe base. There was no mention of the harbors, the marshalling yard, and other installations in the referred to MEW Baedeker List. It is apparent that Bomber Command had not been provided with an update of the target list, as otherwise they would have proudly stated that they had destroyed a submarine hull factory and a ball-bearing plant.

The leaders of Bomber Command must have been satisfied that the job was done, because the RAF never came back for a follow-up visit. During the raid we were also "on camera." One aircraft circled over us and filmed the whole fireworks. The film is marked: "5 Group attack enemy communications at Würzburg 16/17.3.45."[18] Together with the published books it gives more testimony of the catastrophe.

As mentioned earlier, Würzburg was not defended. The Luftwaffe nightfighter controllers announced at 21:20, at a time when the Pathfinders had already marked Würzburg, that the bomber stream heading for the city was a "feint attack."[19] They correctly guessed that Nürnberg was to be raided and sent some of the fighters there. Others were dispatched to Frankfurt to deal with the Mosquitos that were making a diversionary raid on nearby Hanau. Only at 21:24 did it become apparent to the controllers that Würzburg was being bombed and they sent fighters from far away Kassel that attacked the returning bombers.

THE USAAF RAIDS

Bomber Command did not return after 16 March, but the USAAF made up for that. The U.S. Army was advancing eastward and mercifully there were only two more weeks left to bomb us. But hit us they did, and more damage was inflicted and more people succumbed.

On 18 March seven fighter bombers strafed the rubble strewn streets, dropped ten bombs, and killed two citizens. The fighters were part of the Ninth USTAAF which alone on that day made 1,172 fighter sorties over Germany.[20] I remember the raid only too well because again I had a narrow escape. We were working hard to remove the few belongings which had survived in the strangely not burned-out basement of our apartment building. In the street we had a horse-drawn cart, which my father had with much effort persuaded the owner to help us with. Suddenly there was this aircraft noise, explosions not too far away, and machine-gun and cannon fire coming towards us. We dived through the small windows back into the basement and survived. Even the horse and cart miraculously survived.

Two days later, on 20 March fighter bombers returned and raked the suburb of Heidingsfeld. Because it had been incorporated into the city of Würzburg and supposedly as such showed on the Bomber Command target list, it had been 80 percent destroyed during the 16 March raid. Now four days later twenty more bombs fell, killing eleven people.

The northwestern part of Würzburg, called the Zellerau, where most of the army barracks were located, had escaped the main raid fairly unharmed. On 22 March that situation changed. Eight USAAF B-24 bombers of the 2nd Air Division released their bombs, about eighty, high above our cottage. They devastated the Zellerau including the barracks. We saw and heard the bombs coming down—a frightening experience. The official record indicates that 19.2 tons of bombs were dropped and that the target was a secondary one.[21] Strangely, despite the damage only four people were killed. The primary assigned target had been the Giebelstadt Luftwaffe base, south of Würzburg. But when 445 Bombardment Group was to release its bombs another group intersected its course at a lower level and the Giebelstadt target was scrubbed.[22]

The next day, 23 March, fighter bombers came over the city and strafed what seemed worth attacking, but effected little damage.

There followed a lull of three days in which we only saw the planes and their contrails over us without being attacked. But then on 26 March it was our turn again. Eleven B-17s of 1st Air Division of the Eighth USAAF tried to bomb the still intact gas works and the repaired railway station. They dropped 110 bombs of 500 lbs. each, all of which missed and fell on Unterdürrbach, a purely residential village north of Würzburg. The bombers, although, claimed to have hit the target.[23] The orders for the bombers were originally to attack the bituminous gasoline works at Zeitz. Bad weather prevented that attack and the bombers turned to the secondary target of Plauen. Not all aircraft could attack that city and therefore the rest turned to Meiningen. But over that target ranged confusion and eleven bombers turned away to raid Würzburg.

More attacks occurred later in the day when Bomber Groups 322, 344, 386, and 391 of the Ninth USTAAF attacked the marshalling yard at Zell at 3 P.M. About 130 twin-engine bombers dropped 260 tons of high-explosive bombs and caused considerable damage in the yard. The raid was flown at the request of the advancing U.S. Army, which feared that the Wehrmacht was going to stage a counterattack from Würzburg using the railway facilities to bring in the troops.[24]

The final blows came as the U.S. Army approached the city. On 31 March, at the request of the 12th Armoured and 45th Infantry Divisions, two hundred bombers of the Ninth USTAAF dropped 275 tons of bombs on the marshalling yard, the adjacent military warehouses, and the army barracks northwest of the city. The master bomber of Bomber Group 409, one of the six groups attacking, misidentified his assigned target and directed the bombs of his group on the Koenig and Bauer Factory adjacent to the marshalling yard, destroying it completely. The factory was not an assigned target. The warehouses escaped damage but the yard was plowed over some more.[25] In addition, fighter bombers raked the city for about seven hours intermittently, shooting at anything that moved. One of the persons who moved in the city was myself.

I will never forget this raid. I was in the city when it started. No alarm could be heard, because there were no more sirens. The chatter of machine guns and the howl of descending bombs told me unmistakably what was about to happen. I took cover as well as I could and tried to get out of town. But that meant crossing one of the bridges. However they were strafed continuously, as I found out when I came nearer. It would have been like running a gauntlet. I finally crossed after I could hear a mobile siren (mounted on a car) sound the "all clear" in the distance.

Fighter Squadron 527 was one of the many flying this raid and they claimed to have destroyed three aircraft on the Luftwaffe base and four motor vehicles.[26] A total of sixty-five persons were killed in the bomber and fighter attacks this day.

For Würzburg it was the end of the Allied bomber offensive. There followed ground fighting with day-long artillery barrages until 6 April, when the Wehrmacht retreated eastward. Of the six thousand citizens who still lived in the city, another twenty were killed. The Wehrmacht had decided to fight for these ruins. About 300 American and 1,000 German soldiers lost their lives in this useless struggle.

The war seemed over for us and the end had come—but not quite yet. The Luftwaffe could still muster a few planes and twice, German fighter bombers came and tried to attack U.S. Army movements. The damage to the U.S. troops and the city was nil. After that the war had really come to an end for us, and the struggle for a new life started.

Würzburg was dead; 89 percent of its built-up area was destroyed. The British Bombing Survey, the U.S. Bombing Survey, and other sources all agree that it was the worst or second worst destroyed German city of more than 100,000 inhabitants. In the narrative of the official history of the RAF bomber campaign against Germany, Würzburg is not mentioned. It only figures in a reproduced list of the British Bombing Survey.[27] Apparently the military effort was not big enough to merit mention in the official history. That it was one of the most efficient ones appeared not to have mattered.

Part Two

The History of Strategic Bombing

"To study history is to understand
the grand coherence of things."
—Thomas Carlyle

3

The Road to Area Bombing

When Count Zeppelin mounted motors and ailerons on aluminum structures equipped with gas bags, the craft became the dirigible. It was not long before the military latched on to this invention, using it to carry explosives over enemy territory to drop on selected targets.

The real flyer came with the Wright brothers invention. The first heavier-than-air machine took flight at Kitty Hawk, North Carolina, on 17 December 1903. The Wright brothers submitted their design to the U.S. government for military use in scouting and message transmittal. The U.S. government showed no interest. In 1905 the British government was approached, but also failed to react positively. Similar disinterest was shown by the French and the Germans, because the former had the Montgolfier balloon and the latter were developing the Zeppelins.[1]

From 1908 onward the official attitudes changed slowly. The crowned heads of state and chiefs of their armed forces began to watch the aerial demonstrations. Wilbur and Orville Wright performed in European capitals with kaisers, kings, presidents, and assorted dignitaries as awed spectators. Governments and wealthy individuals acquired samples of this new contraption and flying clubs were founded. Even in provincial Würzburg the latest airplanes were demonstrated on what eventually became *Der Flugplatz* (the aerodrome) on the hill east of the city in 1910. By that time the Wright brothers had formed companies with local partners in France and

Germany. The German industrial enterprises AEG and Krupp had formed Flugmaschine Wright GmbH, a limited company, to build planes for, among others, the Italians.

In the Italian-Turkish War of 1912 the Italians used airplanes for scouting, replacing the earthbound cavalry platoon. The Turks claimed that one of the planes dropped an explosive on a Turkish field hospital. If that is true, it was the beginning of aerial bombing.

Tactical bombing means destroying a military object to permit ones soldiers to advance; i. e. tactical bombing happens on the battlefield. Strategic bombing means one attacks far behind the battlefield to destroy military targets, which can be anything from a munitions dump to a weapons factory to a railway station; anything that will enhance and support the enemy's war effort. If one cannot find them or hit them and some bombs fall on civilians—well there the tragedy starts. Yet if to the list of strategic targets is added the morale of the enemy population, the limit of chivalry and fairness in human combat has been exceeded. We are back to medieval times when the rape of civilian populations was the norm. Bombing what has been termed the homefront not only affects the civilians at home but also the soldiers on the front. They are supposed to protect their country which includes their families at home. But they are not there to defend their families.

Aerial warfare started in World War I, became refined, and modern warfare can no longer be considered without it. Air forces of all major powers have become a third armed service (after armies and navies). They operate under the same rules as the two older services.

Once the Wright brothers' invention could carry a load, the military value of the airplane was apparent. Scientists and engineers developed and perfected the carrying capacity, the navigation to the target, and the efficiency of the deadly loads dropped. To reduce the cost of warfare the bomber seemed the ideal weapon, a premise which could please any politician. Conversely it increased the status of the military, gave them more influence in the conduct of wars, and they proved that building bomber fleets had economic and commercial benefits. The bomber commanders promised they could destroy pinpoint targets causing great discomfort in the hinterland of the enemy.

The Germans started it in World War I, failed, killed civilians and, rightly so, were branded mother and children murderers. The RAF tried the same method in World War II. It also failed. The damage done by high-explosive bombs, even when they reached the target, was not what was expected; raids could not be flown at daylight because of enemy defense and finding a pinpoint target at night proved impossible. The bomber generals and marshals were at the end of their rope if they wanted to conduct the war in a civilized manner. Since the military were unable to deliver on their promises they proposed and received permission from the politicians to attack complete cities—to hit anything you have to hit everything.[2] But even that policy did not bring the desired results and fulfill the expectations. The solution was to attack not only whole cities but to burn them to the ground. The fire raid using a mixture of H.E. and incendiary bombs and causing firestorms proved the ultimate answer. It was practiced first by the Luftwaffe over Britain starting in September 1940, experimented with and developed further by RAF Bomber Command from 1942 onward, and perfected by the XXI Bomber Command of the Twentieth USAAF attacking Japan from January 1945 until the end of the war.

Just to make sure that the area fire raids were efficient and successful, the bomber commanders salted them with phosphorous and napalm-filled incendiaries which also had firecracker-like explosives, to assure that the bombs could not be extinguished and that nobody wanted to go near them. To curtail any rescue operations after a raid, delayed high explosives were added.

Such raids were considered to influence the morale of the enemy civilians and thereby add a bonus to the physical destruction. Bomber Harris thought the killing of civilians as in Hamburg was a humane method of warfare because it saved the flower of the youth of Britain from being mown down as in World War I.[3] Such a statement came from the man who was convinced that area bombing decided the war. On the same page of his memoirs Harris points out that 800,000 Germans were starved to death by the British naval blockade in World War I. Does he mean that killing civilians in air raids is a more humane method than starving them to death? An even more extreme position is taken by J. M. Spaight, who states that air power is not a destroyer but a saviour of civilization.[4] One must take into account the date of these statements to appreciate and discount them.

The above view of area bombing was the British version. The U.S. version was, until January 1945, different. General A. Spaatz said in an interview in 1965 that night bombing alone could not have won the war.[5] There was a need for daylight precision bombing as the USAAF practised it. General Ira Eaker said in an interview in 1962 that public opinion in the U.S. did not allow area bombing of German cities, but there was no such prohibitive feeling about bombing Japanese cities.[6]

After World War I, when aerial bombing had been practiced by the major warring powers, a number of people tried to establish what bombing had done and would do in the future. From the empirical development of this weapon system a theoretical base was to be developed to understand the phenomenon better and to make it more palatable to politicians, military staff, and the public in general. The theories were deduced from the latest technical developments and the experiences gained in bombing during the war. Air officers wrote manuals and developed theories for the next war. To mention just a few names on the victorious side of World War I there were Trenchard in the UK, Mitchell in the U.S., and Douhet in Italy.

The most often mentioned of these airmen is the Italian general Giulio Douhet. He was born in 1869. In World War I he advanced to staff officer to advise the Italian general staff on matters of air warfare. Before the war he had predicted (in 1909) that the sky was about to become a battlefield. His criticism of Italian WWI air warfare caused him to be discharged. In 1921 Douhet published the first edition of *Il Dominio dell' Aria*. At the opportune time of 1942 the book was translated and published in the U.S. and, a year later, when the Allied bomber offensive was gaining momentum, in Britain.[7] Long before the translation, his work was widely quoted and absorbed by the bomber officers. Douhet's thoughts were elevated to gospel and referred to in every budget request for air force funds and in manuals of operations.

If one condenses General Douhet's work one must recognize that he had a message, and undoubtedly at the time of his writings, a vision. Based on World War I experiences and technical developments shortly thereafter, the Douhet theorem states:

> Any military power of consequence needs an independent air force.
> The mainstay of this air force must be its bomber fleet.
> When war breaks out, the air force must gain air superiority not only over its own, but also over the enemy's air space.
> As soon as that is attained, the bomber force must ruthlessly attack the enemy hinterland.
> Maximum damage must be done in the shortest possible time.
> The attacks must not only be directed against strategic targets but also against enemy population morale.
> Since bombing is inaccurate and, most important targets are in populated areas, the bombing effort must be massive.
> Bombing of populated areas with high explosives, incendiary bombs and gas bombs will cause popular uprisings to force the enemy government to sue for peace.
> A concentration of attacks in time and quantities of bombs will bring about an early victory.
> Aerial bombs are cheap and will reduce the cost of the war effort.

Analyzing and extrapolating these statements makes one shudder. Certainly they were the considered consequences of experiences gained in World War I. But to elevate them to a proposed policy is, to say the least, against the spirit of the Hague and Geneva Conventions.

As it turned out, Italy, Douhet's country, ignored his teachings.

In World War II, Douhet's theories came into use, but that war was not won because massive bombing of enemy centers caused uprisings. And, to the credit of all participants, none of the bomber fleets dropped gas.

Douhet died in 1930. He did not live to see his native country shadowed by the wings of RAF Bomber Command and the U.S. Fifteenth Army Air Force. Allied raids on Milan, Turin, Genoa, and other cities caused heavy damage and the records show that the population reacted with panic; but there were no uprisings.

Douhet was not the first to expound the bombing theorem. Hugh Montague Trenchard, the RAF chief of staff, had practical experience to prove the same point. His theories and their application in the colonial skirmishes between the two world wars and in World War II have served Britain. When one reads his biography one recognizes a staunch British officer, fighting for king and country.[8] He was born 3 February 1873 and he died 10 February 1956. In recognition of his lifelong services to the military he received a peerage when he retired as chief of air staff in 1929. The ultimate honor for his services came with his burial in the Battle of Britain Chapel of Westminster Abbey.

Trenchard's first posting was in India, where he befriended Winston Churchill after an acrimonious polo game. Their ways never parted from that time onward. Trenchard fought in the Boer War, was badly wounded, and came out of it with a collapsed lung. He recuperated and it shows his strength of will power that he managed to enlist in the Royal Flying Corps in 1912. During World War I he advanced to commander of the British air forces in France under Marshal Haig, and towards the end of the war took over the Independent Air Force.

After the war the British Army and the Royal Navy exerted pressure to have the Royal Air Force, which was established as an independent third armed service in 1917, dissolved and control of all air warfare brought back to their respective commands. This was when Trenchard, then chief of air staff, fought his most famous battles. Trenchard succeeded in keeping and then enlarging the RAF as an independent fighting force. His reasoning was that Britain's "splendid isolation" had ended. As proven during World War I, the island's air space could be invaded at any European power's will in any future war at any time.

Trenchard maintained that Britain needed a strong air force

to defend itself. The defense was not to be waiting for the enemy planes to show on the horizon, but to destroy them at their home airfields. Offense was to be the best defense. Trenchard's theories were similar to Douhet's, but seemingly conceived from personal experience during the war and formed independently of the Italian general's. To survive the next war, in Trenchard's opinion, Britain needed "a strong bomber force to destroy the enemy's hinterland. Attack with these bombers the enemy's civil population to reduce its morale and will to continue fighting."

Although his detractors questioned his literary faculties, one must observe that Trenchard described his theory in short and concise form in submissions to Parliament, in meetings, and in press releases. RAF Bomber Command had not yet been formed when he left as chief of staff, but one can see his hand in Bomber Command's crest, which carries the motto "Strike hard, strike sure."[9] As any survivor of RAF bombing in World War II can testify, they indeed struck hard. The "sure" part is a matter of opinion.

In 1929 Trenchard resigned from the RAF and became commissioner of the metropolitan police of London. But he never lost contact and influence with the RAF. Before and during World War II he made many presentations in public, the House of Lords, and the Cabinet exhorting political and military leaders to have bombers pound Germany with civilian morale a primary target.

Another bomber theoretician was U.S. General William Mitchell. In World War I he had been commander of the U.S. Army Air Services in France. He had befriended Trenchard and was impressed by the latter's theories and successes in bombing cities in western Germany.

Mitchell was born in Nice, France, on 29 December 1879. He saw action in the Spanish-American War in Cuba and the Philippines. At the end of World War I, Mitchell was made a brigadier general. Upon his return to the United States in 1919 he stayed with the army and became an advocate of air power based on his campaign experiences.[10] He proposed an independent air service and suggested the building of aircraft carriers for the navy.

Mitchell, as compared with his contemporary air warfare theoreticians, Douhet and Trenchard, did not expound the value of the bomber as a means of attacking enemy populations. At the time this would have been against America's sense of honor. The problem for him was that the Europeans and the Japanese recognized the importance of air power—and bombing—whereas the United States did not.

The U.S. army and navy establishments, as in Britain, France, and Italy, lobbied against any further development of air power. The struggle became particularly acrimonious when General Mitchell declared that battleships were obsolete and that the coastal defenses of the continental United States should be taken over by an independent air force. It would be cheaper and more effective.

The battle was fought in Congress and in the media. Eventually it was agreed that the Army Air Force should prove its point by sinking some ex-German navy ships which had come into the possession of the United States as a result of the Treaty of Versailles. The tests were conclusive and convincing. But the U.S. government still neglected the development of the air service.

Mitchell became frustrated and vented his critical views in public. In early 1925 he was demoted to colonel and eventually court-martialed in Washington. He was found guilty of insubordination. Mitchell resigned from the army on 1 February 1926. He died on 19 February 1936 and is buried in Milwaukee.

Mitchell's theories of air warfare concerned themselves only with tactical bombing in defense of the United States. His theories were proven correct. During the Spanish Civil War, Republican planes attacked the German pocket battleship *Deutschland*, which was on blockade duties for Franco's Nationalists. The *Deutschland* was damaged and had to leave for home. But the most convincing proof undoubtedly came at Pearl Harbor in December 1941.

In our review of area bombing theories we must turn to the civilian theoreticians who had no World War I experiences to draw upon. Among the most prominent and influential of these civilians was Lord Cherwell. He was Churchill's scientific advisor during the entire Second World War. On 30 March 1942 he sent a minute to the prime minister suggesting that area bombing would break the morale of the German population.

When one studies Cherwell's biography one is left with the impression that his was a very enigmatic personality with a brilliant mind. He was a capable scientist and administrator, a politician and a member of the establishment, but at the same time an aloof, self-centered man.[11]

Frederick Alexander Lindemann—called Lord Cherwell after he became a peer in 1941—was born at Baden-Baden, a southwest German spa, in 1886. His mother was taking the waters at the time. His father was German and his mother American. That she gave birth to him in Germany, not Britain, and his German name, were a lifelong embarrassment to him. After primary education at Blairlodge in Scotland, he was back in Germany for his secondary and university education. For five years he attended the Realgymnasium (high school) in Darmstadt, the capital of the Grand Duchy of Hesse. The archives of the city of Darmstadt contain a letter from a fellow high school student in which Lindemann is portrayed as a withdrawn and arrogant fellow.[12] His biographer says the same thing and mentions that the young student circulated in rather high German society. The Grand Duke of Hesse, a grandson of Queen Victoria, took interest in him and he played tennis with such notables as Kaiser Wilhelm II, another grandson of Victoria, and Czar Nicholas II of Russia.

After high school graduation in 1905 he entered the Technische Hochschule (University) Darmstadt. The archives of this school show that for seven semesters Frederick studied *elektrotechnik*, or electrical engineering, until spring 1908.[13] After Darmstadt, Lindemann took further applied science studies at the Institute of Physical Chemistry run by Professor Nernst, an eminent scientist of his time, at the Königliche Friedrich Wilhelm University in Berlin, now called Humboldt University. In 1911 he earned his doctorate in "philosophy," as applied science was then called. His examiners, Professors Nernst and Planck, both Nobel Prize winners, termed his thesis excellent. Yet in oral examinations both professors and three others gave him only passing grades, and Nernst went as far as to enter into Lindemann's file that there were gaps in his knowledge of physics.[14]

After a lecture tour at the University of Chicago, Lindemann was back in Britain at the outbreak of World War I. In March 1915 he reported for duty at the Royal Aircraft Factory at Farnborough. He learned to fly and his interest in air warfare was kindled. After the war he became a professor of physics at the University of Oxford.

Socially, Lindemann continued to mix with the prominent and well-to-do, and in 1921 he and Churchill met to become lifelong friends. They dabbled in internal (mostly defense) and external politics. In 1933 Lindemann tried to see Hitler, and later Mussolini.

As there was a lack of interest in the British government in air defense and air warfare, Lindemann, with Churchill's help, successfully ran for election as a member of Parliament. From this base he influenced the work of committees and the Air Ministry shortly before World War II. He agreed with the theory that the only defense against bombing attacks was to destroy the enemy's air bases before his bombers could invade Britain.

Lindemann developed a phobia against all things German in his later life and his biographer states that he had an inflexible desire to pulverize Germany in World War II.[15] He let the notion go around that he was not really of German ancestry but that his father was from Alsace-Lorraine.

Churchill passed Lord Cherwell's minute of 30 March 1942 for comments to the minister for air and the chief of air staff, who in turn passed it on to his advisors. There were arguments between Cherwell and Tizard, a fellow scientific advisor, about the arithmetic, but nobody objected to the basic idea of area bombing. The result of the Cherwell minute was a chief of staff committee minute to the War Cabinet, C.O.S. (42) 379 (O), of 3 November 1942, which became the blueprint for the strategic bombing war against Germany.[16]

In 1942 Lord Cherwell became a member of Churchill's cabinet as paymaster general. His political fortunes ebbed and rose with those of Churchill, as did the honors bestowed on him during and after the war. After World War II he was criticized for supporting Bomber Command too much at the cost of the army, navy, and RAF Coastal Command, which was fighting the U-boats.

Lord Cherwell continued his scientific career after the war. He died on 3 July 1957. There is no doubt that Frederick A. Lindemann, Lord Cherwell, had a strong impact on the planning and execution of the bombing campaign. In many documents, briefs, and recommendations, his famous minute to Churchill forms the base.

Another scientist and bomber theoretician was Sir Henry Tizard. His and Cherwell's paths crossed many times and not always peacefully. Tizard was born at Gillingham, Kent, on 23 August 1885. He graduated in chemistry from Oxford in 1908 and went to Professor Nernst's institute in Berlin for postgraduate studies.

After one year in Berlin, Tizard returned to Oxford in 1909. At the outbreak of World War I he joined the Royal Flying Corps and became engaged in aeronautical research. In 1916 he was dispatched to France, to the headquarters of the RFC, to study the accuracy of bombing. To nobody's surprise, he stressed that first of all finding the target, and then hitting it, were the biggest problems of aerial bombardment.

After the war Tizard continued scientific work at Farnborough, the main base of the RAF. The RAF establishment particularly appreciated the fact that he was a pilot and hands-on scientist who had personally tried out many of his theories. He occupied various government and academic positions, and in 1935 Londonderry, the minister of air, appointed him chairman of the Committee for Scientific Survey of Air Defence. This was during the time when Hitler and Göring were boasting about the newly established Luftwaffe. Rightly so, there was concern in the British government as to where this saber rattling would lead.

The most important and consequential work Tizard performed in the Air Defense Committee was the installation of the radar system and its connection to the RAF's Fighter Command. All was well with the Air Defense Committee until Churchill succeeded in having Lindemann appointed to it. Because of old personal animosities, Lindemann blocked everything Tizard proposed. In September 1936 the Air Defense Committee was dissolved and a month later reconvened without "The Prof," as Lindemann was called.

At the same time, another committee chaired by Tizard recommended to the Air Ministry and the Committee of Imperial Defense means to improve Bomber Command. By 1936, in response to the British perception of a growing threat from the Luftwaffe, the British government had decided on the long-range four-engine bomber. But bombs, bombsights, and navigational aids were neglected. This situation continued until well into 1940, and as we will see later caused the escalation of the bomber war. Tizard's Bomber Committee recognized the shortcomings and made recommendations. But when World War II broke out, Bomber Command was still short of the means to perform its intended work.

After Churchill became prime minister in June 1940, Tizard's position became difficult, causing him to resign the chairmanship of the Defense and Bomber Committees; but he retained his position as advisor to the Air Ministry. In that capacity he made unfavorable comments on Lord Cherwell's minute to Churchill about dehousing the German civilian population. There followed a polite but pointed exchange of letters between him and Cherwell. Tizard disagreed with the calculations but not with the principle. In other words he subscribed to the theory of area bombing and its well-known consequences as seen in the blitz. He was all for this form of warfare, only he doubted that Bomber Command had enough resources to carry it through. Until such means were made available, Tizard proposed to concentrate on chasing U-boats. He told Cherwell, "I don't really disagree with you fundamentally, but only on the matter of timing."[17]

Until the end of the war Tizard continued as advisor to the Air Ministry and the Ministry of Aircraft Production. He retired from all political and academic appointments in 1949 and passed away on 9 October 1950. To sum up, Tizard believed in Douhet and Trenchard and did his administrative and scientific best to give his country the means to implement their theories.

Another scientist involved with bombing theories was Lord Solly Zuckerman, or "the Zuck," as he was affectionately called by his friends and admirers. And to the latter I have added myself, after having reviewed his book. Lord Zuckerman was born in South Africa in 1904. In 1926 he went to England to study medicine. After graduation he researched the behavior of apes and monkeys. Between 1932 and 1934 he worked as a research fellow at Yale but then returned to England. At the beginning of World War II he was asked to conduct investigations into the effect of bomb blasts on the human body. Based on his past work he tested apes and goats held in trenches while bombs were exploded nearby. The tests were performed in the Salisbury Plains in October 1939 at the instigation of the Ministry of Home Security.[18] The ministry wanted an assessment of how people would suffer and should react, if still capable, after a bomb had exploded near their air-raid shelter. Lord Zuckerman himself was in one of the trenches, slightly farther away from the exploding bombs than the apes and goats, and he recorded that he suffered no discomfort. His final report stated that there was no visible effect on the animals.

(In this connection, I should mention that the civil defense authorities in Germany advised us not to sit upright with our heads against the wall in the air-raid shelter during an attack. The pressure wave would cause our heads to bash against the wall, and the upright position would expose our lungs. We were advised to lie flat on the floor when and if bombs came down in the vicinity.)

In further studies, Zuckerman found that the German 50-kg bomb was more effective in killing people than heavier bombs of 250 or 1,000 kg. Lord Zuckerman suggested to Lord Cherwell that in order to arrive at recommendations for the deployment of Bomber Command, a study should be used which he had made for the Ministry of Home Security of the bombing of Hull and Birmingham in 1940 and 1941 by the Luftwaffe. Costs and results of the operation of Bomber Command were questioned in Parliament and in military circles at the time. A clear policy had to be developed.

The findings of the Hull/Birmingham Study as published in Lord Zuckerman's book in Appendix 2 indicate:

One ton of bombs kills four people.
Thirty-five people are bombed out for every person killed.
Dwelling houses are destroyed by high explosives and not by fire.
Factories are more seriously damaged by fire than by explosives.
There was no breakdown of morale in either city.

These were only the most important findings. The report was used by Cherwell for his minute to Churchill. There was one detail in the minute which Cherwell overlooked or misinterpreted. Zuckerman said that steady employment and a high rate of wages are the major stabilizing factors for the population. If that applied to Hull and Birmingham, why would it not apply to German industrial workers? Why would they rebel against their leaders keeping in mind not only national feelings but also the experience of high unemployment during the Depression? One wonders whether Cherwell, a recognised scientist, was not out of his depth when it came to drawing sociological conclusions from the effects of his recommended bombing theories. Zuckerman says it was Cherwell who was responsible for the planning and execution of the area bombing policy of World War II.

For Zuckerman it became clear that area bombing was not a way to win the war; in other words, he was at odds with the area bombers. This did not mean that he condemned aerial bombing. He was in favor of precision bombing of strategic targets such as railways and general infrastructure, but not with morale as the main target. Zuckerman's approach to the whole problem was very scientific. He studied the results, evaluated them statistically and then drew impartial conclusions. As an example, he concluded that destruction of railway targets would help to win the war. To destroy a railway center, four 500-lb. bombs must be dropped per acre of the center.[19]

Lord Zuckerman was wrong in only one respect. In his report on Hull and Birmingham he states that most dwellings were destroyed by high-explosive bombs rather than fire. This may have been the case, but probably because the Luftwaffe hadn't concentrated on incendiaries during its raids. Bomber Command later found that the destructive force of firestorms far exceeded its expectations, with Hamburg, Dresden, and Würzburg as fiery examples. Even better proof of the effect of firestorms were the results of the Twentieth U.S. Air Force raids on Japan from March 1945 until the end of World War II. But the planning of the Japanese raids was not based on theory, rather on what General Curtis LeMay, the U.S. commander, had seen the RAF achieve in Europe.

In one respect, Lord Zuckerman was absolutely correct and it would have been to the benefit of friend and foe alike if all the responsible air force commanders had concentrated the bombing campaign on transport targets. Zuckerman, as advisor to Air Marshal Tedder, had succeeded in having the Allied bomber forces destroy the railway system prior to landings in Sicily and the mainland of Italy. Similarly, prior to the Normandy landings the western European railway system was devastated to make it unusable for German troop movements. The Italian landings and the ensuing campaign were a success as railway traffic came to a complete halt.[20] The Normandy landings were a success, and once the bomber leaders reluctantly agreed to attack the German transport system from January 1945 onward, German resistance collapsed. Although, even here there is a caveat: The losses of civilians living next to these transportation targets were considerable. Many people in France and Belgium lost their lives at the hands of their allies.

After the war Lord Zuckerman was put in charge of the scientific part of the British Bombing Survey. As he points out in his book, the survey proved that the bombing offensive was not the determining factor in the defeat of Germany. On the contrary, Lord Zuckerman shows that if his recommendations to raid infrastructure targets such as transport and oil had been followed from the beginning, the war would have been shorter and above all less costly in lives and materials. The report was not appreciated by the Air Ministry and, to this date has never been published. A copy is filed at the PRO.[21]

After the war, Lord Zuckerman returned to his academic career and he died in March 1993. He was a man whose theories were correct, but their acceptance came only after other theories had painfully been proven wrong.

So far in this chapter we have dealt solely with Allied bomber theoreticians, and mostly only with British and American ones. Going through the relevant literature one finds no French, Russian, Japanese, or other nationals who have produced thoughts and theories on the subject. Even in Germany, the country that first practiced strategic bombing on a large scale in World War I, we cannot find a theoretician who advocated area bombing.

Nevertheless, probably the first man to ever propose bombing civilians was German Rear Admiral Paul Behncke, who as early as 1914 suggested to his superior, Admiral von Pohl, commander-in-chief of the Imperial Navy, that German Navy Zeppelins attack England to cause panic and confusion among its citizens.[22] It was to be a military operation without any theoretical background. Pohl and the Kaiser rejected the idea, but not for long.

In World War II, Reichsmarshal Hermann Göring, the supreme commander of the Luftwaffe, approached bombing from an empirical background. He had been a fighter pilot in World War I, with twenty kills to his credit. Ernst Udet, the quartermaster general of the Luftwaffe, had also been a fighter pilot in World War I. He is credited with developing the dive-bomber as a weapon. Udet's and the Luftwaffe staff's idea was that the divebomber guaranteed a higher rate of success in hitting pinpoint targets. As such, it suited the Wehrmacht's aims, and above all its budget, much better than the horizontal bomber.

The only German who could qualify as a bomber theoretician was General Walther Wever, who was chief of staff of the emerging Luftwaffe from 1933 to his death in an aircraft accident at Dresden on 3 June 1936. Wever, an army officer until 1933, was a staunch nationalist who, like the majority of the German people, despised the Versailles Treaty and thought that an historical injustice had been done. His loyalty to the Kaiser's army tradition was very strong and he therefore had little use for Hitler and Göring. But he was convinced that Hitler and the Nazi government could and would rectify the wrongs of Versailles.

As chief of staff of the Luftwaffe he recognised the importance of the bomber, and in particular the strategic bomber. Under his aegis, the German aircraft manufacturers Junkers and Dornier developed what was called the Ural Bomber; long-range aircraft that could strike as far as the Soviet factories behind the Ural Mountains. As an extension of the Douhet and Trenchard doctrines, he theorized that destroying the enemy's armament production potential would stop the supplies to the front line and facilitate the defeat of the enemy army. That his bombers were called Ural Bombers did not mean that he saw only the Soviet Union as a possible future enemy.[23]

Wever's entire outlook on aerial warfare, in his capacity as chief of staff in the early 1930s, is condensed in his speech at the opening of the Air Warfare Academy at Berlin-Gatow on 1 November 1935.[24] In this address he stressed his belief that the Luftwaffe by itself could not win a war. It had to cooperate with the army and the navy. Wever made clear his belief that "The objective of any war is to destroy the morale of the enemy's armed forces."[25]

What Wever meant was to cause destruction in the enemy's hinterland. However—and here he differed from Douhet and Trenchard—he strictly limited his bombing theories to strategic targets and made it abundantly clear that enemy civilian morale was not to be attacked. This thinking was manifested in the "Luftwaffen Dienstvorschrift [Service Manual] No.16," which Wever authored prior to his death in 1935. It was revised in 1940 and applied until the end of the Luftwaffe in 1945. In the 1935 and the 1940 editions under paragraph 186, it stated that "raids on cities with the purpose of causing terror to the civilian population are basically out of order." Only if the enemy persists in raiding German cities in that manner may reprisal raids be permitted.[26] How this instruction was interpreted from 1940 onward by the Luftwaffe we shall see later.

Wever wanted a strategic air force, but even if he had lived, it is doubtful that it would have been created. His untimely death prevented him from becoming a bomber practitioner.

After Wever's death, the Luftwaffe's rearmament accelerated, and his successors, in unison with Hitler's political and military aims, saw in the Luftwaffe a tool for blitzkrieg (lightning war), in which aircraft would support the army, providing fire support for fast-moving armored units.

There were other German air warfare theoreticians who proposed bombing. In May 1933, the Lufthansa director Dr. Knaus submitted a secret document to the German Air Ministry. The civil airline director, turned military expert, recommended how the Luftwaffe should be organised. He explained how the bomber force should attack Paris and the French armament industry in Lyon, Dijon, Besançon, and St. Étienne. Further targets would be Warsaw, Byalistok, and Brest-Litowsk.[27] It is claimed that Dr. Knaus's recommendations were later implemented in the bombing raids in the Spanish Civil War by the Condor Legion of the Luftwaffe fighting on the side of Franco and, in World War II, when Warsaw, Rotterdam, and Belgrade were attacked.

In summing up, one must conclude that there were few men who expounded area bombing on a scientific and rational basis. It was the bomber practitioners from 1914 onward who perfected area bombing on a trial and error basis with devastating results. They were all military men.

4

THE BOMBER PRACTITIONERS

We must now turn to the bomber practitioners. These were the people who conducted the death and destruction which we call the bombing war. But before looking into the lives of these leaders it seems necessary to review the definition "practitioner." They were all military people of elevated rank. They commanded and controlled great numbers of men and machinery and were responsible for the spending of vast sums of money and resources of their respective countries. They dispatched the squadrons that brought death and destruction. Prior to Douhet, Trenchard, Mitchell, et al, with their theories, these practitioners made use of the technical advances in aeronautics to conduct this new type of warfare. In WWI it was the German Zeppelins, Gothas, and Riesenflug-zeuge that spread terror over Britain and France. The Allies were not far behind in retaliating. The men in charge of these carriers of destruction could be called executioners or implementers. They executed and implemented carefully concocted plans of how to hurt the enemy's civilian population. In the process they not only implemented a scheme, they executed thousands of people with their bombs. They were thought to be the instigators and implementors of these mass executions. But were they really? All of them were military men and, therefore, subject to orders from above. As marshal of the RAF, Sir Arthur Harris, the man who sent Bomber Command to Dresden in February 1945, said it was not he who decided to raze that beautiful city, he only followed orders.[1]

Many a military man blamed for disasters defends himself

with pleading that he only followed orders. Orders there must be, otherwise the entire fabric of the military will fall apart. Although, when Fieldmarshal Keitel, the Wehrmacht chief of staff, pleaded "orders" as his defense at the Nürnberg trials in 1946 he was still found guilty and hanged. But that obviously represents the difference between victor and vanquished. Ironically, Harris made his statement at about the same time Keitel put up his defense.

To call the bomber leaders "implementors" appears to be too flat a definition. To call them "executioners" seems too harsh. I prefer to call these men "practitioners." But nobody should ever ask me to call them heroes.

The bomber practitioners we will learn about here received their orders from chiefs of staff, who in turn implemented policy decisions taken by their governments or heads of state. In World War I there were people such as Hindenburg and Ludendorff, who ordered General von Höppner to send the German bombers off. On the Allied side, the Independent Air Force, formed as a separate section of the RAF and commanded by General Trenchard, was directed by the Air Ministry to raid from its base at Nancy, France, any German city within its reach.

Trenchard was at first hesitant about bombing cities. He had commanded the Royal Flying Corps in France, which came under Fieldmarshal Haig. The function of the RFC was tactical air warfare to help the Allies break the deadlock of the trench war. Trenchard was very loyal to Haig and believed aircraft should only be used to support the ground forces. When he was approached to accept command of the Independent Air Force he hesitated. In his biography the story is told that he only accepted when he accidently overheard two high-ranking navy officers, while sitting on a bench in Green Park, London, saying that he should be shot for insubordination.[2] The general accepted and being the true officer he was, he dedicated himself thoroughly to his new assignment. His appointment as head of the IAF became effective in September 1917. By November of that year he was quoted as saying that he wanted to bomb Germany.[3] He had undergone a metamorphosis in compliance with his military calling and the decisions taken by the British Cabinet and the Air Ministry. German cities were to be bombed in retaliation for what the German Army and Navy Zeppelins and the German KAGOHL (*Kampfgeschwader Oberste Heeresleitung*—Squadron of the Supreme Command) had done during the past two years over England.

Trenchard believed in bombing the enemy's populations and thereby attacking their morale until the end of his life. As chief of staff of the RAF he was responsible for the bombing of native and tribal insurrections in the British Empire between the two world wars. He convinced the cash-strapped British government that it was cheaper to quell uprisings in India, Somalia, Iraq, and the Aden Protectorate with bomber squadrons than with sending expeditionary columns into these areas. After the successful pacification of the Mad Mullah of Somaliland by a single RAF squadron in 1920,[4] his conviction of the salutary effect of bombing went so far that he even disobeyed instructions and had villages and towns bombed in Iraq in 1923.[5]

After he retired from the RAF he was still a person to reckon with in the affairs of the Royal Air Force. At the time of the Phony War, from September 1939 to April 1940, when Chamberlain, the British prime minister, ordered strict adherence to the never-signed 1923 Hague Air Warfare Conventions, Trenchard advocated bombing transport targets and cities in Germany by night.[6] In spring 1941 he sent a letter to Churchill urging him to carry on with the raids to Germany and in August 1942 he addressed Churchill again stating that in lieu of an invasion of the Continent, Britain should and could win the war by breaking the morale of the German people. All these pronouncements he had already formulated in the early 1920s when he stated that "if people are subject to sufficient bombing they will compel the Government to sue for peace."[7] He was proven wrong.

There is a plethora of books by German flyers telling about their experiences in World War I. These are descriptions of what the fighting in the air was all about. But none of these books give the background for why the Zeppelins and Gothas dumped their loads on enemy civilians. Looking into the German archives is equally frustrating, because most German

Air Ministry and Luftwaffe files were either purposely destroyed by the Germans or lost when the Potsdam Heeresarchiv (Army Archives) were lost in one of the last Bomber Command air raids at the end of World War II.

Field Marshal Hindenburg, General Ludendorff, and General Höppner were the German bomber practitioners in World War I. There was no deeply considered theory behind their decisions to bomb enemy cities. The idea was to retaliate against the Hunger Blockade and thus to bring the war into enemy territory. These raids were to be against military targets only, so these military men protested. In actual fact, they admitted that civilians would also suffer.

Paul von Hindenburg was born at what is today Poznan, Poland, in 1847. He was a product of the Prussian Junker Class, became an army officer, fought in the Prussian-Austrian War and the Franco-Prussian War, and retired in 1911. The Kaiser called him back for active duty to stem the Russian tide which had entered East Prussia in the early months of World War I. He routed the Russians at Tannenberg and soon thereafter was appointed chief of staff. After the war a memorial was erected at Tannenberg, and when Hindenburg died in 1934 he was buried there. As per the Versailles Treaty he was to be indicted by an international court for war crimes. That part of the treaty, like a few other provisions, fell by the wayside. A German court at Leipzig was to treat the case, but never did. By 1925 Hindenburg was elected president of the Weimar Republic and in January 1933 he made Hitler chancellor. If Hindenburg had been accused of war crimes they would have included his bombing orders. This could have had a salutary impact on the large-scale bombing in World War II.

Eric Ludendorff was the brain behind the Army General Staff and, more so than Hindenburg, must be held responsible for the bombings in World War I. He lived from 1865 to 1937. His biggest feat was that he realized when it was time to quit. In October 1918 he requested the German government ask for an armistice in accordance with President Wilson's Fourteen Points. Although the Central Powers's structure was coming apart with increasing speed at that time, his request was considered treason and he had to flee to neutral Sweden. His exile lasted one year and he returned to a Germany in chaos. This condition must have caused him to see a savior in Hitler. He participated in the 1923 Beer Hall Putsch and from 1924 to 1928 became a NSDAP (Nazi Party) member of the Reichstag.

During World War I the man in charge of the German tactical bombers was General Ernst von Höppner. He was the man responsible for all German aircraft and as such decided on targets and the timing of raids. He had been a career cavalry officer and saw in the airplane a better means of performing reconnaissance than on horseback. In his book, published after World War I, he blames the British and the French for having started strategic bombing.[8] He writes that the Royal Navy Air Service and the Royal Flying Corps attacked strategic targets such as Zeppelin hangars and the Zeppelin Works at Friedrichshafen. He admits that the Germans attacked cities in Belgium and on the Channel coast and even the "fortresses" of Warsaw and Mlawa on the Eastern Front, all located on or near the fighting front. Höppner claimed the German airmen always attacked military targets only, whereas the French attacked, among many others, the "open" city of Freiburg, fifty miles behind the front line on 4 December 1914.

Höppner sent off his machines with orders to aim at military and/or strategic installations, although he admitted that this did not always happen and that civilians were killed.[9] But he showed no qualms because the French had continued to raid German cities, such as Karlsruhe on Corpus Christi Day 1916, killing 110 civilians, mostly children, according to German reports.

Höppner, the bomber practitioner, had convinced himself that his orders were justified as reprisals in accordance with the Hague Conventions. Also, he felt he was only following orders as did many another soldier.

Another bomber practitioner was Britain's Sir John Salmond, who had taken over from Trenchard in France in World War I when the latter was put in charge of the Independant Air Force. Salmond's attitude to area bombing is best shown in his November 1923 letter to Trenchard, in which he defended the practice in Iraq.[10] He first of all hid, as any good bomber practitioner, behind his superiors, some of them high civilian administrators. But then he showed his conviction that bombing civilians and their villages was helping the task of pacifying the area. In other words, don't fight the men, fight their women and children. It is cheaper and less demanding on your own military resources. Many M.P.s in Britain and even Air Commodore L. E. O. Charlton, Salmond's chief staff officer, objected to this type of pacification.

Salmond was active in the RAF until 1933 when he resigned as chief of air staff. This was the highest position an RAF officer could attain and Salmond occupied it for three years. His actions in Iraq were only a small part of his career as an honorable RAF officer, but they added to the proliferation of area bombing as an acceptable form of warfare. One historian has gone so far as to call Sir John Salmond's operations in Iraq a brilliant example of RAF activities.[11] Salmond's influence was felt in the decision-making councils of the Air Ministry until well into World War II. Yet Salmond never came under severe criticism in Parliament or in public as compared with other British bomber practitioners.

RAF pacifying practices were also conducted in the Aden Protectorate, where in 1934 Lord Portal of Hungerford, as he called himself later, became the officer commanding the British forces. Charles Portal was born in 1893. When World War I broke out, he volunteered and before long joined the Royal Flying Corps. He came to the attention of Trenchard and it was he who after the war, when many a military man was out of the service, saw the value of Portal and had him go through the RAF Staff College, the Naval College at Greenwich, and eventually the Imperial Defence College. By 1929 Portal not only had combat experience but had also received an academic training which qualified him for the highest military positions.

In 1940 he was in charge of Bomber Command. It was in this position that he experienced the technical shortcomings of aerial bombing and was later instrumental in finding the solutions. Portal has been quoted as saying that by bombing a large area, some strategic target will be destroyed and no bombs would be wasted.[12] It seemed again a matter of economics to bomb civilians. In reality it was nothing else but a return to the Trenchard Doctrine; nobody admitted it, but the target became the morale of the enemy people.

Portal moved from Bomber Command to chief of air staff in November 1942. In that position until the end of the war he controlled not only the bombing, but all activities of the RAF. He had tremendous responsibilities when one considers what Fighter Command, Coastal Command, and the squadrons stationed outside the United Kingdom did to fight the Axis powers. He not only had to hold up the purely military end of the RAF but also be involved in the politics and economics of the war. He was made a viscount after the war and upon retirement could look back on a successful military career. That area bombing became the major effort of the RAF was not his doing alone. He was egged on and driven into it by public opinion, fellow airmen, and last but not least by Churchill. Portal clearly is on record that he wanted area bombing, with all its implicit damages and casualties. He and Harris believed that Germany could be defeated by bombing alone.[13] Portal was the man in charge and he must take at least some of the blame and a good part of the responsibility.

Sir Charles Portal's ashes rest in an unmarked grave in the churchyard at Funtington, Sussex. If it had not been for the help of the church custodian, I would never have found it.[14] Seen in the proper perspective, Portal deserved better. The marshal of the Royal Air Force had died at his home in West Ashling on 23 April 1971.

Of course, the most prominent British bomber practitioner is the man who commanded RAF Bomber Command from 23 February 1942 until the end of hostilities in Europe—marshal of the RAF, Sir Arthur T. Harris. He was born at Cheltenham on 13 April 1892. His father was a civil servant in India. Harris received his education in the home country and in 1910 went to Rhodesia to farm. By December 1914, as a soldier in a Rhodesian regiment, he was fighting the German Colonial Force in German Southwest Africa. After the rout of the Germans, Harris was called upon to fight the Germans in German East Africa. He refused, made his way to England, and enlisted in the Royal Flying Corps. By January 1916, Second Lieutenant Arthur T. Harris was a qualified pilot and assigned to a squadron chasing the Zeppelins on their raids over England. In 1917 he was posted to France. By 1918 he was back in England, by now a major, to hunt the German bombers. After the war Harris was not demobilized but given a permanent commission. There followed service in India, where he gained his first experience in bombing tribes on the Northwest Frontier. The army restricted that activity by starving the few RAF squadrons in India for funds, spare parts, and recognition as a pacifying force. Harris was so enraged that he threatened to resign. But Salmond had been sent to India to review the situation and convinced Harris to come with him to Mesopotamia to help quell the Turkish-led insurrections there. His biographer praises his exploits in Iraq, which laid the foundations for Harris's later actions in World War II.[15]

By 1924 Harris was back in Britain to attend first the Army Senior Officers School at Sheerness and then to continue his career as commander of RAF units. In 1927 he enrolled at the Army Staff College at Camberley. There followed more postings as commanding officer. He was to return to Iraq to perform similar duties as in 1922-23, but objected and through his normal stubborn persistence avoided a posting that he felt would not further his career. He stayed in Britain commanding a flying boat squadron before being posted to the Air Ministry. From July 1933 onward he worked in the Directorate of Operations and Intelligence. He was involved in the preparation of reports that detailed the defense of the empire against Germany, for a war which appeared likely to happen soon.

Four reports were produced and by 1936, based on an "Appreciation of the Situation in the Event of War against Germany in 1939," the government approved the creation of a strategic bomber force. The interesting part of the report is that it foresaw that bombing alone could not win a war against Germany. The army had to eventually conquer the enemy's lands. Considering that Harris put his name to this report and, taking into account his later unshakable conviction that the bomber alone could force Germany to its knees, it is interesting to note how Harris changed from area bomber after his exploits in the mandates and colonies to strategic bomber in mid-career and then back to full-force area bomber again after 1941. Of course, in 1936 until May 1940 the British government and the public considered killing civilians with bombs as unacceptable. Killing civilians by the proven method of starvation through naval blockade was acceptable because it had been done a few times before. Nobody wanted to be as bad as the Huns had been in World War I when they bombed Britain. The report clearly states that area bombing was to be adopted only after the Germans had started it. It was to be a matter of retaliation, which in accordance with the Hague Conventions was perfectly legal. There remains of course the nagging doubt about what the disciples of Trenchard really thought considering their master's doctrine, i.e. area bombing.

In 1938 Harris took command of No. 4 Bomber Group. Before long he was sent to the United States to oversee the purchase of military aircraft for the RAF. Later in 1938 he took up the post of air officer commanding in Palestine and Transjordan. In his book *Bomber Offensive*, Harris describes how the air force cooperated with the army by circling the rebellious areas to prevent anybody from escaping until the army or police could arrive and solve the problem.[16] There was no bombing of villages as in other Empire trouble spots.

In June 1939 Harris was promoted to air vice marshal. His tour of duty in Palestine was to extend until the end of that year, but he returned to England because of an ulcer. He arrived in August and shortly after war broke out he became commander of No. 5 Bomber Group.

In February 1942 Harris was appointed chief of Bomber Command. By that time the air war had taken a number of turns down the road to brutality and destruction. Harris had instructions to bomb Germany in accordance with the Casablanca Directive, he had instructions from the Air Ministry and, in his discussions with Churchill at Chequers, he received full support from the very top. He convinced himself and others that the bomber could win the war and that an Allied landing to fight the German armed forces and occupy the country was not necessary. Thus began the Strategic Air Offensive against Germany. The main target, ever so unofficially, became German morale. Harris showed his true colors in his book when he said, "the destruction of factories, which nevertheless was on an enormous scale, could be regarded as a bonus. The aiming points were usually right in the centre of the town."[17] After an attack on Cologne, he quoted in a letter to Churchill on 24 March 1942 German sources in neutral Turkey that said "we did a lot of damage and killed plenty of Boches."[18] When one analyzes these statements and looks at them from Harris's point of view, one must admit that he was not just a brutal butcher, as he has been called by many people. If he wanted to kill Germans only, in sort of a body count, he could have attacked small, undefended cities only. The risk would have been smaller and the results even more spectacular. That in the end defenseless cities such as Würzburg were raided and efficiently destroyed is, of course, proof that the military machine works like a bulldozer. There was no stopping Harris from taking his campaign and his theories to the very end. It is his ordering the bombing beyond reason and the call of duty that made his name anathema to many people after the war. He showed no concern for the suffering the attack on morale was causing. Yet, when it came to his own life, he is quoted as being delighted that he did not have to leave his family in an area of Britain, which at the time was still being bombed by the Luftwaffe, when in June 1941 he was sent on a second mission to the United States.[19] It must have crossed his mind that a bomb could make his loved ones suffer.

Harris's biographer, Dudley Saward, portrays him in the best of light. Not so merciful is Charles Messenger.[20] Sir Charles Webster and Noble Frankland in *The Strategic Air Offensive against Germany, 1939–1945* even went as far as not to consult Harris in the preparation of their official history.[21] Yet all agree that he was a dedicated officer, concerned with the welfare of the soldiers under his command, and that he never took a leave while he was in charge of Bomber Command.[22] He had the respect of men in the highest places, such as Roosevelt and Eisenhower, right down to the airmen he sent on these dangerous missions. It was the esteem he commanded in high places that probably caused Portal not to sack him when the two disagreed on target priorities in early 1945. Harris stubbornly continued to order area raids. He was convinced his method would work better and, above all, he finally had all the men, machinery, bombs, and materials at his disposal to prove it. Last but not least, his past exploits, like the first "Thousand

Bomber Raid," on Cologne shortly after he had taken over Bomber Command, had been approved by all. He was even made a Knight Commander of the Order of Bath for that feat on 10 June 1942.

Further proof for Harris that he was right must have been that Churchill was in favor of the area-bombing campaign. It was the prime minister and not the Air Staff or Bomber Command who early in the war wanted the attack on German morale.[23] It must also have occurred to him that his predecessor in Bomber Command, Air Marshal Sir Richard Peirse, was less than eighteen months at that post before he was shifted to a far less important command in India and Southeast Asia. Had this man failed to fulfill, the expectations placed in him and Bomber Command?

In the end Harris, like Portal, was convinced that the bomber offensive against Germany had been a huge success. Without its stubborn prosecution, in his opinion, the Allies would not have won the war. He took this conviction with him to his grave when he died at his home in Goring-on-Thames at age ninety-one in 1984. He is buried in an unassuming grave on the hill east of Goring. As with Portal one would expect a more honorable place for a man who commanded the biggest and longest campaign of World War II. Whether he was right or wrong cannot be the question. He followed instructions, gave orders and over fifty thousand RAF airmen lost their lives. Their exploits and memories alone require respect, which with a measure of judgment must be extended to their commander.

Yet after Harris resigned his command on 28 August 1945, after there was no more fighting, not even in the Far East, he came under neverending criticism, which to this date has not ended. He was not honored as were other great commanders by the Labor government. His biographer, Saward, blames the influence of John Strachey, under secretary of state for air in the Atlee government. Strachey had a background of Nazi and Communist affiliations before the war. Harris considered him a security risk and effected his removal from the Directorate of Bomber Operations.[24] Messenger, in his book *Bomber Harris*, says that the air marshal received all the honors he deserved.[25]

He was raised from Commander of the Order of Bath (KCB) to Knight Grand Cross of the Order of Bath (GCB) in June 1945. On 1 January 1946 he was promoted to marshal of the Royal Air Force, a promotion that was normally reserved for officers who had been chief of air staff. In January 1952 he was made a baronet.

However, the most interesting point in the controversy is his reported opinion that if the Germans had won the war, he would have been indicted for war crimes.[26] After the war and ever since, nobody in Germany has officially called him a war criminal. But nobody was enchanted when in May 1992 a statue of him was unveiled in the center of London. What made that event even more difficult to understand was that the House of Windsor was at the head of the unveiling ceremony with Her Majesty Queen Elizabeth, the Queen Mother pulling the cord on the Union Jack. Why Lady Thatcher, the ex-prime minister, attended is also a question. One can understand that the veterans wanted recognition for their leader and, thereby, for their heroism and sufferings in war and the defamation afterward. But a plaque inside the Church of St. Clement Danes, instead of a monument in front of it, would have been, so many years after the campaign, a fitting honor for all concerned. The statue is exposed, as any outside monument, to graffiti not only from humans but also from birds.

Portal and Harris were the chief exponents on the British side of the bombing war from 1939 to 1945. There were others, such as Air Marshal Saundby, Harris's second in command, the commanders of the bomber groups, and the senior staff at the Air Ministry, such as Bufton and Bottomley. They all played a role in the bombing, but they were even more exposed to be mere implementors of orders from above.

Now we turn to United States bomber practitioners. After Pearl Harbor and after Hitler and Mussolini had declared war on the United States, Generals Spaatz, Doolittle, Eaker, and Anderson moved to Europe and took charge of the U.S. bomber fleets.

The man above these bomber practitioners was General Henry H. Arnold, commander of the U.S. Army Air Forces. He in turn reported to the army chief of staff, General George C.

Marshall. United States government and public opinion was that civilian life was sacred and should not be exposed to deliberate bombing. Precision attacks in daylight were the accepted form of U.S. aerial warfare. Anticipating that enemy fighters would cause losses, the answer was to fly in tight formations and have the bombers equipped with strong defenses. Hence the name of Flying Fortress for the B-17 and Superfortress for the B-29.

Arnold gradually changed the policy and by 1943 he was not "going to pull his punches because some civilian might get killed."[27] After the most destructive-ever area raid (Tokyo, March 1945) had been flown, he sent the responsible commander a congratulatory wire. In the end, Arnold regarded terror bombing and the obliteration of urban centers as necessities of war.[28]

The most prominent commander and bomber practitioner of the USAAF was General Carl Spaatz. He was born on 29 June 1891 at Boyertown, Pennsylvania, went to West Point, and in 1914 joined the U.S. Army Signal Corps. He was sent to France after he learned to fly, and as a fighter pilot had three kills to his credit. Between the wars he occupied staff positions and rose to assistant chief of the Air Corps. In 1942 he was posted to Britain, first to command the Eighth Air Force, then the Twelfth Air Force, next the Northwest African Air Force, and ultimately from January 1944, back in Britain, was chief of the U.S. strategic bomber forces with Generals Eaker and Doolittle commanding the Eighth and Fifteenth USAAF respectively under him. It was in this position that Spaatz gradually and ever so secretly changed from precision bomber to area bomber. He made no great announcements and just went ahead with dispatching the bombers. While in this exposed position he kept out of controversy and always was assured that he was in line with policy and his superiors. He is quoted as saying, "The military man carries out the orders of his political bosses."[29] Like Air Marshal Harris, he carried out his orders and has to be debited with the human losses these actions caused. He was very circumspect in always pretending that only military targets were aimed at and in February 1945 he told his commanders to take special care to maintain that impression publicly.[30]

When the war in Europe came to an end he was transferred to the Far East theater and took over command of the U.S. Army Air Forces there. But most of the conventional bombing and damage in Japan had already been done. He and most other U.S. army and air force generals were opposed to the dropping of the atomic bombs. After the war and after the U.S. Air Force had become an independent service, equal in ranking to the army and the navy, just as General Mitchell had proposed many years before, he became the first chief of staff of the United States Air Force. Spaatz died in Washington, D.C., on 14 July 1974 and is buried in the cemetery of the U.S. Air Force Academy at Colorado Springs, Colorado.

Almost as prominent a bomber practitioner as Spaatz ranks General Curtis LeMay. He was born in West Columbus, Ohio, on 15 November 1906. He obtained a bachelors degree in civil engineering from Ohio State University. While at the university he learned to fly by first joining the National Guard and then enlisting in the Army Air Corps. Next came the Air Corps Tactical School, and before long he was a permanent commissioned officer in the air corps.

LeMay became known as an excellent navigator and is credited with the military and political feat of locating and flying over the Italian oceanliner *Rex* seven hundred miles out in the Atlantic in 1938; just to show the rising Axis dictators what the U.S. Air Corps could do with their four-engine bombers. He also was the navigator of a B-17 that flew non-stop from the United States to Bogota, Columbia, a considerable achievement at the time.

In 1941, while the United States was still neutral, he was in the 34th Bomb Group, which located German submarines in the Atlantic.[31] After the Eighth Army Air Force was established in Britain he was sent over to command the 305th Bomb Group. He flew many missions deep into Germany in the following years, the most significant one being a successful raid on the Messerschmitt aircraft factories at Regensburg. As there were no fighter escorts as yet, the losses to the U.S. bombers were appalling. LeMay landed with a badly damaged plane in North Africa, as had been planned. LeMay is among the few bomber practitioners one may call a hero. He exposed himself and led his men into the inferno which these bombing missions frequently became.

In August 1944 LeMay was transferred to the Far East to take over command of the XXIst Bomber Command. This unit was to become the U.S. air fleet that under his direction first underwent extensive training, next moved to the Mariana Islands, after the air bases there had been completed, and eventually caused havoc in Japan. The tool of destruction was the B-29 bomber.

The bombing campaign against Japan lasted six months and LeMay orchestrated it all from the bomber bases on Tinian, Saipan, and Guam in the Mariana Islands. One city after another, with their easily combustible housing, fell victim to the bombers. The human losses were as great as in Europe, with exact figures difficult to come by in either place.

Like Harris, LeMay defended his campaign, correctly so, saying that he followed orders. As Harris he thought killing untold numbers of enemy civilians was better than losing one of your own soldiers; and as Harris he made many statements to that effect. He is quoted as saying: "I will tell you what war is about. You've got to kill people, and when you have killed enough they stop fighting."[32] His most famous statement came during the Vietnam War, when he was threatening to bomb the Vietnamese "back to the Stone Age." His biographer states that he never said that.[33] Yet in his autobiography LeMay put this comment in writing.[34]

LeMay stayed in the U.S. Air Force and ended his military career as chief of staff when he retired from active duty on 1 February 1965. He died at age 83 in Moreno Valley, California, on 1 October 1990, and is buried in the cemetery of the U.S. Air Force Academy at Colorado Springs, Colorado.

Compared with Spaatz and LeMay, all other U.S. bomber practitioners are minor. They all converted from precision bombers to area bombers and they all can defend their actions with orders from above.

A typical example is Ira Eaker, who as late as 1944 objected to Spaatz, his commander, to the implementation of Operation Clarion.[35] This was to be a superblast of day in, day out USAAF and RAF fighter and bomber missions, tactical as well as strategic, against Germany for no other purpose than to drive home the fact that the Allies had command of the air. (Not that we were in doubt about that at the time.)

Ira Eaker was born on 14 December 1896 at Field Creek, Llano County, Texas. In World War I he became an infantry officer, but soon switched over to the Army Air Force. He held staff and command positions between the wars, both in the States as well as in the Philippines. Not satisfied with a plain military career he attended universities whenever there was time. In 1934 he obtained a degree in journalism from the University of Southern California.[36]

As a bomber practitioner he was one of the commanders of the Eighth Air Force after he had helped create it in Britain in 1942. While under his command, it still adhered to the precision bombing practice. In 1943 he was transferred to North Africa to direct air operations against the German Afrika Corps and to get the Allies into Italy. Once he became commander of the Fifteenth USAAF based in Foggia, Italy, in 1944, the time had come for him to turn at least a blind eye toward terrorizing civilians. Under his command, hundreds of sorties were flown against Balkan cities. Eaker's professional standards had by that time dropped to statements as to "instill a keen civil desire to get out of the war."[37] In 1945 he was posted back to Britain to run the bomber divisions of the Eighth Air Force. He was strongly against attacking targets in the occupied countries when there was a chance of killing civilians. He showed less compassion for the Germans. Eaker retired from active service on 31 August 1947 and died on 6 August 1987.

The first U.S. bomber practitioner was General James H. Doolittle. The "Doolittle Raid" took place on 18 April 1942, when twenty-five U.S. medium bombers dropped their bombs on Japan, some of them into thickly populated areas.[38] Doolittle was in command and this stamped him an area bomber in the eyes of the Japanese.

Doolittle was born at Alameda, California, on 14 December 1896. In 1918 he joined the U.S. Army Signal Corps but saw no action at the Western Front in World War I. He obtained an engineering degree from Berkeley, California, and a doctorate in aeronautics from the Massachusetts Institute of Technology.

Between the wars he was engaged in research and development with such prominent aircraft manufacturers as Curtiss. In 1940 he was back in the service, and based on his engineering background helped auto manufacturers convert to aircraft production. During World War II he commanded all the major U.S. air fleets in Europe at one time or another. As such he could not escape following orders from above. In the sources reviewed for this book I could not find a statement by General Doolittle that indicated a conviction that the attack on morale was justified and would win the war. Like Spaatz, he acted as commanded, but he kept his own councils. Only after Spaatz overruled his objections were nine hundred U.S. bombers sent to Berlin as part of Operation Thunderclap on 3 February 1945. The toll: 25,000 dead Berliners.[39]

Of all the prominent bomber commanders of World War II Doolittle served the longest time. He retired on 28 February 1959 and died on 27 September 1993.

All USAAF bomber practitioners were very anxious to be seen by the general public as chivalrous soldiers doing only what soldiers would do. They saw to it that historians, even the ones chosen by them for their favorable view toward the bombers, were given only restricted access to documents. The result was that accounts on World War II USAAF aerial operations are long on heroic and technical details, but short on the sadder aspects.[40] In contrast, one finds that the exploits of the RAF written by British historians are very comprehensive and openly relate the good and the bad aspects of bombing.

When one turns to the German bomber practitioners of World War II one finds that there were no Luftwaffe leaders as outspoken and determined as Portal, Harris, and LeMay. When German bombers dropped their deadly loads on the cities of the British Isles, the commanders behind these raids were the field marshals in charge of the air fleets based in Western Europe. Under Göring, the supreme commander of the Luftwaffe, there were Hugo Sperrle, commanding Luftflotte 3, and Albert Kesselring, commanding Luftflotte 2. The German air fleets had units attached to them as the military requirements dictated; i.e. they had fighter squadrons, dive-bombers, horizontal bombers, and reconnaissance units. The

Luftwaffe as an army/navy support service had no strategic four-engine bombers. When it was called upon by Hitler after his famous "eraser" speech in September 1940 to terrorize Britain, it proved "barely adequate for the purpose," according to Air Marshal Harris.[41]

Sperrle was born at Ludwigsburg on 7 February 1885. He became a commissioned infantry officer in 1904, but changed to the Fliegertruppe in World War I. Discharged after the war, he was called back in 1935 and made a general of the Luftwaffe. He commanded the Condor Legion in 1936 and 1937 and in 1939 was put in charge of Luftflotte 3. After the fall of France in 1940, he was promoted to field marshal and continued to command Luftflotte 3, which participated in the battle of Britain, the Blitz, and the Baedeker Raids. But he failed to stem the tide of the Allied bomber fleets raiding the Continent. For this failure Hitler dismissed him from active service in late 1944. In 1948 he was tried for war crimes and declared innocent. He died at Landsberg on 2 April 1953.[42]

The other German bomber commander was Albert Kesselring. He was born at Marktsteft, a dozen miles south of Würzburg, on 31 November 1885. His roots were solidly planted in southern Germany.[43] In 1904 he became a commissioned officer in an artillery regiment at Metz, which was then German territory. After the war he stayed with the army until 1933 when he was transferred to the Luftwaffe. He became chief of staff and helped build up that service. When World War II broke out he took over command of Luftflotte 1, which participated in the Polish campaign, and as such he was involved in the bombing of Warsaw. In 1940 he was put in command of Luftflotte 2, which, together with Sperrle's Luftflotte 3 and the smaller Luftflotte 5 based in Norway, attacked Britain. Between them the German air fleets had 875 serviceable bombers.[44] Kesselring is quoted as believing that Britain could have been defeated with air power alone.[45] After the fall of France, Kesselring was promoted to field marshal and in 1942 took over command of all Axis forces in the Mediterranean. Erwin Rommel, the Desert Fox, fought in North Africa under his command. They had many differences of opinion. Kesselring ordered aerial attacks on Malta which caused heavy civilian losses and which cannot be termed tactical raids. He continued in command in Italy until 11 March 1945 when Hitler appointed him Supreme Commander West. Since Kesselring had shown himself as a commander who respected cultural assets by withdrawing German troops from Rome, Florence, and other Italian cities without a fight, it can be assumed that he would have surrendered Würzburg to the advancing U.S. Army had the city not become a pile of rubble.

After the war he was indicted by a British military court at Venice for the shooting of Italian partisans and hostages. He was condemned to death by firing squad. The sentence was commuted to life imprisonment and after seven years he was pardoned. He died on 16 July 1960. Kesselring is described as a staunch German and professional soldier who stood up against Hitler and last but not least against the British judges in his war crime trial in 1947.

Another German bomber commander was Wolfram von Richthofen. He was a first cousin of the famous World War I Red Baron, and at the end of that war was a member of the Richthofen squadron, or "Flying Circus." After WWI von Richthofen studied engineering and obtained a doctorate. When the Luftwaffe was being organized after 1933 he became the first director of the Luftwaffe research and development station at Rechlin. By 1936 he was Sperrle's chief of staff in Spain, and from 1938 until the end of the Spanish Civil War he was in command of the Condor Legion. While still under Sperrle the infamous raid on Guernica took place and von Richthofen is named in literature as the commander of the aircraft that flew the raid. In September 1939 von Richthofen was in charge of the divebombers that descended on Warsaw. Later in the war, von Richthofen commanded other large Luftwaffe formations engaged in tactical operations. He had to leave active service in October 1944 and died of a brain tumor on 12 July 1945.

To sum up the German World War II bomber practitioners, one must state that there was no thoroughly preconceived plan on strategic, area, and morale bombing. The Luftwaffe's top commanders had no bomber background. They had been at best fighter pilots in World War I and four out of the seven top executive officers in the German Air Ministry had been army officers.[46] The two extended strategic bomber campaigns, namely the Blitz against the British Isles from September 1940 to May 1941, and the bombing of Malta from 1942 to 1944, were ad hoc affairs and never executed with the scientific precision of the Allied campaigns against the Axis.

Turning to Italian and Japanese bomber practitioners, one finds no names in archives and literature of any significance. The Regia Aeronautica, the much advertised Italian air force by such people as Italo Balbo in his mass flights to the United States and around the Mediterranean, proved a disappointment after Italy entered the war on the coattails of the German victories in 1939 and 1940.

The Japanese had two air forces but no outstanding bomber commanders in either. The Japanese Army Air Force was responsible for the devastating air raids against Chinese cities in 1938 and 1939. Information on these raids, aside from western correspondents' reports, are hard to find and history has shown that these reports were often filed on unconfirmed information. The Japanese Naval Air Force flew the raid on Pearl Harbor and was engaged in all the major Pacific theater battles. But nowhere can one find that the Japanese leaders and commanders ever planned strategic bombing campaigns or executed any on a large scale.

As said at the beginning of this chapter, the bomber practitioners or, perhaps more euphemistically, the bomber barons, were all high-ranking officers in their respective armed forces. They all have in common that they wanted the best for their countries at the time of national emergencies. They all hide behind orders from above when it comes to facing the huge losses of innocent people, who supposedly were protected by the Hague or Geneva Conventions or at least should have been protected by common chivalry.

To show that aerial bombing can be employed in a professional and military manner one should turn to such eminent leaders as RAF Air Marshal Arthur Tedder and USSR Marshal Zhukov. Tedder was Deputy Allied Supreme Commander under Eisenhower, first in North Africa and later in Western Europe until the end of the war. He is described as an articulate airman with many interests outside the narrow path of his profession.[47] On his insistence Lord Zuckerman's transportation plan was imposed on Harris. Although it cost the lives of many French and Belgian civilians who lived near the railways, the plan restricted German troop and supply movements so badly that "Overlord," the Allied landing in Normandy, became a full success. Tedder believed in bombing strategic targets only. After Dresden he said: "Bombing, YES, but massacre, NO."[48]

Marshal Zhukov, the conqueror of Berlin in 1945, was a Soviet Army commander who expressed his country's view on the application of air power when he told Tedder that the Red Air Force had given "terrific assistance to the artillery."[49]

BOMBING IN WORLD WAR I

POLITICAL EVENTS THAT LED TO WORLD WAR I

To trace the background of area bombing, which was started by the Germans in World War I, it appears necessary to understand the events that led to that war. One must begin with Bismarck proclaiming the Second Reich with Prussian King Wilhelm I its emperor in 1871. The proclamation established Germany again as a nation after Napoleon I had dissolved the Holy Roman Empire in 1806. Bismarck's act, perpetrated in the Halls of Mirrors in the Château of Versailles, offended the French and was one of the many incidents that eventually led to World War I.

If emerging German nationalism was frowned upon by its neighbors after 1871, one should not forget that Britain, France, Holland, Portugal, Spain, Russia, Sweden, and the Ottoman Empire had long before passed the stages of political, economic, and ethnic development. Bismarck's and, after his dismissal by Wilhelm II in 1890, the Kaiser's Reich tried to catch up with them.

The German unification appeared like a burst. Not that this burst made a big conflagration at its beginning. After all, the German kingdoms, grand duchies, counties, earldoms, down to the city states, twenty-five in all, were politically fractured, poor in human and material resources, and militarily insignificant. Individually and in toto they had been attacked, pushed, and bullied over more than two hundred years by the Swedes, the Turks, and the French. That the principalities agreed to yield some of their privileges to a new kaiser was remarkable and viewed with suspicion abroad.

The founding of the new Reich had popular support, but the actual unification was the work of the aristocratic princes who purposely left their legislatures out of the process. There were no civilians at the ceremony in Versailles; it was all aristocracy in splendid military uniforms. Even the constitution of the Reich, promulgated on 16 April 1871, left little power in the hands of the new Reichstag. Despite great cultural, scientific, and economic achievements between 1870 and 1914, Germany was oriented to and guided by the military.[1] Germany was not alone in this situation. Most countries were still being ruled by the dynastic classes and their hangers-on. Liberal constitutions and their enforcement might have contributed to a lasting peaceful period at the end of the nineteenth century.[2]

Germany was not the only country in a struggle for national identity. Italy, like Germany, split into countless little states and beset from all sides by its neighbors, was undergoing the process of unification, the *resorgimento*. Under Cavour and Garibaldi, Victor Emmanuel II of Savoy became king of Italy in 1861, and gradually over the next ten years Italy recovered traditional Italian lands from Austria and France. Except for its inherited glorious Roman history it was a poor country. Italy embarked on recovering the dominant position Rome once had in the Mediterranean. It turned toward Africa and claimed Libya from the Turks, tried to conquer Ethiopia, and tangled with France over Corsica, Algeria, and Tunisia.

In Europe, Germany and Italy were basically the new kids on the block, each in its own sphere. And neither of them played by the rules established by their seniors on the block. Since they were not physically strong, they tried to impress the others with shows of bravura and hard work. The German attitude can best be illuminated by a pronouncement of its foreign minister, Bernhard von Bülow, in the Reichstag on 6 December 1897, when he said: "We also demand a place in the sun."[3]

One of the causes for the rise of the French feeling of *revanche*, which in turn contributed to the outbreak of World War I, was the peace treaty of Frankfurt of 10 May 1871. It required France to cede Alsace-Lorraine, to pay 5 billion goldfrancs as reparations, and have German troops stationed in the Eastern Departments until this sum was paid. Together with the tactless ceremony in the Hall of Mirrors at Versailles and the display of conquered French troop colors in a Berlin military parade in June 1871, French honor and sensibility had been badly trampled.[4] Alsace-Lorraine became the cause celèbre for the French. It was the essence of the *revanche* movement against Germany.

In Germany, Bismarck made the mistake of not grooming and promoting a successor who could take over his aims and policies. It left Wilhelm II at liberty to make a dramatic change in course when he forced Bismarck to resign the chancellorship on 17 March 1890.

Bismarck tried to rein in the demands of emerging industrialists for colonies, which would give them sources of raw materials as well as markets for their products. The trade had gone overseas, was very successful, and the flag had to follow. Germany took possessions in East Africa, today's Tanzania, Southwest Africa, today's Namibia, and in West Africa, Cameroon, and Togo. In the South Pacific, Germany acquired the Marshall Islands, the Marianas, and the Carolines from Spain after it had lost the Spanish-American War and needed money. Germany also took Samoa and the Bismarck Archipelago. In 1898 it forced China to let it have Tsingtao on a lease for ninety-nine years and the adjoining province of Shantung as a protectorate. By 1900, the Kaiser could proudly survey his empire. With all of these possessions under the black, white, and red flag, Germany had caught up with its European neighbors.

The colonies were also to absorb the population surplus. The German population had increased from 50 million in 1890 to 67 million in 1910, an increase of 34 percent; the reason being improved health and living standards.[5] The British, French, Dutch, Spaniards, and others had established areas in Africa, Asia, South America, and the whole continent of Australia to accept emigrants, thus reducing the population pressures in their home countries. Germany and Italy now followed suit. However, that policy proved a failure. Of the 2.85 million emigrants who left Germany from 1871 to 1914, only a mere 13,286 settled in Africa, whereas 2.72 million went to the Americas, most of them to the United States.[6] Similarly, most Italians emigrated to North and South America.

If trade and commerce were to benefit from the colonies, the statistics show that German imports from them never amounted to more than 0.54 percent per annum of the total imports. Nor did exports to the colonies amount to more that 0.73 percent per annum of the total exports.[7] Raw materials also came from other sources. In 1910, when the colonies were thought to pay off the investments and the efforts that had gone into them, only 0.25 percent of the imported cotton and 13.62 percent of the rubber came from the colonies.[8]

It was, of course, not only Germany that exercised colonial politics and acquisitions between 1871 and 1914. There was the Boer War between 1899 and 1902, which resulted in British annexation of the Boer territories in South Africa. That war is famous for the internment of Boer families in British concentration camps. About 25,000 Boer women and children died in those camps.[9] As in German Southwest Africa, where a German expeditionary force quelled the Herero uprising between 1903 and 1907, it was war against women and children, a forerunner of area bombing.

Austria-Hungary occupied Bosnia-Herzogovina and formally annexed it in 1908. It was an act that offended the neighboring Serbs and their Russian supporters, and became another of the many causes of World War I.

In 1899 a German consortium, supported by the government, succeeded in obtaining from the Turks a concession to build a rail line to Baghdad. The line would eventually end in Basra at the Persian Gulf. The Kaiser talked about "my railroad" and a year before, on a visit to Constantinople, he proclaimed himself the protector of the 300 million Moslems of the world.[10] The Baghdad railway annoyed the British because it would give Germany a land/sea route to India and it annoyed the Russians because they had designs on Persia.

The Italians fought the Ottoman Empire in Libya in 1911-12 and established themselves there. This upset the British, who owned the Suez Canal and were heavily engaged in Egypt and the Sudan to protect their sea route to India. Italy also occupied the Dodecanese Islands off the coast of Turkey during the Turkish/Italian War of 1911-1912, but had to retreat afterward.

In 1895 the Italians tried to conquer Ethiopia, but were repulsed. There were overlapping interests for land grabs in West Africa, which were resolved by the Berlin Conference of 1894-95 under the guidance of Bismarck, who had called the interested powers, including the United States, to his capital.

In the Far East, the Russians and the Japanese fought in Manchuria in 1904-05. It was an all-out war, which forced the czar to give up his ambitions to control Port Arthur and the rich hinterland. The Japanese took over Southern Manchuria and made Korea a colony in 1910. The United States took over the Philippines from Spain. In 1898 the emerging German navy entered Manila Bay at the height of the Spanish-American War to show support for the Spaniards. Admiral Dewey, the U.S. commander, had to threaten them with bombardment before they left peacefully.[11]

At the turn of the century the Boxer Rebellion erupted in China. An international expeditionary corps was shipped to China to restore order in and around the foreign enclaves. On the occasion of despatching troops from Bremerhaven in July 1900, Kaiser Wilhelm made one of his many famous gaffes when he admonished the soldiers to behave as the Huns one thousand years before, not to take prisoners, and not to give pardon to the Boxers. The Fleet Street Press started to call the Germans "Huns," and Arthur Harris made many a statement in World War II to the effect that he wanted to kill "Huns."

In 1905 Kaiser Wilhelm, a world traveller, went to Tangiers in Morocco to support German interests in that part of Africa. Bismarck had brokered an understanding of spheres of interest in west and northwest Africa at the Berlin Conference of 1884-85. The Kaiser must have forgotten that.

As Germany was isolating itself or was being isolated (it depends whose history books you believe), it belatedly began looking for some allies. There was Austria-Hungary, the step-brother from the marriage of the First Reich (the Holy Roman Empire); there was Italy, the fellow new kid on the block; and there was the Ottoman Empire, beset from all sides and terminally ill. With the emerging Italians, Germany and Austria-Hungary formed the Triple Alliance and signed three agreements between 1902 and 1912. The basic principal of the alliance was mutual assistance in the event of war.

What also annoyed Germany's fellow great powers were its economic, social, and scientific achievements during this period. At the turn of the nineteenth century, the German states had an agrarian economy and were no threat to the countries that were undergoing the industrial revolution and the benefits that came with it. As an example, when Mr. Koenig was establishing his printing press factory in Würzburg in 1818 he could not find any qualified mechanical tradesmen.[12] Even Germany's infrastructure such as railways was, until 1870, poorly developed and only oriented to the needs of the individual principalities. After 1871 there was a dramatic change. Industries sprang up and their products conquered foreign markets because their quality was good and the cost less. By 1914 the Ruhr Valley produced more steel than Britain, and Krupp steel was on a par with, maybe even better than, Sheffield steel.

Social progress had been made and the population expanded and lived longer. Within the confines of Central Europe, population pressure was building up. Education had improved and, as a result, achievements in medicine, science, and technology were on a par with any in the neighboring countries. As we have seen, Lord Cherwell, Churchill's World War II scientific advisor, was sent to Germany for his education.

In order to protect its trade and commerce, Germany took steps to build up military power. The Prussian/German armies that had defeated France in 1871 were already well-organized units. A German navy did not yet exist. With the founding of the Second Reich the federal government in Berlin had de facto control over the armies of the constituent states and absolute control of the rising German navy.

An incident that annoyed Germany's European neighbors was the construction of the Kiel Canal. From 1895 onward this civil engineering feat connected the Baltic to the North Sea cutting about seven hundred miles of voyage around Denmark. It dashed British military planning, which in case of war with

Germany was based on an expeditionary force sailing past Copenhagen and landing north of Berlin. Any German ship could now be quickly shuttled between the North and Baltic Seas. Next came the First Naval Law of 28 March 1898. Tirpitz, the Kaiser's grand admiral, had convinced his superiors, the Reichstag, and the industrialists that Germany needed a strong navy to protect its overseas interests and assets. This bill was followed by a second one on 8 March 1912, which authorized an even greater German navy. It was to be at full strength in 1920 and second to none on the globe to guarantee Germany's position. These bills were the death knell to any potential understanding between Britain and Germany. The United Kingdom felt threatened.

Regarding the German army, the situation was aggravated by the Reich deciding to maintain a standing army of considerable strength. This not being enough, the German chief of staff, Graf Helmut von Moltke, had the Reichstag pass the German Army and Finance Bill on 30 June 1913. It provided for an army of almost 900,000 men—in peacetime. The cost was to be one billion marks just to establish it. Aside from the affront to neighboring states, when one looks at the cost of this army one must question the sanity of its leaders. Germany had about 67 million people at that time. This meant that 1.4 percent of its population were playing soldier. Not only were these men in their prime not producing anything, they cost money to do nothing useful.

Not only were the army and navy built up, their deployment was just as offensive. Along the western German border railway sidings were constructed to facilitate rapid transfer of troops to these areas. German naval ships were stationed in the Caribbean, the Indian Ocean, the Pacific Ocean, and at Tsingtao in China. Of course other naval powers stationed their squadrons in strategic places also.

General rearmament began. The Russians and French reorganized their armies, Britain built more dreadnoughts. Again, it is a question of who did what first, and the history books give no clear answer.

After Bismarck's dismissal in 1890, German external policies neglected to cater to Russia, which made its turn toward

France. France was not on friendly terms with Germany because of the revanche movement. Britain was still on friendly terms with Germany. But when nephew Willi annoyed his uncle, Edward VII, with his naval policies, Britain joined France and Russia in the Entente Cordiale in 1906. The downward slide to war accelerated and Germany, with Austria-Hungary, became isolated. Nominally Italy, through the Triple Alliance, was on the side of Germany and Austria. This caused the French to move their capital ships into the Mediterranean, where Italy continued to make noises about regaining possessions of the Roman Empire. Britain, on the other hand, which before joining the Entente Cordiale had always felt threatened by the French on its way to India through the Mediterranean, withdrew its capital ships to the United Kingdom. The German dreadnoughts seemed the bigger threat now. The battle lines were being established.

The lines were set up by the ruling governments but with the full support of the public. Nationalism was on the rise. The rulers succeeded in lining up the masses behind them as nations. With the help of symbols and, last but not least, propaganda, the masses were controlled. The media were on the rise and since all Europeans could read, thanks to improved education standards, the masses were behind the desire to teach the Huns, the Boches, the Tommies, the Russkies, etc., whatever the national press called the coming enemy, a lesson—a short one, a powerful one, and a lasting one. The world was ready for war.

THE MILITARY OPERATIONS

The avalanche was set off with pistol shots in June 1914. This was all it took to get the masses moving. The shots fired at Sarajevo in Bosnia-Herzogovina killed the Austro-Hungarian crown prince. The masses were the armies, navies, and above all people that were mobilized in short order. Plans had been made by the general staffs of all the countries that declared war. The German plan was to smash France in a lightning attack through Belgium, finish it off, and then turn on the Russian bear in the east. It was assumed that Britain would stay neutral and pose no problem. Or alternatively, that the British Territorial Army would come too late to assist on the Continent.[13] Marshal Schlieffen's plan foresaw knocking out France within six weeks. What the marshal must have overlooked was the Royal Navy. Would it mothball its ships and let Tirpitz's navy rule the waves from then on? As Clemenceau, the French president, said: "War is too serious a business to leave it in the hands of the military."

What the Germans may not have fully appreciated was that, through the Entente Cordiale, Britain was obligated to help France against Germany. For years there had been staff talks between the two nations forging a plan to march through Belgium into the Second Reich and have it all over and done with in a few months. The Russians in turn were ready to invade Germany and Austria-Hungary, and squeeze Germany from the east. The Japanese were intent on increasing their influence on the Asian continent and eliminating Germany as a competitor in China.

They were all ready and prepared. The heads of state had demonstrations in front of their palaces clamoring for a fight. Volunteers streamed to the armed forces and the troops were sent off with music, flowers, and the blessings of their churches. By the time millions had bled to death on the battlefields, husbands, fiancés, brothers, and sons had either not come back or came back badly maimed; the enthusiasm had evaporated. In 1914 in short order the Germans invaded neutral Belgium, the British Expeditionary Force came across the Channel, the Russians invaded East Prussia, and the Japanese conquered Tsingtao. It was to be by all accounts a short war but it lasted from 28 June 1914 to 11 November 1918—1,597 long days. The costs in lives and money were horrendous. Total deaths were 9.2 million soldiers and 500,000 civilians.[14] Costs, quoting from the available literature, were in 1918 for the British £7 million per day, and for the Germans 180 million marks per day.[15] The total for the entire war was U.S. $603.57 billion.[16]

The war aims of all participants were clear:

> Austria-Hungary wanted to curb Serbia's ambitions in the Balkans.

France wanted Alsace-Lorraine back with Germany as a harmless buffer between France and Russia. This became one of the major aims, particularly after the Bolshevik Revolution in 1917.

Germany wanted a preventive strike to counteract pressure from the East and the West.

Britain wanted the German navy and German competition out of the world.

Russia wanted to help Serbia and acquire an ice-free port in Europe.

Turkey and Bulgaria felt slighted by Serbia after the Balkan War of 1912-1913.

Japan needed land and raw materials.

The wild card in this line-up in August 1914 was Italy. From the French the Italians wanted lands they thought were theirs by historical right, and from Austria they wanted the province of South Tyrol. Despite its obligations under the Triple Alliance, Italy stayed out of the war until 1915, until a secret protocol was signed with the Entente that guaranteed it South Tyrol.

The people who had no designs, neither on their neighbors nor in the economic field, were the Belgians. They were the first to suffer from this conflict and took the worst beating until it was all over.

Of course the planning by the military on both sides had been faulty. Neither side could force a crushing defeat on the other in short order as planned. A long, drawn out conflict was becoming reality. And with it the attitudes hardened. Depending on who one would listen to, the other side started to commit acts contrary to international law, contrary to the conventions, and contrary to humanity.

The British navy imposed a blockade on the Central Powers. The conventions had not outlawed naval blockades. The Declaration of London of February 1909 confirmed that blockades were legal.[17] While the Allies felt justified, the Germans said it was war against women and children, starving them. The Germans retaliated with their U-boats. Again, not outlawed by the Hague Convention of 1907, but a dastardly way of warfare by the standards of the British navy. The Germans not only had invaded Belgium but committed atrocities against its population. At least so the British propaganda told the world. No doubt true to some extent, with the shooting and burning at Louvain as an example, but certainly not so bad that childrens' hands were hacked off, as the British press claimed.[18] The Germans were powerless against this type of propaganda because their overseas cables coming out of the north German port of Emden had been dredged up by the Royal Navy and cut right after Britain had declared war on Germany. The news, particularly in North America, came from Fleet Street. But even then, it is my personal opinion, the Germans were never smart enough to use what can be called the fourth fighting service—propaganda. Attempts were made to outlaw propaganda at The Hague in 1907 but that effort failed and today nobody even thinks of it as immoral in warfare.

The conventions had tried to outlaw discharging explosives from aerial craft. The effort had been stalled and was to be brought up again at the Third Hague Convention in 1914. The war interfered with that meeting, and since there was no code to prevent aerial bombing, and in particular bombing civilians, the road to that new means of warfare was open. But bombing civilians outside the battle zone did not happen until 1915.

The arms race prior to World War I had been on for some time and aircraft had been added to the arsenals. Graf von Zeppelin was building airships, and the Wright brothers' invention was produced widely. By 1910 the major powers had the following aircraft in their armies and navies:[19]

	Airships	Airplanes
Belgium	2	2
Britain	2	4
France	3	36
Germany	9	5
Italy	3	2
Japan	1	2
Russia	3	3
United States	2	2

These numbers appear minuscule, but they impacted military planning. The Germans felt confident that they could avert the French threat of thirty-six planes with their "superior" Zeppelins.

Substantial sums were invested by the major powers. Between 1910 and 1914, budgets for aircraft production for the respective armed forces increased as follows:[20]

	1910	1914
in pounds sterling		
Britain	160,000	1,000,000
France	312,000	1,900,000
Germany	300,000	3,200,000

These sums were small compared with what the German army and navy programs consumed or the cost of the dreadnought fleet in Britain. The Russians were not far behind and they can be credited with the achievement of having the first operational four-engine bomber. By 1914 there were ten Ilja Muromets, built by Sikorsky, the renowned U.S. aircraft designer of later years.

In August 1914, when the war started, the major combatants mustered for the time substantial numbers of aircraft as follows:[21]

	Airships	Airplanes
Belgium	2	16
Britain	0	263
France	10	165
Germany	8	232
Austria-Hungary	1	48
Russia	4	263

Not all historians agree on the absolute numbers. Alexander Boyd says that the Russians had 250 airplanes, or 5 percent less. Von Höppner lists 350 percent more for France, but that number makes the German general appear more heroic for struggling against great odds.[22]

The airplanes were of the wire and canvas type and mostly used for reconnaissance. But it was not long before hand-thrown explosives were dropped from those contraptions.

Within short order all governments and their military staffs recognized the advantage of aerial combat, and as a result there followed a tremendous upswing in the development and production of planes. The Germans continued building Zeppelins, but after substantial losses recognized the advantage of the heavier-than-air plane over the hydrogen-filled airships.

From single-engine scout planes the nations developed single-engine fighters, with engines of undreamed of power, to four-engine bombers by 1917 and 1918. The time from blueprint to flying design was still short. It took no more than three months to have a new type of plane in action at the front. The number of factories went up exponentially, and great sums of money and man-hours were spent. In Germany alone, the increase of factories went from two to eight by 1914, with another five major ones in operation by 1918. The cost also skyrocketed. A simple Rumpler Taube, made by the Flugmaschine Wright GmbH in 1914, cost 25,000 marks (approximately £1,250), in itself a sizable sum at the time. A six-engine bomber cost 750,000 marks in 1917. Aviation became an industry and big business.

The factories on both sides of the war produced aircraft by the thousands as *Il dominio dell'aria* (command of the air), as Douhet called it a few years later, was recognized as a requisite to win the battles in the West. The battles between the opposing fighters, with names such as Rickenbacher, von Richthofen, Fonck, Dallas, and Bishop, have become legend and the subjects of many books. Less has been proudly reported on bombing. It involved different flying machines and caused considerably more losses in human lives. It was a messy business and created no outstanding heroes.

By 1918 both sides had the means to inflict destruction in the other's land. The respective industries had been busy in designing and fabricating improved versions of aircraft that could carry explosives and fire in the form of incendiary bombs into enemy territory. The following long-range bombers were operational and actively deployed:[23]

On the German side:

The twin-engine Gotha, of which about 550 were built between 1916 and 1918. They could carry one half ton of bombs and had a crew of three.

The four- and six-engine Riesenflugzeug, of which thirty-two were built between 1916 and 1918. They could carry two tons of bombs and had a crew of seven.

On the British side:

The twin-engine Handley Page 0/400, of which 507 were built between 1916 and 1918. They could carry one ton of bombs and had a crew of four.

The twin-engine Vickers Vimy came too late to see action before the armistice.

Similarly the four-engine Handley Page V/1500 did not see service in combat. It was to be ready by 1919. It could carry 3.5 tons of bombs.

On the Italian side:

The three engine Caproni Ca5, of which only a few were built between 1917 and 1918. They could carry about one ton and had a crew of three.

On the Russian side:

By 1914 the Russians already had the four-engine Ilya Muromets, of which eighty were built. They could carry a half ton of bombs.

On the French side:

Early in the war the French army had several squadrons of Voisin bombers. They were of the wire and canvas type, had one engine and a crew of three. Maximum bomb load was sixty kg at a radius of 150 miles.

From the above listing it appears that the total number of heavy bombers was still relatively small compared with the number of other combat planes produced in World War I. The records, both in archives and literature, differ slightly, but show great numbers of military aircraft being used by both sides. In round figures from the available sources the following numbers appear:[24]

Number of military aircraft produced by the major combatants in World War I:

Austria-Hungary	5,000
Britain	55,000
France	60,000
Germany	48,000
Italy	12,000
Russia	5,000
United States	15,000

In summary:
For the Entente: 147,000
For the Central Powers: 53,000

The most remarkable aspect of these production figures is that the United States did not start to produce military aircraft until 1917.

That aerial bombing was still a minor effort in World War I is indicated by the fact that of 48,000 German machines, only about 2,000 were bombers, and of these most were single-engine tactical types.

Aerial bombing started on a very small scale in 1914. The German army used its Zeppelins to bomb military installations at Liege, Antwerp, Ostende, Calais, and the Eastern Front. Of particular interest for the Germans were the disembarkation points of the British Expeditionary Force along the channel coast. The Germans always protested that they were only attacking military targets and went so far as to have their pilots carry written orders with them as proof in case they were captured. It was not long into the war, however, before they admitted that civilians could be killed. In the beginning, all of the German bombing on military and not so military targets was by Zeppelins until, as a Christmas present to the British, a German airplane dropped a few bombs on Dover on 24 December 1914. The physical damage was negligible, but the moral one immense. War had been brought to the British Isles from the Continent.

When the German Zeppelins started bombing from August 1914 onward, the British were not far behind. Before the war the Royal Navy had recognized the airplane as an extension of naval guns. The Royal Naval Air Service attacked a Zeppelin shed at Düsseldorf on 8 October 1914. Unfortunately one of the planes flown by Squadron Commander Spencer Grey missed the target and attacked the Cologne railway station instead. Three civilians were killed.[25]

On 21 November 1914, the RNAS was in action again and sent three planes from their base at Belfort in eastern France to Friedrichshafen to attack the Zeppelin Works. One Zeppelin under construction was damaged. As a result the Zeppelin Works reduced their experimental flights over Lake Constance.[26] On Christmas Day 1914, the RNAS raided the Zeppelin base near Cuxhaven. The interesting aspect of that raid is that the Royal Navy used an aircraft tender, i.e. a freighter converted to carry floatplanes on its deck. They were lowered into the North Sea and recovered after the raid. A German Zeppelin scout saw the operation and returned to its base to have the German navy intercept the tender. But the Royal Navy escaped in time. Had the Zeppelin had wireless communication the German navy could have come out earlier.

The French Voisin bombers were used at first for tactical purposes. But on 4 December they attacked Freiburg, a city eighty kilometers behind the front line.[27] There is no record of any casualties and no record anywhere else in literature or archives of the raid. One wonders whether it really happened, because it would have been the first ever air raid on civilians.

By the end of 1914, tactical bombing was being used as a new type of warfare, but on a moderate scale. The war was still, within limits, a civilized undertaking. So much so that the enthusiasm was still there and there was even fraternization of the troops in no-mans land on the Western Front at Christmas 1914.[28]

There were infractions on treaties such as the use of military power against the enemy in the colonies. The Japanese had taken Tsingtao and the British had landed troops in German East Africa and in Southwest Africa. The German navy could not render assistance to any of the colonies. The few ships near these places were on the run, and the bulk of the navy was safely trapped behind the Grand Fleet in the North

Sea. The very raison d'être of the ships, namely to protect German overseas interests, had evaporated. Around the British Isles, though, German battle cruisers bombarded the town of Yarmouth on 4 November 1914 and the towns of Scarborough and Whitby on 16 December 1914, killing 140 civilians in the latter raid. These raids represented a clear infraction of the 1907 Hague Convention.

From literature and documents it is clear that governments and military staffs were looking towards the airplane as a help to win the war. Plans were started to produce bomb-carrying aircraft with bigger loads and longer range. Until the end of 1914 the air war had not deviated much from the conventions. Most civilian losses had occurred in the war zones. They were "incidental," to use Lord Portal's and other prominent military leaders' terms of later times.

Among the military planners and politicians in Britain, Sir William Weir succeeded in convincing the government that the long-range bomber was an even more devastating weapon than the German U-boat.[29] Being an engineer by trade, Sir William also convinced his peers that it was cheaper to drop bombs than fire artillery shells on the enemy. On the German side, as we have seen, there were officers in the admiralty who wanted to use the Zeppelins for teaching the English a lesson. Albeit, it would have to be at night, because daylight tactical raids over the fighting zone had cost the German army four airships by the end of 1914.

Weather and government restraint still held the bombers back, but not for long. The German Kaiser and the chancellor were asked to approve bombing raids. The former hesitated, because he was concerned about losses to life and property of his royal cousins in Britain, particularly in London. However Wilhelm II had no qualms about bombing Paris and other French cities—no human concerns on that front. The chancellor, Bethmann Hollweg, hesitated because he had been ambassador to the Court of St. James and had friendly recollections of that time. He also feared the reactions of neutral countries. In both instances approval was eventually granted.[30] First the Zeppelins and later the Gothas took off for enemy territory with the blessings of the high commanders such as Hindenburg and Ludendorff for the army, and Admiral Hugo von Pohl for the navy. Von Pohl was finally convinced that Admiral Behnke's idea of sending navy Zeppelins to Britain was correct.

As the fighting went on in the trenches, the Germans committed an infraction against the 1907 Hague Convention (Article 23[a] of the Rules for Land Warfare) by blowing chlorine gas at the enemy lines. The first time it happened was on 25 April 1915 during the second battle of Ypres. The submarine war had gone under water, because, against the conventions, Churchill, the first lord of the admiralty, had ordered the installation of guns on merchant ships to blast any U-boat that surfaced nearby to inspect the ship papers and then take the appropriate measures. Churchill also had captured German submarine crews placed in special confinement. Germany retaliated by putting thirty-nine British officers in arrest barracks. By June 1915 Mr. Churchill's successor had to rescind the order.[31] The fighting and conduct of war was becoming tougher.

During the entire war the German position to justify strategic bombing was that it was tactical and only exercised in the war zone. To justify raids on Britain, the attacked cities were declared in the war zone because from them originated supplies for the British Expeditionary Force in Western Europe. The same rationale was applied to France with the additional proviso that some cities such as Paris were also fortresses. That they were many miles away from the actual fighting did not interfere with that reasoning. Besides, German bomber pilots had strict orders to bomb military targets only(!).

The British position was less ambivalent. The admiralty issued a communique on 16 February 1915 that the RNAS bombers had instructions to raid only military targets and avoid dropping bombs on residential sections of towns.[32]

The French and Italian positions were the same as the British and all of them protested that their crews never attacked civilians or non-military targets. They would rather bring their bombs back if they could not identify their targets. In the end, all belligerents protested that their aircraft only executed justified reprisals; in other words, the enemy was to blame. Reprisal raids were flown not only for air raids committed by the enemy before, but also for other infractions. As an example, after the "Baralong Affair" in 1916, in which a German submarine crew was executed by the Royal Navy after capture, the Germans threatened to unleash an unrestricted bombing of British civilians as retaliation.[33]

After German navy airships had raided the Norfolk coast, there were cheers in Germany, but the German chancellor berated Admiral Pohl, the navy commander, for dropping bombs on undefended places and causing bad press in the United States. The Kaiser's original orders placed London strictly off limits for the airships. But he soon changed that to allow bombardment of the London docks, from which supplies were shipped to the Western Front. No residential districts, palaces, public buildings, or monuments were to be targeted. But on 31 May 1915, one Zeppelin let loose without due regard for the Kaiser's orders and dropped bombs over London indiscriminately.[34]

As the war progressed, German army and navy Zeppelins raided London and the Midlands, respectively. The German High Command justified the raids as retaliation against the Hunger Blockade, which was starting to be felt. The German people wanted action and the military were made to oblige. The army would have preferred to use the Zepps at the front for reconnaissance and tactical bombing. There were not enough Zeppelins to do both tactical and strategic bombing. Nevertheless, the military had to follow public pressure and sent Zeppelins off across the Channel from their bases in Belgium. The navy and its admirals were happy to dispatch their Zeppelins from the bases in northern Germany. It was a small campaign, full of confusion, accidents, and uncoordinated sorties.[35]

As the raids continued it soon became apparent that the British government was facing a very negative reaction from the public. Churchill, as first lord of the admiralty, was appointed minister in charge of home defense. He recalled a few fighter squadrons of the Royal Flying Corps and the Royal Navy Air Service from France. Searchlights and antiaircraft guns were installed. A show was required to assure the public that Britain as an island was still unassailable and that it could depend on its navy to keep the war from its shores. There were riots in the streets of London and looting of shops whose proprietors had German-sounding names.[36] Anti-German pressure (not only because of the bombing) went so far that the royal house dispensed with its German name and has called itself Windsor ever since. Churchill had to fire the First Sea Lord, Prince Louis of Battenberg, because of his German name and ancestry. There was talk of reprisals in high government circles. Lord Fisher, who succeeded Battenberg, proposed to shoot one German national in British hands for every British civilian killed by German bombs. In the House of Commons there was talk about bringing downed flyers to trial, or stringing them up outright.[37]

But the Zeppelins kept coming and it was not until the night of 2-3 September 1916 that Lieutenant Leefe-Robinson shot down the first.[38] He received the Victoria Cross and became a national hero. The Germans also had many losses due to accidents and bad weather, and by the end of 1916 the Zeppelin campaign stopped. In 1918 the navy attacked the Midlands again but that effort was small and futile.

During the entire war there were fifty-two Zeppelin raids on Britain with never more than three airships in one raid. Most raids were single sorties. The total weight of bombs dropped was 196 tons, which killed 557 people and wounded 1,358. The material damage amounted to £1.5 million.[39] A total of seventeen Zeppelins were lost in action. The consequential damage was immeasurable. The Germans, the Huns, had become the first to conduct a campaign of terror against an enemy civilian population from the air. They hit not only private homes but also schools, churches, and hospitals. They had hoped to break the morale of British citizens and thereby force the British government to sue for peace.

Nothing of the sort happened. As the bombardment, minuscule as it was by later standards, continued, the riots stopped and public opinion rallied behind the crown and government. But the cries for retaliations reached chorus proportions on all sides. In 1917 Churchill, by that time minister of munitions, issued a statement which declared it unlikely that a people would compel a government to surrender under the pressure of air attack. Good shelters and a strong control by police and military authorities would prevent that.[40] This seems to be the first pronouncement by Churchill on that subject. As we shall see later, he underwent several metamorphoses during his political career, very much to the detriment of civilian populations.

The German navy Zeppelins operated only against Britain. The army Zeppelins were active on all fronts. They bombed French and Belgian "fortresses." Paris was attacked by two Zeppelins on the night of 20-21 March 1915. The crews had received strict instructions to bomb only railway installations, docks, barracks, and factories. Afterward it was admitted that the raid not only hit military targets but also civilians. But, so the argument went, the French had started it all with the attack on Freiburg in December 1914 and only had themselves to blame.[41]

On the Eastern Front, the Zeppelins attacked towns along the front line but not in the hinterland. The Russian reaction was rather strict. They considered all aerial bombing a crime, even when executed against purely military targets. They threatened to either hang or bring to justice any captured Zeppelin crews.[42] This actually never happened. It would also have looked irrational in light of the existence of the Muromets bomber.

French Voisin bombers attacked the Badische Anilin and Sodafabrik at Ludwigshafen in January 1915, and Karlsruhe in February and June 1915.[43] The official reason was given as retaliation against the Zeppelin raids on French towns. These new French raids after the one on Freiburg in 1914 upset German officialdom and the public. There was an official Berlin protest against the attacks on open towns, far from the theater of operations. Historians later justified the raid on Freiburg because there was an airscrew factory. But was it destroyed? The historians do not tell.[44] Worse was to come on Corpus Christi Day in 1916, when French planes struck Karlsruhe again, that time reportedly killing 110 civilians, mostly children who were attending a circus performance. Again it was officially declared a retaliation raid. If retaliation is an accepted fact in international law, is stepped-up retaliation admissable?

The bombers were also employed on other fronts, but on a smaller scale. Between April 1916 and October 1918 the town of Treviso in northern Italy suffered thirty-two air raids by the Austrian-Hungarian Air Force. A total of 1,500 bombs were dropped with a total weight of seventy-five tons.[45] The Austrian-Hungarians also raided Venice many times. World opinion was shocked. What reasoning could have caused an attack on that pearl of human culture? If the industries or dock facilities were to be destroyed, they were far away from the island-city on the mainland side of a long causeway. The Italians also had bombers and raided the Austro-Hungarian naval base of Pola on the Istrian Peninsula. Even the Russians performed a strategic raid. In 1917 a navy tender with float-planes was sent close to Constantinople to attack the dam on Lake Terko.[46] The planes tried to disrupt the water supply to the city, but hitting dams is not an easy task, as the RAF learned in World War II. The Lake Terko raid was the only Russian foray into strategic bombing. They had the Ilya Muromets, the first four-engine bomber ever built, but they did not use it.

The main strategic air battlefield was Western Europe. The planning and clamor for bombing increased in pitch and by 1916 Britain and Germany were sparring off. Both sides had their factories design and turn out planes specifically for strategic bombing. The design parameters for that type of plane called for the highest possible bomb load, the longest range, and good defenses against enemy fighters. This meant multi-engine planes because single-engine planes, which had done the bombing to date, could not be built to these specifications.

The German bomber bases were all in northern Belgium close to the British Isles. The British bases for defense against the German raiders were all in East Anglia and the bomber bases in the beginning were along the entire front in France but later concentrated near Nancy and particularly the Ochey Aerodrome. Germany added another reason for justification of the stepped-up bombing by 1916. It was considered that

defense of Britain would draw on the forces that could otherwise be deployed on the Continent. Since the German
bombers were on the offensive, the defense had to be prepared to meet them anywhere they chose. There was military
logic in that because by the time the war ended there were
about 30,000 British soldiers manning these defenses. That
number represents about two infantry divisions. Against
these considerable forces the Germans never mustered more
than fifty bombers. Bomber fleets raiding Britain were small,
with the biggest raid carried out by twenty-eight Gothas on
the night of 19-20 May 1918. Between 1916 and the end of the
war, the KAGOHL, the squadron that was under direct control of the Army Supreme Command, carried out twenty-
seven raids on the British Isles. As daylight bombing became
expensive in losses, nineteen of these raids were flown under
the cover of darkness. The most effective ones with regard to
civilian lives snuffed out and damage inflicted were the ones
on Folkstone on 25 May 1917, in which ninety-five persons
were killed, and on London on 13 June 1917 with 162 people
killed. The latter raid, in typical fashion, was meant to
destroy docks, wharves, and warehouses in East London, but
there was also a hit on an East End Council School.
"Incidental" losses were 120 innocent school children killed
or wounded.[47] The German communique stated that the raid
was a success in destroying the intended targets. British opinion was undoubtedly that the "Huns" had visited them again.
Public opinion was described as hysterical for both protection
and revenge.[48]

The Gothas and the Riesenflugzeug also raided French
cities, and were frequently used to bomb tactical targets near
the front line. Paris had suffered only isolated small air raids
for two years after the Zeppelin raids over France had been
discontinued because of heavy losses in 1916. However, in
order to underline the impact of the German land offensive of
21 March 1918, Paris was attacked in that month by a greater
force. The civilian toll was 250 people. The material and moral
damage of one such raid was probably negligible.

What brought home to the Parisians that they were unprotected was another German weapon. The front was about 120

kilometers (72 miles) away from Paris. The city could not be considered to be located near the fighting. From 23 March to 9 August 1918, the Germans performed a technical and military feat unsurpassed before and after. They shelled Paris from this distance of 120 kilometers. Whereas area bombing, as we shall see further on, can be interpreted as not being against the Conventions, the shelling of Paris, an open city outside the war zone, was definitely outlawed. By 1917 the losses of German aircraft bombarding French cities had become insupportable. But the clamour for attacking enemy civilians was still there. The answer was a Krupp super gun. Even today its technical details are staggering:[49]

Range:	120 km
Barrel:	34 meters long (the barrel could only withstand 65 firings before it had to be replaced)
Shell:	21 centimeters in diameter; weight was 1 ton
Trajectory:	it took three minutes to travel to Paris
Firing:	frequency of shots was 7 minutes

The first shell was fired on 23 March 1918, for maximum psychological impact at the time of the German spring offensive. The first shot was a complete success, hitting the center of Paris somewhere on the Seine banks as planned. Consternation among French government, military, and the Parisians was enormous. The first three shells killed eighteen civilians and wounded forty-two. Results of firings were passed by wireless to German headquarters by specially placed agents in Paris.

A total of 320 shells were fired into Paris, of which 180 fell into the center and 140 in the suburbs. Total tonnage of shells was 320 tons; a sizeable load of destruction when one compares it with the tonnage unloaded over London by the German airplanes of about ninety tons. One shell hitting Paris on Good Friday, 29 March 1918, killed eighty-eight worshippers in the church of St. Gervais.[50] French authorities asked the Germans through neutral channels to stop shelling during funeral services for these victims; the German military obliged. But in general they were jubilant about their achievements and had no qualms about them—after all, these shells were in retaliation.

In addition to the bombardment by the Krupp gun, Paris suffered a number of smaller night raids from January until September 1918. The purpose was the same as with the gun: to terrorize the French population. About a half million left the city.[51] But neither the artillery shells, nor over four hundred bombs, cracked the morale of the citizens of Paris, let alone France.

Allied endeavors to retaliate against the German attacks were not lacking. Although in the early stages they did not yet have suitable bombers, raids were flown against German cities. This caused a semi-official dispatch from Berlin in June 1917, warning Britain to relocate its population from the vicinity of strategic targets to avoid losses through German reprisal raids.[52]

After the measures taken by Churchill had succeeded in repulsing the Zeppelins, he then faced the Gothas. Churchill issued a report to Parliament that resulted in the appointment of South African Field Marshal Jan Smuts to head a committee to make recommendations on air defense of the homelands and aerial operations in general. The outcome of the committee meetings was that by late 1917 the Royal Flying Corps and the Royal Naval Air Service were combined in the Royal Air Force and put under the jurisdiction of a new Air Ministry. The move was strongly opposed by the army and the navy in general, and by Haig, Trenchard, and Jellicoe, the Home Fleet commander, in particular. They all felt that the airplane's primary role was in support of land and sea operations. The Smuts Committee thought differently and clearly stated that the time had come when wars could be won by air power. In other words, attack the enemy from behind. In January 1918 this credo was seconded by a cabinet committee whose recommendations were to bomb large industrial centers in Germany.[53] The newly appointed minister of air, Sir William Weir, recommended that Trenchard, by then the commander of the Independent Air Force, start up a really big fire in one of the German towns and not be too exacting regarding accuracy of bombing railway stations in the middle of towns.[54]

The Independent Air Force had been formed in early 1918. This new arm in the British war effort was directly responsible to the Air Ministry and was created to carry bombs into the German heartland to destroy factories, and also to destroy morale. Trenchard, as the professional soldier he was, obediently accepted these directions.

Even before the IAF was created, the bombing of German cities with improved planes had begun. In December 1917, Mannheim had been attacked, and in January 1918, Heidelberg, Trier, Rastatt, and again Karlsruhe and Freiburg. The bombing upset Berlin so much that late in 1917 the German wireless service warned the Allies not to continue with these raids.[55] By June 1918 the IAF was fully operational and German cities from Freiburg in the south to Cologne in the north, and as far east as Frankfurt on Main became targets. Fortunately, the range of these bombers went no further east and Würzburg, among other cities, did not suffer.

The impact of the raids was heavy. The German Supreme Command made noises about more retaliation attacks. But resources were already stretched to their limits and Germany was retreating in the west. Later, Ludendorff, while aiming for an armistice, felt that upping the ante in this game would not help his chances. The civilians stood up well to the raids, just as British and French civilians had. There was never a moment of riots or civil unrest. The Air Ministry in London issued a report based on letters taken from German POWs, German newspaper articles, agent reports, and diplomatic sources, which showed that the German population was suffering and complaining about the air raids. It was a document meant to support the bombing campaign and its effect on the German civilian morale.[56] The report turned out to be exaggerated. However, the people's representatives at all three levels of government—the Reichstag, the Landestage, and city councils—sent petitions to the Kaiser, the Supreme Command, and the federal government to stop German raids, thus prompting the cessation of Allied raids.[57] At first their pleas were disregarded, but when Ludendorff pushed for peace, the German bombing campaign slowed down. The last raid on Britain by the Gothas was flown on the night of 19-20 May 1918. The Allied bomber offensive in the meantime increased. The number of British bomber squadrons had grown from five to nine, and Trenchard was appointed commander-in-chief of all Allied bomber forces. Between June and November 1918, the Allied bombers dropped 550 tons of bombs on German cities, killing 746 and wounding 1,843 people.[58] The Gothas and the Giant Planes had killed 835 and wounded 1,972 people in all raids on Britain.

The casualties of area bombing in World War I (including the Zeppelin raids), in Britain and Germany, show the following—for the time unbelievable statistics:

	People killed	People wounded
In Britain	1,392	3,330
In Germany	746	1,843

Before the killing and fighting stopped, there were plans on the part of the Germans to bomb New York with Zeppelins. The IAF was ready to blast Berlin with Handley Page bombers in early 1919.

The Germans had started bombing civilians for their own perceived reasons, but they were hit back and had learned that the morale of a nation cannot be broken by attacking its people with bombs. The British, on the other hand, had inflicted a hunger blockade on the Germans based on their own justifications. The blockade, with the reported number of victims starved to death at about 700,000,[59] and together with the setbacks on all fronts, did achieve its purpose. Civilian morale cracked and, after the German navy began to mutiny on 28 October 1918, revolts broke out all over Germany. The Kaiser abdicated and exiled himself to Holland. The German government sued for an armistice and on 11 November 1918 it was all over—after 1,597 days.

BETWEEN THE WORLD WARS

PEACE AND DISARMAMENT

The Central Powers were literally losing ground and becoming exhausted from the beginning of 1918 onward. Prior to November 1918, one after another of the Central Powers opted out of the war. Bulgaria, which had joined the fray last in 1915, was the first to fall out on 29 October 1918. The Ottoman Empire had entered the war in November 1914 when Russia declared war on it. On 31 October 1918 it sued for peace. Austria-Hungary, the country that had supposedly started it all, followed on 3 November, and on 11 November it was Germany's turn.

The nations were physically, mentally, and economically exhausted. The enthusiasm for war was gone. If it had not been for the United States entering on the Allied side, the war would have come to a stalemate, as the Entente powers of Europe were similarly exhausted.

The cost had been unimaginable in 1914 when it all began. The military loss statistics stagger ones mind. The battle of Verdun cost 362,000 French and 336,000 German soldiers their lives. The German March 1918 Offensive cost the lives of 240,000 British, 92,000 French, and 348,000 German soldiers.[1] For the entire war the British Empire lost 900,000, the French 1.3 million, the Germans 2.3 million, the Austro-Hungarians 1.53 million, and the Russians 1.7 million soldiers. Several thousand Würzburgers did not return. Their names are engraved on the WWI memorial, which survived the WWII bombing but suffered the damage and indignity of being for a while the campground of the U.S. Army.

After WWI, Britain and France were highly indebted to the United States for delivery of war materials. Large areas of Belgium and northern France looked more desolate than the surface of the moon, and for years merchant ships would run into sea mines planted between 1914 and 1918.

On 8 January 1918, President Wilson had proclaimed the Fourteen Points. Taken word for word they represented a reasonable, ethical, and practical solution to the raging inferno of the time. At first nobody took note of them. In October, when Ludendorff asked the German chancellor to arrange an armistice, the Fourteen Points formed the basis for that request. Germany was to lay down its arms under these terms. What eventually transpired was a long way off the course Mr. Wilson had laid out.

But the Central Powers had no choice. They were on their knees and their peoples were in an uproar. Their heads of state were gone or had become powerless. The German delegation under Matthias Erzberger had to sign the armistice agreement in the forest of Compiègne.

Germany immediately had to withdraw its troops from all occupied territories in the East and West and had to surrender Alsace-Lorraine to France. It had to surrender 5,000 field guns, 25,000 machine guns, 3,000 trench mortars, 1,700 airplanes, which included all its bombers, all its Zeppelins, all its U-boats, and 6 battle cruisers, 10 battleships, 8 light cruisers, and 50 destroyers. The term of the armistice was to be thirty-six days, during which the above conditions had to be met. In other words, at the end of the term Germany was to be in no condition to fight again.

The Germans found these conditions a violation of their national honor. However there was more in the agreement. All German troops had to be withdrawn from the left bank of the Rhine, where Allied troops would move in and occupy those territories. The upkeep of these forces was to be paid for by the German government. The question of reparations was left open for a later peace treaty but Germany had to surrender immediately 5,000 locomotives, 150,000 railway wagons, and 5,000 trucks. The return of German prisoners of war was to be left for agreement in the forthcoming peace treaty. Allied POWs had to be returned immediately. The hunger blockade was to continue. That latter clause, Article XXVI, added insult to injury. The war against women and children was to continue. They were being held hostages to ensure that their men behaved. The continuation of the hunger blockade was in clear contradiction of Wilson's Fourteen Points, Article 2, which promised freedom of navigation upon the seas in peace and in war. The 36-day term was extended three times by conventions, the last signed on 16 February 1919 for an unspecified period. On 11 November 1918 the fighting was officially over and the question arose whether the victors had achieved what they had desired.

France had rectified Bismarck's biggest insult and mistake of 1871. Alsace-Lorraine was French again. Germany was no longer a threat to France, but behind Germany's eastern frontier rose a new threat: Bolshevism.

Britain had eliminated the German navy, had under occupation its most valuable colonies, and had blown German commerce off the globe.

Russia had gained nothing and was fighting a civil war.

Italy occupied South Tyrol and has called it Alto Adige ever since.

Japan was an absolute winner at little cost to itself. It expanded its empire at the cost of the Far East and Pacific Ocean German colonies.

The United States had considerable human losses in the meat grinder called the Western Front. But economically it came out on top. It had gone a step further in becoming a world power. Based on Wilson's Fourteen Points it was ready to become the spiritual leader of the world.

Belguim was a nation which had suffered so severely that no retributions could make it a victor.

The First World War was a disaster for both victor and vanquished. Area bombing with its attacks on civilians had started—a new method of warfare had come into practice. The human losses had been relatively small, but for anybody killed by the bombs the loss was absolute.

The armistice agreement of Compiègne understandably

forced the Germans to hand over all bombers, but the Allied bombers were left intact.

What followed next was the signing of peace treaties. Except for Russia, all the victorious powers were invited to Paris for a peace conference. Contrary to the customary niceties of international law the vanquished powers were not invited. This was to speed up the process and avoid any wrangling.

The Paris Peace Conference of 1919 can be compared in some respects with the Congress of Vienna. In 1815 France was utterly defeated after a period of glory and international recognition. An identical situation existed with Germany in 1918. But there the similarity ends. At Vienna, France was treated very gently. It could keep all its territorial European possessions, its colonies, and even the "collected" art and cultural treasures. The British and Austrian delegations insisted on lenient terms. It was the Duke of Wellington who reasoned that a defeated and emasculated nation would rise again in short order to rectify what it would consider injuries, insults, and injustices. The duke, the second in command of the English delegation, insisted that France should not be demilitarized.

The Paris Peace Conference started on 18 January 1919 with the British Empire, France, Italy, Japan, and the United States as major victor powers, and twenty-two associated powers, some of which were not even in existence at the outbreak of the war. They all agreed that the Great War was to be the last one and that conditions must be established to prevent similar ones in the future. To achieve that goal, Germany, the main culprit, must be punished and reduced politically, economically, and militarily to a minor player. Also, all ethnic aspirations of the world's nationalities must be recognized. The main personalities in these dealings were: Lloyd George, the British prime minister; Clemenceau, the premier of France; Orlando, the prime minister of Italy; the Japanese foreign minister; and Woodrow Wilson, the president of the United States. These men and the other delegates each had their own ideas and aims.

Wilson, as the representative of the nation that had come out of the conflict strongest, had his Fourteen Points. Before long he had to retreat, basically because it was argued that the

Huns had shown their real nature at Brest-Litowsk and Bucharest, where they imposed harsh conditions on the vanquished Russians and Romanians in early 1918. The Germans had forfeited any clemency. The victors and their hangers-on were sure of one thing—the Central Powers were to foot the bill. In the surprisingly short period of three and one half months, the document to make peace with Germany was ready. The Germans were invited to Paris at the end of April. There were to be no negotiations, just sign at the dotted line— the hunger blockade would be lifted as soon as they signed. The conditions were just and considerate; they were humiliating and dishonorable—all dependent on from which side one looked at them.

The German delegation protested, delayed, and made counterproposals, but in the end had to sign. It was 28 June 1919. The place was the Hall of Mirrors in the Palace of Versailles, where Bismarck had undiplomatically proclaimed the Second German Reich in 1871. Peace with Germany had been established. But it was a peace that lasted only for twenty years, two months, and two days.

There were enough voices even before the signing that warned that the harsh terms would lead to a new conflict. Individuals like Smuts of South Africa; Keynes, the British economist; Lansing, the U.S. secretary of state; and many others tried to warn the world. The Germans naturally opposed the treaty. They considered it the worst treatment an enemy had received since Scipio Africanus of Roman times had dealt with Carthage after the Third Punic War in 146 B.C.

The treaty was rejected by the U.S. Senate. Wilson, who had come to the peace conference to enshrine the Fourteen Points, had given ground to his international partners. He now faced defeat on his home turf. The state of war between the United States and Germany continued until 1921, when on 25 August a separate treaty was signed in Washington. It did not include a number of the articles that were particularly objectionable to the U.S. legislators and the U.S. public. The United States did, however, participate in the occupation of the Rhineland and in accepting some of the German warships. The United States was also fully in conformity with taking over German properties as far down as trademarks; to wit, the Bayer Cross, which protected also the name Aspirin. It was not until November 1994 that the German Bayer A.G. of Leverkusen bought back the cross for the substantial sum of U.S.$ 1 billion.[2] The Hague Conventions of 1899 and 1907 had made the expropriation of private property of vanquished nations in the Rules of Land Warfare illegal.

China also did not ratify the treaty because it gave Shantung Province to Japan, a decision that was reversed in 1922. Soviet Russia, which had abrogated the Brest-Litowsk Treaty in the dying days of the war, called the treaty a capitalistic plot and moved spiritually closer to the Germans.

Next followed what is referred to as the Châteaux Treaties because peace was signed with every ex-enemy in a different château near Paris. Including the Versailles Treaty they all had a common structure. They all started with the Covenant of the League of Nations and ended with an article stipulating the establishment of an international labor council. In between were all the clauses about reduction of armaments, reparations, new frontiers, and other issues.

As for aerial bombing, all treaties had one important clause: Article 198 of the Versailles Treaty forbade Germany to have any aircraft. The other treaties had similar clauses forbidding the defeated powers to have aircraft, including Zeppelins.

Since the unspoken intention of all treaties was that the world would disarm, outlawing airplanes and thereby bombers seemed a hope for the beginning to a worldwide rejection of area bombing. Disarmament was Point 4 of Wilson's Fourteen. It was unilaterally and contractually imposed on the vanquished. No timely commitment was made by the victors to do the same. If only that had been accomplished, the death of many civilians in the wars to come could have been prevented.

The peace conference officially ended on 21 January 1920, when the Entente Powers and the newly created states had satisfied themselves that the world was set for a better future. But was the world ready?

The Ottoman Empire, which had collapsed in 1918, was reduced to its heartland, Turkey, with territories in Europe and

Asia Minor. The Dardanelles was internationalized under Allied occupation. Cyprus was ceded to Britain. The Dodecanese Islands off the south coast of Turkey were given to Italy. Hedjaz (today's Saudi Arabia), Armenia, Syria, Mesopotamia (today's Iraq), and Palestine became independent states, the latter three after a limited League of Nations mandate. The Kurdistan area was to be subjected to a plebiscite (something that has not happened to this date).

Kemal Atatürk emerged in 1919 as a nationalistic strongman and repudiated the Sèvres Treaty immediately after it was signed. He deposed the sultan, invaded Armenia, and drove the Greeks out of Smyrna. He sent troops into British occupied Mesopotamia causing RAF bombing in response. Atatürk became the father of modern Turkey. Nobody dared to stand up to him and at times there was an undeclared state of war between Turkey and Great Britain. Nobody wanted war, certainly not London and, therefore, repulsions of Atatürk's sallies into Iraq were treated as pacification campaigns of unruly natives.

Atatürk succeeded in tweaking the Allies' noses and they did nothing about it. They suffered him silently. The question arises whether Hitler took a leaf out of Atatürk's book when he started to break the Versailles Treaty in 1933. The Allies signed a new treaty with Turkey at Lausanne on 24 July 1923. It annulled many of the acrimonious terms of the Sèvres Treaty. Above all it gave Turkey back control of the Dardanelles. It also squashed the plebiscite for Kurdistan.

The other Châteaux Treaties were also detested. Millions of Hungarians became Romanian citizens, millions of Sudeten German-Austrians became Czechoslovak citizens, Ukrainians became Polish citizens, and 250,000 Austrians became Italian citizens. The Fourteen Points had foreseen that all ethnic groups should have the right to their own states. What came out of the Châteaux Treaties was the creation of states that included many unwilling citizens of foreign nationalities.

That the honor, pride, and self-esteem of the defeated nations were not considered and intentionally trampled on could perhaps be understood at the time, but it hurt. It hurt the Germans as much in 1919 as the 1871 peace had hurt the

French. It caused lingering resentment from Berlin to Ankara. The unilateral disarmament of the vanquished with no corresponding reduction in arms by the victors created a feeling of national insecurity against pressures from abroad and from within. The creation of the League of Nations without membership of the vanquished peoples showed where the victors placed them.

In the case of Germany, the Allied Control Commission for Reparations settled the total sum payable at 132 billion goldmarks in 1921, with payments to stretch until 1960. In addition, still unspecified quantities of coal to be delivered to France, 26 percent of the proceeds of all exports were to be paid in addition to the 132 billion goldmarks, 200,000 tons of ships to be delivered over five years, and many more still to be defined services and deliveries.[3]

If violation of national and individual pride could perhaps be digested in time, the economic restrictions and exigencies of the treaties soon proved unworkable. The exhausted and starving masses of the defeated nations had the economic foundations knocked out from under them. Riots, putsches, revolts, and general unrest soon started to mark the postwar years. Agitation from the right and the left, particularly from the Moscow-supported communists, soon were the order of the day.

If one acknowledges that the Versailles Treaty was one of the many, if not the main cause of World War II, one must visualize what was imposed on Germany. It had lost 6.5 million of its citizens, i.e. about 10 percent of its population, to states around it. This loss was in addition to the war losses of 2.3 million of its able-bodied men. It had lost one-sixth of its farmland, 10 percent of its factories, and control of the only natural resource it has ever had: coal in the Saar, Upper Silesia, and the Ruhr area.[4] How could Germany create the gross national product in order to allow the government to fulfill the obligations instituted by the treaty?

In addition to these treaty obligations, the German government also had internal obligations. There were war disability pensions to be paid, there was the cost of changing from a war footing back into peace, and there were the war bonds. During the war, the Kaiser's government had begun to accelerate the printing of new money, because the cost of the conflict had become monumental and bonds could not finance it any longer.

Now, after the war and in the face of national and treaty obligations, the government speeded up the presses even more. In 1914 four goldmarks were worth one U.S. dollar. In May 1921 it was 14.8 marks, in November 1921, 62.6 marks, and toward the end of the postwar German inflation it was 62 billion marks to the dollar.[5] In other words, the money my grandparents had saved before 1914 to look after their retirement was worth nothing. The war bonds they had dutifully purchased, not least because they promised good interest, were just pieces of paper. I remember as a youngster playing with stacks of what would be called today monopoly money and collecting stamps with face values of millions of marks. The family's bonds, money, and stamps were eventually consumed in our attic by the firestorm of 16 March 1945.

The German economy collapsed. The established sum of 132 billion goldmarks of reparations, in 1914 goldmarks, was equal to U.S.$33 billion. The U.S.$33 billion did not take into account the value of the lands, foreign assets, merchant navy, coal deliveries, occupation levies, etc. The men in charge of hammering out these conditions at the peace conference were politicians such as Clemenceau, Lloyd George, and their advisors. Under the circumstances it seems justified to turn the tables on Clemenceau and his comment about war being too serious a business to leave to the military. Perhaps peace is too serious a business to leave to the statesmen. Perhaps a Duke of Wellington at the Peace Conference of 1919 would have been as judicious as in 1815.

Germany defaulted, and as a result French troops occupied the Ruhr industrial area on 11 January 1923. They took control of practically everything, from factory operations to public administration. Germans had to provide food and billeting, commodities that were very scarce already. Even bordellos for the occupying troops had to be established.[6] A number of Germans were shot because they did not obey the 7:00 P.M. curfew. On 31 March, during an anti-occupation demonstration at the Krupp Works at Essen, another fifteen Germans were killed. Anti-French feelings reached a postwar high throughout Germany. The rising politician Adolf Hitler made the occupation the theme of every one of his speeches.

Fortunately, cooler heads prevailed on the Allied side. Charles G. Dawes, a prominent U.S. statesman, banker, and head of the Reparations Committee at the time of the Ruhr occupation, pushed through a plan in 1924, which first of all forced the French to evacuate the Ruhr. Next the plan extended the payment and Dawes arranged for bridge credits to the German government. Germany borrowed 33 billion goldmarks, which in the turmoil before and after World War II were never repaid. Of the imposed 132 billion goldmark reparations, only 36 billion were ever paid. But even that reduced sum proved fatal. After the 1923 inflation had been brought under control by such economists as Hjalmar Schacht of 1946 Nürnberg war crime fame, the world recession of 1929 was the next blow. By October 1932 there were 7.5 million unemployed in Germany.

Yet there were some bright spots on the cloudy horizon. There was growing sympathy for Germany. French, British, and U.S. troops pulled out of the occupied Rhineland four years earlier than the treaty stipulated. Germany was allowed to join the League of Nations on 28 September 1926.

International respect and understanding for Germany was on the rise. It was partly fueled by genuine appreciation and partly by economic and political realities. The 60 million people in the heart of the Old Continent could not be left in limbo and ignored. In foreign politics Germany's star was on the ascent. But in internal politics there was still absolute chaos. The integrity of the Reich had been attacked by revolution, separation attempts by individual states, and paramilitary putsches. Among the latter was Hitler's Munich Beerhall Putsch of 9 November 1923. By the mid-twenties there were many parties of all colors and persuasions, but the struggle for power was in the hands of the Social Democrats, the Communists, and the National Socialists. They fought heated and at times bloody battles. There was a constant change of government in Berlin and thus no consistent central authority. As Churchill said, if the victorious powers of World War I had not gleefully supported the abdications of the Hohenzollerns, the Habsburgs, Wittelsbachs, and all of the German princes, there might never have been a Second World War.[7] On 30 January 1933, the Reichpresident Hindenburg, of World War I military fame, entrusted Hitler with the government of the Weimar Republic. The Nazis were legally brought to power in accordance with the constitution that had been adopted by the German National Assembly at Weimar in 1919. The new government offered restitution of law and order, economic stability, restoration of German integrity abroad and at home—in short everything the ordinary citizen craved. The party program was a masterpiece of statements and promises of social correctness. However, like many a political instrument it was just a piece of paper, no more, no less.

The new government called for elections on 5 March 1933. The National Socialist Party gained a small majority in the Reichstag, and on 24 March introduced a bill that abolished the immunity of the Reichstag members. It looked innocuous. But it was the beginning of the Nazi dictatorship. They marched off enough Communist and Social Democrat deputies to Konzentrationslager and then passed any law in the Reichstag they pleased. From there to the beginning of World War II followed one after another of Hitler's bluffs and blunders, all of which need not be repeated here as they are well-known history.

Not all Germans were enthusiastic about the "New Order." But many supported Hitler because he did bring order to the political scene. He reduced unemployment and, last but not least, he mitigated and eventually abrogated the Versailles Treaty. It was that miscarriage of a peace treaty that caused the conditions that brought Hitler and his rowdies to power. But how did they arrive there? They were a penniless gang of extremists, disappointed with the political, social, and economic performance of the post-WWI German government. They had neither the clout nor the monetary means to go anywhere. Yet they soon had the funds to support an ever-increasing political apparatus. Not too many documents and books exist which indicate from where the funds came. Hitler promised strong government, he promised to fight for German

Lebensraum in the East, with a simultaneous destruction of the threat of Communism. He spelled it all out in *Mein Kampf*. In short he appealed to the people who could finance him. As an example, in 1932 the Deutsche Bank provided Hitler with a Junkers Ju-52 trimotor plane complete with a pilot, Captain Hans Bauer.[8] Since the chaos in Germany appeared threatening to Central Europe, even French sources such as the Sécurité and the firm of Schneider-Creusot financed the National Socialists.[9] Even Henry Ford supported the Nazi Party financially.[10] Neither Hitler, the poor 1913 emigrant from Austria, nor his cohorts alone could have had the means for the 1923 putsch or the later election campaigns. If, with sufficient financial support he came to power, there would not only be law and order, there would be markets and profits for his supporters.

By the time 8 May 1945 came around, everybody had learned a painful lesson. Hitler had promised to recreate Germany and in one of his many hour-long speeches in 1933 he said: "Give me twelve years of time and you will not recognize Germany again." He could not have been more correct. On the morning of 17 March 1945, after Bomber Harris had sent No. 5 Bomber Group over Würzburg, I could not recognize my own city any more. It and all the major cities of Germany had been converted into piles of rubble.

Had there been an amenable peace treaty in 1919, there might not have been a Second World War. There would not have been a Hitler government in Germany. Of the many statements made by Ribbentrop, Hitler's foreign minister, one was certainly correct. Before he was marched to the gallows at Nürnberg in 1946 he said: "How can anyone blame Germany for her government when it was the Versailles Treaty which produced such a government."[11]

BOMBING AND REARMAMENT

In Articles 8 and 9 of its constitution the League of Nations recognized the need for disarmament. This objective came as a direct result of the fourth of Wilson's Fourteen Points in which he proposed reduction of armed forces to the lowest level consistent with domestic safety. Domestic safety meant defense and by definition eliminated offensive actions. Having the Covenant of the League in the Châteaux Treaties, and Articles 8 and 9 in the League Constitution gave the Central Powers the assurance that they would not be alone in disarming. The preamble of Part V of the Versailles Treaty specifically indicates that.[12]

Allied Control Commissions traveled the width and breadth of the loser countries to ensure that they were in compliance with disarmament. But soon, either because they mistrusted each other or they felt the need to codify peace and armaments, conferences were called among the victors to establish ranks. Britain, with its world-spanning navy, was intent not to lose its preeminent status at sea. The 1921-1922 Washington Naval Conference, and later conferences in London on the same subject, set the numbers and sizes of capital ships Britain, France, Italy, Japan, and the United States could have. At the Washington Conference the participating governments recognized that the threat of aerial war still existed and that some codes and limitations had to be set up for its conduct. The participants of the conference condemned aerial warfare, but could not agree on outlawing it. Therefore, a Committee of Jurists was established to draft rules, which would then be ratified. The committee met in The Hague on 11 December 1922, and by 6 February 1923 a proposal for the conduct of aerial warfare containing sixty-two articles was ready. Article 17 stated that the 1907 Hague Convention on Maritime War would also apply to aerial warfare. That meant no bombardment of cities was allowed. Article 22 forbade aerial bombardment for the purpose of terrorizing civilian populations. Unfortunately, the jurists' work never advanced beyond a draft, not even proceeding to protocol, the step ahead of a binding treaty. The French government in particular rejected the draft, on the grounds that the existing conventions already covered the conduct of aerial war. In the end, everybody from Hitler to Chamberlain and Roosevelt paid lip service to these rules at the beginning of World War II, and conveniently forgot about them shortly thereafter.

In 1924 the League of Nations condemned aggression as a

means of politics. Theoretically that derailed the Clausewitz definition of war. If the politicians had come to the end of their ropes they would still have to talk to each other under the aegis of the League. The 1928 Briand-Kellogg Pact even went further by declaring war illegal as an instrument of national policy. In 1925 after France had invaded the Ruhr in 1923, Germany, under its chancellor Stresemann, felt threatened and a treaty was signed at Locarno, Switzerland. It guaranteed the borders of Germany created by the Versailles Treaty and was signed by all of Germany's neighbors, old and new. In 1920, Austria, Bulgaria, and Hungary were graciously admitted to the League, followed by Germany in 1926. Turkey, the trouble-maker of Sèvres and Lausanne Treaty fame, was admitted in 1932, and in 1934 the ultimate pariah, the USSR, got in. Now the League of Nations was almost complete. Almost, because the United States, the father of it, and Switzerland, the host of it, had not joined. They never did.

General disarmament, one of the main purposes of the League, was slow in proceeding. Not until 1926 was a preparatory commission established to flesh out the meaning and details. It foundered on technical details and definitions of what reserves and war materials meant. There was also the French insistence that Germany's armed forces would always have to be inferior to the French forces. Finally, in February 1932, a disarmament conference began at Geneva. All League members were represented as well as non-members, the United States and the Soviet Union. Germany had pushed time and again for this conference. It and its WWI allies had implemented their contractual obligations, but the other treaty partners had not only failed to disarm but increased their arms. Germany felt threatened. The forces surrounding Germany were colossal in both quantity and quality. In 1928 the German army had 100,000 men. Around it were 755,000 French, 595,000 Italian, 614,000 British, 212,000 Czech, 263,000 Polish, and 600,000 USSR soldiers. Germany had no tanks; France had 2,500. Germany had no military aircraft; Britain had 1,300 and France 1,800. On its eastern frontiers Germany faced about 1,700 USSR, Polish, and Czech aircraft.[13] Some of the Russian bombers had a range of 1,400 kilometers and could carry two tons of bombs.

Why the world was in arms at that time is difficult to understand. Seemingly there was this ingrained fright of the German army marching again, but the Allied Control Commission could and did verify that there were no more than 100,000 soldiers in Germany. There was the danger of Soviet Communism, but that was more a psychological threat than a military one. There was a noticeable shift of Japan and Italy moving away from the Entente to threaten, respectively, Chinese and U.S. interests in the Far East, and British and French interests in the Mediterranean.

The conference began at Geneva on 2 February 1932. On 9 February the German chancellor Brüning pointed out in a lengthy address that Germany felt itself endangered. Especially threatening appeared the state of Czechoslovakia, with airfields for bombers to reach any point in Germany. Added to this was the fact that Soviet bombers could be brought to the Czech airfields in short order. It was one year before Hitler came to power and German external politics were still of the type described as "hat in hand." The German government wanted assurance that there would be no threat from that massive military ring around its territory.

Before long, the disarmament conference agreed that gas warfare, bombing, and limitations on arms needed to be codified, and proposals were tabled for discussion. Of particular interest were proposals to regulate bombing. The preparatory committee had upheld the existence of air forces. This seemed an understandable point, taking into consideration the Trenchard Doctrine, Douhetism, and the successes of colonial pacification. The Germans objected. In February they proposed a complete prohibition and destruction of air forces, and as a consequence that dropping bombs from aircraft be outlawed.[14] Aside from the military point of view, it also made economic sense for the Germans. They had no air force and if the terms of the conference would allow them to have one it would cost money.

The French proposal of February 1932 called for an international peace force and the complete abolishment of strategic bombardment. Tactical air warfare including tactical bombing was to be allowed. The British proposal of 7 July 1932 also suggested the elimination of aerial bombing.[15] The accounts of what exactly was proposed, discussed, and rejected vary between historians.

The Germans were not to be granted equal rights. They walked out in autumn 1932. By December they were back after agreeing to a period of five years before Germany could increase its armed forces. The French disagreed and insisted on an eight-year period, which caused the Germans to walk out a second time on 14 October 1933. By that time Hitler was chancellor, and he declared Germany's exit from the League.

The main factor that prevented the outlawing of bombing was a revised British proposal to permit bombing for policing in colonies and League-mandated areas. This provision was completely rejected, primarily by the United States, but also by Spain, Norway, the USSR, and Germany. It was to be either complete prohibition of bombing or none at all. After Germany had walked off, the conference stalled and world rearmament started.

As an international body, the League was in decline from 1933 onward. Germany, which until that time is often referred to as the Weimar Republic, had honestly sought to broker disarmament, together with an equal status for itself.

Disarmament and bringing bombing under control became a dead issue. Hitler made a few proposals to limit the menace. Two times in 1935 he proposed limiting strategic bombing, and in 1936 he transmitted such a proposal directly to the British government.[16] But nobody believed him because his strongman tactics, such as occupying the Rhineland in March 1935, denouncing the Versailles Treaty, and announcing that Germany was rearming in general and in the air in particular, scared everybody. The road to Armageddon was open. Everybody became afraid and started to rearm in earnest.

Not all victorious nations had demobilized after the Great War. There were enough conflicts after "the war to end all wars" to keep the military and their suppliers employed. In 1918 the Russian civil war was still raging. The Entente tried to interfere and sent 40,000 troops and combat planes into Murmansk and Archangel.[17] A British aircraft carrier with its planes kept the Red Fleet at anchor in Kronstadt outside

Petrograd (as it was then called). The Japanese moved into Vladivostok. The RAF sent two squadrons to assist the White Russian General Wrangell to conquer Tsaritsyn (later called Stalingrad).[18] The Bolsheviks employed the leftovers of the World War I Imperial Air Force to fight the White Russian forces and their Entente supporters. The four-engined Ilya Muromets with its three thousand pound payload was the main bomber.[19] The newly formed Polish state fought the Soviets in 1920, but there was little air combat in that conflict.

Similarly, there were few if any air actions when the Greeks at British behest invaded Anatolia in Turkey in 1919 and were expelled in 1921. The Chaco War between Bolivia and Paraguay from 1932 to 1935 cost 100,000 lives and 140,000 wounded, but no air action was reported.[20]

However, the concept of bombing civilians had not been forgotten. The imperial/colonial powers discovered that it had a salutary effect on rebellious natives, their rifle toting warriors, and their families. The minor perpetrators of these peace missions were the French and Spaniards in their Moroccan dependencies from 1923 to 1934. The Italians did the same in Libya between 1923 and 1933. The major perpetrators were the British under the able guidance of Lord Trenchard and such effective commanders as Salmond, Game, Portal, and Harris.

The United States, although politically it would never consider itself a colonial or imperial power, also let its eagles fly. From 1919 to 1923 U.S. aircraft chased insurgents and bandits (or national heroes?) in Santo Domingo and similarly chased bandits in Haiti from 1923 to 1938.[21] These were minor actions that received very little publicity.

On the other hand, the British colonial air actions have been well publicized; not only the actions themselves, but also their political, economic, and military background. Bombing developed into such a fine art that many RAF air marshals from Trenchard to Harris were proud of it until the end of their lives. After World War I the Royal Navy and the British army took up an extended political campaign to have the RAF abolished as an independent armed service. Churchill as air minister and Trenchard as chief of air staff fought the First Sealord Admiral Beatty for years. The fight with the army was not as acrimonious because Churchill was also minister of war, i.e. minister of the army. Lloyd George, the prime minister, was determined to cut defense spending to a minimum after the horrendous debts incurred during the war. He decided and proclaimed publicly that Britain would not be involved in another major war for ten years and therefore needed only minimal armed forces. The "ten year rule," as it was called, appears incongruous in the light of the Châteaux Treaties.

The Cabinet was pressing the RAF, questioned its needs and the proposed budget of £66 million in peacetime 1919. The long-established army and navy services wanted the Royal Flying Corps and the Royal Naval Air Service respectively back under their commands to use them for tactical air operations. They did not want the independent RAF to perform reconnaissance and frontline support and perhaps be told that it could not be done. The lobbying was intense with Churchill vacillating, even going as far as to propose a defense ministry (with himself as minister) that would control the three services, and Trenchard staunchly upholding the need for an independent RAF. The fight went on for years. Trenchard won, created the RAF as it is known today, and has since been called its "father." His organizational and command skills are apparent in not having army titles for the officer corps and gradually involving the RAF in British Empire military control. Trenchard succeeded in employing it in an economical manner to quell local colonial unrest.

The bombing started in 1919 when Afghanistan declared one of its holy wars and together with the tribes in the northern Indian frontier area began to threaten India's security. Handley Pages were sent to India and attacked the rebels and their villages. The RAF resources were sparse and there was no thanks from the army for their work. One Handley Page V-1500 bombed Kabul on 24 May 1919.[22] Dakka was also bombed as was the city of Jalalabad for three days in May 1919. There were heavy military and civilian losses. The RAF contingent was under the command of Air Vice-Marshal Sir Philip Woolcott Game. He has been described as more ruthless in his bombing methods than the bombers of World War II. The

Punjabi town of Guyranwala was bombed and strafed with machine guns, killing twelve people. The action was investigated in London and found not only justified but necessary.[23] India and its frontiers had to be kept safe within the British Empire, although the cost of it was also a consideration. The 1919-20 skirmishes required 29,000 combat troops and 34,000 auxiliaries to supply them.

Trenchard, who had only twenty-five squadrons, stationed nineteen of them permanently across the empire. Eight were in India, three in Mesopotamia, seven in Egypt, and one distributed to naval stations such as Malta.[24] He drew a masterpiece of political and strategic distribution of limited resources.

By 1920 another sore had opened on the British Empire's body. The Mad Mullah of Somalia, who during the Great War had challenged British rule, made trouble again. The cost of pacifying the region was estimated in the millions of pounds sterling and the dispatch of two divisions. A single RAF squadron of eight planes was finally flown from Egypt and routed the mullah by attacking his strongholds and villages. The cost was £77,000, a real bargain.[25] The mullah fled to Ethiopia and was killed there.

From 1920 until the 1930s a further trouble spot for the British Empire was the Middle East. The Sèvres Treaty had mandated Mesopotamia, Palestine, Transjordan, and Yemen to the United Kingdom. What it really meant was that the indigenous peoples of these regions exchanged their Turkish masters for British masters. These people had cooperated with Lawrence of Arabia and with the French to defeat the Turks. Freedom from foreign rule and independence had been promised. They may have heard of Wilson's Fourteen Points, but they were sacrificed to big power imperial politics at the Paris Conference. Independence was like a fata morgana in the hot desert air. For Britain the mandates were a consolidation of the route to India, the crown jewel. No more upstart continental power would build a railway to the Persian Gulf and thereby control the land access to India. In London, Churchill had changed portfolio and become minister of colonies. In March 1921 he convened a conference in Cairo to find a solution to the rising unrest in the mandated areas. These lands were theoretically under the umbrella of the League; yet France and Britain treated them as colonies. In Mesopotamia and Palestine alone Britain maintained eighty army battalions in 1920. They performed costly police actions that did not fit into Lloyd George's budget. At Cairo, within one week Churchill persuaded everybody to let the RAF do the policing. As proven in Somalia, it was faster and above all much cheaper. Politicians and military brass were elated; the RAF because their star was rising, the army and navy because they were rid of a difficult task. Aerial bombing had taken a great step forward.

Reports reaching Britain soon spoke of aerial attacks on tribal encampments in Mesopotamia and of machine-gunning the inhabitants. Churchill wanted the pilots court-martialed. Trenchard ignored him and had the political administrators in Iraq back him up. The new policing method was cheap and successful.[26] Tens of thousands of rounds of ammunition were fired and about one hundred tons of bombs dropped. The RAF losses were eleven aircraft from rifle fire and fifty-seven due to accidents.[27]

The policing by the RAF throughout the British Empire went on until the outbreak of World War II. The Northwest Frontier of India was a permanent trouble spot. The RAF flew into Kabul in 1928-29 and airlifted six hundred British and European nationals out to safety in India.

The effectiveness of bombing the insurgents spoke for itself. In the Middle East, the eighty battalions were reduced to six as ground support troops for the RAF. Eight RAF squadrons of nominally ten aircraft each took over the policing duties. Salmond, the last RFC chief on the Western Front, took over as commander in Iraq. The problems with the natives dragged on for years and were far from over when the Luftwaffe appeared as a threat on the horizon of Iraq in World War II.

The method of pacification raised indignant voices in the Westminster Parliament but Trenchard and successive air ministers persisted in letting the bombs fall. The Cabinet agreed and in 1927 designated the RAF to police the Aden Protectorate, thereby allowing the reduction of armed forces to one British battalion, one Indian battalion, and one RAF

Squadron.[28] In 1928 the Imam of Yemen captured two sheiks friendly to Britain. The one RAF squadron brought the Imam to heel within one week at the cost of about £8,000.[29] Portal had become the commander of the British forces in Yemen and Aden, and when new trouble erupted in 1934 he quelled it in three months by bombing the insurgent villages. A total of twenty-eight tons of high-explosive and incendiary bombs were dropped, eighty of which were fused for delayed explosion. The latter killed seven people when they tampered with them, although no other losses were incurred through the bombing. RAF losses were zero.[30] The report Portal sent to the Air Ministry was praised highly and helped its author on his road to the highest post in the RAF.

In India, the policing carried on into World War II, when RAF planes fired on protest rallies five times in August and September 1942.[31]

The pacification of rebels and their kin by the RAF was a brutal undertaking. It included not only bombing of towns and villages but the destruction of crops, cattle, water supplies, and anything that supported life in the insurgent areas. It was extremely successful. It confirmed the Trenchard and Douhet doctrines.

The RAF, that new and untraditional third service, had proven its usefulness. Admiral Beatty, its most vociferous opponent, had to concede defeat. Trenchard was winning not only because he saved the country millions of pounds but also because he could persuade the government that in a future war defense of the home isles and victory was no longer the prerogative of the navy. In numerous meetings and papers he hammered out "the Trenchard Doctrine." When it was applied at full force in World War II it showed that bombing defenseless tribesmen was one thing, bombing an enemy nation of equal technical sophistication was very costly and did not bring fast victory. But in the twenties, Trenchard and the RAF survived. One of the many reasons was that the French air force, at the time the mightiest and best equipped, was considered a threat to Britain. If a superior French air force bombed the British people hard enough they would force the government's hand.[32] British government policy supported the existence of the RAF and particularly bombing as an inexpensive method of policing their empire. Hence, the British stance at the Geneva disarmament conference. The bomber could not be outlawed and the British public was warned to be prepared for bombers coming over the island in the event of war. Prime Minister Stanley Baldwin went as far as to say in a speech in the House of Commons on 10 November 1932 that "the bomber will always get through."[33] One wonders what the victims of the Luftwaffe Blitz of 1940-41 thought of that statement. If there had been an international agreement to limit bombing, many of Baldwin's countrymen might not have been killed by German bombs. But the British attitude after World War I was that air attacks outside the battle zone could not be prohibited.[34]

The Spaniards also dropped explosives on insurgents of the Rif Rebellion in the early 1920s. The conflict spilled over into French Morocco and lasted till 1926. In the end the French deployed 85 battalions and 22 squadrons with a total of 160 planes.[35] Similar problems erupted in Syria, which France had accepted as a League mandate in April 1920. French colonial troops were brought in to fight the Druzes. Damascus was bombed on 20 October 1925 whereby the Moslem section of the city was badly damaged and 1,416 civilians killed. French sources published a toll of only 150 killed.[36]

Italy was another country to use its air force, the Regia Aeronautica, on people who had no means of defending themselves against this menace. After Mussolini had assumed power in 1923 he turned into the dictator that history knows. He sought to restore Italy to a world power. He declared the Mediterranean the *mare nostrum* and thereby set a collision course with the Royal Navy patrolling the sea route to India via Suez. The Italian navy and air force were built up. Italy needed markets and land for its surplus population to settle on. During World War I it had lost control of the interior of Libya, taken from the Turks in 1912. From 1923 onward Italy was involved in an ongoing fight with rebellious tribes that lasted till 1932. Whole villages and their flocks were herded into five large concentration camps where thousands of them died. A 160-mile-long fence was erected along the Libyan-Egyptian border to prevent supplies coming into the colony.

The Regia Aeronautica controlled the fence and attacked any Libyans still at large, whether men, women, or children.[37] Under Balbo, who became governor of Libya in 1933, and after the "pacification" had been completed, Italian colonists came to settle.

Ethiopia, which neighbored the Italian colonies of Eritrea and Somalia at the Horn of Africa, became the next target of Mussolini's expansion. It had been invaded by Italy in 1895 but the aggressors had been repulsed in the battle of Aduwa. A border clash was engineered in December 1934, and by October 1935 the Italian army and air force had brought enough men and equipment through the Suez Canal to commence an invasion. Whether it was in the interest of the shareholders of the Suez Canal Company to let these forces pass is a moot point. The League tried to stop the conflict but failed. Similar presentations by the British and French governments failed. Sanctions were agreed upon but not enforced. Nobody wanted to be too hard on the Italians. There was also anxiety that the Regia Aeronautica would bomb London if it came to an open conflict.[38] Mussolini, like Hitler a few years later, had succeeded in bluffing the international establishment about the strength of his air force. There had been the impressive long-range mass flights of bombers with refueling stops under the command of Italo Balbo from Rome to Chicago and Rome to Rio de Janeiro.[39] But there certainly were no planes to reach London and return without refueling. By May 1936, Ethiopia was firmly in Italian hands. The role of the Regia Aeronautica has been described as purely tactical but one must question that when one learns that among the 320 aircraft employed, a good portion were state-of-the-art bombers such as the Caproni 101, Ca 133, and Savoia SM81. These multi-engine bombers dropped mustard gas on helpless Ethiopian troops and towns, despite the June 1925 Geneva Protocol that outlawed the use of poison gas, and of which Italy was a signatory.[40] The international press reported that the RA attacked many hospitals; but that kind of news was to be expected.

The guns were barely silent in Africa when the Spanish Civil War broke out. For years the political situation in Spain had been unstable. By July 1936 there were political murders of

Republican and Falangist personalities, and soon thereafter came uprisings in many Spanish cities in support of either camp. General Francisco Franco, the military commander of the Canary Islands, flew into Spanish Morocco and took charge of the Moroccan army. In order to transport his troops to southern Spain he appealed directly to Hitler for transport planes. Within a few days he had twenty German Ju-52 trimotors flying his Moroccans to Seville. It was a technical feat and constitutes the first major troop airlift in history. A total of 15,000 troops were ferried from Morocco to the Spanish mainland.

The Spanish Civil War is known in history for the atrocities committed by both sides. It is also known as a proving ground for the modern arms of Germany, Italy, and the USSR, and further for the senseless slaughter of civilians at Guernica and Barcelona by Luftwaffe and Regia Aeronautica planes, which were fighting on the Nationalist side.

The atrocities inflicted on innocent Spanish civilians started in July 1936 at the very beginning of the war and continued until the war ended in April 1939. The Republicans within a few months killed 12 bishops, 4,184 priests, 283 nuns, and 2,365 monks.[41] After the capture of Badajoz by General Yagüe's Moroccan troops in August 1936, this venerable Nationalist general, after whom a street is named in Madrid, had 4,000 people shot.[42] These outrages caused international outcries and galvanized the attitudes governments took toward the two opposing sides. The League stayed clear of involvements, last but not least because it was almost defunct and powerless. Britain, France, and the United States adopted a policy of non-intervention. Under Mussolini, Italy saw an opportunity to rope Franco into its orbit and make Spain an ally in the Mediterranean. Germany sympathised with the Falangists and was afraid that if the Republicans won, the USSR would have a foothold in Western Europe. The USSR pretended not to involve itself but supported ideologically and materially the Republicans. The lines of political, economic, and military interests were drawn by the summer of 1936.

Britain, France, the United States, and other countries permitted their nationals to join the International Brigade, which on many fronts put up strong resistance to the Nationalist advance. On the Nationalist side, the Italians came in early. In July 1936 they sent twelve Marchetti S.81 Pipistrello bombers, complete with crews.[43] Total Italian support until the end of the war amounted to about 50,000 troops and over 700 planes of all types.[44] German help was crucial in getting Franco started on the mainland and continued until April 1939. In the beginning the German effort was clandestine and German military personnel traveled to Spain in civilian clothes. In November 1936 the Condor Legion was formed and 12,000 troops landed at Cadiz. They were mostly Luftwaffe personnel but there were also tank crews and antiaircraft and artillery gunners.[45] By the time it was over the Germans had up to 16,000 men in Spain on a rotating basis. In all, they supplied 285 aircraft, from lumbering Ju-52 transport bombers and obsolete He-51 biplane fighters to the modern Ju-87 Stuka divebombers, Me-109 fighters, and He-111 bombers of World War II fame.

Stalin's USSR was enamored by the Republicans's anticlerical and Communist stance and in July 1936 decided to weigh in against the Fascists. By October 1936 Russian freighters had unloaded 50 tanks, 20 armored cars, and 108 fighter planes at Cartagena. The planes, mostly I-15 and I-16 fighters, and tanks, came complete with crews, who like the Germans arrived in civilian dress. The fighters went into action in November and helped to stall Franco's drive to Madrid.[46] By midwinter of 1937 the USSR had 433 planes in Spain, which represented two-thirds of the Republican air force.[47] The preponderance of fighters in the USSR/Republican air force in Spain resulted in a temporary air superiority, which lasted until the Condor Legion and Italian Aviazione Legionaria were equipped with better fighters. The USSR supplied a total of 1,409 planes between 1936 and 1938, of which 1,176 (83 percent) were destroyed. The Spanish air force before the civil war was small. Of about 277 planes of all types, 214 ended up with the Republicans and 63 with the Nationalists.[48]

The cost to the Spanish people for the "help" from both sides was immense. The national gold reserve, valued at U.S.$788 million, was sent to the Soviet Union for safekeeping. The Soviets paid themselves from it for the war materials and services they had supplied.[49] At the end of hostilities the

Soviets claimed that they were still owed over U.S.$50 million. Spain never saw its gold again. Another U.S.$250 million was sent to France for material help. The Germans were paid in iron ores and minerals, which they needed for the build-up of their armaments. They also obtained control of mining companies, ensuring that they would get paid.

The air force actions during the Spanish Civil War were mostly tactical. Where bombing occurred it was in support of imminent ground assaults. The Republicans had few bombers because the main force consisted of Russian planes. The USSR's Red Air Force had huge bombers, which would have been useless for tactical support and easy prey for enemy fighters. They had few medium bombers such as those the Condor Legion and the Aviazione Legionaria had been equipped with. Only 340 aircraft of the 1,400 supplied by the USSR were medium bombers of the SB-2 and R-5 type.[50] There were isolated bombing raids by the Russian/Republican Air Force against Seville, Zaragossa, Valladolid, and Salamanca.[51] To the chagrin of the Republican military commanders, most of these raids were executed without authorization. The Nationalists, due to the help of their fellow Fascist supporters, regained air superiority by the end of 1937.

Strategic bombing on a large scale did not fit this war, because it was brother against brother, and destruction of industry, infrastructure, and residential areas would have been counterproductive. The victor would have to pay for their reconstruction before he could use them again.

Franco, on his own initiative and the advice of his foreign supporters, tried to wrest control of Madrid from the Republicans in late 1936. He had himself proclaimed head of state of Spain and needed the capital to bring credence to the title. There were numerous air raids on Madrid, causing frightful civilian losses. Exact casualties were never established, but some sources indicate 2,200 to 2,500 killed and 4,000 wounded.[52] At the time, the superior Russian fighters inflicted heavy losses on the slow Ju-52 bombers. The advance on Madrid stalled and the city did not fall to the Nationalists until early 1939.

When Madrid could not be taken by late 1936, Franco shifted his campaign to the north to gain control of the Basque region. Nationalist troops pushed northward with the tactical air support of the Condor Legion and the Aviazione Legionaria. These air units were under the direct control of Franco, who had his headquarters at Salamanca at the time. The chiefs of the Legions were assigned to these headquarters. Day to day operations rested with the chiefs of staff in the field, who, in the case of the Germans, was Colonel Wolfram von Richthofen. The instructions from headquarters were clear and unambiguous. Prepare for a rapid ground force advance without too much consideration for civilian losses. Smash the morale of the opposing troops.[53] Some historians maintain that the Condor Legion was not only a proving ground for German armaments but also was to establish the impact of bombing on civilian morale. No proof for the latter statement has been found in the archives at Freiburg or Koblenz. Richthofen, in a diary covering his entire sojourn in Spain, also mentions nothing.[54] There was no need to prove the merits of area bombing. The RAF had shown on a large scale in the League mandates how expedient bombing civilians can be on morale.

The tactical air strikes in the north soon gained notoriety because they killed many civilians, and as a result were reported as terror raids by the Republicans and the international press. One of the major raids occurred on 31 March 1937 on the city of Durango. It left 258 people dead.[55] The most infamous air raid occurred on 26 April 1937. Guernica, a small town of immense importance to Basque history, was the target of planes of the Condor Legion and the Aviazione Legionaria from 4 to 7 P.M. All aircraft were under the direct command of von Richthofen. He had cleared the raid with Salamanca and timed it to prevent the retreat of Republican troops through the town; at least that is what intelligence had told him. The raiding fleet consisted of twenty-three Ju-52, four He-111, one Do-17, and three Savoia-Marchetti bombers. They dropped forty-five tons of high explosives and incendiary bombs, one-third of the total being incendiaries.[56] Following the bombers came the fighters, ten He-51, six Me-109s, and twelve Fiat Cr-32s. They spread terror among the defenseless and fleeing inhabitants with their machine guns. There were no Republican troops in town; the intelligence had been incorrect. The bridge over which they were to escape was not destroyed. In all, 1,645 civilians were killed and 889 wounded.[57] These figures were released by the Republican press, while the whole raid was hotly denied by the Nationalists. Franco claimed that the Republicans had set the town on fire. In his diary, von Richthofen makes scant mention of the raid. Under the date of 26 April he mentions only that there was a raid on Guernica and strafing of troops in the town. The entry for the next day says that the fighters were back over the town and that it was in flames. For 28 April he states that Guernica "*soll total zerstört sein*" (Guernica "is supposedly totally destroyed"). But in the same entry he claims that the "Reds" have torched the buildings. For 4 April he mentions that sixty tons were dropped on Red troops without indicating where, and the Durango raid is not mentioned at all in his diary.

Many historians have attempted to clarify what really happened at Guernica. The accounts vary from the above Republican statements to Franco's version. Analyzing the facts and reports one cannot deny that the raid happened. The word went out that the Huns had been let loose again and had shown their true colors. Von Richthofen has been blamed for it all, and his later involvement in the bombing of Warsaw did not help his image. What on first sight seems strange is the number of victims. Guernica had 5,561 inhabitants. There were no shelters and there was no air-raid warning system. The forty-five tons of bombs, according to Lord Cherwell's scientific calculations in World War II, could not have killed 1,645 people. However, it was market day in Guernica on 26 April and the population had swelled to about 10,000. Still, 16.5 percent fatalities with only forty-five tons of bombs dropped from mostly auxiliary bombers would have made Bomber Harris proud a few years later. Other sources maintain that one hundred people were killed.[58] Evaluating available statistics, one would find that it took only 0.027 tons to kill a civilian at Guernica whereas later during the Blitz the Germans needed 0.25 tons and Bomber Command required 0.2 tons at Würzburg to achieve the same grisly results.

The news spread like wildfire around the world. Berlin was

embarrassed and kept silent. The Goebbels-controlled press never mentioned the raid. Eden, the British foreign secretary, called in Ribbentrop, the German ambassador in London, and proposed an international inquiry. Franco, with the connivance of the Germans, declined. World opinion later coupled Guernica with the German bombing of Britain in 1940-41, and the idea that it was a trial run for the Luftwaffe has persisted since. What made Guernica truly famous (big by standards of the time though small by World War II standards) is Picasso's huge painting called "Guernica." He produced it on the orders of the Republicans shortly after the raid. Its abstract mysticism has fascinated millions of viewers, and the event would probably long have been forgotten were it not for the painting and its odyssey from France to the United States and to Madrid. In 1946 at the Nürnberg war crime trials the former Basque minister of justice, Jesus Leizaola, tried to have charges included for the destruction of Guernica.[59] The request was declined. A consideration must have been that, as in all raids in the Basque region, the Condor Legion did not act alone. The Aviazione Legionaria also participated.

The Guernica raid had tainted the Luftwaffe's reputation. It should never have happened. It was not the only raid in the Spanish Civil War which caused civilian suffering, although in absolute numbers it caused the most losses, provided the quoted numbers are correct.

Barcelona was bombed between 16 and 18 March 1938. Barcelona, like other Republican-held ports on Spain's Mediterranean coast, was the entrance point for help from the USSR. The Nationalist, Italian, and German navies tried to blockade it. The Republican navy and air force fought back and Russian planes bombed the German pocket battleship *Deutschland* at Ibiza on 29 May 1937. As a reprisal, German naval units shelled the port of Almeria two days later, raising the question why innocent civilians had to suffer for a military action they had nothing to do with. Barcelona had strategic value and the raids in March 1938 must be considered strategic because it was not until January 1939 that the city became a battlefield.

The initiative to bombard Barcelona was taken by

Mussolini without consultation or approval by Franco. Mussolini was upset by Hitler's annexation of Austria and in general felt that the Germans were stealing the show everywhere. He wanted to prove that Italy was a force to be reckoned with.[60] Specific orders were issued not only to aim at the harbor installations but also at residential districts. The raids lasted forty-four hours and were carried out by planes of the Aviazione Legionaria stationed at Mallorca. Six Condor Legion hydroplanes also participated. Over 1,300 people were killed and more than 2,000 were injured.[61] The international outcry was immense. Britain, the Vatican, and even Hitler pressed Franco to stop the slaughter. Franco in turn was furious with Mussolini and requested him not to issue direct orders to the Italian soldiers in Spain.[62] Whereas the Guernica raid must be considered a tactical operation, albeit gone completely wrong by design or accident, the Barcelona raids were designated terror raids. Why, it is impossible to understand.

During the course of the Spanish Civil War there were many minor raids that caused civilian casualties. Reviewing the files of the Condor Legion one reads that they, of course, always hit their assigned military targets such as harbors and railways.[63] There were instructions for fighters on how to attack moving trains from the last wagon toward the locomotive. It does not say that a difference should be made between a passenger and a freight train.

While the war in Spain was going on in Europe, the Second Sino-Japanese War was raging in the Far East. In 1931 Japan took over northern Manchuria and established the last Chinese emperor, deposed by the 1911 revolution, as emperor of the new puppet state, Manchukuo. Relations with China continued to deteriorate and by 1937 the Japanese army and air force had invaded the northern Chinese provinces from Manchuria. The Second Sino-Japanese War had started and would continue until the Japanese surrender in August 1945. From 1937 onward Japanese forces advanced along the Chinese coast and took possession of all major cities from Peking to Canton. Fierce battles developed around the major cities and the Japanese army and navy air forces went into action. The army air force deployed about 300 planes and the navy air force about 230 based on carriers off shore. Against them stood about 100 Chinese fighter planes.[64] There was no planned strategic air war, but civilian losses were substantial because bombing was performed without any consideration of civilians. Except for the raids on Chungking, the far away provisional Chinese capital, the most notorious raids occurred around the battlefields. The Chungking raids were strategic, because they happened far away from the front lines. The city was attacked two hundred times with a total of 3,717 sorties.[65] In the summer of 1939 during four months of continuous attacks four-fifths of the city was destroyed. Japanese planners had expected that with the destruction of Chungking, China could be blasted out of the war and its people would rebel. It did not happen and the morale of the citizens actually improved.[66]

Other major cities suffering from the Japanese air forces were Nanking, Hankow, Canton, and the Chinese sections of Shanghai.[67] Chinese civilian losses between 1937 and 1945 amounted to 77,105 killed and 78,394 injured.[68] Between July 1937 and March 1940, Japanese aircraft flew 9,786 raids with a total of 43,000 sorties. They dropped 142,000 bombs and killed 51,000 Chinese citizens during that period.[69] Nanking was particularly hard hit. In late 1937, twelve hundred bombers dropped five hundred tons of high explosives, a considerable tonnage at that time. The bombing represented the prelude to the plundering and raping of that venerable city.

The international media reported the outrages of the major raids and soon presentations were made in Tokyo to stop the carnage. The British, French, and American efforts succeeded in having Japan agree to the establishment of sanctuary zones. By November 1937 such an area had been created in Shanghai next to the Foreign Concessions. A quarter of a million Chinese civilians fled into this area and were safe. The Japanese faithfully observed the immunity of the place. Similar zones were created in other major cities and have been credited with saving tens of thousands of Chinese lives.[70] A similar scheme would have made World War II less ruthless. It was proposed in 1939, but the belligerents all found reasons of their own not to pursue it.

With the bombing experiences of World War I, the raids occurring afterward, and with the political developments in Europe and the Far East, it is easy to understand that after the breakdown of the Geneva disarmament conference, many nations began to be concerned about their safety. Rearmament commenced and every nation blamed the other for having started it. Rearmament, of course, meant building up air forces, because attempts to outlaw or limit them had been prevented. To what degree the respective air forces were built up and received funds from the treasuries depended on whether the air force was an independent service or attached to the army or navy. It also depended on whether Douhetism was considered a fact of modern warfare or was belittled by the two tradition-al services. When the leading airmen were free of the shackles of the conservative army generals and navy admirals, they could convince legislators that air forces, and bombers in par-ticular, were needed. In Britain, the RAF had become inde-pendent in 1918. France created an independent air ministry in October 1928, which became responsible for all matters con-nected with flying, both military and commercial.[71] L'Armée de l'Air became an independent service in 1933. The Soviets set up a Bureau of Commissars of Aviation and Aeronautics in November 1917, a few days after they had seized power from the Mensheviks.[72] Similarly, Hitler, a few days after becoming chancellor, created an Air Commissionary with Göring as its head in March 1933. Mussolini, after his march on Rome in 1922 and being made prime minister by Victor Emmanuel III, created the Regia Aeronautica in 1923 and made Italo Balbo its first minister in 1929. The Japanese air forces remained part of the navy and army, respectively, until the bitter end in 1945. In the United States, as we have learned previously, Mitchell tried to convince Congress to create an independent U.S. Air Force. It did not happen until 1947, after World War II.

Of the above listed states, Britain became the most bomber-oriented, with a ratio of bombers to fighters of 2:1 in 1932 and a total of one thousand planes.[73] This ratio was maintained and manifested in the establishment of RAF Bomber Command in July 1934.[74] In France, the ratio of bombers to fighters was kept at approximately 1.6:1 until 1928, with a total of 1,540 planes.[75]

The French military leaders never believed in the Douhet Theorem. In 1923 Marshal Fayolle, the air force inspector general, defined the purpose of the French air force as providing tactical support for the army.[76] The bomber was to operate in connection with the artillery in the battle zone. Air superiority was to be a prerequisite for that. This in turn meant a well-equipped and numerous fighter force. The French, like their fellow major powers, suffered from a shortage of funds, and therefore a purely defensive air policy appeared the solution.

In the USSR the situation was governed by the geography of the country. In the tradition of the Muromets bomber the Soviets developed new large and long-range bombers. By 1930 they had about eight hundred Tupolev TB-3s. It had a range of thirteen hundred kilometers, could carry a bomb load of one ton, and had a crew of six.[77] Because of its size it could be easy prey for modern fighters, and as a result the Soviets developed bombers carrying up to five fighters, which could be launched and retrieved in flight. Some of these planes operated until 1942 behind enemy lines.[78] Despite these technical feats, the Soviets decided, as a lesson of the Spanish Civil War, that the role of the Red Air Force was to be tactical. The Soviets were afraid that long-range bombers could not only be brought down by enemy fighters, but also by electromagnetic beams. The Russian engineer Grammatshikov had experimented in that field in 1924 and had obtained promising results.[79] In the years before World War II the USSR had the biggest air force, but only few strategic bombers.

The Italians let their air force deteriorate after World War I, from five thousand planes and several thousand trained pilots to about one hundred obsolete machines.[80] By 1926, under Mussolini this number had been increased to three hundred, and after 1932 the build-up continued, supported by a budget equivalent to U.S.$40 million.[81]

German air force developments had come to a dead stop with the signing of the Versailles Treaty. Supposedly all front-line planes had been surrendered after the armistice in November 1918. In 1920 there were still about fourteen hundred planes and approximately two thousand Air Corps officers and men in the German army.[82] The German government called this force *Polizeistaffeln* (Police Squadrons) and maintained they were required to keep law and order. The Paris-based Allied Control Commission went along with this explanation, presumably for fear of a Communist takeover in Germany. Once the putsches in Bavaria and the Rhineland had been quelled, there was no further need for the Polizeistaffeln. The German government tried to obtain permission to keep them, but the Control Commission turned the request down in April 1920. It ordered the disbandment of the formations and their soldiers in twelve days.[83] Since General von Seekt, chief of staff of the German army, had a keen understanding of the importance of air warfare not all of the two thousand flying personnel were demobilized. Von Seekt created the *Sondertruppe* (special formation), which was entrusted with the planning of logistics for a re-establishment of the army air force. Many officers joined that group to eventually end up as Luftwaffe leaders in World War II. The planes had to be dismantled and scrapped. But again, not all of them came under the wrecking ball. Many were hidden in barns and industrial sheds and surfaced after 1933. These were mostly single-seat fighters. There is no record of bombers being hidden; they would have been too big. The German government passed a law that made hiding World War I army planes punishable, but the law was just window dressing for the benefit of the Allied Control Commission.

The Sondertruppe became part of the Reich War Ministry. It kept track of the hidden planes, prepared lists of spare parts stores, and investigated the old aircraft factories and other suitable industries for possible rapid conversion to plane production should the need arise. The correspondence with these factories refers to "production of motor vehicles."[84] Despite Versailles, demobilization, and appalling economic conditions, Germany was psychologically quite prepared to fight should it be attacked, from the east or the west. When the Ruhr occupation came about, armed resistance was considered and the War Ministry ordered one hundred fighter planes from the Dutch firm Fokker.[85] Delivery was to be taken after fighting had started. Similarly, the German navy ordered ten seaplanes from the Heinkel factory in Sweden and had them stored under a private address in Stockholm Harbor.[86] The Ruhr crisis was peacefully settled before Fokker could deliver. The legal implications of the orders to Fokker and Heinkel in light of the Versailles Treaty would have been a challenge to any lawyer. The Germans had title but not possession of the planes.

The next step in the clandestine rearmament of the *Reichswehr*, as the German army was now called, was a secret addendum to the 1922 Rapallo Treaty with the Soviet Union. For the world to see, Germany and the USSR recognized each other and made a number of political and commercial agreements. Not known until much later were secret clauses that allowed the German army to establish training schools in Russia for air force and tank personnel. The air force school was located at Lipetsk west of Moscow and operated from 1924 until 1933, when Hitler ordered it closed. Fifty of the planes purchased from Fokker were sent there. Selected officers and men were transferred to receive combat training, after having attended private flying schools in Germany for basic training. The German flying schools were financed and operated by the army, although on the outside they looked like commercial enterprises. The airfield at Würzburg had such a school beginning in the 1920s. From 1927 to 1935 it was directed by Ritter von Greim, a Reichswehr officer in civilian clothes. Von Greim was a WWI fighter pilot who became the last commander of the Luftwaffe in 1945.[87] The Lipetsk school was staffed by 160 German instructors and over the years trained 450 flying personnel.[88]

The Lipetsk airfield and the tank school at Kazan served not only for training, but also for development and trials of weapons manufactured under whatever ruse could be employed to escape the watchful eyes of the Allied Control Commission in Germany. A further part of the secret agreements was the delivery of Russian ammunition and other war materials to Germany. Reports reached the British press, but nothing was done about it by the Allied governments.[89] Also in the Rapallo Agreement was a provision that Junkers, the German aircraft firm, would establish a plant at Fili, near Moscow, to produce military aircraft for the German army. It was a fully self-contained factory with a capacity of producing three hundred machines per year.[90] The USSR was to receive five percent of the production as compensation and royalties. The rest was to be transferred to Lipetsk. The enterprise was only partly successful because of problems with the BMW aero engine production and misunderstandings between the Russians and the Germans.

Junkers, the owner of the Fili factory, was interested not only in surviving on German army orders, but also pursued the production of commercial aircraft. The Rapallo Treaty allowed the establishment of a German commercial airline from Sweden via Moscow to Iran. Junkers developed and provided the planes. But it appeared that not all was commercial. The Ju-52 airliner, cum auxiliary bomber of Spanish Civil War fame and transport plane of the Luftwaffe until 1945, came out of this scheme.

In 1926, when the International Air Agreement was signed in Paris, Germany had the most efficient air lines in Europe. By that time the Versailles Treaty had permitted return of control over German air space to the German government, as well as the construction of commercial aircraft. Their capacities and technical specifications were still very much limited, but the Germans rose back into the air. The War Ministry took advantage of that by having soldiers in civilian clothes become airline pilots, gaining flying experience before sending them to Lipetsk for combat training.

The Germans also had not quite given up on the Zeppelins for military purposes. This was at the time when the United States was experimenting with air ships as flying aircraft carriers, launching and docking fighters in flight. The Germans developed two huge Zeppelins, which undertook commercial flights to such distant places as Tokyo and Rio de Janeiro. Regularly scheduled service from Frankfurt Rhein/Main Base, the forerunner of today's Frankfurt Airport, to Lakehurst, New Jersey, near New York, was established. It took sixty hours in considerable comfort, albeit no smoking allowed, because the whole ship was kept afloat by hydrogen gas. It all ended in disaster when in 1937 the *Hindenburg* went up in flames at Lakehurst with heavy loss of life. Filling the airships with helium would have been the answer, but helium was only available in commercial quantities in the United States, and sale of such a strategic commodity to Nazi Germany did not come about. It was the end of the "Zepps," and the military and commercial benefits they had once represented.

The German War Ministry soldiered on. The planning and secret scheming to create a Luftwaffe continued. Specifications were issued for a night bomber to carry a 1.5-ton bomb load.[91] The whole planning operation was disguised within a *Luftschutzamt* (Civil Defense Department).[92] All officers and soldiers wore civilian clothes, particularly the ones at the German flying schools and the staff on their way to the Russian training centers. The monies for the Luftwaffe came from the army budget. When later, in the early 1930s, not enough could be clandestinely diverted, the Reichswehrminister requested money from the budget of the Transport Ministry, under the pretext that the funds were to be used for commercial aviation.[93]

When Hitler became chancellor on 30 January 1933, and three days later appointed Hermann Göring *Reichskommissar für Luftfahrt*, the creation of the Luftwaffe was all devised and ready to roll; and speed was of the essence. It had to be done very secretly because there was still lip service being paid to the Versailles Treaty and, more important, the Geneva Disarmament Conference was going on.

German aircraft manufacturers, who had struggled along the path of survival since 1918, were suddenly being given funds and orders. The situation in the aircraft industry after the war had seemed hopeless. The Versailles Treaty outlawed production of military planes even for export, and the construction of commercial aircraft was permitted only after 1926. Many of the manufacturers folded, whereas others established foreign subsidiaries such as Junkers in Russia, Dornier in Italy, and Heinkel in Sweden.[94] After 1933 the industry suddenly received massive orders from the government to build up the Luftwaffe. The equivalent of U.S. $10 million was approved by the cabinet on 9 February, eleven days after Hitler became chancellor. In the first six months of 1933, a total of U.S. $12.5 million was appropriated.[95] Erhard Milch, the ex-Lufthansa Airline president turned secretary of state of the recently established air ministry, issued strict orders to disguise the

Luftwaffe build-up. Air force personnel continued to wear civilian clothes.

The modest plans of the old Reichswehr Ministry Sonder-truppe were revised. Suddenly, struggling factories such as Junkers and Dornier had to work double shifts to meet the goals for 1934. These included, for delivery by October of that year, 210 bombers, 65 fighters, and, most important, 872 trainers.[96]

The Luftwaffe was also intended to have a strategic role, as first planned by General Wever. Prototypes of four-engine bombers were developed and called "Ural bombers," a clear indication of what their purpose and destination would be. After Wever's accidental death and after Hitler's plans toward Eastern and Western Europe had jelled, it was decided that the Luftwaffe would remain a tactical force, and further development of long-range bombers was stopped. Dornier's four-engine bomber Do-19 was scrapped, and Junkers's Ju-89 became a four-engine commercial airliner.

The real turning point in the history of Europe came in March 1935 when Hitler openly declared the Versailles Treaty null and void. He confirmed that reparation payments, suspended since 1931 for economic reasons, would be suspended indefinitely. German troops marched into the demilitarized zone west of the Rhine. General conscription was reintroduced, with every able-bodied young German man to serve two years in the *Wehrmacht*, as the Reichswehr was now called. The personnel strength of the German army thereby increased from 100,000 to 500,000 men. And, last but not least, the veil of secrecy was pulled off the Luftwaffe. Not only did the Luftwaffe become the third fighting service of the Wehrmacht, it was shown to international visitors and its actual strength exaggerated with considerable boasting. Between 1935 and the outbreak of World War II, Göring and Milch did their utmost to bluff foreign visitors. This took grotesque forms, such as cramming as many fighters as possible into an airport where French military dignitaries stopped for refueling on a visit to Germany. At the Zurich Air Show, Germany displayed souped-up models of its latest bombers and fighters, which at the time were still in the prototype stage. When the British government representatives Simon and Eden visited Hitler in 1936, they were told that the Luftwaffe had surpassed the RAF in bomber and fighter strength. In 1937 Göring confided to the visiting Lord Trenchard that he hoped that his German fighters would never have to fight RAF fighters, because the German models were so superior.[97] Göring went as far as to put on a sonic recording of divebombers, telling Trenchard that this was the noise of events to come.[98] Further shows were staged after the annexation of Austria and Czechoslovakia, on 15 March 1938 and 17 March 1939 respectively. While Hitler reviewed the parades of army troops in Vienna and Prague, the Luftwaffe appeared overhead in great numbers as part of the spectacle. Of the 540 planes over Vienna, 270 were bombers. The bluffing worked. It scared Germany's neighbors, and such displays entered the arsenal of Hitler's diplomatic weapons.

In the United States there was very little planning for an air force in the 1920s and early 1930s, very much to the dissatisfaction of General Mitchell and like-minded military personnel. This attitude changed after the Geneva Disarmament Conference had failed and major nations around the globe began to rearm. U.S. military planners started to be concerned about Italian and/or Japanese navies appearing on the horizon of the U.S. east and west coasts. In 1934, the Boeing company of Seattle had succeeded in winning a competition for a long-range, four-engine bomber which could fly out over the oceans and intercept enemy navies. By 1938, quantities of this bomber, the deadly B-17 of World War II, comprised a large portion of the USAAF. At the time it was the only four-engine, long-range bomber in the world.

In Japan, the army and the navy maintained firm control over their respective air forces, with the result that bombing was considered tactical·and not strategic warfare.

After the failure of the Geneva Disarmament Conference, every country rushed into the arms race and the major powers began to build up their air forces. There were differences in the theories and equipment. Britain led the way in deploying the bombers. France, Russia, Italy, Japan, and Germany looked at bombers as a tactical weapon and the United States perceived the bomber as a long-range coastal defense weapon.

The sophistication, and with it the cost, of an aircraft had risen exponentially since air warfare had begun in World War I. A British aircraft engine manufactured in 1935 would require 8,000 to 9,000 man-hours. These were five times as many hours as required for a 1918 aircraft engine. By around 1938, an up-to-date bomber consisted of 70,000 individual parts, which in turn required 6,000 to 8,000 drawings. The manufacture of a plane without its engines needed 14,000 to 18,000 man-hours.[99] Not only had the costs escalated, the nations' resources were taxed to the limit.

The armament race started before the Geneva Disarmament Conference failed in 1933. Who started it is a moot point. Every nation was pointing the finger at the other, and each claimed that its own efforts were dictated by self-defense. Most historians prove in one way or another that rearmament was started by Hitler as soon as he came to power. The renowned British historian A. J. P. Taylor claims that German rearmament until 1936 is a myth.[100] This view is supported by R. J. Overy, who maintains that British rearmament started before Hitler came to power.[101] Other sources show that the German military budget for 1935 was U.S. $3 billion, whereas Britain and France had budgeted U.S. $610 million and $730 million respectively.[102] The same source indicates that for that year the budgets for the respective air forces were: Germany, U.S. $900 million, about 33 percent of total military budget; Britain, U.S. $140 million, 23 percent; France, U.S.$160 million, 22 percent. As the race speeded up, the military budget figures had increased by 1938 to: Germany, U.S. $4.7 billion with 1.55 billion, 33 percent for the Luftwaffe; Britain, U.S. $1.76 billion with 420 million, 34 percent for the RAF; France, U.S. $850 million with 170 million, 27 percent for L'Armée de l'Air. Yet another source shows that in 1934 Germany had the lowest armament budget as a percentage of gross national product.[103] The figures quoted indicate: Germany 1.8 percent, France 8.1 percent, Britain 3.0 percent, Russia 9.0 percent, and Japan 8.4 percent.

Misinformation and disinformation played a great role in this race. Churchill claimed that by 1936 the German government was spending U.S. $3 billion annually on rearmament.[104] A. J. P. Taylor claims that total German rearmament between March 1933 and March 1939 cost U.S. $10 billion. This averages to U.S. $1.66 billion per annum, slightly more than half the amount Churchill had stated. But then in 1939 Hitler bragged that he had spent U.S. $22.5 billion, a $3.75 billion average per annum to build up the Wehrmacht.[105] Can one blame politicians, military planners, and historians for believing Hitler? From the political and economic point of view, rearmament made sense. It kept alive old hatreds and alleviated unemployment.

There is no doubt that all major nations participated in the arms race. Even in the United States, a country far away from the hot spots of Europe, the armament fever was recognized. The Neutrality Act of 1935 forbade the sale of arms to countries waging war. However, there was no restriction on selling arms and particularly airplanes to anybody who was only preparing for war and who could pay for them. Payment had to be in cash if the purchaser was not current in payments on World War I debts, which no country was.[106] Soon the orders for planes poured in from France and Britain. The industries of these countries could not meet the targets of their respective air armament plans. There was no money in either the British or French treasuries, but the threat to peace was considered such that gold reserves, sale of government assets, and budget deficits were used to pay for the purchases.

Statistics show how rearmament fever gripped the nations after 1933. Not only were arms produced, but also new divisions created and equipped with these arms. In 1933 the major powers had the following bomber fleets: France, 320; Britain, 390; Italy, 270; USSR, 410; USA, 300.[107]

Germany, because of the Versailles Treaty, had none at the time. Smaller countries surrounding Germany did not yet feel threatened and had only small bomber forces: Belgium, 30; Czechoslovakia, 40; Poland, 28; Norway, 6. Countries having no bombers at all were: Holland, Switzerland, and Spain.

Based on a German source, the picture had changed by 1936. Total frontline aircraft including bombers were: France 2,515; Britain, 1,270; Italy, 2,100; USSR, 4,700; USA, 1,800; Japan, 1,300.[108]

The source, a Luftwaffe publication, gives no indication of what Germany had. One can understand that because on one hand the Germans wanted to show that they were threatened by the armaments of neighboring nations. On the other hand, Hitler and Göring had already used the bluff of Luftwaffe strength to intimidate other countries. In the first case a low figure was politically useful and in the second case a high figure was equally effective. The above source lists the air force strengths of Poland and Czechoslovakia as 765 and 650, respectively.

The speed with which the major powers increased their air forces is best shown when one compares aircraft production of 1938 with 1939:[109]

	1938	1939
France	1,382	3,163
Germany	5,235	8,295
Japan	3,201	4,467
Britain	2,827	7,940
USA	1,800	2,195
USSR	7,500	10,382

What is not clear from the above table is whether some of the aircraft produced were sold to other countries. Britain, Germany, Italy, and the United States exported planes. For example, the Finnish Air Force had Blenheim bombers; Yugoslav Me-109s fought Luftwaffe Me-109s over Belgrade in 1941; France bought one thousand U.S. Curtis P-36 fighters in 1938; and prior to World War II Britain purchased Lockheed Hudsons from the United States. In 1933 Göring bought eighty-five aircraft engines from Armstrong-Siddeley/UK under the pretext that they were to power "police aircraft."[110]

Much has been written about the arms race before World War II. The statistics of what was produced vary. German publications, even of post-WWII vintage, stress low expenditures on the German side. British, U.S., and French sources state exactly the opposite for German rearmament. To confuse the issue even more, there are East German sources with references to USSR and other Communist literature, which are slanted against both the Fascists and the Capitalists.

The time from the 1918 armistice to the invasion of Poland by the Wehrmacht on 1 September 1939 was one of continuing

crises, of political and economic turmoil, and the growing resignation among all people that another war was inevitable.

In Europe and the Far East, Germany, Italy, and Japan,
united in the Axis Pact with the professed aim of expanding
their political and economic bases. The start had been made
with the invasions of Manchuria, China, and Ethiopia, and by
Germany abrogating the Treaty of Versailles. Between 1935
and 1937 Hitler consolidated his power in Germany, and to
many people in the world he appeared as a shining example
of how to pull a country out of the Depression. He even
signed a naval treaty with Britain which guaranteed the superiority of the Royal Navy over the Kriegsmarine (the German
navy). But then in March 1938 Austria became part of the
Greater German Reich. The union was forbidden by the
Versailles Treaty, but no actions were taken. In September
1938 the long-festering problem of the Sudeten-Germans/
Austrians in Czechoslovakia was brought to a boil by Hitler.
War almost broke out in Europe. The Sudeten-Germans/
Austrians were a rather tragic problem of history. They were
Austrians until 1918 when their land became part of the
periphery of Czechoslovakia. They were denied joining up
with Germany because they were Austrians; they could not
join Austria because of their geographical location; and the
Czechs needed them to add real estate to their country. There
were demonstrations and suppressions with a number of
deaths from 1920 onward. Many books have been written
about how it all happened and why the Munich Agreement
momentarily saved the world from Armageddon. Hitler's
bluffs had worked and he could tell the German people that
he had corrected another injustice of Versailles.

In March 1939, despite Hitler's assurances that he had no
more territorial ambitions, he sent the Wehrmacht into the
Czech part of what was left of Czechoslovakia. After the
Munich Agreement, Benes, the first Czechoslovakian president, had resigned after not having been consulted about the
agreement. There was the perceived threat to Germany of
USSR bombers soon being staged at Czech airfields.[111]
Czechoslovakia was in turmoil and Hacha, the new president, asked Hitler for help.[112] He obliged, and the century-old

Czech dream of an independent state collapsed. The protectorate of Bohemia and Moravia was created, and the threat of Russian bombers operating from there was eliminated. The never-mentioned advantage for the Czech people of the protectorate was that it kept them out of the battles of World War II and prevented the bombing of their cities, except for some USAAF raids on Prague, Pilsen, and Brüx in 1944-45. Slovakia became a sovereign nation and Poland and Hungary helped themselves to small pieces of Czechoslovakia. While he was at it, Hitler also took away the Memel District from Lithuania, which had been given that country by the Versailles Treaty.

Mussolini was not to be outdone by his Fascist friend, and he occupied Albania in April 1939. It gave him a base from which to revive old differences with Greece.

Next, Hitler cancelled the naval treaty with Britain. This alone must have scared everybody in Britain, because the Kaiser's old naval threat raised its head again.

Next in his *"Drang nach dem Osten,"* Hitler tackled Poland and the question of the Polish Corridor, which separated East Prussia from the Reich. It was again a problem created at Versailles and many people, Germans as well as others, saw it as such. As in the Sudeten, it caused ethnic tensions and eventually 5,400 Germans living in the Corridor paid for it with their lives.[113]

Hitler's bluffs and threats increasingly met resistance abroad. Yet still the world had some hope that Hitler, the soldier of the trenches of World War I, would not push mankind into another disaster such as any modern war would bring. He professed that he had no designs in Western Europe. As proof of that, one can point to the Siegfried Line, or in German, the Westwall. It was a line of pillboxes and tank traps built in 1938-39 from the North Sea to the Swiss border. It took a national emergency program to build it, with thousands of men drafted to swing shovels and pick axes and to pour concrete. The line stared into the face of the French Maginot Line, a similar and useless waste of national resources as was proven during World War II. Many historians state that Hitler was serious in not wishing a confrontation with the West. If that was so, he utterly failed by his actions, threats, and bluffs. His biggest mistake must have been to sign a nonaggression treaty with the USSR in August 1939 to solve the Polish question with attacks from the east and the west. Viewed from the capitals of the democratic states, this meant that the dictators of the world governed lands from Berlin via Moscow to Tokyo.

On 1 September 1939 Hitler declared war on Poland in a speech to the Reichstag, whose deputies, by now being all true Nazis, cheered wildly. Compared with 1914, these representatives of the people were the only cheering crowd. The German people and the world bowed their heads in sorrow and fear.

Bombing in World War II

Hitler had barely announced the state of war between Germany and Poland when a few hours later President Roosevelt sent an appeal to Britain, France, Germany, Italy, and Poland pleading for the well-being of innocent civilians. He referred to the maiming and death of thousands of defenseless men, women, and children by ruthless bombing from the air during the past few years. The appeal said that this had sickened the hearts of every civilized man and woman and profoundly shocked the conscience of humanity. Roosevelt continued that, if this form of inhuman barbarism was resorted to, hundreds of thousands of human beings would lose their lives. He addressed his appeal to the belligerents in the hope that their air forces under no circumstances would bombard civilian populations and unfortified cities. An immediate reply was requested.[1]

Hitler replied forthwith, stating that the appeal represented a humanitarian principle that completely corresponded with his own view. Britain and France issued a joint declaration confirming that they were in full agreement with Roosevelt's appeal. Chamberlain, the British prime minister, had made a statement in the House of Commons on 21 June 1938 that Britain, in the event of a war, would adhere to the recommendations made by the Commission of Jurists in The Hague in 1923.[2]

Of the three statesmen mentioned above, only Chamberlain kept his word, albeit by default. After he resigned in May 1940, his successor, Winston Churchill, let the bombers loose and was later joined by the two others in killing hundreds of thousands of innocent people. None of them is known to have shown the slightest remorse for abandoning a civilized approach to warfare.

In September 1939, on the surface the appeal boded well for the masses who had been indoctrinated that enemy bombers would appear over them as soon as war broke out. The only country that can proudly say it did not participate in this warfare is France. At the Geneva Disarmament Conference, France had stated that banning bombardment was not necessary because it was forbidden by the existing conventions of The Hague and Geneva. The French point of view is best supported by a speech French General Maxime Weygand gave at Chatham House, England, on 16 May 1939. In it he said that bombarding defenseless people smacks of cowardice and is repugnant to the soldier. He further said that people ordering such actions cannot be very brave.[3]

After 1 September, Britain and France sent Germany an ultimatum to pull back from Poland or be in a state of war with them in forty-eight hours. Hitler hoped that the Western nations could be bluffed again. He was wrong.

The German army pushed through Poland and within weeks was in front of Warsaw. There followed the first aerial bombardment of a city in World War II. Historians have proven that Warsaw was a fortified city with more than 100,000 Polish troops inside to defend it, and that the Germans sent numerous requests to the Polish commanders for a peaceful and honorable surrender. There was no reply. Next followed leaflets dropped by the Luftwaffe with the same offers, and after that, leaflets advising the citizens to leave the city. Again, no reply. The efforts to obtain a peaceful surrender lasted from 16 to 24 September. On 25 September about 200 Luftwaffe Stukas, 30 old Ju-52 bombers, and a number of ground attack aircraft bombarded Warsaw. They unloaded 500 tons of high explosives and 72 tons of incendiaries. Some of these bombs fell on German army positions.[4] At the express orders of Göring the crews had to aim at military and infrastructure targets only. Of course, such orders had been routine ever since World War I. Yet the deportment of the German bombers in

Poland is vindicated by a report of the French air attaché, who informed his government that the Luftwaffe had bombed in conformity with the rules of warfare. The report was dated 14 September and therefore does not cover the raid on Warsaw of 25 September. Warsaw was certainly in the war zone and its bombardment could be justified, particularly after the many appeals to surrender. Polish sources had proudly stated that it was a fortress and would be defended until final victory. The unfortunate political aspect of the bombardment is that it was executed by airplanes. Had the Germans used their artillery to destroy the intended targets, the Hague Conventions would have applied and, legally at least, sanctioned the raid. But bombers used as long-range artillery caused the devastation, at the very beginning of another great European war, and that aroused world opinion and damned the Luftwaffe into infamy. Exact casualty figures have never been established. Some sources claim that 26,000 people were buried in the rubble after the surrender of the city.[5] Considering the tonnage dropped and that the majority of bombs were delivered by dive-bombers, one is inclined to question this figure. Whatever the casualty rate, civilians were killed by aerial bombs. The dread-ed threat had become a reality. The Warsaw raid became the first stepping-stone to the bombing war. It was a tactical raid and not a strategic one. The world did not yet make a distinc-tion of that kind. As in World War I, the Huns had again thrown the first bomb.

The invasion of Poland was a masterpiece of blitzkrieg as envisaged by the German military planners. It proved that an air force must support army operations. Poland was conquered in three weeks. But it was not only the Wehrmacht that occu-pied Poland. The USSR invaded Poland from the east on 17 September. Theoretically, Britain and France should have declared war on the USSR, since they had obligated themselves to guarantee Polish borders in spring 1939 and entered into a state of war with Germany to fulfill that commitment. They did not. Taking on two dictatorships at the same time was obviously too much.

Since there were already tensions with the Japanese, declaring war on the USSR would have fortified the Berlin-

Tokyo Axis by adding a solid land bridge in between. Although the Japanese and the Russians did not see eye to eye, there had been Soviet support for China since 1937 and a minor undeclared war between the two of them in the Far East. After all the posturing of the Japanese army in eastern China, the Soviets established a bomber force in Eastern Siberia that was ready to attack Tokyo if necessary. In July 1938, Japan and the USSR fought each other at Lake Khasan about eighty miles southwest of Vladivostok. From June to September 1939 a border dispute broke out at the Khalkin River, a tributary of the Amur. In the first instance the opposing forces were little armies of division strength, whereas in the second instance the fighting became more serious with about five hundred planes involved on both sides.[6] There are no records of bombing civilians. The Japanese Army Air Force was thoroughly trounced by the Red Air Force, and, on the ground, General Zhukov, of 1945 Berlin conquest fame, made his name in Soviet military annals by routing the Japanese army. Both countries maintained diplomatic relations during the time of fighting and the desire to avoid a full state of war eventually resulted in a USSR/Japanese non-aggression pact signed in April 1941. Undoubtedly Stalin was looking west for a coming dispute with Hitler's Germany; the Ribbentrop Pact of August 1939 notwithstanding.

Stalin did not waste time implementing the dishonorable secret annex to the Ribbentrop Pact, which allowed the USSR to occupy eastern Poland and the three Baltic States of Estonia, Lithuania, and Latvia. When Finland resisted Russian actions, the USSR declared war on it. The world, but above all Germany, had deserted these four countries, governments, and people who had formed a bulwark against the expansion of Bolshevism.

The Winter War, as history has been calling it, lasted from 1 December 1939 to 13 March 1940. Finnish forces fought a heroic and strategically superior battle, but in the end it was the masses of the Soviet men and materials which forced Finland to sue for peace. It lost large tracts of land and nobody had come to its help. British planning under Churchill, then the first sealord, was considering invading northern Norway and advancing through Sweden to help Finland. Another plan the Western Allies considered was to bomb the oil fields at Baku from British bases in Iraq. Neither plan was implemented. There was only assistance from countries such as Sweden and Italy in the form of volunteers and war materials. Germany remained neutral and held up a shipment of Italian planes at the port of Stettin.[7]

The Red Air Force did not lose time in showing that it had bombers. On the first day of the conflict it flew a bombing raid on Helsinki from its recently acquired base on the Estonian island of Saremaa.[8] Before long there were many raids on more Finnish towns, ports, and railways. Eventually the USSR deployed 2,500 planes that dropped 7,500 tons of high explosive bombs and incendiaries. Against this stood a minuscule Finnish air force of less than 100 planes, later augmented by foreign purchases and help to about 250. Russian losses were between 750 and 900 aircraft, whereas Finnish losses amounted to about 70.[9]

The Red Air Force flew a total of eight hundred raids on Finnish towns and villages. Civilian losses were 956 killed and 1,850 wounded. The cities with the heaviest losses were Helsinki and Viipuri with ninety-seven and sixty citizens killed respectively.[10] Bombing and war had come together again at the expense of innocent civilians.

Germany's strict stance of neutrality in the Winter War has left a question mark. Why did Hitler and his foreign minister, Ribbentrop, not scheme to have Britain and France declare war on Russia? Germany's professed reluctance to fight the West, with a small dose of skillful diplomacy could have caused history to take a different course. Unfortunately, Britain and France not only let Poland down, but Finland also.

1939 TO APRIL 1940: THE PHONY WAR

While the fighting and annexations were going on in northeastern Europe, the war in western Europe was scarcely noticeable. On 3 September, a few hours after Britain and Germany had entered into a state of war, the air-raid sirens in southern England sounded. Was the propaganda threat spread by the

British press before the war that the Luftwaffe would immediately attack London coming true? It was a false alarm. The air attaché to the French embassy in London was flying from France over the Channel and had set it off. Embarrassing as the incident may have been, it proved that Britain's warning system was working.

Before the war a British commercial plane had made flights over German territory and taken pictures of strategic targets such as military airports and industrial installations.[11] From 1936 the Air Targets Sub-Committee of the Industrial Intelligence Centre had established priority targets, which identified in detail the location and capacities of aircraft factories, oil refineries, power generating stations, railway yards, and other strategic targets.[12]

When war broke out, RAF Bomber Command was not yet equipped to conduct a strategic bombing offensive, but it was ready to attack isolated military targets on enemy soil. Most of the squadrons had twin-engine bombers such as the Wellington, Handley Page, and Blenheim. From the first day they conducted daylight raids against the German navy in the Heligoland Bight and the German home ports. Chamberlain's instructions, that targets must be clearly identified as military, were scrupulously adhered to; last but not least, because there was fear of unleashing German retaliation. This went so far that German warships in the harbor of Wilhelmshaven were not attacked because they were berthed too close to residential dwellings.[13] The results of these sorties were dismal and the losses heavy. German fighters shot down many of the bombers, which had inadequate defense weapons. Deeper penetration into German territory would have been prohibitive. Before long the RAF abandoned its raids on the German navy. Daylight bombing had to be abandoned and precision bombing of military targets was beyond the capabilities of Bomber Command because, despite all of the committees, their eminent scientists, and many technical achievements, development of navigational aids had been neglected. RAF aircraft flying in cloudy weather or by night depended on dead reckoning and astral navigation. The resulting inaccuracies caused many bombs to be dropped far away from legitimate targets.

Bomber Command, despite all the monies that had been spent to make it a fighting force, felt checkmated by the losses incurred in daylight operations, its inability to navigate at night, and the restrictions imposed on it by the government. Many of the targets identified by the Air Targets Sub-Committee were in heavily built-up German towns and they could not be located or bombed without inflicting German civilian losses. It was the commander-in-chief of Bomber Command, Air Chief Marshal Sir Edgar Ludlow-Hewitt, who devised an alternative way of waging air war. It was the first attack on the morale of the German people.[14] From September 1939 until April 1940, Bomber Command flew numerous sorties at night over German cities, dropping propaganda leaflets. The cities were mostly in the Rhine/Ruhr area, where there were known to be German workers with strong Socialist and Communist sympathies. It was a waste of time and effort because again many targets were missed and the leaflets ended up in open country. Although historians might disagree, the German people were so overfed with propaganda from both sides that they believed neither. The bomber crews did not like the raids because that was not what these young men had joined the prestigious Bomber Command for. The raids were given the derisive name "nickelling."

Chasing German ships on the open sea continued. There were raids on naval and commercial craft but the results were disappointing and continued to be costly, even though they were flown far off the German coast. As an example, on 18 December 1939, quoting RAF records, 22 bombers attacked German shipping and 15 planes did not return. The German report of that encounter lists 44 bombers attacking and 34 being lost.[15]

The period from the end of the Polish campaign until 9 April 1940, when German forces invaded Denmark and Norway, is called the Phony War. The Phony War was fought mostly at sea with little action on land and severe restrictions imposed on the combatant air forces by their respective governments. Nobody wanted to throw the first bomb, lest the enemy unleash a campaign of retaliation.

On the German side the fear of retaliation was just as pronounced. One day before the invasion of Poland, Göring advised in his Order No.1 that Luftflotten 4 and 6 should commence hostilities against Poland at 04:45 on 1 September 1939. Luftflotten 2 and 3 were ordered to guard the western frontiers of Germany in the event that hostilities should arise with Britain and France.[16] The neutrality of Belgium and Holland was to be strictly observed; small enemy formations were not to be pursued over neutral territories and combats of larger formations over these countries was subject to approval by Göring himself. The orders for the Luftwaffe units in the west were to guard the Ruhr industrial area, playing a strictly defensive role.

On 3 September, Göring followed up with Order No. 2, which strictly forbade raids on British soil and made attacks on British naval and merchant ships subject to his approval.[17] Even attacks on troop ships crossing to France could not be flown. Yet a day later, Göring approved a raid by two bombers on an aircraft carrier in the harbor of Shearness. On 10 September 1939, even Hitler issued orders not to cross the western border of Germany. It is obvious from these orders that the German High Command was concerned about not having enough aircraft to fight any British or French raids on Germany while Luftflotten 4 and 6 were engaged in Poland.

As soon as victory in the Polish campaign was a certainty, most of the Luftwaffe formations were relocated to the west. In his Order No. 4 of 23 September 1939, Göring reiterated that any air war would have to be started by the British and/or French air forces. But British naval units in the Heligoland Bight could be attacked, and preparations were made for retaliation raids on still-to-be-determined British towns if the RAF should attack German cities.[18] Similar planning was to be effected for retaliation raids against Paris and Marseille in the event L'Armée de l'Air was to bomb Germany.

Reconnaissance flights over Britain were authorized because the Luftwaffe had prepared target folders before the war but had no detailed plans for how to attack such targets.[19] These flights were a nuisance to Britain as much as the "nickelling" aggravated the Germans. It went so far as to cause Göring to declare in a speech that he did not mind the leaflets but the Luftwaffe could and would prevent any bomb drop-ping on German soil. Just before war broke out he had made his famous "Maier speech" at Essen on 10 August 1939, saying that his name would be Hermann Maier if an enemy bomber reached the Ruhr.[20]

Through October and November, German policy still was that only military targets should be aimed at, although the list of such targets now included naval units in their bases, ship-yards, and harbor installations in all major British ports.[21] The Royal Navy had chased all German commerce from the high seas and the blockade of Germany was again in full swing. The German U-boats did their part to repeat the World War I coun-terblockade of the British Isles, and the Luftwaffe extended that campaign by attacking the ships in the harbors. Signif-icantly, the orders excepted the London docks. Only tank farms, refineries, grain silos, flour mills, etc. in places such as Liverpool, the Manchester Ship Canal, Bristol, Cardiff, and similar harbors were to be attacked. Great emphasis was placed in the orders not to cause civilian casualties.[22]

The blockade of the British Isles was heightened by orders in December 1939 that all ships within thirty miles of the British coast could be attacked by day and night. On the other hand, ships sailing through Norwegian waters, irrespective of their nationality, could under no circumstances be attacked, since Britain had not interfered with the iron-ore ships from Narvik to Germany. The ore was vital to the German arma-ment industry, and neither the German navy nor the Luftwaffe could protect these shipments.

The winter of 1939-1940 was one of the harsher ones in recent history, and the weather contributed to the prolongation of the "Phony War." Only occasionally isolated aircraft of the RAF penetrated into southern Germany, and in Würzburg we were forced to spend time in the air-raid shelters. I will never forget when there was a low-flying plane over Würzburg dur-ing one of the alarms and we could hear its engine noise in the shelter. We were scared, but nothing happened. Not even the flak batteries that were guarding the city opened up. Würzburg, technically and legally speaking, was at that time a defended city and could have been attacked. The 88mm heavy flak, well hidden and inaccessible to the public eye on the hills surrounding the city, only fired once, when they shot blanks to herald, the new year at 24:00 on New Years Eve 1939 following a good German custom. Later, when we really needed defending, there was no more flak.

With the new year the war got tougher. Hitler had made offers to Britain for peace. The royal houses of Belgium and Holland had tried to mediate between both sides, and even Mussolini, still neutral, attempted to stop the war. In Britain nobody believed in Hitler's approach and the circles around Churchill, at that time the first lord of the admiralty, defeated any possible moves by the Chamberlain government in that direction. On 16 December 1939, Churchill submitted to the Cabinet a plan to cut Germany off from its Scandinavian iron ore supplies.[23] It would extend the war to Norway and possibly Sweden. Minefields would be placed in Norwegian and Swedish waters, forcing ships carrying ore to Germany to sail into international waters, there to be captured by the Royal Navy. Any qualms about infringing on international law, Churchill said, should be weighed against Britain fighting to uphold the League of Nations principles, and small countries would go under if Britain did not win the fight against tyranny. Norway might object, but then Britain would cancel the lucrative contract the Norwegian Merchant Fleet had to transport oil to the United Kingdom.

Norway, a peace-loving country, trying to keep neutral and placate the belligerents by giving them equal concessions, was being dragged into the conflict. British preparations for landings in Norway began on 16 January 1940. British planning foresaw a landing in northern Norway and Sweden to cut off the German ore supplies, and at the same time provide help to the Finns in their fight against the USSR.[24] The occupation of Narvik was planned for the end of March 1940. Minefields were to be laid in Norwegian territorial waters on 29 March 1940, albeit with the proviso to avoid any confrontation with the Norwegian navy.

German planning was not far behind and started on 27 January. Inside Norwegian territorial waters the Royal Navy had boarded a German navy supply ship trying to return to a

German port. There had been other threats to Norwegian neutrality and the ore supplies from Narvik. On 3 April the British Cabinet learned that 400,000 German troops were ready in Stettin, Swinemünde, and other German Baltic ports to sail north.

The Royal Marines were ordered to sail to Narvik on 8 April.[25] In a naval race, ten German destroyers with three thousand mountain troops on board arrived there first. On 9 April 1940 the Phony War was over.

1940: TWO BLITZKRIEGS AND THE START OF STRATEGIC BOMBING

On 17 March 1940, in preparation for the invasion of Norway, the Luftwaffe was ordered to mine the British naval base at Scapa Flow in the Orkney Islands and to destroy the Royal Navy oil tank farm on Lyness Peninsula.[26] This purely tactical operation caused the first civilian losses on British soil. The British air ministry jumped at the opportunity to retaliate and ordered the first attack on German soil. On the night of 19-20 March, the Hörnum seaplane base on the Island of Sylt became the target of fifty bombers dropping twenty tons of high explosives and 1,200 incendiaries. Later reconnaissance photos showed that the damage was minimal.[27] Whereas previously both sides did their utmost to prevent civilian losses, the restrictions on bombing were now gradually reduced. The Luftwaffe had bombed several harbors during the Phony War, but no civilian losses were reported. Chamberlain's orders were still in force, but Bomber Command had at least once the chance to implement the Trenchard Doctrine. It had been chafing to do that since 3 September 1939.

The Scandinavian campaign ran its course with heavy damage to places such as Narvik, Kristianstad, Oslo, and Stavanger. The RAF and the Luftwaffe were in action over all these places. The Wehrmacht occupied Denmark and Norway in short order and evicted the British expeditionary force which had landed a few days after 9 April at Andalnes instead of Narvik. The battle for Narvik took longer. Allied forces landed there belatedly and then withdrew because they were needed in France.

Churchill had promised the Cabinet that the Royal Navy and Royal Marines occupying Norway would fatally weaken Germany. As did his Dardanelles plan in 1915, it failed. But this time Churchill's political stock was higher and he was not sent on a political vacation.

On 10 May 1940, Germany struck out west and invaded Belgium, Luxembourg, and Holland. The planning for that strike had become known in early 1940 when a German courier plane with high-ranking officers strayed into Belgian airspace and had to make an emergency landing. In the luggage of the officers were found the complete plans for the invasion. It was a repeat of the old Schlieffen Plan of World War I, which foresaw invading France from the north. Again, the unfortunate Belgians and Luxemburgers—and this time even the Dutch—were dragged into a conflict they wanted no part of. It was the Germans that did the invading, but documents show that France and Britain also had plans to march through these countries to occupy the German Ruhr area. There had been comments in British government circles that Britain's frontier was at the Rhine; i.e. the Rhine was the starting point of the present war. These comments had been published and discussed in Dutch papers.[28] Already in July 1934 the British foreign secretary had indicated in the House of Commons that Britain would have to occupy the Low Countries to deploy aircraft there for the defense of London.[29] In November 1939, Britain and France had completed their Plan D, which called for placing their troops in Belgium if the Wehrmacht attacked France.[30] In early 1940, after the German plane had landed in Belgium, the Belgian government turned down a request by Britain and France for staff talks to let Allied troops pass through its territory for an attack on the Reich.[31] The proposed Allied invasion of a neutral country had at least been publicized and discussed with this country. The German invasion came without such niceties.

The German campaign to enter northern France via Holland, Belgium, and Luxembourg developed as planned. But then on 14 May 1940 at 15:00, there occurred what can be considered the start of area bombing in World War II.

The German invaders of Holland had made fast progress

except in Rotterdam, where a contingent of parachute troops was trapped in the city. Overall, Rotterdam would soon fall, but in the meantime the paratroopers might be wiped out. The German commander sent envoys to the Dutch defenders proposing surrender to avoid further bloodshed. If no surrender or answer was forthcoming, the city would be shelled and bombed. The deadline passed, and one hundred He-111 medium bombers took off from their north German bases. While the bombers were on their way the Dutch commander surrendered the city. As agreed between the German army and the Luftwaffe, the bombers were advised by wireless to return to base. But only forty-three received the message and the others continued. As an additional safeguard it was agreed that the approaching bombers should watch for flares from the ground troops to signal "proceed" or "abort." There were clouds and the fifty-seven bombers did not see the flares signaling "abort." On a strictly defined triangle north of the Maas bridges, the bombers unloaded ninety-seven tons of high explosives consisting of 158 bombs of 500 pounds and 1,150 of 100 pounds.[32]

The international press reported that thirty thousand people were killed. The BBC seized upon that figure and we were told in their German broadcasts that an atrocity had been committed. An atrocity it no doubt was, although the German army had tried to avert it and the number of victims was later established at about nine hundred. The bombed area was swept by a fire, which left experts wondering how it could assume such proportions. The people of Holland and the citizens of Rotterdam in particular had suffered losses that in a nation observing strict neutrality should never have been inflicted. Until 10 May, Holland had guarded its neutral status impeccably toward both sides. Planes infringing on Dutch territory were forced to land and crews and machines were interned. One straying RAF bomber was even shot down when it refused to land. The crew survived and was interned until 10 May.[33]

Why Hitler decided to invade Holland is beyond comprehension. From his point of view one can understand that he violated Belgium/Luxembourg neutrality to enter France as in World War I. A neutral Holland would have been of such advantage even if Germany had won the war. The iron-ore ships from Scandinavia would have been beyond destruction by the RAF once they entered Dutch waters. For the ore to get to the Ruhr it had to pass through Rotterdam. It was the most economical route. Finally, Holland would have been a legal barrier for the RAF bomber streams in later years.

In Britain, Chamberlain had resigned and Churchill had become prime minister. The thirty thousand casualty figure and other German raids were judged by the Cabinet to allow retaliation. On 15 May the air ministry was authorized to order raids on German soil east of the Rhine. Before that date, RAF Bomber Command and bombers of the Advanced Strike Force stationed in France had flown ground support raids on German communications and advancing army units from the Rhine westward. The losses of the Advanced Strike Force were extremely heavy. Between the 10th and 15th of May, seventy-one Battle and Blenheim bombers were dispatched. Only thirty returned and most of them were badly damaged.[34] Now the bombers were finally free to attack German targets as had been planned for years under the Trenchard Doctrine. Before the fateful date of 15 May, during the night of 11-12 May, thirty-seven Hampden and Whitley medium bombers had made the first raid on a German city. The aims were rail and road communication centers.[35] Four civilians were killed including, unfortunately and ironically, an English woman living in the attacked town of Mönchen-Gladbach.

Why the Rotterdam raid caused the British Cabinet to implement reprisals and not the much heavier Warsaw raid, is open for speculation. Warsaw suffered from 572 tons of bombs, whereas Rotterdam received only 97 tons. One reason may have been that propaganda, the fourth service in modern warfare, grabbed the Rotterdam raid and exaggerated it beyond its actual dimensions. British public opinion wanted retaliation. The international press called it the first terror raid of the war. Does that exculpate the Luftwaffe for the Warsaw raid? In either event, the raids were tactical in support of ground operations. They were not planned strategic terror raids. But by any interpretation, they caused heavy civilian losses and because of that left the Luftwaffe with a bad reputation. Luftwaffe senior and junior personnel did not approve of terror raids, but after Rotterdam the stigma stuck to them.[36]

The blitzkrieg in the West, the third after Poland and Norway, took its course. Belgium, Luxembourg, and Holland were overrun in short order and after a daring dash through the Ardennes by German panzers, the British Expeditionary Force (BEF) was encircled at Dunkirk. There are conflicting interpretations of what happened next. One line is that Göring persuaded Hitler to let the Luftwaffe pound the British troops on the beaches into surrender. The other line states that Hitler wanted the British troops to escape because he still hoped for a peace settlement with London. The facts are that the German army halted its attack, that the Luftwaffe did considerable damage to the troops, and not least to the city of Dunkirk. Most important, the BEF escaped, although leaving all its equipment behind.

While the campaign in the West was unfolding, RAF Bomber Command flew an ever-increasing number of strategic raids against targets in Germany. Reports indicate that most crews bombed their assigned targets of railway yards, troop assemblies, oil refineries, etc.; so the RAF files in the Public Record Office, London, state. The German reports of the time talk about little damage, bombs dropped on open cities and far away from any legitimate targets. The obvious facts are that Bomber Command had at the time only medium bombers, whose crews could locate their targets only with great difficulties at night and even in the few daylight raids still being flown. There was little damage in Germany, although a number of civilians were killed. The German leadership ignored the raids, but the population began referring to the supreme commander of the Luftwaffe as Hermann Maier.

France, Britain's suffering ally, objected vehemently to the RAF campaign against Germany. Gamelin, the French supreme warlord, was afraid of German retaliation against French cities. L'Armée de l'Air was in no position to defend its homeland. From its leading position after World War I it had deteriorated by the early 1930s to an obsolete force. In August 1939 it had only 575 fighters and 300 bombers and many of them were stationed overseas.[37] French industry and orders from the United

States doubled that number by June 1940 because the active replenishment program started in 1935 by nationalizing the aircraft industry was just coming into full swing.[38] But the fall of France could not be prevented.

The Luftwaffe had bombed the industrial suburbs of Paris on 3 June 1940. The aim was the Citroën Works; they were damaged and the human loss amounted to 254 people killed.[39] Further raids were flown against French aircraft factories and the harbor of Marseille to prevent the arrival of reinforcements from Africa.

On 10 May 1940, the day the German West Offensive started, Freiburg, the German city that had suffered several times in World War I, was attacked. Three medium bombers dropped 69 bombs, killing 25 civilians and wounding 24. The Goebbels press reported that people on the ground had clearly identified the planes as French. Until the end of the war German propaganda blamed the French air force for having started the bombing war against German cities. The facts were quite different. The mayor of Freiburg traced some of the shrapnel to German bomb manufacturing plants. It was soon found out, but never officially acknowledged, that three Luftwaffe He-111s had lost their way to Dijon, France, with orders to bomb the airfield there. Through clouds they identified the wrong target. The French were horrified to be falsely accused of the raid and braced themselves for German retaliation. It never came.[40]

L'Armée de l'Air and l'Aéronautique Navale did fly a few raids into Germany. During the night of 7-8 June, a single naval bomber found its way to Berlin and bombed a factory in the suburbs. Two days later, the same plane attacked the Heinkel aircraft factory at Rostock on the German Baltic coast. L'Armée de l'Air flew raids against the BMW Works in Munich and the chemical factories at Ludwigshafen on 4-5 June.[41] Reports indicate that they found their target and did some damage at Ludwigshafen. The raid on the BMW Works is not recorded, neither in the BMW nor the city of Munich archives.[42] The question arises why could the supposedly ill-equipped French bombing force find and hit its assigned targets, whereas RAF Bomber Command missed them most of the time, as later investigations showed.

On 5 June, l'Armée de l'Air issued orders to stop raids into Germany, basically for fear of German reprisals and also because the few planes left could be better applied by attacking tactical ground targets. L'Armée de l'Air was fighting in the north against the Germans and l'Aéronautique Navale took over fighting the Italians in the south.

Mussolini, encouraged by his friend Hitler's successes, did not want to be left out of the spoils of the impending French defeat, and declared war on France and Britain on 10 June. Italy was still exhausted from the wars in Ethiopia and Spain, but taking booty from the French, particularly Corsica, Tunisia, and Djibuti, seemed an easy gain. The Regia Aeronautica bombed French air bases and other military installations in southern France and North Africa with limited success.

Mussolini was soon taught a lesson as to what war was all about when RAF Bomber Command, a day after Italy entered the war, started to fly raids into northern Italy. The nights of 11-12, 15-16, and 16-17 June, Wellingtons, Whitleys, and Hampdens raided Turin, Genoa, and Milan.[43] Turin reported seventeen people killed and forty injured. The Italians were obviously caught by surprise because the cities had not been blacked out. The RAF planes had to fly from airfields in Britain, with refueling stops on the Channel Islands, because the French objected strongly to raids being flown from their homeland. At one time they even barricaded a runway in southern France to prevent RAF planes from taking off.[44]

After the British Expeditionary Force had successfully escaped from Dunkirk, the fall of France could not be stopped. The French government decamped to Bordeaux and on 16 June requested through diplomatic channels in Madrid conditions for a ceasefire.

Franco, the Spanish dictator, emulated Mussolini and declared Spain a "non-belligerent" country, one step beyond being "neutral." He seized the internationalized city of Tangier and communicated to Hitler that he wanted all of French Morocco and Gibraltar and was willing to enter the war on the Axis side. It is ironic that the French government hoped for good terms through Franco's offices.

Three days after requesting armistice terms the French government asked that bombing of French cities, in particular Bordeaux, be suspended. Apparently the request was delayed in diplomatic channels and the Luftwaffe proceeded with a raid on Bordeaux planned for 19 June.[45] The raid was to destroy harbor installations but, as happened so often, the bombs missed and killed sixty-three civilians. The German government was embarrassed about the raid and particularly the treatment it received in the U.S. press.

An attack on harbor installations was justified because the French were evacuating their air forces and navy to their colonies in North Africa. British representatives visiting Bordeaux tried to persuade the French military to pass these forces to British control.[46] Germany, on the other hand, was concerned that they might under one flag or the other continue to fight the Axis. As it turned out, the majority of the French air force and navy were transferred to French North Africa and in particular the more modern planes and ships.

The armistice that was signed at Compiègne on 22 June clearly stipulated that no planes, ships, and colonies had to be surrendered. Hitler did not want French honor to be hurt. The fact that he then chose Compiègne, including the very railway carriage in which Germany had surrendered in 1918, for the French surrender of 1940 does not follow that line. Why he, the head of state of Germany, had to be present at the beginning of the negotiations is also difficult to comprehend. His French counterpart, General Huntziger, was a senior army commander and had the authority to sign the document.

If the French thought that the fighting was over for them they experienced a rude surprise on 3 July. French navy ships in British-controlled ports were seized on or before that date. On 3 July a Royal Navy squadron appeared outside the French naval station at Mers-el-Kebir, Algeria, and demanded surrender of the ships at anchor. Among them were three battleships. The French admiral refused. There followed a short bombardment in which one battleship blew up with the loss of more than one thousand sailors, one ran aground and lost about two hundred sailors, and one escaped into open waters. History books are very critical of this unfriendly action against a former ally. On 24 September the Royal Navy

Sir Charles Portal seen here when he was Britain's Chief of Air Staff in 1940-1945.

Sir Hugh Trenchard

Marshal of the RAF
Sir Arthur T. Harris

Monument to Harris
at St. Clement Danes
Church, London

USAAF Bomber Generals in World War II

Curtis Le May

H. H. Arnold

Ira C. Eaker

Carl Spaatz

James Doolittle

Würzburg after reconstruction in 1980s

Würzburg in May 1945

Würzburg 1648, after Thirty Year War

Downtown Würzburg in April 1945

Source: top–Original etching by Meriam, 1648.
bottom–Stadtarchiv Würzburg

One of the many churches destroyed in Würzburg in 1945.

The Riemenschneider Madonna survived the firestorm but then disappeared and has never been seen since.

Kürschner Hof in downtown Würzburg about 1938

Kürschner Hof in 1945

Source: top–WIM Lichtbildstelle
bottom–Photoverlag Gundermann, Würzburg

One of the author's family's businesses in 1937.

20 February 1945, firefighters working to extinguish the burning stationery store belonging to the author's father.

Wesel, Germany, before World War II in 1939.

Wesel, Germany, after World War II in 1945.

Above: Mass grave of 3,000 men, women, and children killed during the bombing raids on Würzburg, Germany. Only about 1,300 were identified.

Right: 2,500 Allied air crew are buried at Dürnbach, Bavaria.

Downtown Würzburg after reconstruction.

Source: WFL-GmbH, Rottendorff/Würzburg

attacked the French fleet in Dakar. Vichy France was very upset. Eighty bombers of the French North African Air Force raided Gibraltar with fifty-five tons of high explosives in retaliation the next day.[47]

If the French also thought that they had not lost any territories, except having to suffer the temporary occupation of northern and western parts of France until a peace treaty would be signed, they had another surprise. On 28 June 1940 Hitler visited Strasbourg and on 15 July ordered Alsace-Lorraine to be incorporated into the German customs boundaries. It became a de facto annexation without the niceties of a political declaration.[48] When Hitler had declared war on Poland in the Reichstag speech of 1 September 1939 he said that Germany had no territorial intentions in the West. He broke his word again. The echoes of 1871 and 1914 seemingly did not reach Hitler's ears.

Western Europe had been overrun in a blitzkrieg. Holland, Luxembourg, Belgium, and large parts of France became "occupied enemy territory" and, already during the campaign, were subjected to bombing by the RAF. The German theory that an air force's role was to support ground operations had been proven correct. Douhet's and Trenchard's theories and feeble attempts to implement them, had not stemmed the German advance.

If the Polish campaign and the Phony War can be called the first phase of World War II, the campaign in the West was the second. In the first phase, bombing was still very restricted. In the second phase it escalated and set the scenario for further escalation. The Luftwaffe had done its share of raids. L'Armée de l'Air had been very careful not to prompt German retaliation. The RAF had been given carte blanche to attack Germany and thought it was hitting only legitimate targets.

The losses to the respective air forces were considerable. The RAF lost 166 bombers and 219 fighters. French losses amounted to 218 bombers and 508 fighters. Luftwaffe losses came in at 635 bombers and 457 fighters.[49] In essence the Germans had won, but at a price to their air arm. The French air force had been eliminated and the RAF and the Luftwaffe were now staged against each other from Norway to the Channel coast.

The next phase was the threat of invasion of the United Kingdom. Some historians state that Hitler never wanted to cross the Channel. The facts are that the Wehrmacht never planned or equipped for a cross-Channel operation. The Kriegsmarine, the German navy, was no match for the Royal Navy. There were no German landing craft and not even a marine corps. Hitler made speeches and clandestine approaches to inveigle Churchill and his cabinet into peace talks. There is even speculation that his deputy's (Rudolf Hess) flight to Scotland in 1941, to persuade the British government, was purposely planned by both and not the madhatter's trick of Hess alone, as the world was told.[50] The full truth will not be known until the Hess files at the Public Record Office are declassified in 2017.

But in 1940, how could Hitler be believed, when at the same time he openly concentrated troops, aircraft, and barges in the Continental Channel ports, and had exercises conducted for the invasion. Who could believe him when the U-boat campaign increased in ferocity and German long-range aircraft patrolled on shuttle missions between newly acquired air bases in France and Norway, the western approaches to the British Isles? It was the Focke-Wulf FW-200, dubbed by Churchill the scourge of the Atlantic, which accounted for 580,000 tons of lost shipping in 1940 and a further 1 million tons in 1941.[51] Hitler's stick and carrot scheme convinced Britain even more that it had to fight, although the prospects were grim. The only hope lay in the entry of the United States on Britain's side, and there were many signs that this was about to happen. Germany's anti-Semitic stance and its open agitation in German communities in South America scared the leaders of the U.S. government. As a result U.S. neutrality became less neutral.

While the RAF continued to bomb targets in Germany and the occupied territories, the Luftwaffe started on 15 August a campaign to soften up southern England with raids on fighter bases, communications, and many other legitimate targets. On 1 August, Hitler had given the order that starting on 5 August (Eagle Day) air superiority over southern England had to be established in four days. Weather and Luftwaffe technical problems delayed the start to 15 August. Instead of four days, the battle of Britain lasted until early September. Like Britain over the Reich, Germany had clandestinely sent planes over England before the war to take pictures of military installations.[52] The targets to bomb were known and many of them were destroyed or damaged.

The campaign brought heavy losses to both sides and was finally won by RAF Bomber Command. It was the time of the famous Churchill pronouncement that so much was owed by so many to so few. Bomber Command with the help of radar had fought a heroic battle. The two German Luftflotten, under Kesselring and Sperrle, respectively, mustered about 820 fighters, Bomber Command had 600. But the RAF was fighting on its home ground, whereas the German fighters could only spend short periods over southern England to shield the bombers, before being forced to return because of limited fuel capacities. It was a tough battle but facts prove that Churchill's statement was one of many wartime propaganda pronouncements.

The Germans learned in short order what Bomber Command had experienced the year before. Bomber formations flying in daylight take dreadful losses. The Luftwaffe was not equipped for this kind of war. It had no long-range fighters to protect the bombers. Losses on both sides were: RAF, 550 fighters; Luftwaffe, 956 fighters and bombers.[53] Damage caused by the German bombs did not entail serious interruptions of RAF operations and life in general. Yet, it was recognized later by the Air Ministry that, if the Luftwaffe had continued bombing the RAF fighter bases, it would have succeeded in the battle of Britain. In an Air Ministry communication it is stated that the Luftwaffe made a mistake in calling off the attacks.[54]

In the months after the fall of France, RAF Bomber Command continued bombing Germany. This was justified by Churchill and his government as the only possible means of fighting the Reich. This is not entirely true, because long before the Normandy landings in 1944, Allied commandos frequently raided the occupied European coast from Narvik to Bordeaux; the Dieppe raid being the most famous. In addition, it was London that organized and, with the help of the RAF, supplied the national resistance movements in Western Europe. Both schemes engaged considerable German forces and the latter was, strictly speaking, against the Conventions. It hardened the attitude of the occupiers and has left ill feelings to this day.

The Air Ministry gave Bomber Command instructions on what to attack based on the Air Targets Sub-Committee of the Industrial Intelligence Centre. After 1936, a total of sixteen Western Air Plans had been developed. Four spelled out the most likely scenario and indicated what should be hit. The Western Air Plans W.A.1, 4, 5, and 6 defined as targets the Luftwaffe, communications, war industry, oil and aircraft factories.[55] For months between June and December 1940, the bombers flew into Germany at night and dropped their bombs. Oil was the main target, but because the number of attacking bombers was small and that number scattered over many targets, the damage was limited.

Bomber Command was still flying twin-engine bombers. The rearmament program, started in 1933 with ever increasing numbers of aircraft coming into active service, was still in progress. British aircraft factories were expanded and started working around the clock. For 1940 the British War Potential Program had projected a production of 16,000 planes.[56] To this had to be added the deliveries from the United States, which stood at 14,000 aircraft and 25,000 aero engines on order in August 1940.[57]

That oil was the Achilles heel of the German war machine was correctly recognized early in the war. If its destruction had been persistently executed, the war would have ended sooner. But in summer 1940 Bomber Command had to spread its resources over such target systems as barges in the Channel ports, airfields in the occupied countries, and helping Coastal Command and the navy to chase U-boats. The German fuel situation had always been difficult. It is best shown that despite its famous armored divisions, the majority of the German army still depended on the horse. There were more horses in the German army in World War II than in World War I.

The Luftwaffe, for all its proclaimed strength and efficiency, was always just able to keep its planes fueled. In 1934 it depended entirely on imports for its high-octane fuel. In 1936-

37 the U.S. Ethylgas Corporation built a plant in Doeberitz to produce octane 86 gasoline. By 1939 synthetic plants were in operation using coal as a base. But one ton of fuel required six tons of hard coal, which had to be mined and transported.

In case of war the demand of the Luftwaffe was estimated to be 100,000 cubic meters per month. In 1939 there were stores of 400,000 cubic meters. At that time Germany could produce 20,000 cubic meters per month and imported 9,000 cubic meters per month from Romania. Stores and production were only sufficient for a blitzkrieg.

Another problem was transport. The Luftwaffe needed 9,000 tank cars, but had only 5,200 at the beginning of the war. Production, transport, and storage of fuel was a problem for the German air force.[58] By the end of 1940 Germany had captured another 200,000 tons of aviation fuel in the countries of Western Europe. There were now stores of 600,000 tons that were widely scattered and could not easily be transferred from one theater of operation to the other. A concentrated and continual attack on German oil would have been a knockout blow at the beginning of the war. It was not until late 1944 that this was realized and even then Bomber Harris still thought that area raids were the way to bring Germany down.

Bomber Command continued its raids on many cities, which annoyed the German leaders including Göring and Hitler. On 4 September 1940 the latter exploded in a speech to his rubber stamp parliament in Berlin. He screamed that Germany would escalate the bombing war for every ton dropped over its territory and that *"wir werden ihre Städte ausradieren"* ("we shall erase their cities"). I will never forget his hysterical emphasis of the word *"ausradieren."* On that count, two years later, we were wondering whether the British did not have the better eraser.

During the battle of Britain, Hitler had given strict orders that London was not to be bombed. Now that order was rescinded and there occurred another step forward in the bombing war. Some historians claim this was exactly what Churchill had wanted and intended with the inaccurate bombing of German cities, because the publicity would draw the United States into war.[59]

The RAF bombings from 11 May 1940 onward were always considered deliberate acts of terror by the German government. Before the war the RAF had boasted that it could inflict damage to selected targets. When it missed them it seemed logical that it was done with a purpose. German propaganda published a White Paper on RAF raids, which thoughtfully avoided references to civilian losses, lest the people get upset, but mentioned such "dastard" willful destruction of heritage assets as the garden pavilion of Göthe at Weimar and Bismarck's mausoleum at Friedrichsruh.[60] Bomber Command must have been thrilled to be credited with such accuracy. Statistics show that from October 1940 till February 1942, Bomber Command killed an average of 219 Germans per month and destroyed about 120 buildings in the process.[61] The number and the types of aircraft available to perform these raids was limited. On paper there were 532 twin-engine bombers in service; actually available for operations were rarely more than 150.[62] But these relatively few and small aircraft flew raids whenever weather and moonlight permitted them. The main targets were still to be oil installations. Air Marshal Peirse, who had taken over from Charles Portal as chief of Bomber Command on 5 October 1940, was also commanded to attack vital war industries in German and Italian cities, continue laying mines, and attack German military installations across the Channel; an invasion still being feared for 1941. Peirse protested that he could not possibly raid all these targets, with the result that damage was scattered and annoying to the Germans, but not much more.

By contrast, the German Luftwaffe now initiated what has ever since been referred to as the Blitz. After the battle of Britain had to be called off because of heavy German losses and with no foreseeable success in sight, the bombers of Luftflotte 2, commanded by Field Marshal Kesselring from Brussels, Luftflotte 3, commanded by Field Marshal Sperrle from Paris, and Luftflotte 5, commanded by General Stumpf in Kristianstad, Norway, were let loose on Britain. In total these air fleets had about 770 serviceable machines between them.[63] Depending on the distance to the target, these twin-engine bombers could carry a bombload of about two tons maximum.

Before Eagle Day the Luftwaffe had restricted itself to attack shipping targets in an effort to cooperate with the U-boats in the blockade of the British Isles. After Eagle Day it was RAF airfields, radar stations, and transport. But now the Luftwaffe let loose with a vengeance. We were told it was retaliation and nothing else that brought about the increased bombing of still supposedly strategic targets. The RAF raids, maiming and hurting Germans and their possessions, would now be legally responded to with equal killing, maiming, and destruction. The Conventions allowed for that.

To bring this situation into perspective, one has to compare the respective operations. Bomber Command was lucky to be able to dispatch about 150 bombers on the long distance raids into German territory. Berlin in particular was a long way from the bomber bases. The distance to Italy was even longer. The German air fleets on the other hand were based just across the Channel and many squadrons could fly two sorties daily. German raids on British targets from Eagle Day onward could muster as many as 1,700 sorties per day, fighters and bombers. The raids on London started on 7 September 1940. Three hundred bombers of Sperrle's command appeared over the city in the early evening. The intended targets were the dock lands which were undoubtedly hit, but the terror aspect becomes apparent when one learns that 30 percent of the bombs were delayed action, with up to fourteen hours lapse before they would explode.[64] From 7 September until 13 November, London was bombarded every night. A total of 13,000 tons of high explosives and 12,000 incendiary canisters were dropped. Other cities were raided too and the most famous raid is the one on Coventry on 14 November 1940, when 450 bombers discharged 500 tons of high explosives and 880 incendiary canisters.[65] Civilian losses were appalling, mainly because there were few adequate air-raid shelters. In the raid on Coventry 554 people lost their lives. In the raid on London on 15 October over 400 perished. Hitler's eraser was at work but, if he thought it would stop British raids on Germany and/or that morale in the UK would crack and force the British government's hand, he soon realized his miscalculation. In 1940 the Luftwaffe dropped 37,000 tons of bombs on Britain and the

RAF 10,000 tons on Germany.[66] On the score of causing civilian losses the Luftwaffe was leading. By November 1940 German raids had killed more than 15,000 British civilians, whereas in six months of bombing Germany in 1940 the RAF had killed 975 Germans.[67] The Blitz was not justified retaliation, it was an escalation in the bombing war.

British official policy, as expressed in the media and the House of Commons, was that the targets in Germany were of a military and strategic nature. Although not publicly announced, this changed on 16 December 1940 when the first RAF area raid was authorized. It was to be a retaliatory attack for the raids on Coventry and Southampton. Crews were instructed to hit the center of Mannheim. Of 134 bombers dispatched, about 100 attacked the target. The German report listed 34 people killed, 81 injured, 1,266 bombed out, and about 500 residential dwellings destroyed.[68] Compared with what the Luftwaffe could deliver, this was small retaliation.

The morale of neither people wavered and the respective governments became convinced that their own people had superior moral qualities. Bomber Command was still hampered by a lack of good navigational equipment which resulted in missing targets or hitting the wrong ones. The Luftwaffe on the other hand could place its bombers within four hundred yards of the intended target with the help of radio directional beams crossing over the target area. British historians report that damage to strategic targets in Britain was substantial. It surprised the Air Ministry and RAF staff. One historian goes as far as to state that the Germans did not even intend indiscriminate bombing of civilians.[69]

As part of a sideshow of the Blitz one must mention the Italian participation in it. Mussolini, never to be outdone by German successes, dispatched against German objections a small air fleet of the Regia Aeronautica to the Channel coast. From 25 October 1940 to 5 April 1941 the RA had eighty-seven fighters and seven-eight bombers stationed at Belgian airfields. They flew raids against southern England cities and in five months dropped about fifty-five tons of high explosives.[70] The operations were sporadic and historians on both sides of the Channel seem to belittle the effort. Part of the Italians's problems was that their aircraft were technically inferior to the Hurricanes and Spitfires. The existence of the Italian contingent at the time of the Blitz and its actions against Britain caused Churchill to declare in the House of Commons on 30 September 1941 that the RAF should bomb Italy, with the intent of knocking it out of the war; and particularly Rome because the RA had bombed London.[71] It never had, but that was a fine point which a man like Churchill could ignore when it came to condoning raids on the Eternal City.

By early 1941 the mutual bombing campaigns were at a crossroad. The RAF was increasing in strength and the Luftwaffe was declining. In Britain the long-range planning for an effective bomber force became reality. The four-engine Halifaxes, Stirlings, and later the potent Lancasters began to arrive in numbers. The British Commonwealth Air Training Plan, initiated in Canada at the beginning of the war, provided the necessary crews. There was a basic difference in theory of the needs of the respective armed forces to win the war. The personnel strength of the British army was 2.9 times that of the air force. The figure for the German army was 4.5 times. Britain was to win the war through a strong air force. Germany, with its blitzkrieg theories, was to win the war through its army with the Luftwaffe playing a supporting role.

National mobilization of all resources commenced in Britain the moment war started. Big and small industrial plants were converted to aircraft production. Large car manufacturers switched to aero engines. Rolls Royce to this day produces aircraft engines. Modern mass production methods were employed, women were drafted into the industry, and the whole effort was put under Lord Beaverbrook, the press baron and friend of Churchill, who became head of the newly formed Ministry of Aircraft Production. From a delivery of 7,940 aircraft in 1939 the output of the United Kingdom based industry alone, i.e. without deliveries from the United States and Canada, rose to 15,000 in 1940, 20,000 in 1941, and leveled off at an annual production of 26,000 in 1944. A similar steep increase occurred in the fabrication of aero engines.[72]

Technical development was also pushed. The lack of proper navigational equipment was overcome with systems such as

Gee and H2S which allowed locating targets with almost pin-point accuracy. New plane types were developed with the Mosquito being the ultimate multipurpose craft as bomber, fighter, and reconnaissance machine. There was clear and single-minded determination and guidance from the Cabinet down that the Royal Air Force was the most important instrument in the arsenal of the nation. Scientists and industrialists were brought in to develop and increase aircraft production.

By contrast German attitudes and performance were con-fusing and ill directed. German national mobilization did not occur until after the fall of Stalingrad in January 1943. Things began to look bleak and Goebbels asked a crowd of ten thou-sand in the Sportspalast of Berlin on 18 February 1943 "do you want total war?" The claque jumped to its feet, raised their right arms in the Nazi salute and roared "*jawohl.*" Before that event Hitler had decreed that life in general and supply of consumer goods and services should be as normal as in peace-time. In late 1940 the German leadership was convinced that the war was as good as won. No effort was to be made to increase the military strength. The Luftwaffe was to continue the war with the plane types it had and production quotas were sufficient. The three German armed services each had their own armament programs with no coordination of man-power and material resources between them. The aircraft industry, except for the Junkers Company, was still in the con-trol of private individuals and there was little coordination with regard to production, types of machines, and allocation of resources. Overall planning had been placed in the hands of Ernst Udet, a WWI fighter ace, who created a monstrous bureaucracy. Hitler gave orders without consultation and, as regards the Luftwaffe, these orders were often contradictory. As an example one must consider the jet fighter development. The Me-262 was to be a fighter. He wanted it to be a bomber. When it finally came into service in late 1944 as a fighter it proved lethal to U.S. bomber formations. But it was too late to make a decisive impact. Comparing German aircraft produc-tion with British output, one finds that German production was low. In 1939 the output was 8,000 planes, in 1940 it rose to 10,000, in 1941 to 11,000, in 1942 to 15,000, and then in 1943 and 1944 jumped to 25,000 and 40,000 respectively. In these years the Germans finally realised that the air offensive of the Allies needed to be responded to and the rise in output is due to increased fighter production.[73]

The respective aircraft industries of both Britain and Germany employed during the war years approximately the same number of people. But the output per manhour was much higher in Britain thanks to the employment of modern production methods. In Germany it was still the old-fashioned master-apprentice principle. In Britain it was mass production by semi-skilled workers. Few German women entered the war industry. Up to 80 percent of the workforce in the aircraft industry were foreigners. Some of them volunteers, most of them forcefully brought to the Reich, and a considerable number were concentration camp inmates. Morale must have been a problem. But surprisingly, quality and quantity of production were high.

German air force strength in March 1940 was 3,692 machines. By March 1941 the number had declined, instead of going up, to 3,583, and a year later it was down to 2,872.[74]

1941: More Blitzkriegs

In 1941 German military planning had to divert a considerable part of its resources and time to help Mussolini. Italian troops invaded Greece from their bases in Albania on 28 October 1940. More than 100,000 Italian troops started to march.[75] They were supported by 187 RA aircraft, 55 of which were three-engine bombers. The Greeks had 150 aircraft of which 29 were bombers. Air raids in both directions started in November when Italian bombers, among other targets, hit Salonica killing two hundred civilians. The Greeks attacked Italian bases in Albania, reportedly only hitting airports. Britain became involved in the fighting and occupied Crete on 29 October 1940, a day after the Italian campaign had started. The RAF flew support for the Greeks from Malta by attacking Italian ports. Before long the Italian forces were pushed back into Albania and Mussolini's fortunes appeared bleak. He could not emulate his fellow dictator's blitzkriegs.

In the meantime Hitler, who was planning on invading

Russia, tried to secure the southern flank and oil supplies from Romania by political maneuvers. The USSR had forced the Romanians to cede Bessarabia, the Bulgarians felt threatened, and both accepted German military help in materials and German troops stationed on their territories. Yugoslavia was to join the Axis, but that political feat faltered on the objections of the Serb majority in the Yugoslav ruling circles. Hitler had to delay the thrust eastward to establish his southern front and to help the Italians. In December 1940 Luftwaffe units had already been stationed on the Italian Dodecanese Islands off the Turkish coast and had flown raids against Alexandria and the Suez Canal. German transport planes had ferried 30,000 Italian troops from Italy to Albania.

One feat of the RA should be mentioned here because it was one of the few strategic air strikes this force ever made. In true Balbo long-range flight fashion, Italian bombers attacked the oil installations on Bahrein Island in the Persian Gulf. For the return flight they refueled in Eritrea an Italian colony at that time still in the hands of the Italians.[76]

By 6 April 1941, German diplomatic efforts with Yugoslavia had come to an end and in typical Clausewitzean fashion another blitzkrieg was started. It lasted only a few weeks. Yugoslavia surrendered on 17 April and Greece on 21 April. By June the island of Crete was also in Axis possession. The Luftwaffe and the Regia Aeronautica played their supporting roles attacking military installations clearly identified by clandestine overflights long before the hostilities started.

The worst and most infamous raid of this latest blitzkrieg happened on the first day when 484 bombers and Stukas of Luftflotte 4 dropped 360 tons of bombs and incendiaries on Belgrade. Whereas all other raids can be termed tactical, the Belgrade raid was clearly strategic. Many innocent people were killed and the Luftwaffe did not help its reputation formed by the western media as a tool of horror. German and Austrian historians, however, consider the raid a tactical strike. The enigmatic chief of German counterintelligence, Admiral Canaris, for reasons of his own had warned Yugoslav General Simovic of the planned raid.[77] Civilian losses were high but have never been clearly established. Churchill wrote that 17,000 bodies were in the ruins.[78] Tito's biographer, V. Dedijer, is quoted as listing 3,000 bodies buried, and the war crimes tribunal in 1947 against the commander of Luftflotte 4, Generaloberst Alexander Löhr, accused him of 1,500 deaths.[79] Another source quotes a figure of 2,271[80] and still another quotes 4,000.[81]

In a strange and implausible argument, the RAF flew two retaliation raids for the Belgrade attack on Sofia, capital of Bulgaria on 6-7 and 12-13 April 1941. Wellingtons of 37 Squadron based at Mendini, Greece, dropped about thirty tons of high explosives on railway targets and adjacent residential areas.[82] Bulgaria was not in a state of war with Britain until 12 December 1941.

With the defeat of Yugoslavia and Greece another blitzkrieg had been won but at the cost of having stretched Germany's limited resources further. The Wehrmacht was now spread from North Africa, where Mussolini also had to be bailed out, to the North Cape and from the Atlantic Coast to a line from East Prussia to the Danube Delta.

And then came the fateful day of 22 June 1941, a Sunday. I will never forget that morning when I switched on the radio and on came Goebbels informing the world that Germany was making a preventive strike against the USSR. In the family we agreed that this was the beginning of the end for Germany. Germany was fighting on two fronts again, something Bismarck had successfully prevented, the Kaiser had not seemed to care about, and Hitler now purposely started.

Stalin became the hero of the Great Patriotic War and Churchill and Roosevelt, the democratic leaders of the world, had the world's foremost communist suddenly as an ally. Despite the non-aggression pact of 23 August 1939, the conflict between the USSR and Germany was unavoidable. The ideological concepts of the two states were diametrically opposed. But there was also the economic aspect of it. Already during World War I the East was recognised as the future for Germans. August Thyssen, the German steel magnate, had advocated to the German government in September 1914 that areas as far away as the Crimea and the Caucasus be annexed because they had manganese and other valuable ores. Ukraine is known for its agricultural riches and its coal deposits. Ludendorff, the

German chief of staff, saw these areas as settlement colonies for Germans in 1918.[83]

Hitler's government seemed to be programmed from the beginning to strike out east. He should have considered that Karl XII of Sweden and Napoleon I had marched in that direction before with disastrous results. On the other hand, he may have looked at the conquest of the American West as an example of how a nation secured Lebensraum. France, from Louis XIV to Napoleon I, had tried the same by invading Germany.

Goebbels said it was a preventive strike. Postwar historians speak of a brutal surprise attack on the USSR. But was it really? More and more historians using now available Russian documents maintain that it was really a question of weeks before the USSR would have struck out west. It appears as if it was again a situation as in Norway in April 1940, when German troops arrived before the Royal Marines. Victor Suworow, a Russian army officer who defected to the West before Communism collapsed, gives many detailed examples and lists orders issued by Stalin and his top staff which confirm this.[84] The German historian Werner Maser refers to further documents prepared by Russian officers such as Zhukov and Wassilevski.[85] The German strength was estimated at one hundred army divisions. The USSR was deploying 259 army divisions at its western borders leaving 45 divisions to defend its other frontiers. The Red Army had about 5 million soldiers facing 3.5 million German and allied troops.

The facts are that the Soviet Union was concentrating its military forces in the west from 1940 onward. Why were they there? Were they to strike out west and if not why were they unable to stem the inferior German forces? The Red Army seemed to have been taken by surprise. Millions of Russians were killed or taken prisoners and thousands of Red Air Force planes were destroyed by the Luftwaffe in the first few months of the campaign.

There can be no doubt that the reason for the USSR forces being in position was to extend world communism and to return to the age-old Russian desire for an open, ice-free access to the oceans. There can be no doubt that the clash between the two nations was to happen sooner or later. The only question that remained was who would strike first. Goebbels may have been right, for once.

The Russian armed forces were prepared for war. They had superior numbers of tanks and artillery and these were of better design. The Red Army had twelve times more guns than the Wehrmacht and seven times more tanks. The Soviet air force was the strongest in the world. It had about 17,000 planes, about five times as many as the Luftwaffe. The German aggressors had only about 1,500 tanks and 6,000 guns.[86] Twenty-three million Russians worked in the war industry which consumed 43 percent of the national budget in 1941.[87] Aircraft production alone was slated to reach 1,500 machines per month in 1941. The industry was working around the clock to reach this goal.[88]

Based on past blitzkriegs, Hitler calculated that by the end of 1941 the USSR would be defeated and he could then turn west again to finish off Britain. He was utterly ill-informed about Russian strength and intentions. It was believed that the USSR armed forces were leaderless because of the 1937 purges when 90 percent of the generals and admirals were executed on trumped-up charges of treason. In addition about 35,000 lower-rank officers were shot. German estimates of armaments understated Soviet strength. Assessment of the Red Army performance in the Winter War against Finland confirmed these findings. Since October 1940 the Luftwaffe had flown many high-altitude reconnaissance flights over the USSR, but obviously they had not revealed the full picture. Many of the Soviet armament factories were then already behind the Ural Mountains, beyond the range of the German planes. Hitler must have been so sure of his coming success that he ignored the possibility of having the USSR attacked by Japan from the east. The Soviet/Japanese non-aggression pact of 13 April 1940 explicitly eliminated that.

The blitzkrieg developed as planned with German successes and advances despite numerical and material inferiority. The Luftwaffe claimed to have destroyed 7,500 Soviet planes in the first few months. This supposedly represented 70 percent of the order of battle of the Red Air Force in the west.[89] But this success had its price. German losses were 774 aircraft representing 60 percent of its order of battle. When winter came, the

German army was still outside Moscow, had not occupied Leningrad, and in short was stuck first in mud and then in snow and ice. Troops and their equipment had not been equipped for that contingency, losses and reversals mounted and the blitzkrieg had failed.

There followed three years and four months of the most bitter fighting the world had ever seen, with horrendous losses of men and materials on both sides and in the end with the Red Army meeting the U.S. Army at the Elbe River in Germany in early 1945.

At the eastern front the war in the air was ferocious but developed mostly along tactical lines. The majority of the Soviet planes were army support machines, many of them of obsolete design. The USSR aircraft industry operating at full capacity was in the process of replacing them. The Luftwaffe learned in short order that the high Soviet losses did not guarantee air superiority because new and better planes were rising like mosquitos out of the Pripet Swamps.

When the blitzkrieg came to a halt in the winter of 1941-42 the Luftwaffe was weaker than when it started in June and German industry was in no position to re-equip it quickly.

When the campaign started the Red Air Force had only about eight hundred long-range bombers. They were stationed far behind the front lines and escaped destruction. Soviet air strategy after the Spanish Civil War had abandoned bombing and concentrated even more than the German high command on having the air force play a support role for the army only. This meant that there were few strategic bombing raids flown behind the German lines. During the entire war the Soviet strategic bomber force flew 215,000 sorties, but only about 7,400 were directed against targets such as Berlin, cities in East Prussia, Bucharest, and Helsinki.[90] The rest were tactical support raids which resulted in heavy losses at the hands of the superior German fighters.

Soviet strategic raids continued until 1945 but there does not appear to have been a basic plan to bomb targets or cities. The intensity of the attacks, particularly the early ones was small. In the three raids on Berlin in 1941 only thirty tons of bombs were discharged. There were several raids on the

Romanian oil fields at Ploesti and in February 1944 there were three major raids on Finland involving up to 850 aircraft of all types to force Finland out of the war. A total of 2,386 tons of high explosives were dropped.[91] Similarly, to force Hungary to quit, four raids with a total of 1,129 sorties were flown against Budapest in September 1944.

Few publications and documents can be located which describe the actions of the Soviet strategic air forces; there was not much action. By contrast German strategic air actions were substantial. Moscow in particular suffered because it was another place which Hitler vowed to *"ausradieren."* Mass raids were flown between 21-22 and 24-25 July 1942. During the first raid alone 104 tons of high explosives and 46,000 incendiary bombs were rained down on the city. But Moscow was ready. There were 600 fighters, 796 antiaircraft guns, and numerous searchlights in position.[92] Of the 127 bombers executing the first raid, 22 were shot down; a loss rate that could not be tolerated. Therefore, after the first heavy raids the Luftwaffe put aside the "eraser" and returned to tactical warfare. To the praise of the Germans, downtown Leningrad was not attacked by the Luftwaffe. Of the magnificent structures of that city only the Kirov Theatre was damaged by artillery fire during the long siege. The Winter Palace with the Hermitage, the gold-domed cathedrals of Kazakhstan and of St. Isaacs and many other monuments survived the war. But the palaces outside of Leningrad were completely destroyed because they were in the war zone. The Soviet Baltic Fleet penned in at Kronstadt was repeatedly attacked and the battleship *Marat* was sunk by a Ju-87 divebomber on 23 September 1941.[93]

The Luftwaffe losses were mounting as the campaign progressed because Soviet resistance in the air and on the ground increased. There were still concentrated actions which involved hundreds of German bombers and caused great damage. In June 1942 the raids on Sevastopol, the USSR naval base in the Crimea, rained 2,246 high explosive and 23,800 incendiary bombs on that city.[94] In addition the city was shelled by the biggest caliber German guns. On 23-24 August 1942, six hundred German bombers raided Stalingrad. Losses in civilian lives are quoted as 40,000.[95] However this figure appears very high and, as the original Warsaw, Rotterdam, and Belgrade accounts, may be based on unconfirmed media reports. The USSR did not publish any figures on air-raid civilian losses. But civilian losses there must have been many. The raids on Sevastopol and Stalingrad can be termed tactical because both cities were in the path of the advancing German army. But the magnitude of them and the inherent losses of civilian lives make them atrocities. Also, if they were to be justifiable in accordance with the Hague Conventions, demands for surrender should have been issued first as before the Warsaw and Rotterdam raids.

It became apparent to the German leaders that Russia could fight back. Before the advancing German army 1,500 factories and 10 million workers of the industry west of the Ural mountains were relocated east of those mountains. Some relocated aircraft factories produced again only three weeks after they had been unloaded at their eastern destinations.[96] Output of the Soviet aircraft factories rose steadily. By June 1944 the production reached 3,300 planes per month. The strength of the Red Air Force had climbed to over 24,000 machines, an overwhelming number over the Luftwaffe. There was also a steady flow of American made planes coming in via Alaska. Roosevelt, who had declared the United States the arsenal of the democracies, ordered these deliveries to a peoples democracy while the United States was still neutral (and had laws to prevent such sales). Until 1945 the USSR received about 18,500 U.S. and British built aircraft.[97]

By early 1943 masses of tanks, guns, and aircraft pushed the Wehrmacht back. General Korten, the Luftwaffe chief of staff, tried to assemble a force that would strike behind the Urals. It was a feeble attempt and resulted in raids on the Molotow Tank Factory at Gorki, the Saratow oil refinery, and the city of Jaroslavl in June 1943.[98] About 1,100 sorties were flown and about 1,500 tons of bombs dropped. It was hoped that the bombings would also have an effect on Russian morale. But the raids could not be sustained. The Luftwaffe was too occupied with tactical warfare and it also lacked long-range bombers.[99] The halfhearted attempt at quickly developing a four-engine plane was a failure. The Heinkel He-177 became more of a threat to its crews than to the enemy.[100]

With the major strength of the German air force deployed in Russia after June 1941, the operations in the west dwindled to nuisance raids on Britain. Sperrle was still in charge of Luftflotte 3. His bomber force was reduced to about 150 planes of which only 100 may have been serviceable. They attacked cities from the Channel coast up to Hull, but the tonnages delivered were never more than fifty tons per raid. It was terror on a small scale, even though the terror was extended by the intermittent shelling of Dover by the coastal batteries placed at the Pas de Calais from 1941 onward. Some 148 civilians were killed in these bombardments which rained down without warning.[101]

The Luftwaffe was also busy in other places and had to spread its resources. In the Mediterranean, Malta became a major target. German troops under General Rommel had been dispatched to North Africa to shore up retreating Italian forces. To supply these units the ships had to pass the island of Malta, a major British stronghold between Gibraltar and the Suez Canal. La Valetta, the principal port, was pounded for years by the Luftwaffe and the Regia Aeronautica. These raids must be termed strategic, because they were not in the immediate battlefield and there never seemed to have been plans to land on the island. It was a formidable fortress and it was hoped that it could be isolated by air action. The plan almost succeeded, had it not been for the heroic defenders and the equally heroic ships and their crews which brought in supplies. The damage to this ancient and historic place was substantial and over 4,800 civilians lost their lives in three years of bombing.[102]

As 1941 progressed Bomber Command continued to fly raids into Germany and Italy, all the time hitting and/or missing the intended targets. At first the targets were oil, transportation, and aircraft factories. As the German U-boat campaign in the Atlantic became more threatening, U-boat bases on the west coast of France and shipyards in northern Germany were added to the list. The Operational Record Books of the RAF at the Public Record Office in London speak of damage inflicted and increasing numbers of bombers dispatched. German records published and referred to in the Bomber

Command War Diary (BCWD) speak of limited damage and, by later standards, still small civilian losses. I remember well the reports in the German media of increasing terror raids on innocent citizens and villages. Goebbels was walking a tightrope. To call the British, and Churchill in particular, war criminals—as he did—he had to admit that the bombers were coming through and that German antiaircraft defenses could not prevent them. The facts were that, for instance, on a raid on Nürnberg on 12-13 October 1941 for which 152 aircraft were dispatched, only a few bombs fell on the city killing one person. But villages from ten to ninety-five miles away from Nürnberg were bombed; villages of no strategic significance and obviously attacked by aircraft lost or misguided by German countermeasures.[103]

The losses to the German civilians were by that time not as accidental and incidental as the British public was made to believe through their press. On 9 July 1941 Peirse, the Bomber Command chief, had received instructions from the Air Ministry to attack the transportation system and from then on, in addition, the morale of the civilian population.[104] In other words, to the many target systems identified in Western War Plans before 1939, morale of the population was added as a destroyable entity. If it cracked because of human and material losses the citizens would force the German government's hand. There is, of course, one basic fallacy in this assumption—the more people you kill the fewer there are to force an end to hostilities. Although British morale did not crack during the Blitz, the Air Ministry thought German morale would. If one assumes from this attitude that the British government considered its people superior, one must not forget that in World War I German morale did crack. After about 700,000 people had starved to death because of the naval blockade, revolts broke out in November 1918 and forced the German government to call for an armistice.

Depending on the weather and many other circumstances, such as bomber crew experience, the German civilian losses were mounting. Hamburg suffered eight deaths on 12-13 March 1941. A night later 51 died and at Kiel 125 died on 8-9 April. The number of sorties and the bombloads were increasing. Whereas for all of 1940 Bomber Command had delivered

10,000 tons of bombs, six months later an additional 18,000 tons had been dropped. But the effort came with a price. From 3 September 1939 to 14 July 1941 one thousand bombers had been lost.[105] If the only way to attack Germany was by air, and many political and military leaders thought this was the way to win the war, to continue and succeed Bomber Command losses not only had to be replaced but the number of planes had to be increased. A delegation was sent to the United States. Air Vice-Marshal Arthur Harris headed the RAF delegation. His post as deputy chief of the air staff was taken over by Air Vice-Marshal Bottomley.

Despite the increased sorties of the bombers, there was no sign of Germany slackening in its war efforts. On the other hand there were the glowing reports of the air crews of targets burning and designated installations destroyed. Upon Lord Cherwell's instigation, D. M. Butt, a civil servant in the War Cabinet staff, was appointed to review photographs taken from bombers during the raids. Only photographs of crews reporting to have bombed the targets were used. Few bombers were equipped with cameras at that period. Over four thousand photos of one hundred night raids in June/July 1941 were evaluated. It was found that depending on the moon only between one in four to one in fifteen planes were within five miles of the target. The report, completed in August 1941, was a blow to Bomber Command and its leader, Sir Richard Peirse. The government decided to assess the bomber offensive and a halt to all major operations was ordered. It appeared that German reports of little damage were correct. There followed a period of reprieve for the German cities.

In the second half of 1941 British fortunes declined further. Rommel threatened the Suez Canal, the Soviet Union seemed in danger of collapsing, money was running out for paying war materials coming from the United States, and the U-boats were roaming the Atlantic with ever-increasing success.

The United States was still neutral but providing support despite legal barriers imposed by Congress. President Roosevelt, who had concerned himself solely with domestic matters until 1939, considered it politically prudent to shift his attention to foreign affairs. He saw a threat to democracy in the

Axis Powers, which included Japan, whereas in Britain he perceived a bulwark against this evil. His New Deal had been a limited success. There still were millions of unemployed and their votes were needed.

When war broke out in Europe the nations of the western hemisphere under the guidance of the United States signed the Declaration of Panama which provided a security zone of three hundred miles around the continent in which no fighting could take place. This suited most Americans who were loath to being dragged into another European conflict. But the U.S. administration considered a war with the Axis powers inevitable, particularly once Germany and Italy conquered the United Kingdom. War would then come to the shores of the United States. Therefore Britain had to be saved and at the same time U.S. defense had to be established.

Like the rest of the world the United States had begun to rearm after the collapse of the Geneva Disarmament Conference. The start was later and the momentum smaller in the beginning. The B-17 four-engine bomber, the Flying Fortress, went into serial production in 1936. The B-24 four-engine Liberator came off the drawing board in 1937 and entered service in late 1939.[106] In early 1939 Congress appropriated $300 million to increase the Army Air Corps from 1,700 to 5,500 planes.[107] In 1940 Congress voted $11 billion for general rearmament. U.S. aircraft production that had been as low as 437 planes in 1934 jumped to 2,195 in 1939, to 6,000 in 1940, and eventually to 96,000 in 1944.[108] Increasing the U.S. armed forces had dual benefits. It brought the United States out of the Depression and it showed any potential aggressor that it would face resistance. The expenses were financed through government credits.

Supporting overseas democracies still had to jump the hurdle of the Neutrality Act. Roosevelt convinced Congress and the general public that by helping Britain and France and being prepared at home, the United States could maintain its neutrality and keep out of the war. The Neutrality Act was amended in November 1939 to allow deliveries to nations at war. American industry, as in World War I, could employ people, reap profits, and through that, support the democratic principle. The development of the United States as a first-rate economic world power could continue. Foreign deliveries had to be on a cash basis. Britain sold assets such as Argentine railways, South African gold holdings, and domestic gold reserves to pay the bills.

In foreign politics the U.S. administration turned a blind eye to the British occupation of Iceland in May 1940 while all the time condemning the Axis grabs of European real estate. Secret staff talks were started with Britain after the fall of France. Three senior U.S. officers visited Bomber Command in August.[109] Capital Royal Navy ships were refitted in American east coast shipyards, a clear breach of neutrality. Over 30,000 British children were brought to the United States to be safe from German bombs.

In December 1940 Henry Morgenthau informed the U.S. president that Britain was rapidly running out of cash. There would be no money, no arms deliveries, and Axis victory was rising on the horizon. With no deliveries, U.S. industry would decline, unemployment rise, and American shores would be the next to be attacked. The answer was Lend-Lease, brilliantly pushed through Congress. Britain could breathe easy, support, both material and psychological, was increasing. Roosevelt sent envoys to Churchill with secret messages promising help.

When the British admiralty wanted to lease U.S. ships to transport troops to the North African theater, the U.S. government graciously provided U.S. navy ships at no charge.[110] On 7 April 1941 all German and Italian ships in U.S. ports were seized to prevent any acts of sabotage. On 11 April 1941 the U.S. security zone was extended to twenty-six degrees west thus bringing almost the whole of the Atlantic from west of Iceland and the Azores under the control of the U.S. Navy.[111] No official announcement was made to the Axis Powers causing confrontations between German submarines and the U.S. Navy with the loss of ships and men. After U.S. and British staff talks in March 1941 and the extension of the U.S. security zone, the U.S. Navy took over the guarding of convoys. The U.S. craft operated out of the new bases the United States had acquired from Britain from Newfoundland to the Caribbean for the delivery of fifty old U.S. Navy destroyers. All of these operations had to be done clandestinely because they were against the Neutrality Act of 1935.

In summer 1941 more and more of U.S. neutrality crumbled. Because Britain needed to deploy more troops in the Middle East it was evacuating Iceland. U.S. Marines took over from the British army. Roosevelt and Churchill met at Placentia Bay, Newfoundland, to proclaim the Atlantic Charter. It was basically a rehash of Wilson's Fourteen Points promising freedom from fear, of the seas, and other freedoms; above all self-government to all nations. It seemingly applied to victors and vanquished of the present war. As in 1919, the vanquished were not permitted to enjoy the benefits of the Charter in 1945. The unofficial but very significant parts of the conference were the secret meetings of the military staffs.

Roosevelt through General Arnold, commander of the U.S. Army Air Force, had four senior officers prepare what has gone into the history of bombing as the Air War Plans Division AWPD-1 Plan. It had been worked out in cooperation with the RAF in Britain and covered the following subjects:[112]

> Air defense in the Western Hemisphere
> An air offensive against Germany
> Strategic defense in the Pacific Theater
> Air support for the invasion of Europe
> After the defeat of Germany, a strategic air offensive
>   against Japan

History unraveled as foreseen and planned at Placentia Bay. Germany tried desperately to avoid a war with the United States. The German navy wanted its U-boats to fire back when attacked by U.S. destroyers. Hitler forbade such actions. But they happened and the two countries continued on a collision course. The shooting increased and was reported as acts of defense against the Nazi aggressors. By November 1941 Roosevelt had no problems having the 1935 Neutrality Act repealed. This meant war-like U.S. operations could be brought out into the open.

In the Far East a similar collision course was apparent with Japan. U.S./Japanese negotiations were still going on when

Japanese carrier planes bombed the U.S. naval base at Pearl Harbor on 7 December 1941. The world was told that the attack came without a declaration of war. This was true because the Japanese diplomats in Washington had their instructions muddled and saw the U.S. foreign secretary after the raid had happened. The Japanese had started an undeclared war by default. Whether the U.S. government knew about the impending attack on Pearl Harbor is a moot point and has been the subject of several studies.

Back on the Atlantic side Hitler lived up to Germany's obligations under the Tri-Partite Pact and declared war on the United States on 11 December 1941. It could not have pleased Roosevelt more—Hitler again the aggressor. Churchill was delighted and saw the fulfillment of his diplomatic efforts. Hitler, the master diplomat, had now brought the 400 million people of the British Empire, the United States of America, and the Soviet Union against 100 million Germans. The major Allied powers controlled 60 percent of the world manufacturing capacity. Germany with its allies controlled 17 percent.[113] No fast blitzkrieg could overcome these potentials. If Hitler had hoped that the United States would first try to direct its war efforts against Japan his intelligence sources had let him down. If he had hoped that Japan would also live up to its obligations under the Axis Pact and declare war on the USSR, he again had miscalculated. How the German government and military leaders thought they could win this war is beyond comprehension. It showed their incompetence and arrogance, and for that alone they should have been brought to trial.

1942: TURNING OF THE TIDE

Allied fortunes continued to decline for a while. Pearl Harbor for all its callousness was a tactical raid, intended to knock out the U.S. Pacific fleet as a threat to Japanese conquests in Southeast Asia.

It was the United States which started area and indiscriminate bombing in the Far East. Out of frustration over the continued setbacks, twenty B-25 twin-engine bombers were loaded on the aircraft carrier *Hornet* and dispatched once they were within striking distance of the Japanese islands. The operation was under the command of Colonel James Doolittle and has entered history as the "Doolittle Raid." On 18 April 1942 the bombers scattered their loads over the Japanese islands, did little or no damage, and most of them landed in China as previously arranged with that new ally. It was a stunt of no military significance, but of considerable publicity value at home. The public were told that only military targets were destroyed. At that time this was still the true and professed policy of the U.S. Army Air Force.

Over in Europe in early 1942 the British chiefs of staff reconfirmed that the bomber was the only weapon with which to fight Germany and Italy. But the revelations of the Butt Report resulted in changes. Air Marshal Sir Richard Peirse was replaced as commander of Bomber Command by Air Marshal Arthur Harris on 23 February 1942. Opinions are divided as to whether Peirse was made the scapegoat for the poor performance of Bomber Command. He was appointed commander of RAF forces in India, certainly a step down from the most prestigious post of commander-in-chief of the bombers. The planners at the Air Ministry could not blame themselves for not having supplied the RAF with modern navigational equipment, for giving them bombers that had no defense against fighters shooting from below and machine guns of inferior caliber, and for implementing the Trenchard Doctrine with unsuitable planes.

The decision to continue bombing and put it in the hands of a forceful leader had several reasons. The Allied armies were in no position yet to land on the Continent and fight the Axis armies. It was feared that there would be a repeat of the trench warfare of 1914 to 1918 as a result of any assault in Western Europe. The USSR demanded such an assault as a relief on its front. Churchill sent messages to Stalin assuring him that the attack would come but that in the meantime Germany would suffer a bombardment unseen before. The messages made it clear that not only would the German war effort be reduced, but that the people living around these installations were to suffer from the Allied bombs. Similar messages went to Roosevelt whose reactions to bombing civilians are not recorded.

From the prime minister via the Air Ministry, Bomber Command was given clear instructions. Since precision bombing had not worked day or night, area bombing was to replace it. As Harris interpreted it: In order to destroy something you have to destroy everything.[114] The air staff pretended that area bombing was a temporary measure until experience and technical means would allow return to precision bombing.[115]

In the meantime many documents and statements were issued to convince everybody that an attack on morale would win the war. On 14 February 1942 Bottomley, who had become the scribe of the Air Council, had instructed Bomber Command in Bombing Directive No. 22 to focus operations on the morale of the enemy and in particular on the industrial worker.[116] The directive lists the targets and even gives the tonnages of bombs required per square mile and number of inhabitants of the major cities to be blasted. At 50 percent efficiency, i.e. bombs hitting the target, a square mile needed seven tons and eight hundred inhabitants needed one ton. All Harris had to do was do the soldier's thing and follow orders. Just in case the instructions were not clearly understood, Portal followed them up with a memo to Bottomley the next day stressing that the aiming points were to be built-up areas and not, for instance, dockyards or aircraft factories.[117] On 29 October 1942 this was followed up with a directive from the Air Ministry to all RAF home and overseas commands on what could and could not be attacked in enemy occupied countries and what could be bombed in German, Italian, and Japanese home territories. The list of restrictions in enemy occupied countries is understandably long and ambiguous. The instructions on enemy home territories comprised one single paragraph and said: Bomb everything and particularly morale.[118]

Improvements were coming and it would have seemed fair to let Peirse prove his mettle as commander. Instead he was replaced by a man who had shown since his early military career that he was a singleminded soldier who would follow orders, stick with them, and implement them beyond any second thoughts.

Indiscriminate bombing had been encouraged some time

before. Air Vice-Marshal Saundby, a senior officer in the Bomber Command staff, instructed Air Vice-Marshal Slessor, commander of No. 5 Group, in case the target could not be found to drop bombs on "any good looking built-up area" instead of bringing them home, "to get at least some sort of benefit out of the sortie."[119] As early as 13 October 1940 Churchill had voiced his satisfaction with the Foreign Office for turning down a Red Cross offer to investigate German and British bombing.[120] He was afraid Britain would fare worse and bombing would have to be discontinued. Sinclair, the minister for air, had suggested that the less-qualified bomber crews should drop their bombs from greater height.[121] On 31 October 1940 Churchill told Portal that the morale of the Italian people should be considered a military objective.[122] The pronouncements on area bombing continued into 1941 when the chiefs of staff endorsed a memo from Trenchard to Churchill recommending German morale as a target. They proposed attacks on transportation because railway facilities are always located in big population centers. By hitting them Bomber Command would swat two flies with one stroke. German morale would soon break; last but not least because it was inferior to British morale.[123]

One should of course not assume that all these British leaders were relishing the thought of their enemies' blood. An honest attempt had been made to identify vital targets in the German war industry. The Ministry of Economic Warfare had specified among many other targets the U-boat engine works of MAN in Augsburg, the spark plug factory of Bosch at Feuerbach, and the ball-bearing factories at Schweinfurt. If all these factories could have been 100 percent destroyed, as the MEW assumed Bomber Command was able to do, the German war effort would have collapsed. But Bomber Command, despite the heroic performance of its crews, could not find and/or hit the targets. Upon the urging of Lord Cherwell a new commission under Mr. Justice Singleton was formed to investigate how Bomber Command could best be employed. The report, dated 20 May 1942, was inconclusive and, although it caused some elevated heartbeats at High Wycombe, resulted in no new instructions to the bombers.[124] It confirmed that attacks on morale had started by stating that on the four consecutive night raids on Rostock from 23-24 April 1942 onward the Heinkel aircraft factory was a subsidiary target. The aiming point was the *Altstadt* (Old Town), destroyed with laudable success.[125]

But even when the target was found and hit, damage was often small and Bomber Command losses were high. When twelve Lancasters attacked the MAN works at Augsburg on 17 April 1942 in a daring daylight raid, seven bombers did not return. When I worked as a summer student in that factory in 1947 I was told the bombs had all missed. I could see for myself that there was little destruction in the factory area, whereas the inner city showed the results of the night raid of 25-26 February 1944 when 584 Lancasters and Sterlings and 10 Mosquitos unloaded 2,000 tons of bombs and incendiaries in two waves destroying 24 percent of the dwellings and killing 1,500 people.[126]

A way had to be found to make bombing pay and produce results. If there was a vital industry within the limits of a German town raze the whole place and as a benefit destroy the industry. The error in this thinking was that most German city centers were built long before the industrial revolution and industries were located on the outskirts of or completely outside the city. Oil refineries, the original targets, were situated in open country. Being large plants they occupied areas which could be easily found. Area bombing of the large refineries at Leuna, Thuringia, would have had a strategic effect without killing civilians.

But the collective thinking of the leaders had shifted to attacking morale. Early in February 1942 Archibald Sinclair had submitted a paper to the Cabinet proposing area bombing. It had no empirical basis and actually, based on the Butt Report, it should have suggested abandoning bombing. Sinclair convinced the Cabinet and Bomber Directive No. 22 was issued.

Churchill, who had been a staunch protagonist of bombing ever since he had been minister for air after World War I, turned to his scientific advisor, Lord Cherwell, to prop up the decision with some figures. The Germans had provided the facts. Professor Zuckerman evaluated the results of the Birmingham and Hull Luftwaffe raids and Cherwell extrapolated them. His memo to Churchill of 30 March 1942 confirmed the decisions taken the month before.[127] What Cherwell had not included in his memo was Zuckerman's finding that neither at Hull nor at Birmingham did the bombing cause panic or anti-social behavior.[128]

While Harris, after his appointment as Bomber Command chief in February 1942, immediately went about to prove himself as a forceful military leader and implemented the instructions of Directive No. 22, the Air Ministry and chiefs of staff produced more papers which consolidated the area bombing campaign. These papers also showed the government what was needed in planes, gasoline, bombs, etc. to carry out the attacks. Allotting the resources to Bomber Command caused a stir from the army and the navy, but Churchill, the ultimate arbiter as prime minister and minister of defense, put his weight behind Portal, the RAF chief of staff.

The chiefs of staff concluded in their meetings in 1942 that Bomber Command must be increased. Until that point had been reached the bombing should be concentrated on transportation targets. Harris ignored that suggestion and started area bombing with raids on Lübeck on 28-29 March 1942, on Rostock on 23-24 April, followed by the one thousand bomber raid on Cologne on 30-31 May. That raid snuffed the lives of 469 civilians. It seems that while the chiefs of staff wanted the destruction of transport, Harris decided to dispatch as many Huns, as he liked to call Germans, as possible. Always following orders, of course, and apparently taking advantage of the confusion at the top, rewarding him in due course for not following orders. In a memo requested by Churchill, Harris points out what Bomber Command had done to date, the date being 28 June 1942. Correctly he refers to the mine-laying operations, the attacks on German naval and commercial shipping with the resulting reduction in German navy operations in the Atlantic, the deployment of German nightfighters, flak guns, and 3 million men to combat the RAF bombers, the destruction of industries in the German towns attacked, and the destruction of French factories working for the German war effort. The most interesting part of the memo regards the recognition that transport is one of Germany's "most pressing problems."[129] But he gives scant information on past and planned attacks on this target system.

German reaction and reprisals to the first mass area raids was swift but rather anemic. The Luftwaffe had no strength in the west. It launched small raids on British places which had little or no defenses. In late April and early May 1942 Exeter, Norwich, and York were bombed. In the second raid on Exeter three hundred civilians were killed. After Rostock, Bath was hit, but then again the Luftwaffe losses were too high. What has been called the (German) Baedeker Raids were abandoned. Britain could sleep quietly again.

On 22 September 1942 the RAF staff issued a report entitled "The Development and Employment of the Heavy Bomber Force."[130] By deduction of the results of the survey done by Professor Zuckerman and including the Coventry raid, the authors of this blueprint for applying "attack on morale" on the German civilians, came to the following conclusions:

> 42 German towns, each with 100,000 inhabitants or more, must be destroyed.
> The 42 towns are inhabited by 15 million people.
> One ton of bombs is required for each 800 people.
> Each town must be attacked once per month over a six month period.
> 4,000 bombers will be required to perform this task.
> Allowing for 25 percent of bombers hitting the target, 75,000 tons of explosives will have to be dropped monthly.
> At the end of this period the towns will be destroyed beyond recovery.
> Germany will cease to function both militarily and on a civilian level.
> The people will rebel.

The paper endorsed the attack on morale as the weakest point in the German war machine, but thoughtfully admits in paragraph four that "attack on morale is not a matter of pure killing."—(Would the Germans have known that, it would have given them great comfort.)—At the end of paragraph four the air staff justified their recommendations by referring to the results obtained in "the small wars in which the Air Force has been continuously engaged."

The paper states the war could be over in six months. No landings on the Continent would be needed. Any other implications about the Russians moving into Europe or the Americans coming to help is not mentioned but must have been in the minds of the politicians.

This paper proves many historians incorrect who blame Harris for the ensuing slaughter. It was the air staff headed by its chief of staff Sir Charles Portal who issued the blueprint. Portal is on record as having informed Churchill et al that the enemy would surrender after six months of the proposed intensive attacks.[131] True to the Douhet/Trenchard Doctrine, the war could be won with no greater effort than giving the RAF 4,000 bombers and 450,000 tons of bombs. Contrary to Douhet, there was no mention of using poison gas. Nor is there mention in the report of how many planes would not return for their next sortie, nor how many people would be left in the leveled towns to defy Hitler and his Gestapo.

The report was passed around and since it had Lord Cherwell's memo to Churchill as its father, Tizard, Cherwell's rival, published a memo in which he voiced disagreement. It was not on humanitarian grounds that he disagreed, rather the arithmetic was faulty.[132] A further point made was that in late 1941 and early 1942 Bomber Command had lost as many air crew as it had killed Germans.[133] The body count had resulted in +/- zero.

By 14 October 1942 the air staff issued another paper which stated in its opening paragraph that now six thousand bombers, including the American bomber fleet, could reduce resistance to an Allied landing in Western Europe to the point where such landing would succeed.[134] The target date for the landing is shown as 1944. Suddenly the masters of the air admitted by implication that cracking morale, which was still the main objective, would not end the war after all.

The fight for allocating resources continued. The British army and navy pointed out that transporting the raw materials and overseas produced planes, the gasoline, and the bombs to Britain would take enough personnel to man four army divisions.[135] To transport the 1¼ million tons of 100 octane aviation fuel would take 154 tanker loads away from the fuel supply coming by convoys to Britain.[136]

The most significant document for what bombing was meant to be was sent to the War Cabinet from the chiefs of staff committee on 3 November 1942 under file C.O.S. (42) 379 (O).[137] It was signed C.P. leaving little doubt the author was Charles Portal. The fourteen page script lists the old arguments that the German war industry must be destroyed. The number of German cities had been increased to fifty-eight and the tonnages to be dropped were now 90,000 tons per month by December 1944. This was written in November 1942. By earlier estimates of 1942 the bombing campaign was to end the war in six months.

The most brutal aspect of the document is paragraph seventeen: "Civilian casualties are estimated about 900,000 killed and 1,000,000 seriously wounded." Twenty-five million Germans would be rendered homeless, i.e. about 25 percent of the German population at the time. The document apparently passed without any comment on the human losses through the chiefs of staff and through the Cabinet. This aspect of killing civilians continued with Portal until after the war when he declared the then known number of 600,000 killed as incidental losses in an address to Winchester College in late 1945.[138]

Evaluating the viscount's statements and deductions one can find some strange inconsistencies in his November 1942 submission:

> Appendix I: The 58 German towns house 17.5 million people.
> Paragraph 17: 25 million Germans would be dehoused.

Were the Allied bombers to attack more than the fifty-eight towns? Even assuming that the towns would be 100 percent destroyed, the figures do not add up.

In paragraph six he says that the German bombing attacks were examples of inferior techniques, not well planned and effected only a fraction of the damage per ton of bomb compared with what can be done now.

Even if one disregards the British propaganda reports of

the German area raids meant for United States consumption, one must recognize the ferocity of the Luftwaffe bombings of British civilians. Now the RAF was to do even better.

The document was a position paper for the RAF for the forthcoming Casablanca Conference. It admitted by inference the failure to date of the theory that Germany could be bombed into submission. It proposed an even more devastating campaign to reach the original goal. It also showed the British position vis-a-vis the American ally.

At the Washington Conference of the chiefs of staff in January 1942 it had been decided to carry out a combined USAAF/RAF strategic bombing campaign against Germany.

By August 1942 the U.S. Eighth Army Air Force had established itself in Britain and on 17 August had started bombing occupied France, with the railway yards at Rouen the first target. French civilian losses were 140 killed and 200 wounded.[139] The basic U.S. air strategy was founded on daylight precision raids flown by bomber formations which could defend themselves against enemy fighters. The B-17 and B-24 bombers had heavy defensive armament and losses over Western European targets were as small as expected. It was strict U.S. policy that civilian lives should not be targeted.

The blueprint for American operations was the Air War Plans Division AWPD-1 document. It spelled out the resources needed and the main targets. Under paragraph 4.a.(1) it listed "Possible Lines of Action":[140]

a-Disruption of a major portion of the electric power
    system of Germany
b-Disruption of the German transportation system
c-Destruction of the German oil and petroleum system
d-Undermining of German morale by air attack of civil
    concentrations

To leave no doubt what the authors meant by item d above they had said in paragraph 3.d: "As German morale begins to crack, area bombing of civil concentrations may be effective." Such were the recommendations. Nobody can have any argument with items a to c above. As regards paragraphs 3.d and 4.a.(1).d one may ask in general whatever happened to the chivalrous American attitude never to hit a man when he is down and, in particular, how do these paragraphs correspond with Roosevelt's telegram of 1 September 1939?

In August 1942 Roosevelt had requested an update of the plan and the result became AWPD-42. It specified 154 targets to be destroyed and keep destroyed. Airplane assembly plants, aluminum, and magnesium had been added to the original plan. A total of 6,834 U.S. bombers stationed in the United Kingdom and the Near East would be required to fly a total of 66,045 sorties. As in the Air Ministry papers, victory was forecast six months after the plan was started.

1943: THE BOMBERS ARE COMING

Next followed the Casablanca Conference in January 1943. Roosevelt and all his senior army and navy officers were there, including General Spaatz, the commander of the Eighth USAAF. Churchill was there with Portal, among others, but Harris was not invited. The conference which was about planning general operations, had two special aspects which affected German morale. During a press conference Roosevelt purposely or inadvertently said that the Axis Powers would have to surrender unconditionally. This put wind into the sails of Goebbels who was whipping up German morale in light of the recent military setbacks everywhere. The other aspect was the "Combined Chiefs of Staff Directive for the Bomber Offensive from the United Kingdom" of 21 January 1943 in which it was clearly established that the primary objective of the U.S. and British bomber fleets would be the progressive destruction and dislocation of the German military, industrial, and economic system and the undermining of the morale of the German people where their capacity for armed resistance was fatally weakened.[141]

The American bomber leaders, such as Spaatz, Eaker, and Doolittle followed these instructions. They had the B-17 and B-24 bombers fly in tight formations by day over Europe, identify the strategic targets, and unload. The Americans were under pressure from the British to participate in the night area bombing campaign. But from the top of the USAAF leadership down this request was declined and frowned upon for mostly military, but also humane reasons.

For RAF Bomber Command the Casablanca Directive made no change. Harris in his unique position interpreted it that he had to continue to hit German industrial targets and since they were, in his opinion, in or near big cities, he would continue with area attacks. His attitude is best shown by his own statements, before and after the conference:

> To destroy something you have to destroy everything.
> The destruction of factories could be regarded as a bonus.
> The aiming points were usually right in the centre of the town.[142]
> In spite of all that happened at Hamburg [where 50,000 civilians died], bombing proved a comparatively humane method.[143]
> I kill thousands of people every night. [To a police officer who had admonished him that his speeding might kill somebody.][144]
> In normal warfare practise, in besieged cities, if they did not surrender, every living thing in them was in the end put to the sword.[145]

The latter statement puts Harris into the category of field commanders of the Middle Ages. Yet Harris first of all believed that area bombing with him in charge would end the war. He had the ear and encouragement of Churchill whom he often visited at Chequers, the prime minister's country home not far from High Wycombe, the Bomber Command headquarters. And lastly, Portal was all for area bombing, although, like a weather vane, he changed direction a few times, depending on the political winds.

Under the circumstances, the RAF bomber offensive continued at night. When Harris took over in February 1942 he laid on missions with up to 120 mostly medium-size bombers. Many cities in the Ruhr and at the German coast were bombed. Next, the fire-raising technique was developed because it was easier to burn a city than to blow it up.[146] The Germans considered the Lübeck and Rostock raids as the first real terror raids. Forces of 234 and 161 aircraft were sent to Lübeck and Rostock respectively. Since they were harbor cities, they were easy to find and Harris sunned himself in the success of the missions. The one-thousand bomber raid on Cologne on 30-31 May 1942 was a bit of a stunt because Harris had to borrow planes from Coastal Command and the training units to rake up that number. Despite the references to this raid in the Portal paper discussed earlier, the results were much smaller than the RAF thought. Nevertheless, when news reached Göring of the damage and the number of aircraft involved, he refused to believe that such a raid could be flown. The next one-thousand bomber raids on Essen and Bremen were failures because, as before, the targets could not be identified. Instead the bombers unloaded all over the countryside.

But the means of Bomber Command were improving. More airplanes and better navigational equipment came into action. From the erratic bombing raids in 1940-41 the missions turned into the beginning of the bomber offensive against Germany as described by Webster and Frankland.

Upon Portal's insistence and against Harris's advice, a pathfinder force was established. Using the OBOE and H2S navigational equipment it began to locate the target cities with great accuracy.

In accordance with Churchill's instructions of 31 October 1940 to consider the morale of the Italian people a "target," bombers were dispatched in still small but ever increasing numbers to north Italian cities from October 1942 onward. Cities like Genoa, Turin, Milan, and La Spezia were hit. Industrial damage and civilian losses were the same as in Germany. Losses to the bombers were smaller because the Italians had no nightfighters and were not as far advanced as the Germans in their radar systems. The flight paths led over Vichy France which had no air force to defend its neutrality. Harris says that the effect on Italian morale was enormous. About 300,000 people, half the population of Turin, fled the city after the second attack.[147]

Despite the Portal paper to the Cabinet outlining how Germany alone would be attacked, demands on Bomber Command to attack other targets continued. The German U-boat campaign was still in full swing and on 14 January 1943 an order was issued, signed by Bottomley, to area bomb the submarine bases in the French Atlantic ports.[148] The German navy had built bombproof pens for the U-boats so no damage occurred to them. But the cities around the pens were devastated and many innocent Frenchmen were killed. Earlier the destruction of three German submarines under construction at Le Trait caused the death of two hundred Frenchmen working on them.[149] Lorient took the brunt of these raids, followed by St. Nazaire.

On the German front, Bomber Command penetrated deeper into the Reich. Berlin, many flying hours away from the bases in Great Britain, became a regular target. With the fast new Mosquito bomber even a daylight raid was launched to delay a Nazi rally in which Göring and Goebbels were speaking. The German radio and newsreel reported glowingly on the speeches, but said nothing about the interference caused by the bombers. Of the many improvements which were coming to Bomber Command, the Mosquito bomber must be considered one of the most significant.

When rearmament started in the early 1930s the RAF did not wish to depend alone on the heavy bomber to carry out the Trenchard Doctrine. Orders went out to the De Havilland factory to develop a small bomber which would be faster than any enemy fighter and could evade them by flying higher. The outcome was a plywood covered plane, a masterpiece of British engineering. The plane could travel as fast as 415 miles per hour at 39,000 feet. Only the late model German FW-190 fighters could match the speed, but not the service ceiling. The Me-109 could not match the Mosquito at all and only the Me-262, the first operational jet fighter, could perform better in all respects than the Mosquito. This new bomber could carry 4,000 pounds of bombs, only a quarter of a Lancaster load, but its aim was 100 percent accurate most of the time. The Butt Report had shown how inaccurately the four-engine bombers placed their bombs.

With the help of the OBOE system, a Mosquito could place its load within three hundred feet of the target. When the Danish Resistance requested destruction of the Gestapo headquarters in Copenhagen, the Mosquitos did the precision job with minimal damage to the surrounding area. Similarly, they hit a diesel engine factory in Copenhagen on 27 January 1943 with the loss of only one aircraft. Mosquitos mined the narrow Kiel canal causing problems in supplying the northern end of the Russian front and the passage of ore ships coming from Sweden. Another successful raid was flown on 27 May 1943 at dusk when eight Mosquitos destroyed 90 percent of the Zeiss Works at Jena and, most notably, killed only seven persons.[150] In the end Bomber Command had ten squadrons of Mosquitos and used them effectively for precision, diversion, and nuisance raids.

In other words, the RAF had a tool from mid-1942 onward that allowed them to hit what they wanted. Harris gives scant credit to the capabilities of this revolutionary aircraft in his "Dispatch on War Operations," causing the air staff in their comments on the dispatch to rectify that fact.[151] The question arises, why was Bomber Command not equipped with more Mosquitos to perform a precision strategic campaign which would have destroyed German industry without the heinous losses of innocent civilians? Certainly the cost to the British war effort would have been much less. Since accuracy of bombing was better, fewer bombs would have been required. A Mosquito had two air crew, a Lancaster seven; the Mosquito was a wood covered plane, the four-engine bombers needed scarce aluminum; radar signals are absorbed by wood but reflected by metal. Harris defended his neglect of the Mosquito bombers with statements that many more Mosquitos would have been needed to deliver the same loads as the heavies.[152] Had he ever considered the greater accuracy and smaller waste of bombs?

By mid-February 1943 Bomber Command had done its duty on Lorient, having dropped four thousand tons of bombs and completely destroyed the city. St. Nazaire's turn came by the end of the month. It was attacked several times until April at which time it was realized that the U-boats could not be touched in their pens and that the only effect of the bombing was French civilian losses.

Despite Pathfinders, OBOE, and H2S, the accuracy of bombing sometimes still left a lot to be desired; fortunately for those who thereby escaped the bombs. On 3-4 March 1943, 417 bombers were dispatched to raid Hamburg. The Pathfinders made a mistake and the town of Wedel, thirteen miles from Hamburg, was destroyed instead.[153] Hamburg only suffered lightly, presumably because a few bombers did not follow the Pathfinders markings. But following Saundby's musings, there was at least some benefit gained out of a failed mission. Wedel, with an important naval clothing store the only real strategic target, was a field of ruins.

From March till July 1943, Harris tried to wipe out the Ruhr industrial area. Great damage was done to the Krupp Works at Essen and the cities of Dortmund and Duisburg. Civilian losses rose and with them the inadvertent killing of Allied prisoners of war and foreign workers voluntarily or forcibly staying in these towns. Other towns were attacked to keep the German defense spread out. The war was coming closer to Würzburg when Frankfurt, 120 kilometer west, was raided on 10-11 April by five hundred aircraft. Noteworthy raids of the time were the destruction of the Eder and Möhne dams on 16-17 May. A bouncing bomb had been developed to skip over the water until it hit the dam, where it sank and exploded at a set depth. It was a raid of immense bravery by the crews involved. Of the nineteen planes dispatched, eight did not return, putting the raid into the same class as the MAN-Augsburg raid months earlier. Over 1,200 people, again including many foreign workers, drowned in the flood waves rushing down the valleys. But the main damage was consequential because German hydro dams from that time onward were only kept half full, reducing the generation of badly needed power.

Another raid had very tragic consequences. On 15-16 July the Pathfinders missed the Peugeot motor factory at Montbeliard, France, by seven hundred yards causing the bombers to hit the workers' houses instead of the factory; 123 Frenchmen who undoubtedly thought the war was over for them were killed and 336 wounded by their former allies.[154] In a similar raid on the Renault factory at Billancourt in March 1942 the French losses were 367 killed and 341 badly injured.[155]

Including the missions into occupied Western Europe, over 24,000 Bomber Command sorties were flown between early March and end of July 1943 from which over one thousand aircraft did not return.[156] Most of these losses occurred over the Ruhr which caused Harris to call off the attack on the German industrial heartland. The Ruhr continued to function until the end of the war, albeit under tenuous conditions.

The next major operation of Bomber Command was the battle of Hamburg from 24 July to 3 August 1943. It was a full success from Harris's point of view. The battle was fought together with the Eighth USAAF which blasted the city during daytime. The gory details of that operation need not be repeated here. There is ample literature in both English and German which describes how 50,000 civilians died.[157] Four major raids were directed against the city by Bomber Command at night and the Americans flew 252 B-17 sorties in two days. Bomber Command's aiming points were the residential areas, whereas the Eighth USAAF had selected industrial targets. Bomber Command released 10,000 tons of high explosives and incendiaries from over 3,000 aircraft. As a result the second largest German city (1.5 million) was well over 60 percent destroyed, about 50,000 people were killed, and 87 bombers were lost.

The low loss rate for the bombers of about 2.9 percent occurred because "Window" was used for the first time. Millions of small aluminum stripes were thrown from the attacking planes to completely thwart the German radar defense. Speer, the German armament minister, is quoted as saying that a few more raids like the Hamburg one would have forced Germany to surrender. He said that after the war and from many of his pronouncements some historians cannot help getting the impression that he was currying favor with his captors. But the fact remains that it took Hamburg industry only months to return to production, under the circumstances an incredible achievement, thanks mainly to Speer's ingenious talent for organising the German war effort.

There can be no doubt that, had Bomber Command been able to keep up the pace of destroying the principal German cities and keeping them destroyed, the German war effort would have come to a standstill. But there were never enough planes. The piecemeal destruction of the cities allowed the Germans to recover and carry on. If the industries, as listed in the famous memo

No. 22, had been obliterated by precision attacks, it would have been finis Germaniae. One must ask again: Why were there no more Mosquitos produced and employed and why did bombing civilians seem the only solution?

On 17-18 August 1943 Peenemünde, the German rocket research center, located at the Baltic Coast, was attacked by 596 aircraft. A feint raid by other aircraft had drawn the German nightfighters to Berlin. The main raid was a full success and caused many months delay in the start of the rocket campaign.[158] Unfortunately again, of the approximately eight hundred scientists and workers killed, about five hundred were Polish or other foreign workers. Of the attacking aircraft forty were lost, mainly because Berlin is not too far distant and the Luftwaffe realized quickly where the action was. For the first time German nightfighters participated that were equipped with *schräge Musik* (literally, inclined music), cannons that could fire obliquely upward from the fighter. The RAF bombers, when attacked from below, had no defense in that direction.

A few days after Peenemünde, Harris returned to the area bombing technique and tried to tackle Berlin. On 23-24 August, 727 bombers flew to the German capital. Forty did not return, i.e. 7.9 percent, which proved too high a loss rate. The marking had been poor and the raid was a failure. The next two raids on Berlin were equally unsuccessful and Harris abandoned for the time being the battle of Berlin. But other German cities such as Mannheim, Nürnberg, Hannover, and Kassel were severely damaged in the coming months.

Italy was also not forgotten and the northern Italian cities had their share of raids. Churchill had specifically approved Portal's plan of 1 December 1942 which called for 4,000 tons of bombs to be rained on Italian cities. The plan also foresaw a daylight raid on the Palazzo Venezia, Mussolini's home and office.[159] It was realized in London that Italy was never in a position to wage a war against the Western Allies. The situation worsened when Mussolini declared war on the Soviet Union and sent troops to the Eastern Front.

After Italy entered the war in 1940, the Mediterranean had become a major theater of war. The formidable Italian navy, particularly its submarine fleet, was feared by the British. But reverses of military fortunes had gnawed at Italian morale. Although he was a dictator, Mussolini was afraid of his people and did not wish to subject them to hardships. Food rationing was not introduced until 1941 after the first food riots had occurred at Carignola in January of that year.[160] Italy which had only 2.7 percent of the world's manufacturing capacity, continued on a peace basis to keep its population happy. Between January 1940 and April 1943 Italy manufactured only 10,545 aircraft.[161] In the Macchi C-202 it had a first-class fighter, but only 1,500 were ever produced.[162] There was no flak to defend the cities and only a rudimentary civil defense organization.

The RAF had no problems in attacking Italian cities by day or night. Southern Italian cities were bombarded from Egypt and Malta. Bomber Command stationed in the United Kingdom flew 1,800 sorties to northern Italian cities and dropped about 3,300 tons of bombs. Losses were sixty-six aircraft or 3.7 percent, well within the 5 percent rate accepted by Harris.[163] By September 1943 the raids had reduced Italian industrial production by 60 percent.[164] About 10,000 Italians had been killed in the bombing campaign between June 1940 and September 1943.[165] Distribution of goods had broken down in southern Italy. Professor Zuckerman, as advisor to Air Marshal Tedder, who was in charge of the U.S. Northwest African Air Forces and the RAF Mediterranean Air Command, after careful study had recommended that an all-out attack on the Italian railway system would facilitate the Allied landings in Italy. Whereas in the north, Harris blasted the industrial cities, in the south Tedder immobilized the transport system. In early September 1943, after the Allies had successfully landed, Mussolini was deposed by his own party and the king. Marshal Badoglio, his successor, sued for peace and Italy was out of the war. Depending on who one believes, it was either the breakdown of morale due to the bombing in the north or the collapse of infrastructure in the south that caused Italy's quest for peace. Harris could breath easier because one theater of war for Bomber Command had ceased to exist. But Zuckerman had proven what an attack on transport could do to assist an amphibious landing.

The Eighth U.S. Army Air Force had continued in the meantime to fly its missions over the occupied countries. After the first raid, which targeted the railway installations of Rouen, the B-17s and B-24s were sent over an increasing number of targets in Western Europe. The U.S. bomber doctrine called for destroying strategic targets. Since the aircraft had to fly high, they saturated them with high-explosive bombs. The planes always flew in tight formations, identified their aims, and unloaded what we called the bomb carpet. Accuracy was remarkable. The USAAF could drop 70 percent of their bombs within one hundred feet of the aiming point.[166] Morale was not on the U.S. target roster—at least not yet. The losses to the bombers were small on these missions. Luftflotte 3, still commanded by Field Marshal Sperrle and stationed in France, had only 328 fighters. Most Luftwaffe dayfighters (764) were in Russia and the nightfighters (456) were stationed mostly in northwestern Germany to combat the night bombers.[167]

The Americans occupied seventy-seven air bases in the United Kingdom and had all of Northern Ireland for themselves. Like Iceland, the air bases in Northern Ireland were taken over from the British before the United States entered the war. In neither case was an official announcement made, leaving the possibility that German forces would attack neutral U.S. installations.

The U.S. bombing campaign followed the Casablanca Directive and the Pointblank Directive issued on 14 May 1943. The former was seemingly an effort of the staffs of both air forces. The latter, although it was purported to have the approval of British experts, had been produced by "Operations Analysts consisting of eminent United States experts."[168] It was a lengthy document that reiterated the parameters of the bombing war and updated the plan of action. It included what RAF Bomber Command was to do and confirmed its attack on morale. Interestingly, Harris, in his "Dispatch on War Operations," does not list this document as having been received.

The document outlines in detail which targets the USAAF would destroy and lists the required resources to do so. It lists the U.S. bomber fleet strength as 944 heavy bombers in June 1943 and 2,702 by March 1944. Based on the experience in the three months before the directive was issued, 100 bombers were necessary to destroy a target placed in a 1,000-foot radius. Tight formations were required to ward off the German fighters. U.S. fighter escort is mentioned, but not clearly defined. One target system stands out as excluded compared with the earlier AWPD-1 and AWPD-42 documents—morale.

Although the Eighth USAAF participated in the raids on Hamburg in July/August 1943, their attacks on shipyards and factories resulted in less than 1 percent of the total Hamburg civilian losses.[169] For all their valor, the American bomber crews paid dearly when it came to deep penetration raids in daylight. On 17 August 1943 the Schweinfurt ball-bearing factories and the fighter factories at Regensburg were the targets. The targets were damaged, but of the 376 planes dispatched, 60 did not return, and many of the ones that did make it home were beyond repair. It was an expensive lesson as 550 air crew were either killed or captured.[170] One plane fell in a built-up area of Würzburg, killing the crew but causing no losses among the inhabitants. Schweinfurt, located only forty kilometers northeast of Würzburg, brought the bombing war closer to us and we hurried to the air-raid shelters from then on whenever a daytime alarm was sounded. Before that nobody had paid much attention.

These two raids brought to an end the U.S. doctrine of self-defending bomber formations. It is not reported, but the RAF bomber commanders must have said: "We told you so." What was badly needed was a long-range fighter plane that could accompany the bombers on their daytime missions and ward off the increasing number of German fighters. The Pointblank Directive indicated that the German fighter defense might number three thousand planes by 1943. The directive also stressed as one of the principal targets the German aircraft industry. This implied but did not spell out in so many words that air superiority was the key to the success of the directive. The experts should have read Douhet's book. As it turned out German fighter numbers increased dramatically. In 1943 over nine thousand single-engine fighters were produced.[171]

To keep fighting, the American air force leaders returned to the less defended targets in the occupied countries. But here a new problem arose. Bombing marshalling yards, U-boat pens, and factories, even with the best intentions, caused losses among the friendly populations. The workers were warned to stay away from these places. But here again, the experts disregarded the realities of life. Twenty-five thousand Frenchmen worked for the maintenance of the German submarines in the French Atlantic ports. The factories of Phillips in Eindhoven, Holland, and the factories of Schneider Creusot, Peugeot, and Renault in France employed thousands more. The men had to work to make a living. They could stay away a few days, but not extended periods in anticipation of a raid which might or might not come. Although, no doubt, the occupied nations wished a demise of the German occupiers, once their places of work were destroyed so was their livelihood. As a result, there were posters printed in France which showed Roosevelt as "assassin."[172] Two major raids were on Rotterdam on 31 March 1943, where 400 were killed and on Antwerp on 6 April 1943, with 2,000 dead. Many other Western European cities were attacked. Some of these raids did real damage and at least engaged the German fighters and flak. From 1943 onward the Eighth USAAF could deliver substantial tonnages of bombs. In 1942 it was mostly France which received the loads; 1,681 tons or 96 percent of the total. In 1943 Germany received 27,152 tons, France 17,977, Belgium 1,162, Norway 1,497, and Poland 358.[173] But as we shall see later, this was only the beginning. The raids were all purportedly strategic to damage the German war effort and above all of precision nature. Unfortunately they also caused great losses among innocent people in the occupied territories.

Despite the AWPD-42 listing morale as a recognised German target, there was much soul-searching among the U.S. air force leaders. From their own ethical point of view, they were not only concerned about killing women and children, they also had to look over their shoulders toward American public opinion. Their British counterparts did not have that second problem because, despite all the protestations that there was no control, the UK government had a firm grip on what was published. Last but not least, Lord Beaverbrook, a member of the Cabinet, owned a sizeable number of British newspapers.

However there were U.S. planes, bombs, and crews sitting in Britain to fight the enemy. On 10 October 1943, after some deliberations, the Eighth flew its first area attack. The center of the city of Münster was the aiming point. This raid set the precedent for employing the U.S. bombers in bad weather, which was now approaching, by using airborne radar. The device was still very inaccurate, but that did not matter as long as it identified a major city area.

The Eighth bombarded many targets in 1943 with missions to such distant places as southern Norway, East Prussia, and southern France.[174] The U.S. bombers based in Britain were by now not the only U.S. force that could attack the Germans and their remaining Allies. Instead of being stationed in the British mandates of Palestine and Trans Jordan, as envisaged in AWPD-42, a considerable number of bombers were now located in Algeria, Libya, and Tunis, much closer to potential targets. It was the Northwest African Air Force (NWAAF) under General Spaatz. Command of the Eighth USAAF had been turned over to General Doolittle. Spaatz's bombers provided mostly tactical support for the invasion of Sicily and mainland Italy.

As the Allies moved up the Italian peninsula, the NWAAF became the Twelfth USAAF, continuing its tactical role. Spaatz had been transferred back to Britain as the equivalent to Air Marshal Portal, to be in charge of all European Theater USAAF operations. General Eaker was put in charge of the Twelfth and under him was also placed the newly created Fifteenth USAAF, consisting mostly of heavy bombers and intended to conduct strategic warfare. Its base became Foggia northwest of Bari, Italy, its main supply port.

The designated targets of the new bomber fleet were in southern Germany and the Balkans. There had been two marginally successful raids against the Ploesti/Romanian oil fields on 12 June 1942 and 1 August 1943. There was damage but the losses were severe. Fifty percent of the bombers on the first raid and 33 percent on the second raid did not come home.

The air war against the Balkan allies of Hitler started in November 1943. If, as some strategists tried to prove, attack on morale had knocked Italy out of the war, it was now time to try the same treatment on the Bulgarians, Romanians, Hungarians, and any government and people who fought on Germany's side against the USSR and the Western Allies. On 27 February 1944, General Norstad, director of operations for the Mediterranean Allied Air Forces, issued a bombing directive for U.S. and RAF forces to attack Bulgarian cities, Budapest, and Bucharest. Precautions were to be taken to avoid the appearance of terror raids.[175]

On 14 November 1943, the Fifteenth USAAF made its maiden major strategic raid with ninety-one B-25 medium bombers attacking Sofia, the Bulgarian capital. It was the first of many devastating raids on the major cities of the Balkan countries.

1944: BOMBING UNRESTRICTED

The year 1944 started with the Luftwaffe trying to retaliate against Britain and the ceaseless pounding Bomber Command and the USAAF were enacting on Germany and on the strategic targets in German-occupied territories. From the badly depleted bomber forces in Russia several squadrons were moved to the Channel coast to begin a renewed attack on London on 21 January. It was to be a repeat of the Baedeker Raids of 1942. The effectiveness of the campaign was small but the propaganda value on both sides considerable. German reports played up the successes and British media called for more destruction in Germany to eliminate the Luftwaffe once and for all.

The Baby Blitz, as history has been calling the feeble Luftwaffe bombing effort in 1944, lasted until 29 May 1944. The man in charge was the young Luftwaffe General Peltz, who had been personally picked by Hitler for his élan. He had Göring monitoring him at his headquarters in France. But the Reichsmarshal soon disappeared when the results were not as expected. Peltz, who also had Sperrle as his superior, had been given 447 twin-engine bombers of Luftflotte 3, which made twelve attacks on London and the southern counties.[176] A total of two thousand tons of high explosives and incendiaries were dropped and caused some damage and apprehension. Interestingly, many of Harris's area-bombing tactics were employed, but the two thousand tons were paltry in comparison with what the RAF and the Eighth USAAF delivered to Germany in the same timespan. RAF Fighter Command's nightfighters, together with the improved antiaircraft defense, ruled the air over southern England. Over two hundred of Peltz's bombers did not return. Although he had received some reinforcements, this campaign, like the original Blitz and the Baedeker Raids, faltered and had to be abandoned because of unsustainable losses. The order of battle of Luftflotte 3 had been reduced to 144 bombers. For the third time proof had been brought that the Luftwaffe was not a strategic weapon. Hitler, Göring, and the Luftwaffe staff took the lesson and practically abandoned strategic bombing, a type of warfare they had never understood or mastered, as compared with the Trenchard-trained Britons and the Americans who imitated them later. German planning now concentrated on the defense of the Reich and, despite the damage to many aircraft factories, the production of fighters soared to unprecedented heights.

Under Speer, fighter production was standardized, materials were allotted, and the total war syndrome finally caught up with German industry by introducing double shifting. Single-engine fighter production rose to 25,800 by the end of 1944, a figure which was not expected by the Allied war planners.[177]

While Peltz's bombers tried to make an impression, Harris initiated his biggest and costliest campaign of the war. The battle of Berlin had been started on 18-19 November 1943 when 440 Lancasters were dispatched. It was only a limited success because the city was covered by clouds, its location was beyond the range of OBOE, and the Pathfinders had made scattered markings. The H2S device did not work well on an indistinguishable inland target like Berlin. The raids in the following months suffered from the same conditions until they were abandoned on 24-25 March 1944, when 811 four-engine Lancasters and Halifaxes Mark III dispatched suffered a loss rate of 8.9 percent. A total of sixteen missions were flown to Berlin ranging in dispatched aircraft from twenty-two Lancasters providing a spoof raid for the assault on nearby Magdeburg on 21-22 January 1944 to the 811 mentioned above. Most raids involved 500 to 700 bombers. Despite the difficulties, there was damage in the city. Government buildings, industrial plants, the railway system, and the Kaiser Wilhelm Gedächtniskirche on Kurfürstendam, still visible today as a monument against area bombing, were damaged or destroyed. During the battle 8,120 bombers dropped about 30,000 tons of high explosives and incendiaries and killed about 10,000 people against a loss of 493 aircraft.[178]

Harris, who was very outspoken against panacea targets such as oil, ball-bearings, molybdenum, etc., because of the difficulties in finding them and the losses incurred, blissfully convinced Churchill and Portal in letters in November and December 1943, before and during the raids, that wrecking Berlin from end to end would cost Bomber Command 400 to 500 planes, but would cost Germany the war. Surrender would be inevitable by 1 April 1944.[179] The battle of Berlin must be considered one of his panacea targets like the Ruhr and others. He was right, panacea target bombing did not make the Germans throw in the towel. Harris's superiors all the way up to Churchill let him continue the area campaign, seemingly convinced that the strategy would eventually work.

While the battle of Berlin raged, many other cities were visited, partly to divert the German defenses and partly because the Air Ministry wanted them attacked to avoid a general recovery of German industry. Harris even laid on a raid on the ball-bearing town of Schweinfurt with 734 sorties on 24-25 February 1944. The Eighth had pummeled the town the day before with 266 B-17s, but this time under long-range fighter escort, probably P-51 Mustangs available since December 1943, to avoid a repeat of the disaster of 17 August 1943. Harris was right, the Schweinfurt raid was not a success.[180] Other cities hit were Leipzig twice, Stuttgart three times, and Frankfurt four times. All of these raids were major operations causing substantial damage but also losses to Bomber Command. The worst raid was on Nürnberg on the moonlit night of 30-31 March 1944 in which 795 bombers participated and 95 were lost, 11.9 percent of the force dispatched. It was a controversial raid, not only because it caused little damage to Nürnberg, but because there was suspicion that the Luftwaffe fighters had been tipped off.[181] Was there a mole at High Wycombe?

During the period of November 1943 to 31 March 1944, the RAF bombers had flown about 29,500 night sorties delivering about 78,500 tons of bombs on targets in Western Europe and losing 1,117 aircraft in the process.[182] In January 1943, during the Baedeker Raids on Britain, the BBC German broadcast had warned us that for every pound dropped by German planes, British bombers would drop one ton.[183] The Baby Blitz had dropped 2,000 tons on Britain in four months. The 78,500 tons dropped by Bomber Command at about the same time do not come anywhere near the figure of 4 million, as extrapolation of this boast would indicate.

Allied planning for storming the shores of Western Europe had taken concrete forms by early 1944. It had become obvious that Germany was not to be defeated with the available bomber forces. Neither the RAF nor the Eighth USAAF had enough resources to bomb German centers continually. The report prepared by the Air Ministry on 22 September 1942, predicting that 4,000 bombers attacking forty-two German towns once per month over a six-month period would cause German surrender did not work out. Bomber Command could not even repeat its most effective raid, the battle of Hamburg. There were about 4,000 bombers in Britain and Italy, but weather, target finding, German defense, and crew problems had not been factored into the optimistic planning of the experts.

The Allied army and navy leaders had, of course, never accepted Bomber Command's predictions. "Overlord," the codename for the Allied landing in France, was pushed onward despite the resources that were spent on the bombing war. There were also political considerations. If Germany collapsed while there were no Western Allied troops on the Continent, the Russians would walk right to the shores of the Atlantic, with nobody to stop them. Age-old Russian designs for an ice-free access to the high seas, and the more recent desire to subject Europe to Bolshevism, would become a reality. Without doubt Churchill must have remembered the predicaments of 1919 when he, as minister of war, tried to stem the Bolshevik tide. Instead of Hitler, there would be Stalin as the master of the Continent.

The army and navy commanders could point to a successful landing in Italy, although thanks to Hitler's Atlantic Wall they could expect considerably more resistance on landing in France. Like the Westwall (the Siegfried Line) the Atlantic Wall was nothing but a hastily constructed string of bunkers and gun emplacements around the major Atlantic ports. The disastrous Dieppe raid had proven their worth, but more so by faulty planning of Combined Operations than by the strength of the fortifications. Many a Canadian soldier paid the ultimate price for this folly. The raid proved that, without a prior bombardment of the shore defense and cutting of lines for reinforcements, a landing was at best doubtful.

After landings in Italy an investigation was launched to evaluate their success. To nobody's surprise it was found that Professor Zuckerman's plan to smash the Italian railway system was the main factor.[184] A similar plan of destruction of coastal defense and railway centers in France and Belgium was submitted to General Eisenhower, by that time the supreme commander of allied forces in Europe and his deputy, Air Marshal Tedder. Both endorsed it wholeheartedly based on the Italian experience. The instruments to carry out these attacks were to be the U.S. and British strategic bombers. But there a long drawn out fight started. The bomber leaders, Harris more than Spaatz, objected violently and listed numerous arguments. The list included the fact that their forces were not trained for precision bombing, that Bomber Command had no experience in the necessary daylight operations, that there would be countless deaths among French and Belgian civilians, and so on. These circles were supported by the Air Ministry, the prime minister and the British Cabinet, including scientists such as Lord Cherwell.

The argument was won by Eisenhower/Tedder and in April 1944 Bomber Command under Harris and the Eighth USAAF under Doolittle were placed under Tedder who issued orders as to which targets were to be destroyed. What followed until 6 June, the date of the Normandy landings, was a successful destruction of the Belgian and French railway systems. Hundreds of raids were flown day and night against railway yards, from Orléans to Lille and as far east as Aachen in

Germany. Despite little Luftwaffe resistance, many raids were as inaccurate as before. One of the first, on 9-10 April on the railway yard of Lille, cost the lives of 456 French people.[185] Two-thirds of the freight cars in the station were destroyed but many bombs fell on nearby houses inhabited by railway personnel. There were other raids that were successful and did not cause any losses.

Zuckerman had been asked prior to the railway campaign to estimate the possible losses to the friendly civilians living near the targets. Based on sixty-nine installations to be hit, his estimate was 12,000 killed and 6,000 wounded.[186] Air Ministry estimates had placed the figure at 40,000 killed and 120,000 wounded. Zuckerman states that actually about 10,000 were killed. This seems a low estimate when compared with the total of 65,000 French civilians alone killed by Allied bombing in the entire Second World War. Perusing the Bomber Command War Diaries one cannot escape the observation that the most effective raids and least costly on civilian casualties were the ones that were carried out by Mosquitos entirely or with Mosquitos as target finders. The campaign was a full success and is credited with preventing German reinforcements from arriving in time at the Normandy beachheads.

Bomber Command had dropped 42,000 tons of bombs on thirty-three assigned targets. The Eighth USAAF had been assigned forty-five targets but attacked only twenty-three, dropping 11,600 tons.[187] The losses to Bomber Command were 203 aircraft out of a total of 8,800 sorties, i.e. 2.3 percent, well within Harris's limit of 5 percent. The referred to source claims that the French and Belgian populations did not resent the losses in lives and chattels. Consulting other sources one must put a big question mark behind that statement.

As made clear to the bombers at the beginning of the campaign, they were free to continue with their raids on Germany when possible. Bomber Command flew about 15,000 such sorties, almost twice the number of sorties flown on the "Overlord" targets. Cities such as Düsseldorf, Karlsruhe, Duisburg, and many others were attacked. On 26-27 April 1944, Harris even launched another panacea raid on Schweinfurt; equally unsuccessful as the previous ones. The

Eighth also continued with daylight raids against German targets but all under heavy fighter protection. The diversion of the bombing from Germany to the railway targets had allowed German industry and defense to recover. The supply of the Wehrmacht in the east and the west still functioned.

Once the Allies had successfully landed on the beaches in Normandy, the bombers were directed to ground support operations. They attacked German troop concentrations, ammunition dumps, gun emplacements, and airfields to prevent airborne reinforcements from arriving. Many a French town was ravaged and places such as Caen, Le Havre, and Lorient afterward looked like bombed-out German towns. Bomber Command again could not always hit its assigned targets for the same reasons and excuses as before. Harris was proved right when he said his command was not equipped and trained to perform tactical work when his bombers dropped their loads on Canadian troops. The worst destruction was rained on the city of Caen. German troops were supposedly entrenched in the city, and together with massive artillery fire were to be pulverized. In actual fact there were few Germans in the city and the pulverizing left as dark a blotch on the RAF as Warsaw and Rotterdam had on the Luftwaffe. Caen was a mistake. It was a tactical raid gone wrong. Yet no media reported on the consequences and details of the raid on 7 July 1944 and subsequent raids on nearby villages. Caen itself received 2,650 tons of bombs[188] and lost 2,000, and perhaps as many as 15,000, citizens.[189] The city was 60 percent destroyed and the rubble posed problems for the advancing Allied troops. British wartime propaganda handled it under the motto: "Do like Dad, keep Mum."[190] In 1962, Würzburg and Caen became partner cities based on the experiences and devastating senseless destruction they both had suffered from American and British bombers. Caen, like Monte Cassino and Wesel, are typical examples of the bombers having gone amuck by being plowed over several times. There were no Wehrmacht units in these places, there could not be because they were piles of rubble after the first raids. As an example, Wesel was raided eleven times by the USAAF and ten times by the RAF.[191]

About half the effort against targets in France, Belgium, and Holland was to support the advancing Allied ground troops. The other half were missions flown against a new German threat to the United Kingdom.

The Allies knew that at Peenemünde flying bombs and rockets were being developed. The successful precision raid of 17-18 August 1943 had delayed their development, but not stopped it. After the raid, research and production was moved to places in Austria, and caves and salt mines in Thuringia. The V-1 flying pilotless bomb was ready for action and let loose on 12 June 1944, six days after the Normandy landings. Intelligence and aerial reconnaissance had identified the launching sites being built earlier. About one hundred of them had been constructed with the help of 40,000 French and other foreign workers. But doubts about the existence and danger of the V-1 had been brought up by Lord Cherwell and thereby delayed instructions to Bomber Command to destroy the launching sites and the adjacent storage facilities. The campaign against them started on 16-17 June after a number of these bombs had landed in southern England. From then on it was a steady effort to wipe out this danger. The Doodle Bomb, as it was called, was a slow-moving pilotless aircraft with a jet engine. Its flight path and destination were programmed into it at the launching base. It carried a one-ton bomb load, had a ceiling of 3,000 meters, and a range of 250 kilometers with a speed of 500 kilometers per hour. By no stretch of the imagination was it a weapon which would turn the fortunes of war. It could be spotted on radar and shot down by antiaircraft guns and by faster fighters. It had a high failure rate, but it also had the advantage of being cheap to produce and was of an unsophisticated design.

Over 30,000 of these flying bombs were produced, mostly by slave labor in underground factories. About 20,000 had been fired between 12 June and 3 September 1944 when Allied ground forces overran all the launching sites in northern France. But launchings continued until 29 March 1945 from sites located further back. Southern England and London in particular were hit about 10,000 times, i.e. 10,000 tons of high explosives came down and 5,864 people were killed.[192] Later

Antwerp became the target after it had been captured by the Allies. About 4,000 V-1s were sent there and together with the later-appearing V-2 killed about 3,000 people.

Next came the V-2 rocket, first launched against London on 8 September 1944. This weapon was completely different from the pilotless aircraft described above. It was a liquid fuel rocket and the forerunner of the ballistic missile. It had a warhead of one ton, a range of 290 kilometers, a speed of 6,000 kilometers per hour and reached an apogee of 97 kilometers. Its flight path was radio controlled. The monster was 14 meters long and 1.5 meters in diameter.[193] The firing required it to be stood up straight on a mobile pad as a launching base. It was a sophisticated machine which could not be intercepted as it traveled faster than sound and could not even be expected in advance, because it literally fell straight from heaven out of the stratosphere. About 6,000 of these rockets were built, but only about 3,000 were fired against enemy targets. London again was the main target, with 1,300 directed against this metropolis. Paris received about nineteen and about 1,200 were aimed against Antwerp to disrupt Allied supplies to the advancing ground forces. Human losses in London were 2,855 killed and 6,268 wounded.[194] Why Paris had to suffer again as at the end of World War I, no doubt adds to the idea of German *Schrecklichkeit*.

The V-weapons had a long history of development and were originally meant as tactical field weapons. After many false starts they obtained Hitler's personal support and were destined to become *Vergeltungswaffen*, weapons of retribution, for the ever-increasing bomb loads coming down on German cities. They did considerable damage and caused grievous harm. They were truly outside any of the conventions of warfare, because they were utterly inaccurate. Their flightpath was known, but the atmospheric conditions in this path could only be guessed at. Together with the technical shortcomings in their performance and the weather conditions at the target area, the V-weapons were a limited success.

Aside from bombing the V-1 launching sites, the Allied military commanders turned a blind eye to the new threat and left the civilians to their own devices to endure the danger. Churchill became concerned about the V-weapons and made plans to use poison gas as retribution for the retribution.[195] The threat to people within the range of these weapons lasted until March 1945. The Wehrmacht purposely set up V-2 launch pads in populated areas like The Hague, Holland. They used the surrounding cities as hostages against bombing the launching installations. The pads in The Hague were to be destroyed by bombers on 3 March 1945, but as so often happened, the real targets escaped unscathed and 800 innocent Dutch citizens were killed. The Dutch foreign minister in London lodged a formal protest with the British foreign minister on 7 March and indicated that the Dutch population was becoming very "anti-Allies" as a result of continued inaccurate bombing.[196]

On 20 July 1944 there was a remote chance that the fighting, bombing, and killing could be stopped. A group of German officers made an attempt on Hitler's life. It failed. The courageous and patriotic conspirators paid with their lives. Through international channels they had solicited the support of the Western Allies. They were ignored. Roosevelt's unconditional surrender order seemingly included all Germans, pro and contra Nazis. The irony is that if area bombing was to cause the Germans to force their government's hand, the movement needed leaders. Here there were potential leaders risking their lives and their honor. All resistance and partisan movements in German-occupied territories received Allied and Soviet support. But in Germany the conspirators not only had to struggle against their internal enemies, but against their external ones as well.

The aerial campaign to make the Germans rebel continued and increased to Armageddon proportions. The bombing not only cost hundreds of thousands of German lives, it also cost the lives of many young Allied airmen. The failure of the Western Allies to support the German resistance movement and the failure to recognize a chance to make morale bombing pay through this support has, to the best of my knowledge, never been investigated by any historian. There is no limit in hypothetical human and material savings that would have occurred had the war ended shortly after 20 July 1944.

Würzburg certainly would not have come up for destruction at High Wycombe meetings.

The bomber commanders were given their freedom again from SHAEF in mid-September. The day-to-day tactical bombing was to be continued by the British and American tactical air fleets which had been assigned from the beginning of Overlord to the invasion forces. They were comprised mostly of fighters and medium bombers. On 21 September, Harris wrote a letter addressed to "Dear General of the Army", i.e. Eisenhower, in which he buttered up to Ike saying how proud he and Bomber Command had been to serve under SHAEF and thanked him for the leadership. Back came a letter addressed to "Dear Bert," i.e. Harris, calling him a great soldier and man.[197] Seemingly all differences of opinion about using Bomber Command and the Eighth USAAF, as voiced by Spaatz and Harris in January 1944, were forgotten. The bomber chiefs had heeled and nobody could argue with the success.[198]

While the bombing of strategic and tactical targets went on in northwestern Europe, the Fifteenth USAAF under General Eaker based in Foggia, Italy, continued the campaign to demoralize the people of the Balkan states. Bulgaria, which had never formally declared war on the USSR, suffered numerous raids. A total of 40,000 bombs fell on that country killing 1,720 citizens.[199] Sofia, bombed on 14 November 1943, was further raided on 10 January 1944 by 143 B-17s, and the following night by 44 RAF Wellingtons. Raids continued, culminating in a raid by 300 heavy U.S. bombers on 4 April 1944, when 1,400 railroad cars were destroyed. But the majority of the bombs fell on Sofia itself.[200] Bulgaria was invaded by the Red Army in September 1944 and shortly thereafter changed sides and fought the Wehrmacht on the side of the USSR.

Similar raids with even bigger losses to civilian lives were flown against Bucharest and Budapest. Bucharest was attacked eighteen times killing 4,111 civilians.[201] The twenty-seven attacks on the Ploesti oil fields cost 700 lives. In all about 7,000 Romanians were killed by Allied bombs.

American bombing policy had changed. The main target had become the civilian population and any damage to strategic targets was a bonus. Whereas only a year before the

American leaders had scoffed at this inhuman British attitude, they now adopted it themselves. After all, morale bombing had been part of the AWPD-42 plan. The people in the Balkan cities did not react as predicted. Whereas before the bombings there was a sympathetic undercurrent for the Allies among the populations, fed by the Voice of America and BBC propaganda, there now was a hostile feeling and the Americans and the British were called hypocrites. It was the same as had happened in France. Why was it necessary to kill friendly civilians? Why this ruthless smashing of cities? The Russians made big propaganda gains out of this by pointing out that their air force was only being employed to attack tactical targets and those only with precision. The Russians painted themselves as liberators in general and from the capitalist bombers in particular. Just the same, the USSR ground forces benefited greatly from the destruction of the transport system. By August 1944 Romania was out of the Axis camp, not because of the bombing of its civilians, but because Soviet troops had overrun the country.

Hungary was bombed heavily by the Fifteenth USAAF and the RAF from April to November 1944. In twenty-nine air raids on Budapest and its suburbs, over 7,000 Hungarians were killed.[202] Hungary also was knocked out of the war, not by bombs but in February 1945 by the Red Army.

The Balkan campaign of the Allied air fleets has been given little publicity. It was devastating, but small compared with what happened in Germany. Similarly, little is known about what bomber actions happened over Italy after its surrender in September 1943. Neither the postwar British nor the U.S. Bombing Surveys deal with the raids on Italian cities. The Fifteenth USAAF attacked Rome, Naples, Milan, and many other cities. An estimated total of 50,000 Italian civilians were killed by Allied bombs until the fighting in Italy stopped in February 1945.[203] The figure includes 500 Italians who had taken refuge in the papal residence of Castel Gandolfo outside Rome, a place internationally recognised as territory of the Vatican, a neutral state.[204]

An interesting feature of the American bombing campaign in Europe were the shuttle raids. The bombers raiding the aircraft factories at Regensburg on 17 August 1943 had started from Great Britain and landed after the raid in North Africa. This way they could avoid the concentrations of German fighters over northwest Germany and Holland on the way home. On the return trip the bombers could attack targets close to the North African bases and be better maneuverable when they faced the fighters again. A similar plan was to be implemented to attack targets in eastern Germany by running shuttle raids between USAAF bases in Britain and Italy and Poltava, a city near Kiev in Ukraine. This worked until 21 June 1944. The Luftwaffe had reconnaissance planes follow the bombers and when during the night of 21-22 June seventy-three B-17s were parked at Poltava, German bombers dropped 110 tons of bombs on them and destroyed forty-seven.[205] About 200 He-111s and Ju-88s had carried out the raid.[206] Had the Allies followed Douhet's theories and achieved complete air superiority, the shuttle raids would have worked.

From summer 1944 onward, the skies over Germany were full of the contrails of the high-flying U.S. bomber formations during daytime and full of the drone of the British bombers by night.

By summer 1944 the attitude of senior USAAF officers had changed completely. In 1943 General Arnold had already espoused the British theory that killing civilians will make the survivors force their government's hands.[207] The source lists the qualms many senior officers expressed in performing and ordering this kind of warfare. The American leaders were very well aware that they were approaching a public relations problem. The British, with the help of German propaganda, were pilloried all over Europe as ruthless killers. Any historian who extols French, Belgian, or Dutch understanding for the bombing of their citizens and their homes must have talked to the wrong people. Now the Americans, as had already happened in the Balkans, were falling into this same category. The public, both in Britain and the United States, was told by the "free" press that only military installations were being targeted. American public opinion and ethics could not have it any other way. But the bombers being frustrated in their promise to win German surrender singlehandedly could see that their methods did not work. Why the Americans who had seen the British approach not yield any results after years of tremendous efforts and losses had to join in morale bombing is difficult to fathom. Considering that the American military has always been under the tight scrutiny of the American public, they had the additional task of deceiving their own citizens.

There was a great exchange of letters, opinions, and proposals on how to win the war from the air. These discussions involved military leaders from the president down to Doolittle and Eaker, the commanders of the Eighth and Fifteenth USAAF respectively. In the final analysis it transpired that Roosevelt accepted terrorizing enemy civilians,[208] that Arnold would not want to conduct the air war without it, and that Spaatz accepted it, but hid behind Eisenhower who approved anything that would finish the war quickly.[209] They all agreed that it was not a good American attitude. It had to be hidden from the public, but hopefully the end would justify the means.

Allied intelligence networks must have had their agents in the attacked cities. Was it not reported to the planners of the bombing operations that there was never an incident of rebellion after a heavy raid? The people took the pounding docilely with few outbreaks of emotion. My own emotions and experiences at Würzburg were certainly along these lines. If one believes Goebbels's propaganda, there was even hostile reaction towards people who complained. A week after the heavy RAF raid on Bochum of 4-5 November 1944, a man was lynched by his fellow citizens because he criticized the German conduct of the war.[210] There was no need for continuing the attack on morale. It had been proven ineffective.

On 25 September 1944, new directives were issued from the Air Ministry and the leader of the USAAF to attack oil and transport targets in the following order of priority:

> Petroleum industry with special emphasis on gasoline and
>   its storage
> Rail and water transport systems
> Tank production plants and depots
> Motor transport production plants and depots

Only as an alternative were industrial targets to be attacked if weather or other conditions prevented attacks on the primary targets.[211]

It appears from that order that somebody at the higher levels had realized that morale bombing had not worked. But the back door was left open in the event the oil and transport target systems would not work either. Portal, in chameleon-like fashion, insisted that Harris follow these instructions. Forgotten were his follow-up to Bottomley's memo of 14 February 1942 defining the aiming point as the city centers and his submission to the Cabinet of 3 November 1942. Harris in turn plowed along in his old groove and ignored what his chief had ordered. There followed an acrimonious exchange of letters between these two officers. It went on from November 1944 until February 1945, culminating in Harris offering his resignation on 18 January 1945.[212] If Portal would have had the courage to let Harris go, many an innocent civilian life would have been spared and Würzburg would not have been destroyed.

The targets outlined in the instruction of 25 September were legitimate and important installations. Without oil and transport the German war machine could not function. Marshalling yards and oil refineries occupy large areas and the bombers, both U.S. and British, had by that time the means to locate them in good or bad weather and hit them with precision. Because of the land they required, they were located outside of city centers and the exposure of civilians was therefore much smaller.

After the bombers were released from SHAEF, a Combined Strategic Target Committee was formed which took over from all previous institutions such as the Ministry of Economic Warfare in giving instructions on which targets to bomb. Zuckerman said it lacked expertise and experience. Zuckerman particularly criticized the qualifications of the committee members, pointing out that in civilian life they had no training to scientifically evaluate the targets and the weight of attacks required. The members came from such diverse fields as publishing, breweries, tobacco firms, and coal merchants.[213] However the primary targets, oil and transport, were assessed correctly by the committee, although there was nothing new about this. What was wrong with the committee was that on a weekly basis it produced lists of alternate targets to open the above referred to back door. Spaatz and Portal should have dissolved the committee after it had identified oil and transport and the other two manufacturing targets and insisted on implementation of these recommendations. After the war it became clear from captured German documents that the shortage of fuel for the Luftwaffe became insupportable.[214] In interviews after the war Speer said that had oil been persistently attacked, presumably during the entire war (not only from late 1944 onward), Germany would have been rendered powerless. As it happened, because the refineries were not bombed consistently, German fuel production increased fourfold between 1939 and the end of 1944.[215]

But fuel also had to be transported to the fronts. Transportation was the Achilles heel of the German war effort. It took about one freight train per day with fifty cars with twenty tons capacity each to supply a fighting German army division. In June 1941, Germany and its allies marched 130 divisions into USSR territory; for the army alone 130 trains per day had to reach the fighting front. The further the German army advanced the longer the turnaround of these trains; if they came back at all. Another problem the German Reichsbahn faced in Russia was the different track gauge. The Russian gauge is wider than the Central European gauge. If, as happened, the rail bed was narrowed to make German trains run, there were numerous operating problems in stations and marshalling yards. If the rails were left as they were, all goods had to be transferred to captured railway stock. The supply of the Eastern Front amounted to a huge transport problem. This was no secret and openly advertised by banners at every railway station in the Reich saying in huge letters: "*Räder müssen rollen für den Sieg.*" ("Wheels must be turning for victory.")

In the Reich, coal had to be transported to power generation plants. Hard and brown coal generated 80 percent of German power. Coal was needed to make iron and steel from the iron ores shipped in from Sweden, France, and Spain. It took 115 tons of coal to produce one heavy tank and six tons to distill one ton of gasoline.[216] As for oil, after the loss of the Romanian fields at Ploesti, Germany depended entirely on synthetic fuel oil. There were huge plants all over Germany and many of them were heavily guarded by antiaircraft guns. They kept producing, because Harris, Doolittle, and Eaker did not attack them as planned. Aircraft fuel production actually rose from 10,000 tons in September 1944 to 49,000 tons in November of that year.[217] Whether the raids were not flown to permit German production to rise and thereby permit continued resistance against the Russian advance, as claimed by Groehler, is a moot point. Coal and its transportation was a bottleneck. Again that was clearly advertised because everywhere there were posters exhorting people that no wastage of coal should be tolerated—"*Kämpft den Kohlenklau*" ("Fight the Coal Thief").

The Allied ground advance in the west came to a halt in September 1944 because they also had a transport problem. Antwerp, the nearest port to the front, was in Allied hands, but its access was blocked by German possession of the Scheldte estuary. Rotterdam had not yet been liberated and the liberated French ports of Le Havre and Cherbourg had been heavily bombed. Brest, also heavily damaged by bombs, was hundreds of miles away from the front. The railway systems of France and Belgium had been devastated. Seemingly, even without daily bomber interference, transport posed a problem for Allied warfare.

The Allied bomber fleets inflicted heavy damage when they raided oil and transport targets, but they did not concentrate on these installations. The morale attacks continued and increased in frequency. Old favorites of Bomber Command in the Ruhr were plowed over again such as Duisburg, Essen, and Dortmund. Farther afield, Stettin and Kiel received their share of bombs and when they ran out of big and important industrial towns, the bombers crushed smaller places such as Heilbronn, Bonn, and Freiburg. German civilian casualties were mounting and one of the worst raids was on Darmstadt on 11-12 September 1944, when more than 12,000 people were killed by 226 Lancasters.

Bomber Command also continued to fly tactical raids on French Atlantic ports still held by German troops, on V-weapon sites, and as far away as Norway. On 28-29 October

1944, an attempt was made on the U-boat pens at Bergen. The pens were not damaged but fifty-two Norwegians were killed by stray bombs.

In summary, Bomber Command, while attacking tactical targets for Overlord, also flew 4 percent of its raids in 1944 on oil targets, 10 percent on transport, but 19 percent on urban areas.[218] Between mid-August and the end of the year the bombers made 72,881 sorties and dropped 265,708 tons of bombs; 696 aircraft did not return.[219] The total bombload discharged by the British bombers flying from the United Kingdom was 525,500 tons in 1944.[220]

Many of the American bombs fell on U.S. investments in Germany. The Opel/General Motors factory at Rüsselsheim west of Frankfurt and the Ford factory at Cologne took heavy hits. How U.S. shareholders reacted to the losses of their foreign holdings is not reported. The distillate works of Leuna and Poelitz had been built with earnings of Standard Oil, New Jersey and Royal Dutch Shell in the late 1930s when these moneys could not be exported because of German foreign currency restrictions. The plants operated unimpeded for the German war effort until late 1944.[221] There are no reports how U.S. banks viewed damage to the plants on which there were still outstanding loans.

The total tonnage of bombs discharged by the Eighth USAAF over enemy held territory was 387,500 tons in 1944.[222] Adding Eighth USAAF and RAF Bomber Command bombloads, one arrives at 913,000 tons of bombs. To this total must be added the tonnage dropped by the Fifteenth USAAF of 260,000 tons. Well over 1 million tons of bombs rained down on Europe in 1944; and these were bombs falling only on strategic and area targets.

There was no doubt that Germany was about to lose the war. But there were still a few last jerks and convulsions of the dying body, such as the V-weapons, the battle of the Bulge and, on 1 January 1945, a sweeping Luftwaffe fighter bomber raid on Allied airfields. Obviously the war was not yet over. When General George Marshall, the U.S. chief of staff, visited SHAEF in October 1944, he told air force leaders that he had doubts about their priorities being correct. He wanted them to abandon long-range strategic bombing objectives and concentrate on knocking Germany out by 1 January 1945.[223] The logic seemed crystal clear. Why destroy the backyard when you are fighting at the front door to enter the house. The Allied air force leaders went back to the drawing board and devised a plethora of plans with codenames such as Clarion, Thunderclap, Hurricane I, Hurricane II, and a few others. Despite Marshall's clear statement, they all maintained strategic bombing, called for increased attacks on oil and transportation, and foresaw an increase in these efforts. They all contained the idea that a powerful show of air strength over even the remotest parts of Germany was necessary to convince its people to roll over and die.

The culmination of all the deadly air warfare planning and execution in World War II must be the fighter attacks on anything that moved in Germany. The fighters had so far played their assigned role of defending the bomber formations in daytime, to make tactical attacks in the front area, and to shoot down any intruding enemy planes. They fought the increasing numbers of German fighters that attacked the U.S. bomber formations over Germany. These were heroic fights, which nobody wishes to belittle. The Allied fighter pilots had a slight advantage because they were better trained. They received two hundred hours of instructions before they were sent into battle. Luftwaffe fighter pilots, because of lack of fuel and the necessity to bring them into action, received only one hundred hours of training.

The bombing by day and night continued with ever increasing intensity. But now at daytime came swarms of fighters circling above like the gathering of vultures over a carcass.[224] Many an ex-fighter pilot has written about his exploits, how he downed German fighters and attacked Luftwaffe airfields, bridges, and other military targets. Many boast about how many locomotives they dispatched, but without saying that in the process they shot up passenger cars and the people in them. No mention is made that they first made sure that the locomotive was hauling a freight train, a legitimate target. There are accounts of Germans and foreign workers who describe how some fighters first came down so low as to practically look into the windows, getting up in the air again and then blasting the train. Worse still are accounts where the train had stopped and the passengers fleeing into the fields were raked by the guns.

The RAF made a science out of attacking rail and motor transport. From a report for the period of December 1944 to March 1945, it is apparent that attacks lasted only two and a half to three seconds, during which the fighter blasted the target over a flight path of 600 to 700 yards.[225] No doubt these fighters wreaked tremendous damage. From October to year-end 1944 there were over 2,000 raids on German railway stations and marshalling yards; 1,700 trains were attacked, 3,000 locomotives, 7,600 freight cars, and 4,400 passenger cars were destroyed.[226] Although it was not always easy shooting; many German trains had flat cars attached with antiaircraft guns on them. It was not only Germans who were the victims. In their enthusiasm it appears that USAAF fighters had attacked trains, houses, and civilians in German-occupied countries. The director of USAAF Intelligence pointed this out to the director of operations of the Eighth USAAF. The deputy commander of the Eighth, F. L. Anderson, replied that some pilots may have been over-zealous and that in the future they would only strafe Germans.[227]

What is mentioned nowhere in English literature and Allied archives is how many farmers were attacked in their fields, the total of civilians killed in passenger trains, the individuals chased on isolated roads, and other such exploits. One pilot boasted about having killed twenty-five cows.[228] Their endeavor to hit anything that moved in Germany, as they had been instructed by their superiors, went so far as to strafe a column of marching POWs, killing eleven officers and wounding forty-two.[229]

Bombing and shelling innocent POWs, their own comrades, happened a few times. One of the most cruel was when on 23 December 1944, fifty-five U.S. officers and twenty-six enlisted men were killed by the Eighth USAAF as it bombarded the POW camp Stalag XII near Limburg.[230]

The magnitude of the fighter campaign can be appreciated when one peruses Carter and Mueller's *Combat Chronology 1941-1945*.[231] Thousands of these planes were sent over

Germany from mid-1944 onward to either first raid specific targets or protect the bombers and then be allowed to attack targets of their own choosing.

As part of the unrestricted bombing there were attacks on neutral countries mostly followed by diplomatic exchanges between the governments of the bombers and the bombed. Settlements were negotiated, ranging from the sale of radar equipment by Britain to Sweden and at the same time release of interned RAF aircrews,[232] to a compensation payment of U.S. $14 million to Switzerland by the United States in October 1949.[233] The first such bombing happened on 4 September 1939 when the RAF attacked ships in the Kiel Canal. One plane went 110 miles astray to the north and dropped two bombs on the Danish town of Esbjerg killing two neutral citizens.[234] The last unintentional raids happened in early March 1945, when the Eighth USAAF attacked the cities of Zurich and Basel in Switzerland on the same day, dropping forty tons of high explosives and incendiaries. Spaatz was sent by Roosevelt to Switzerland to apologize.[235] Swiss papers voiced indignation and did not accept Spaatz's explanation of bad weather. The U.S. government considered it prudent to pay $4 million immediately in damages. The countries suffering most from the overflights and bombing were Sweden and Switzerland.

Crossing over southern Sweden by Bomber Command on their way to German targets had become a routine matter. During the entire war, between 6,000 and 8,000 infringements of Swedish air space by at times tightly flown RAF bomber streams took place.[236] The Swedish government protested frequently in London but let it be known that this was just a routine matter and should not be taken too seriously. Sweden had a difficult position to maintain its neutrality. In 1940-41 the Germans forced it to let their troops pass through its territory on their way to Norway and Finland. On the economic front Sweden did not want to lose its market in Germany for ball-bearings and iron ore. Therefore, there was the attempt to make concessions in both directions, although with the decline of German fortunes it became clear that the Western Allies received more favors. After the war, RAF Marshals Tedder and

Harris were sent to Sweden to express the RAF's gratitude for Sweden's help in letting the bombers fly part of their routes unmolested by flak and nightfighters over neutral territory.[237] Sweden's help went so far as to allow the installation of air navigation wireless stations in the British consulate at Malmö.[238] Berlin protested in Stockholm that Sweden did not enforce its neutrality, but these protests were also halfhearted because Germany did not wish to lose the ball-bearings and high-grade iron ore.

On occasion Sweden did attempt to enforce its neutrality. During the entire war eleven German, six British, and two U.S. warplanes were shot down when it was not clear whether they might attack Swedish towns.[239] On the other hand, Sweden accepted many Allied bombers which took refuge from pursuing German fighters or were too damaged to return to their bases in the United Kingdom. The Swedish Defense Staff went as far as to send instructions to the Air Ministry on how to approach Sweden for emergency landings.[240] By July 1944 a total of ninety-four Eighth USAAF bombers had landed in Sweden and were interned.[241] Many of the USAAF and RAF crews were allowed to return to Britain, whereas others were interned and maintained their planes, which were returned after the war to their respective countries.

Switzerland suffered the most from the bombers. Like Sweden, it had difficulty maintaining its neutrality. It protested vehemently about overflights and bombings of its territory. There were about 6,500 intrusions into Swiss air space by Allied and Axis planes during the war.[242] Like Sweden, Switzerland had commercial interests to defend which included earnings from the transit rail traffic via Switzerland between Germany and Italy, and imports from Spain via Switzerland to Germany. While in Swiss territory these trains were supposedly safe from Allied bombers. But not always, because both the RAF and the USAAF deliberately attacked trains and railway stations within Switzerland. The attacks were part of the Allied political and military maneuvers to force Switzerland to reduce trade with the Axis Powers. In January 1945 alone, 53,000 tons of coal were shipped via Switzerland to Italy and about 700 tons of clothing, food stuffs, and textiles went the other way to Germany; all safely outside the vulnerable Brenner route through Austria.

Though the RAF had stopped bombing Switzerland after 1940, the USAAF continued to violate and purposely attack Swiss air space. On 24 April 1944, one hundred U.S. bombers flew over Schaffhausen causing both human and material losses. The Swiss were defenseless against such numbers. Stragglers were shot down and many planes were forced to land. In the end there were over one hundred U.S. bombers and their crews interned in Switzerland. Men and machines remained there until the war was over, in adherence to international laws. The price paid for such correctness was bitter for a country that wanted no part of the war: about sixty people were killed, about one hundred wounded, and at least six hundred lost their homes.[243]

1945: GERMANY

The new year had come but "The Marshall Plan" had not materialized. On 1 January 1945 the USSR and Western Allied armies stood at the frontiers of Germany. In World War I, Hindenburg and Ludendorff had thrown in the towel at that moment. They had Wilson's Fourteen Points to support that move. In World War II, Hitler had made it clear that Germany would fight to the bitter end. We would all go down in a Wagnerian *Götterdämmerung*. He had Roosevelt's unconditional surrender and the hideous Morgenthau Plan to support his view.

Conditions on the German homefront had deteriorated considerably by 1945. All able-bodied men were in the Wehrmacht and many would never come back as the obituaries in the daily papers showed. Würzburg with its multitude of military hospitals was full of wounded and convalescing soldiers. Food rations were declining, the stores were empty of merchandise, and many were closed by order of the authorities to free their employees for the war effort. The mood of the women, children, and old people left in the cities was depressed. There was no enthusiasm for anything and people were careful not to express any opinion because "Big Brother" was watching. The bombing raids and now the strafing by the fighters was endured stoically and there was no visual sign of revolt as there had been in November 1918.

The bombing increased in intensity. On 3 February nine hundred B-17s of the Eighth USAAF attacked Berlin in daytime. The raid was part of "Clarion Call," a plan hatched by the top military and scientific advisors calling for intensified bomber and fighter raids on all German urban areas, big and small, to finally convince the population that the war was lost and that the German government should be forced to give up. Berlin was clouded over and the loads were discharged on inaccurate radar readings. There was material damage and a death toll of 25,000 Berliners. As a sequel General Marshall personally ordered a raid on Munich in southern Germany to show that no place could be a haven for the millions of refugees streaming west ahead of the advancing Russian armies.

The fighter strafing increased and victims of raids on trains near Würzburg were buried in the municipal cemetery. Passenger trains were attacked at Winterhausen on 13 January; Marktbreit and Seligenstadt on 15 January, killing fifty people in the train at Marktbreit and an unknown but sizeable number at Seligenstadt. The Gemünden railway station was destroyed on 30 January. On 2 March fighters dived down to shoot at farmers in the fields.[244] All these places are located within a twenty kilometer radius of Würzburg. The war and its victims were brought to Würzburg. Cities within one hundred kilometers of Würzburg, such as Aschaffenburg, Frankfurt, and Nürnberg had been damaged heavily.

A new list of the Combined Strategic Target Committee of 8 February put Berlin and Dresden in the first two places.[245] Since the Americans had blasted Berlin already, Harris selected the second city and ordered a double raid on Dresden for 13-14 February. Many books have been written about this operation, the details and the sufferings, the lead-up and the aftermath, including the USAAF participation in them.[246] The USAAF came the next day and bombed the smoking ruins and the parks where the survivors had sought refuge. The biggest horror of these raids were the attacks of the Eighth USAAF fighter bombers. They strafed people in the open who had escaped to the Elbwiesen, the flats of the Elbe River passing through Dresden and people in the parks and on the roads leading from the city. They attacked columns clearly marked with the Red Cross insignia.[247] No records can be found in U.S. archives about this slaughter. The action reports in the files of the AFSHRC at Maxwell Air Force Base speak of locomotives and railway cars destroyed, of tractors and trucks, and mention even the killing of two horses, but nothing of the humans deliberately shot at, as confirmed by many eyewitness reports contained in the literature.

The number of identified victims reached 35,000. For years bodies and parts of them were excavated and many historians believe the often quoted figure of 135,000 victims to be closer to the mark. If this figure is true the Dresden raid exceeds the established worst casualty rate of 87,000 in a single operation on 9-10 March 1945 on Tokyo. Even the immediate death toll of the atomic bombs caused fewer losses. Dresden has been and will be remembered for the military mind having run amok. The soothing words by Air Marshal Sir Robert Saundby in the foreword of David Irving's book are scant comfort. His position as second-in-command of Bomber Command leaves no doubt that he participated in the planning of the night raids and the coordination with the USAAF. The delayed second wave of RAF bombers guaranteed a maximum of terror. Bomber Command dropped 1,478 tons of high explosives and 1,182 tons of incendiaries. The Eighth USAAF delivered another 771 tons into the smoking inferno.[248] The city was 59 percent destroyed in twenty-four hours of raids. The Americans came back two more times, on 15 February and 2 March, to add to the chaos.

The missions of the RAF continued. Of the more successful raids the one on Pforzheim on 23-24 February is noteworthy, because it killed 17,000 people. Four days before American troops entered Cologne, that city was attacked again in two waves by 858 aircraft. The raid was not a tactical strike coordinated with SHAEF. The city was not even on the list of the Target Committee of 8 February. It was one pile of rubble which was turfed over again with hundreds of bodies left for the Americans to dispose of.[249] Cologne was the first major city where Western Allied ground troops encountered difficulties in advancing because of streets full of bomb craters and rubble.

They also found that the German command organized stiffer resistance in cities that were already destroyed.

Bomber Command was not letting up. Essen and Dortmund received more than 4,000 tons of bombs each in daylight raids in early March. The USAAF revisited Berlin on 28 March leaving behind about 1,000 tons of explosives. Nürnberg was bombed again in February. The names and numbers of the many places which were attacked before the war was over on 8 May would fill pages.

The Allied bombers had an easy approach to their targets as most of the flight path was now over friendly territory. But German fighters by day and night still had to be reckoned with. In particular the first ever operational jet fighter, the Me-262, was feared, because it could strike with unheard of speed. There also was a last show of strength of the German night-fighters on 3-4 March. About eighty Ju-88s followed the bomber stream into England and attacked the landing RAF bombers at twenty-seven airfields. Twenty bombers were shot down when they thought they were home safely. Three German fighters came down too low and crashed. It was the last Luftwaffe action over British soil in World War II.[250]

The Wehrmacht was out of fuel and supplies, and in general in disorganized retreat. The attack on oil and transport, although only carried out halfheartedly, was one of the many thrusts that made the German army expire. Of the 182,000 tons of bombs dropped on Germany in the months of January to April by Bomber Command only about 5 percent fell on oil targets and 3 percent on transport. Of the 188,000 tons dropped by the American bombers 63 percent fell on industrial and transport targets.

The fighters continued to strafe anything that moved as they had been instructed. As late as 7 March 1945 RAF Fighter Command issued a further target policy in which it was expressly stated that nothing could be attacked in still German-occupied Holland, Denmark, and Norway. But anything could be attacked in Germany, except "that the provisions of the Red Cross Conventions are to continue in force."[251] The document is signed in the name of Air Officer Commander-in-Chief Fighter Command Sir Roderic M. Hill. The reference to the Red Cross

Conventions is meaningless because not until after World War II were Red Cross Conventions signed concerning air warfare.

In many accounts of the air war it is said that the fighter attacks on German civilians in 1944-45 matched what the Luftwaffe had done to Belgian and French refugee columns in 1940. Against these statements one must hold Göring's instructions of 1940 that Stukas and fighters attacking marching columns must ascertain their military character before firing on them.[252]

Comparing the Fighter Command order with Göring's order clarifies at least the tenor of orders issued. My own experiences and those of members of my family certainly vouch for the bestiality of these fighter attacks. More than once did I have to dash into the ruins of Würzburg to avoid the bullets raking the street I was on. My aunt and cousin were on a field path near Krefeld when an RAF fighter came down and hammered them. They survived except for a few scratches. It is these aspects of the fighter bombers which require a special mental effort to dispatch to the annals of history which this study has set out to achieve. Bombing was an impersonal thing both for the bomber and the bombed. They never saw each other. Fighters were a different story. They took aim at people across short distances. The reactions of the civilians often included lynching a downed fighter pilot; which was no more despicable an act than the strafing by the fighter pilots. Both persons placed themselves outside the conduct of warfare, although both could claim that they only followed orders. In the case of the German lynchers, there were orders from Himmler and Goebbels to do just that. (The fate of a U.S. fighter ace at the hand of a trigger happy German with a shotgun evokes compassion, but in the final analysis also understanding of the tragedy.)[253]

The public in the United States and Britain were still told that all bombing was against military targets only. There had been debates in the House of Commons in February 1944 when the bishop of Chichester questioned RAF bombing methods. Vera Brittain, the well-known British writer and pacifist, had published a thirteen-page article in the magazine *Fellowship* in March 1944 in which she quoted British, neutral, and German newspaper reports to show how ruthless and ferocious the bombing was. The report caused a stir in Britain and in the United States, but was soon forgotten and Vera Brittain was ostracised in her country for being unpatriotic. On 6 March 1945 British MP Richard Stokes, who had been critical of pronouncements on the bombing policy in the House of Commons since 1942, rose again to question the government. On 18 February an article appeared in the U.S. daily, *St. Louis Post Dispatch*, in which the correspondent reported after an interview with a high-ranking RAF officer that the Allies had now made the long-awaited decision to adopt deliberate terror bombing of German population centers. This article burst like a blockbuster into the Air Ministry, SHAEF, and U.S. government offices such as the Ministry of War and others. Air Commodore C. M. Grierson had let the cat out of the bag in a press briefing at SHAEF a few days after the Dresden raid. The report was immediately and forcefully denied by government and military leaders such as Secretary of War Stimson, Eisenhower, Spaatz, and Archibald Sinclair.

The truth continued to be repressed and hypocrisy extended even into military records as seen with the raid on Würzburg. The instructions from High Wycombe to No. 5 Bomber Group for the raid on Würzburg on 16 March stated that the attack was: "To burn and destroy an enemy industrial centre."[254] The title block of the film made from one plane of No.5 Group during the raid says: 5 GROUP ATTACK ENEMY COMMUNICATIONS AT WURZBURG 16/17.3.45. Harris was against this camouflage of the actual purpose of bombing German cities. He requested the Air Ministry to publicly assess the area campaign not the least of it to confirm the bomber crews, who knew they were killing enemy civilians, in their duties and the open support of their government.[255]

Voices were raised and questions began to be asked. Churchill, the seasoned politician, saw the writing on the wall and sent a minute to Ismay, the chief of defense staff, on 28 March in which he questioned "the bombing of German cities for the sake of increasing the terror, although under other pretexts."[256] When the minute reached the Air Ministry and Bomber Command, another blockbuster exploded. Portal,

Harris, and all the bomber practitioners protested violently about being taken to task by the very man who for years had instructed them to attack morale or civilians under whatever pretext. The ever-diplomatic Portal persuaded Churchill to withdraw the minute and substitute it with a less abrasive one by 1 April. The bombers' sun was beginning to set and Churchill was back full circle to where he had started in 1940 when taking over from Chamberlain, who had decreed no bombing of civilians.

The truth was, as reported by many historians, the USAAF and Bomber Command had run out of targets. The war in Europe had come to an end because the Allied armies had conquered it all. It was the ground troops from the east and the west that sealed the fate of Germany. The bombers had persisted far beyond the point of necessity, long after any advantage could be gained, either tactical or strategic. They persisted simply for the sake of destruction for its own sake. They had wreaked havoc unheard of in human history. Some of them, like Harris, fell into disgrace, others, like LeMay, rose to the highest levels of the military profession.

1945: Japan

Japan, like Germany and Italy, had faced the problems of industrialization, population surplus, and no markets for exports and imports. It had to expand beyond the home islands to live and prosper, but found that there was no room and tolerance for its forays. In reviewing literature and documents for this study one finds only one author who recognizes the dilemma of Japan, but by omission nobody allows Germany and Italy the same benefit.[257]

The war with Japan had started with the bombing of the U.S. Pacific fleet at Pearl Harbor on 7 December 1941. After the disastrous setbacks for the Allies in the early years, the tide had turned and Japan had been forced to go on the defensive.

The threat of the combined military power of the Axis had not materialized. There was hardly any coordinated effort between Germany and Italy on one side and Japan on the other. Japan was singleminded in its objectives and refused to support its allies. After the defeat of the Sixth German Army at Stalingrad in January 1943, Germany officially requested some action in the Far East. The Japanese ignored the request. Japanese disregard for its allies' problems went so far as to allow, before December 1941, U.S. ships and later neutral ships to sail into Vladivostok to deliver war supplies to the USSR.[258]

Japan, which had entered the war with resources which were insufficient for a long war, as Germany had, became squeezed for supplies. The Japanese islands have no natural resources. Japan was in the center of an expanded empire with vulnerable supply routes. Everything for war production had to be brought across the seas.

The U.S. Navy launched a submarine campaign, which had all the ingredients and features of the German U-boat battles of World Wars I and II. It caused immense Japanese shipping losses, with the result that aircraft production alone could not keep up with the losses in battle.

The Japanese army and navy air forces were never meant to be anything but tactical weapons. They were designed to support the land and sea battles. As in Germany there were no heavy four-engine bombers. Japanese bombers were all twin-engine, had a maximum bomb load capacity of one ton, a maximum ceiling of 35,000 feet, a range of about 2,000 miles, and no more than four machine guns for defense against fighters.[259] The enemy the Japanese air forces was facing was far superior in equipment, numbers, and training. Between December 1941 and August 1945 the Japanese air forces lost 38,000 planes. The Americans lost 8,700.[260]

The U.S. Naval Air Force with its carrier-based planes had been instrumental in the demise of the Japanese navy at Midway, Coral Sea, and other battles. The employment of the U.S. Army Air Force in defeating Japan did not reach a planning stage until 1943. In November 1943 the Committee of Operation Analysts submitted an in-depth report on Japanese industry and commerce. It had been requested by General Herny H. Arnold in March that year.[261]

At the Sextant Conference in Cairo in December 1943, it was decided to transfer two hundred B-29s to Chungking to destroy half of the Japanese steel production located in Manchuria, Korea, and Kyushu.[262] It was called the Matterhorn Plan, but was never fully implemented. Bombing from China started in May 1944. The distances were too great and the supporting services for a modern air fleet could not be established in China.

In March 1944, General MacArthur and Admiral Nimitz submitted campaign plans for the conquest of Japan. Both plans foresaw a supporting role for the USAAF. The Nimitz Plan called for the capture of the Mariana Islands south of Japan and to build bases there for the B-29 bombers. The USAAF generals from Arnold downward were unhappy about the assigned role and convinced General George Marshall that the B-29 was unsuitable for tactical work. But the Nimitz Plan was adopted and at the same time the Twentieth USAAF was created with the intent of a strategic air campaign against Japan.[263] The Twentieth USAAF was to have 1,000 to 1,500 B-29 bombers and an unspecified number of fighters. The bases on the Marianas were to be operational in December 1944.

By early 1945 U.S. army, Marine, and navy forces were evicting the Japanese from one island after the other, coming ever closer to the Japanese home islands. The campaign was a U.S. effort with some help from the Australians and New Zealanders. No British forces were involved because they were still engaged in Europe. The U.S. thrusts were commanded by Admiral Nimitz and General MacArthur. They planned and conducted naval, land, and amphibious campaigns approaching the Japanese islands from the southeast and southwest respectively. They hoped to make Japan surrender having realized the futility of further combat; failing that, they hoped to reach positions for invading the Japan mainland.

Early in 1945 Admiral Nimitz had his navy air force carriers sail closer to the Japanese islands as the Japanese navy had been practically defeated. Nimitz's planes attacked coastal towns but did little damage. There were ninety aircraft carriers and escort aircraft carriers with 14,000 planes, part of them stationed on recently captured Okinawa Island, pounding away at the southern Japanese harbors.[264]

The situation was different for the U.S. Army Air Force units dispatched to fight in the Far East. Until late 1944 they

were providing tactical support for ground and navy operations in China and the Pacific Islands. The Twentieth Air Force
flew first from Burma to later establish itself in southern China.
Since 1941, before Pearl Harbor, General Chennault had organized the Flying Tigers to help Chiang Kai-shek. The impact of
these operations was minimal. The USAAF generals in
Washington with General Arnold at the top were unhappy
with the assigned roles and results. Arnold had spearheaded
the development of the B-29 bomber from 1939 onward. It
could operate at 35,000 feet and carry a bomb load of ten tons
over a distance of 4,200 miles.[265] It came too late for the war in
Europe, but after many setbacks it was ready in numbers for
bombing Japan, which had been the original thought behind
its creation. With its high ceiling it was out of the range of
Japanese flak and fighters.[266] All that was needed was an air
base close enough to Japan to bring this super plane into
action.

When Arnold had the Committee of Operations Analysts
study where Japan was vulnerable, they had few facts to go
by. The Japanese had been very circumspect in keeping their
industrial and infrastructure build-up away from foreigners'
eyes. The limited information available came from Japanese
publications, reports of visitors to Japan, and such farfetched
sources as insurance policies of British fire underwriters. As in
Britain earlier in the war, the knowledge and judgement of scientists, industry leaders, and high-ranking civil servants was
engaged to recommend how bombs could best be employed
to defeat the enemy. And, in this particular case, how to defeat
him without making costly landings on each of the main
Japanese islands. It was the landing aspect that frightened
U.S. planners, because they expected Japanese resistance until
the last piece of real estate had been conquered. The potential
losses of these amphibious operations based on the island
hopping campaign in the Pacific were estimated at 500,000
lives. This is the figure which was quoted many times by
President Truman after the war as justification for releasing
the two atom bombs. At the same time, Churchill, with typical
hyperbole, even raised that figure to 1.2 million.[267] U.S. military planners were more realistic and estimated it would take

46,000 lives, much less than the politically tainted figures of Truman and Churchill used for justifying the horror of the atom bombs. But even 46,000 U.S. lives justified an aerial campaign which would avoid amphibious landings.

The committee reported in November 1943 that merchant shipping, aircraft and steel plants, and urban industrial areas would be the most important targets.[268] Having done their homework properly, they observed that urban centers in Japan were and are constructed differently from European centers and would be more susceptible to fire than to blast bombs. The U.S. had excellent incendiary bombs in its arsenal which spewed fiery napalm. This made attempts to extinguish them impossible. Napalm was as humane a liquid as the phosphorous jelly in the RAF incendiary bombs. Both stick to anything, skin, wood, steel, masonry, etc. Fire would spread quickly through the wooden structures of Japanese housing centers and it was hoped the effect on morale would be as still anticipated in Europe at that time. U.S. Air Force planners never deviated from that moment onward from fire and morale raids as the means of beating Japan into the proclaimed unconditional surrender.

In 1943 the USAAF still lacked the necessary airfields to implement such a policy. However Arnold and his staff persisted that they could win the war for the United States. What had eluded them in Europe would work in Asia. As Portal in the UK in November 1942, they had made an estimate of Japanese to be killed—584,000.[269] Members of the Committee of Operations Analysts, which prepared the report for Arnold, had no comment on the humanitarian aspect of the estimated fatalities. They considered them as incidental as Portal had. The USAAF would prove its mettle and its generals would be heroes by winning the war, albeit at the cost of 584,000 civilians. What the supreme commander of the U.S. Armed Forces thought of this plan, in light of the fact that not one Japanese bomber had ever purposely attacked U.S. civilians and in light of his telegrams to the leaders of the warring nations in early September 1939, is not documented.

Not all USAAF generals were in agreement with firebombing. General Haywood S. Hansell, co-author of the AWPD-1, commander of XXI Bomber Command operating out of the recently established bases on the Marianas, wanted to destroy the Japanese aircraft industry. This required precision bombing, which was extremely difficult under the meteorological conditions over the Japanese islands. It required higher fuel use and smaller bomb loads than the experts had expected. There were further technical problems that caused the operations directed by Hansell to be a limited success. Arnold replaced him with General Curtis E. LeMay on 20 January 1945. And that is when the firebombing of Japan really started. Hansell was to become LeMay's second in command, but refused the position.[270]

Hansell's replacement looks like the scenario of Peirse's replacement as commander of RAF Bomber Command in February 1942 with Harris. Neither Hansell nor Peirse had been given the means to conduct air wars like their successors. And, both successors were of the singleminded obsession that they would go into the halls of history as the deciding military leaders in ending World War II.

By November 1944 U.S. forces conquered the Mariana Islands south of Japan. Immediately huge air bases were constructed to accommodate the B-29 fleets on the islands of Guam, Tinian, and Saipan. The implementation of such a project within a short period of time is proof of the managerial and technical capabilities of the United States. On 29 November 1944 the first B-29s were sent off to Tokyo, 2,000 nautical miles away, to make an experimental fire raid. Raids on Nagoya and other cities followed. They were all small in scale and results.

When LeMay took over from Hansell he sent his crews through a rigorous training program which not only improved their technical performance but also the spirit of the men. All publications on LeMay agree that he was a man of leadership with a hold on the morale of his subordinates down to the last enlisted man. He still faced problems with the techniques of raiding cities and with the small bomb loads his planes could carry to fly to and back from the distant enemy islands. LeMay realised that he was in charge of an expensive and sophisticated weapon system, and that high expectations were placed on him by his boss, General Arnold in Washington, who was in direct command of all the bombers on the Mariana Islands. He was also aware that both MacArthur and Nimitz were trying to have his bombers under their respective commands to ensure that their campaigns would end the war. If he wanted his place in history he had to please Arnold and proceed with setting civilians on fire. He is circumspect and apologetic in his memoirs about killing civilians, bringing in historical examples from antiquity where whole conquered city populations were slaughtered by the victors. But like all bomber practitioners, he defends killing "their" civilians in order to save "our" soldiers. For a civilian amateur historian (i.e. the author) there is a gap in understanding the military ethics of such attitudes.

The U.S. military planners only recommended fire bombing, leaving the final approval with its humanitarian aspects to higher levels.[271] There was the general belief that all of Japan was one vast cottage industry, with a drill press in every home to make war supplies. LeMay observed burned-out drill presses, like stumps in an area of forest fires, when he visited Yokohama after the war.[272] No doubt this cottage industry was a feeder industry, ineffective as it must have been from the point of view of quality control, distributing raw materials and collecting the end product. Steel, aluminum, tanks, airplanes etc. could not be produced that way. Names and factories such as Mitsubishi, Ishikawashima-Harima, and others existed then and continue to exist. Most of them survived the war suffering little damage.[273]

A further argument for attacking urban residential areas was the declaration by the Japanese emperor in June 1944 that every Japanese citizen, man, woman, and child, young or old, was a soldier in the defense of the homeland. Women and children took training in opposing the invaders when and if they were coming.[274]

The destruction of Japanese cities started in earnest in January 1945. The plans had been laid out and all LeMay, and to a lesser extent the U.S. bomber forces now stationed on recently captured Okinawa, had to do was follow orders. Before the war was over in August 1945, 153,000 tons of bombs were dropped over Japan, 75 percent of them incendiaries.[275] Over sixty major Japanese cities were burned down during this campaign. The USAAF had adopted the Douhet Doctrine.

Yet daylight and high-level attacks still showed limited success in the early operations. Although Japanese home defense was inferior compared with German defense, the B-29s had to fly high and the carrier-based navy aircraft took losses. Japan never had more than 500 daylight fighters and they had to be stripped of all armaments to reach the B-29s at their operating altitudes. The Japanese fighters had to ram the American bombers, meaning for every kill there was one less fighter. By March 1945, one hundred and two B-29s had been lost, about 5 percent of the available U.S. bombers.[276] To reduce losses, in March 1945 in a bloody and costly battle, U.S. Marines occupied Iwo Jima, an island halfway between the Mariana bases and mainland Japan. U.S. fighters could from then on escort the bombers on their missions.

Tokyo became the main target in the early operations and in February and March 1945 large areas were burned down in daylight attacks from great heights. The results were not enough to satisfy LeMay and Arnold. Night raids were instituted on 25-26 February when 172 B-29s dropped 453 tons of incendiaries and wiped out one square mile of the capital.[277] What followed was the most devastating air raid in the Far East campaign and possibly in World War II depending on what casualty figure one applies for the Dresden raid in February 1945. LeMay had secured Arnold's permission for an all-out night raid on Tokyo to be flown with aircraft which had been stripped of their defensive armaments to increase their bomb load. About 280 bombers came down to 8,000 feet and unloaded over an area of seventeen square miles of the capital. The area was Akasuka, a workers' district purposely selected to affect the morale of the working class. The estimated population density of the district was 103,000 people per square mile and conceivably as high as 135,000 in some areas. The target area was well clear of upper-class dwellings and several miles away from the large Imperial Palace grounds, which had been declared off limits by President Roosevelt. The bombers dropped 1,665 tons of incendiaries and high-explosive bombs.

The raid lasted over three hours with General Power flying as master bomber and photographer over the area for two hours. No account is given of his impressions of the holocaust perpetrated under his direct command. About seventy-five Japanese nightfighters rose to fight the raiders. They brought down one U.S. plane and antiaircraft fire brought down two. Another twelve were lost en route.

One million people lost their homes, 40,000 were injured and, as established in the postwar U.S. Strategic Bombing Survey, 87,793 people lost their lives.[278] Hap Arnold sent a congratulatory wire to LeMay the next day.[279] It was a huge success considering the devastation achieved with the means employed. RAF Bomber Command required a much bigger effort to cause the destruction of Hamburg and Dresden.

What it was like on the ground is described in detail in Hoito Edoin's and Robert Guillain's books.[280] The description of the inferno in general and the accounts of individuals who escaped it do not differ from accounts in books about Würzburg, Hamburg, London, Dresden, etc. The firefighting and civil defense services were overwhelmed within minutes of the attack, whole city quarters were engulfed in flames causing a searing heat and combining into a roaring firestorm. If caught in the middle there was no escape. People became stuck in liquid asphalt and were burned to cinders. Jumping into a canal to extinguish the napalm on one's skin did not help because there was soon no more oxygen to breathe.

The magnum air raid of 9-10 March was not the last for Tokyo. LeMay's bombers came back on 13-14 and 15-16 April dropping a further 4,000 tons of bombs and destroying an additional eighteen square miles. In May they continued and by the end of the war fifty-six square miles of Tokyo lay in ashes.

Other Japanese cities were not spared either. Yokohama, Kobe, Nagoya, and Osaka were burnt. In all sixty cities were destroyed to an average of 43 percent. Some of these towns had no military or economic significance. To the honor of the bomber planners it must be said that such famous places as Nara and Kyoto with their valuable cultural assets were not destroyed. Kyoto was spared at the express orders of Henry Stimson, the U.S. secretary of war.

Immediately after V-E day in May 1945, a commission was sent to Germany to assess the results of the bombing war and to recommend actions for a speedy victory over Japan. To nobody's surprise, they proposed destroying the Japanese transport system.[281] Their recommendations had no impact on the rolling fire campaign. To stop a military steamroller takes time. The bombing campaign against Japan was on its way and it has been assessed by historians as one of the bloodiest military operations in human history.

Its crowning effect was the atom bombing of Hiroshima and Nagasaki in August 1945. Reams of paper have been inked about the moral, political, and military issues behind President Truman's decision to unleash such destructive power. Should the Japanese have been warned, or should there have been a demonstration blast in a remote area? Was the A-bomb necessary at all since the Japanese government had already put out peace feelers to the still neutral USSR? Or was it a means for the United States to impress the Russians, the next adversary just below the horizon? These questions will be debated for a long time to come. Stalin had officially informed the Potsdam Conference on 28 July 1945 that the Soviet government had been approached by the Japanese government about a peace proposal originating from the Japanese emperor.[282] There would still have been time to stop the bombing on 6 August.

American military leaders were mostly against letting the bombs go, because they knew Japan was about to surrender. Arnold, Spaatz, and LeMay, in particular, agitated against it. From their point of view, as commanders of large fleets of bombers, this is understandable. If one single bomber could do what normally took hundreds of aircraft, there would be no need and future for most generals. It would take 210 B-29s delivering 2,100 tons of bombs to produce the same effect as the one bomb from the *Enola Gay*, the B-29 that released the bomb on Hiroshima.[283]

The Twentieth USAAF had a list of cities selected for the atomic bombs. In order of sequence they were Kyoto, Hiroshima, Nigata, and the Kokura Arsenal.[284] Mr. Stimson, the minister of war in Roosevelt's cabinet, had visited Kyoto between the wars and insisted that it not be destroyed. Hiroshima took its place and Nagasaki was bombed because the assigned target for the second bomb could not be clearly located.

The bombing of Japan was a gruesome affair. As in Europe, many civilians were killed. The estimates run from 330,000 to 900,000 Japanese dead and up to 1.3 million injured.[285] The two atom bombs destroyed two entire cities, but the conventional bombing had flattened an area thirty times larger.[286]

When it came time to sign the armistice on board the battleship *Missouri* in Tokyo Bay on 2 September 1945, it was the army General Douglas MacArthur who presided over the ceremony. The air force generals figured in the background.

World War II was over and all experts agree it was not the bombers who had won it.

Part Three

The Effect and Effectiveness of Strategic Bombing

"Military action is important to the nation—
it is the ground of death and life,
the path of survival and destruction,
so it is imperative to examine it."
—Sun Tzu, *The Art of War*

MILITARY AND CIVIL DEFENSE

The well-organized and equipped German nightfighters were not in action over Würzburg on 16 March 1945. The German controllers fell victim to Bomber Command's spoofs and directed the fighters to Hanau and Nürnberg, allowing the Lancasters to cross and unload over Würzburg unimpeded. Since all flak had been withdrawn long before the raid, the bombers faced no dangers.

Civil defense of Würzburg was well-organized but completely overwhelmed by the magnitude of the raid. The developing firestorm could not be contained. Communications collapsed and civil defense units concentrated on guiding people out of the inferno of the inner city to the river and the Ringpark.

MILITARY DEFENSE

When the German High Command initiated bombing Britain, France, and Belgium in World War I, and when international and German opposition to this new and uncivilized warfare grew louder, Hindenburg defended his decision with the correct statement that the few German Zeppelins and bombers kept considerable Allied forces engaged to shoot them down.

In World War I, the "masterbomber" of World War II, Arthur Harris, was in charge of a flight of RFC fighters to hunt first Zeppelins and later Gothas day and night. In 1916 over 19,000 soldiers were stationed in southern England in antiaircraft services including 110 aircraft which otherwise would have been available on the Continent.[1] By 1918 there were 304 antiaircraft guns, 415 searchlights, and 11 fighter squadrons of a nominal 24 aircraft each deployed in the Greater London area alone. A further 176 guns, 291 searchlights, and 5 fighter squadrons were stationed in the Northern Defense Area.[2] These considerable forces would face single sortie Zeppelins and later a maximum twenty-eight Gothas per raid.

Conversely, when the RFC and the Independent Air Force started to retaliate against the German hinterland, considerable German military forces were withdrawn from the battlefield. The British bombers had the advantage of a much shorter route to Germany from their French bases and they could raid a much larger area in western Germany. The Germans had to locate and spread their fighters and antiaircraft guns over a greater number of cities than Britain. By 1918 there were 896 guns, 454 searchlights, 170 fighters, and 327 barrage balloons deployed in Germany. Over 24,000 soldiers were required to man these defenses. Of the nearly 4,000 bombing sorties dispatched to German territory in 1917 and 1918 the German defense brought down about eighty Allied planes.[3]

Evaluating the above statistics one can see the futility of the military planning and conclusions. Both countries claimed correctly that a bomber offensive would draw enemy forces from the battlefield. The offensive forces, i.e. aircraft, required to invade enemy territory were a fraction of the opposing defense forces. But both countries had to station about the same number of men and war material on their home soil to defend themselves. In other words, militarily speaking the calculation came out plus or minus zero.

The means of destroying enemy bomb-carrying aircraft in World War I were rather basic. The intruding enemy was spotted by visual or acoustic means. A ground network of communications would first of all decide on friend or foe. Next, courses and possible targets would be established and the defenses, ground-based and airborne, would be scrambled. In a clear daylight raid the fighters and flak guns would train on their targets. At night the action was far more a question of luck. If an enemy bomber was "coned" by a searchlight it became a visible target for the nightfighter. The guns could only fire barrages in the path of the bombers. If lucky the enemy bombers would fly into the cables of barrage balloons, but the fighters normally had to grope in the dark, unless there was moonlight.

The organizations to detect intruding enemy aircraft in England were the Observer Corps and fighter sweeps. In Germany there was the Flugmeldedienst (aircraft detection service). In both countries these services reported to the military.

The fighters on both sides were single-engine, single-seat bi-planes of the same type used on the front. The antiaircraft guns were first converted field guns mounted on swivel bases, but later the first antiaircraft guns as they were employed in World War II appeared. The dreaded and effective WWII German 88mm gun came into action in late 1918.

Once World War I had been brought to its bitter end, and as governments struggled with budgets and the looming threat of the next war, Trenchard expounded his doctrine. After his retirement as chief of air staff, committees evaluated technical and scientific developments and thanks to men like Tizard, and also to a degree Cherwell, fighter squadrons were created and radar stations built. By the time of the battle of Britain in 1940, fighters and radar stations had been brought under the capable command of Air Marshal Sir Hugh Dowding, the first commander-in-chief of Fighter Command. It was this combination which doomed the Luftwaffe attack on the RAF installations. Military defense had been streamlined. There were superior fighter planes such as the Hurricane and the Spitfire and they could be guided by the radar stations. British radar could detect aircraft flying at 15,000 feet and over, well inside France, the Low Countries, and the North Sea. Closer to the British Isles, aircraft could be spotted flying as low as five hundred feet. The maximum range of Sir Robert Watson-Watt's device at the beginning of World War II was about one hundred miles.[4]

By 1939 there were 53 fighter squadrons, 2,232 heavy and 2,000 light guns, 4,128 searchlights, and 1,450 balloons in Great Britain.[5] Originally Fighter Command was not equipped for night combat. By early September 1940, when Hitler decided to let the Luftwaffe bombers start the Blitz, there were ten squadrons ready to receive them. Again, they could be guided by radar, which works well day or night, fog or clear weather.

On the German side, propaganda tried to convince the people that there was a continuous, 50-kilometer-deep flak belt behind the Siegfried Line, as part of the western defenses. No enemy bomber would penetrate that zone. The belt supposedly extended from the North Sea to the Swiss border. There was no such belt. When war broke out, there were sufficient anti-aircraft guns and listening devices to station them around many western German cities. But that was all. There were experimental radars (one of them called the "Würzburg" for some unfathomable reason), with a maximum range of forty miles. There was no tie-in to the fighter squadrons. The German fighter formations were not specifically organized to defend the Reich. Their main task, as for the rest of the Luftwaffe, was to provide tactical support for the army.

All major nations had modern fighters by 1940-41 in the following numbers: France, 400; Italy, 150; Japan, 500. Facing each other at the start of the battle of Britain were: the Royal Air Force, 600; the Luftwaffe, 820.[6]

These aircraft were single-engine monoplanes, which could reach speeds up to 400 miles per hour, could climb up to 20,000 feet within five to six minutes, and had up to eight machine guns mounted in fixed positions in their wings. Their ceilings were maximum 40,000 feet, i.e. about 10,000 feet higher than any bomber could climb.[7] They were praised for certain features, which supposedly made them superior to other designs and which were played up by the media during the war. The Japanese Zero fighter had great maneuverability, but lacked armor plate to protect the pilot, and its fuel tanks were not rubber lined (self-sealing). A tracer bullet penetrating into the fuel tank made it blow up. The first Spitfires had only .303" machine guns, whereas the first Messerschmitt Me-109 had three 20mm cannons. The Spitfires could turn more easily, but when the shells of the Me-109 hit there was considerable destruction. In other words, there were limitations in design which could not be overcome without reducing another feature.

As the war progressed, improvements were made to make fighters more effective. In 1944 the first jet fighter, the

Messerschmitt Me-262, made its appearance. With its superior speed it was feared by the USAAF bombers.

When it was realized that daylight bombing was too risky and costly, the RAF in October 1939, the Luftwaffe in August 1940, and the USAAF only later in the Pacific War in 1945 had to switch to night raids. Both Britain and Germany created in short order nightfighter squadrons, which consisted of heavier aircraft, mostly twin-engine types. With the help of ground-based radar stations and control centers, they were directed towards the bombers; onboard radar devices brought them closer, but the final engagement was visual. There are numerous accounts by bomber and nightfighter crews describing the viciousness of these fights.

As the war progressed, sophistication of electronic devices to detect, approach, and destroy an enemy aircraft became legendary. Gone were the days when Britain considered, at the recommendation of Lord Cherwell, hanging steel nets seeded with aerial mines from barrage balloons hoping that, like a fly going into a cobweb, the enemy aircraft would run into these defenses.[8] The methods of deceiving the enemy's electronic defenses also reached proportions which were at times brilliantly scientific, at times just plain smart. The Hamburg raids in July 1943 were successful because the German radar stations had been put out of action by aluminum strips scientifically dimensioned to interfere with the wavelength of the German radar sets. Tons of these strips, called Window, were released from the bombers and floated to earth. On the other hand, when the German ground controllers switched one day from males to females, because Bomber Command had been giving misleading instructions to German fighters with transmissions from Britain, Harris had expected it and had German-speaking ladies on the air immediately.

When the Germans launched their V-weapon campaigns the United Kingdom was mostly unprepared. The relatively slow V-1 could be brought down by fighters and flak. But against the V-2 there was no defense.

Britain and Germany had the most sophisticated military defenses of all belligerents in both world wars. During World War II the Luftwaffe made 2.6 million fighter sorties against the

1.44 million day and night Allied bomber sorties.[9] The most successful ace of Luftwaffe nightfighters, Heinz Wolfgang Schnaufer, shot down 121 RAF bombers, and most surprisingly survived the war.[10] A restriction Hitler put on the operation of the German nightfighters, not permitting them to pursue the RAF bombers to their illuminated landing bases in Britain, was considered a boon by Harris. It allowed his bombers to return with ease. Hitler wanted the German people to see the wrecks of the bombers; a real folly when one considers that many came down in isolated and sparsely populated areas.

On the other hand, a mistake Harris made was not to gain air supremacy at night over Germany. Both Douhet and Trenchard in their doctrines state that air supremacy is a milestone in a bomber war. Harris, of course, was too much in a hurry to knock Germany out of the war. He took the risk, at considerable cost to his men and planes.[11]

Italy had few nightfighters and few antiaircraft guns. It had no radar system to detect penetrating aircraft, because what radar existed had been developed and was controlled by the Italian navy. As a result the RAF had easy cruising over Italy.

Japanese military defenses were equally lacking. Most of the army and navy air forces's fighters were engaged at the perimeter of Japanese military operations. It almost appears that neither service saw its duty to be to defend the home islands. What fighters there were stationed at home could not fly high enough to engage the B-29s. Similarly, most Japanese flak could not reach the operating height of the B-29 bombers. South of Japan there were few locations available for early warning radar installations. Iwo Jima and the Bonin Islands were the only ones, but were lost during the USAAF bombing campaign. Coordination between radar operations and military and civil defense was poor. When the XXI USAAF Bomber Command raids began in late 1944, Japan had only five hundred dayfighters and about fifty nightfighters to defend the home islands.[12]

As the antiaircraft guns became more sophisticated, the bombers were forced to unload from greater heights. Their accuracy in hitting targets decreased, and surrounding areas were subjected to damage. It was a fact the bomber generals and marshals did not and could not admit. No bombsight could compensate for all the meteorological conditions a bomb had to descend through. Conversely, a flak shell had the same problems, although the gunners knew their meteorological conditions. That meant that bombing and defense against it became more scattered, obviating some of the praised technical advances.

Over German territory in World War I, fighters and antiaircraft guns brought down about equal numbers of Allied planes, thirty-six by flak and thirty-five by fighters.[13] Of the thousands of Allied planes destroyed over Germany in World War II, no statistics could be found listing losses through fighters or flak.

When the government of the USSR requested the opening of a second front in Western Europe from 1942 onward to relieve the pressure of the Wehrmacht on Russian territory, the Western Allies argued that the bomber offensive represented such a front. It was claimed, as in World War I, that the bombers tied large numbers of men and war material to the defense of the Reich. There is no doubt that fighters and antiaircraft guns were drawn from the East. In 1944 only 22 percent of the Luftwaffe fighter force was stationed in the East where it was desperately needed to combat the ubiquitous Soviet ground attack plane Sturmovik. In the West, 60 percent of the Luftwaffe fighters were engaged to fight the RAF and USAAF bombers and 18 percent were deployed in the Mediterranean theater.[14] Equally hard felt in the East was the assignment of the 88mm flak gun to the defense of German cities. The 88 was used in the East as an antitank gun against the overwhelming number of Soviet tanks.

As for the dislocation of manpower, the picture was equally grim. Over 750,000 men were engaged in the defense of the Reich. They included the fighter pilots and their maintenance staff. Manning the antiaircraft defenses was alleviated by the employment of 30,000 Luftwaffe auxiliaries, school-age boys sixteen to seventeen years old,[15] and 50,000 Russian POW's who thereby escaped the deadly conditions of the POW camps.[16] There were further untold numbers of Croats and members of other nations who were friendly to the German cause. These boys and men were trained to fulfill the work of gunners, ammunition carriers, etc. They were effective under the command of a few German soldiers who were not suitable for frontline duty. (Quite a few of the USAAF bombers lost in the 1943 Schweinfurt raid were shot down by high school classmates of mine who had been delegated to the flak positions there. Three of them were killed in the raid.)

German cities protected by antiaircraft guns suffered fewer casualties. The number of people killed in undefended cities could be as much as ten times higher.

Considerable further manpower was engaged in repairing bomb damage to infrastructure and industry. Again many foreign laborers, some of them conscripted, some of them engaged voluntarily, were supervised by Germans, who otherwise could have worked in the armament industry or could have been drafted into the Wehrmacht.

The Western Allies' claim that the bomber offensive tied up large resources away from the front lines and industry is correct, though Speer, the armament minister and the Wehrmacht found many ways to soften that aspect of the bombing war.

CIVIL DEFENSE

In World War II, the moment the bombs, incendiaries, and phosphorous canisters came down, the civilians were on their own. Ideally, but certainly not always, they had been warned by the sirens and had moved to air-raid shelters. While the raid was progressing, they could do nothing but hope. Hope that there would not be a direct hit, hope that they would not be trapped in their shelter, hope that their home would be spared, and hope that it would soon be over. The end of a raid, when one could safely or otherwise leave one's shelter was always hard to judge. If the sirens were still working, they only sounded the all-clear after the last bomber straggler had disappeared. That could be a long time, during which fires would spread, façades would tumble, and time-delayed bombs would continue to spread terror. Waiting in the shelters for the fires to subside could be particularly deadly when bomber commanders had scheduled a second raid for an hour or two later.

Before World War II many countries initiated civil defense measures. The most extensive ones were taken in Britain and Germany. Other countries like France, Italy, and Japan did not spend much money to protect their citizens. As an example, the destruction of a part of Rotterdam by a small German bomber force was only possible because there was not enough fire-fighting equipment and no civil defense.[17]

In Germany, preparations for civil defense began shortly after World War I. The Versailles Treaty did not allow antiair-craft guns. There was no military defense, and protection of the citizens had to depend solely on civil defense. From January 1928 to September 1931 there were exercises in various German cities assuming bomb, incendiary, and gas attacks on industri-al installations. In December 1928 the ministry of the interior was made responsible for all civil defense. An aerial surveil-lance and warning system was established.[18] Sirens were installed after trials of warning the population with red flares proved impractical.[19] But serious efforts to create protection for the citizens from bombing did not start until 1933 after Hitler came to power and started rearming Germany.

Göring, who had been appointed minister of aviation, also became responsible for civil defense. The Luftwaffe took over the warning system, which meant that the civil authorities depended on the military. In 1935 the Civil Defense Law was promulgated which made every person, even foreigners, living in Germany subject to the implementation and ordinances of civil defense. A massive number of orders were issued:

> The local police were put in charge of all measures.
> Fire brigades were modernized and motorized.
> A technical emergency service was created, complete with heavy equipment to effect rescues and repairs.
> In every house a defense group was formed from the inhabitants.
> These people had to be trained 104 hours per year.
> Attics had to be cleared of combustible materials.
> Home owners had to provide hand water pumps, sand bags, etc.
> Basement shelters with airtight doors and windows were built.

Adjacent buildings had to have emergency passages between them in the basements.

Everybody had to buy a gas mask; price RM 5.00.

There were periodic civil defense exercises complete with black-outs.[20]

Over 12 million people were trained in civil defense which would include slaking fires with sandbags or hand-operated water pumps (a futile exercise considering even the first fire raids of Bomber Command, when thousands of incendiaries were dropped over a small area), to giving first aid.

Luftschutz, air defense, became a major national effort. Pamphlets, posters, radio programs, and other means of media could be seen or heard everywhere. Money was spent by all levels of government to install a system of protection for the ordinary citizen. Obviously, the authorities did not trust the capabilities of the military defense apparatus. In 1933-34 German industry spent about RM 4 million to protect its factories. During the same period German towns spent about RM 10 million.

Würzburg, as all German cities, had to spend from its tax revenue considerable sums to install and perfect its civil defense system. In 1939 RM 227,223 were expended, lesser sums between 1940 and 1943 (the Wehrmacht was winning the war), and RM 296,517 in 1944 when the chances of being bombed became greater. The total was RM 1.1 million which was used to train civil defense forces, to construct public shelters for hundreds of people, to construct big water ponds in public places (as reservoirs for the firefighters), to purchase and tear down houses to make fire escape routes, to correct damages caused by air raids, and to help other bomb-damaged cities.[21]

Civil defense underwent a steep learning curve during the war in Germany. The above mentioned water ponds and fire breaches were installed based on experiences of other cities. They saved thousands of lives during the main raid on Würzburg. People jumped into the ponds to escape the heat and sparks.

Separate instructions and conditions were established for the German railways, the postal system, and certain important industries. The idea was that these institutions should function normally as long as possible prior to a raid, even at risk to the workers.

Not all areas of Germany were treated equally when it came to protecting the citizens. Rural areas were assumed safe from air attacks and no provisions were made. As the bomber offensive intensified it became clear that the in-house shelters were mostly inadequate and a program was begun of building bunkers of heavy reinforced concrete above and below ground. Cities in the Rhineland and Ruhr industrial area were selected to have bunkers for up to 20 percent of their population. Some bunkers had capacities for up to 30,000 people. Cities far away from the RAF bomber bases and cities with little or no industry were excluded from the bunker program.[22] Würzburg, for example, did not have a single bunker air-raid shelter. Instead, underground passages of the medieval fortifications were opened and offered good shelter. But there were few of them because the wall and moat system of Würzburg had been demolished in the late nineteenth century.

The bunker program had to compete for concrete and other building materials with the construction of the coastal defenses along the Atlantic, the repairs to bomb damages, relocation of industries underground or to safe areas, and last but not least with the construction of seven headquarters for the Führer. One located in Silesia and never finished consumed 257,000 m^3 of concrete alone.[23]

Another part of civil defense was the evacuation of non-working citizens, particularly children, to areas considered safe. The welfare section of the Nazi Party orchestrated the evacuation of 5 million Germans, i.e. 5 percent of the Reich population of 100 million in 1939, to locations in eastern and southern Germany, including to the Protectorate of Bohemia and Moravia (now the Czech Republic).[24] Dehoused citizens were also transferred to such places and frequently, in the latter stages of the war, experienced a second dehousing as the bombing moved deeper into Germany.

In Britain, civil defense was also taken very seriously. As in Germany, it was shortly after World War I that the British government felt Air Raid Precautions (ARP) had to be instituted.

As Prime Minister Baldwin stated in 1932—the bomber will always get through. In May 1924 an ARP subcommittee was formed in the Home Office under the chairmanship of Sir John Anderson, best known for the shelter named after him. The air staff of the Ministry for Air provided the committee with estimates that London could receive 450 tons of bombs in the first seventy-two hours of a new war. This information was based on extrapolation of World War I facts and assessment of latest technological developments. It was estimated that in the first month of a new war London would suffer 25,000 fatalities.[25] The committee concerned itself with disposing of such an unheard of number of bodies and estimated that 20 million square feet of lumber would be needed per month to fabricate coffins. The supply not being possible, mass graves were considered as was burning in great funeral pyres.

By 1938 the tons of bombs that could come down on London alone were estimated at 3,500 the first day and 700 tons daily thereafter.[26] These figures were discussed by the Cabinet and Parliament, and above all laundered in the Fleet Street Press. Figures of 200,000 casualties in the first ten days and reports of fleeing refugees being machine-gunned from enemy planes were spread and, naturally, scared the population. Any intelligent observer, even without access to intelligence information, could assess that 700 tons per day would require 350 of the Luftwaffe twin-engine bombers to fly every day the circuitous route to London. The first day with 3,500 tons delivered would have brought an air show of unprecedented proportions. Even if the bombers violated the neutrality of the Low Countries, where the bombs, the planes, and the gasoline could come from was not explained. It is unfortunate that the media spread such hysteria, which contributed to the hostility on both sides before the war. However, the threat was there, as Hitler and Göring showed with the parades over Vienna and Prague.

Faced with such grim prospects, the British government had to act. The Home Office was authorized to enact ARP measures. A net of air warden posts was set up. Each was responsible for several blocks of a city. It was staffed with volunteers who would ensure black-out regulations, provision of hand operated fire pumps, distribution of gas masks, of which 50 million were issued/sold before the war, etc.[27] During and after a raid, the warden post was to report damages and summon help. Help was available through voluntary three-man fire parties manned by inhabitants of the affected area and equipped with hand-operated fire pumps. From outside the area heavy rescue units including fire brigades could be called. The latter, depending on what the municipality had provided them with, could be useful or helpless vis-a-vis the bomb damage. The hand pumps were no more effective in Britain than in Germany against the sophisticated fire raids and the incendiaries. Also, only 8,500 were delivered in Britain before the war.[28] A paramilitary Civil Defense Guard was formed which had, by the time the Blitz came, about 2 million volunteer members.

To protect its citizens the British government did not appear to be as thorough as the Germans. Responsibility for coping with the results of an air raid, from burying the dead, to looking after the bombed out, to repairing damages, was spread between the ministries of Health, Home Security, Transport, and others.[29] Coordination of rescue efforts was said to often be lacking.

The provision of air-raid shelters consisted at first mainly of delivering unassembled Anderson Shelters to houses that had at least a small yard in the back. The shelter was made of corrugated sheet metal and required a hole to be dug in the yard with the excavated soil placed on the roof of the assembly. There was room for up to four people inside. Bunks were provided to wait out the alarms. Comfortable it was not. There was dampness inside, overcrowding when there were more than four people to the house, and not the least, poor ventilation. Many people preferred to stay on the lower floor of their houses.

A similar uncomfortable shelter was a steel box, 6½ x 4 x 2 feet high placed in the basement, if there was one, or the ground floor. It was called the Morrison Shelter after the Minister of Home Security. One crawled into it when danger loomed, but against the blast of a heavy bomb it offered no protection.

People living in apartments found shelter in basements if there was one, or on the ground floor with no protection against a direct hit. The most secure shelters were the stations of the London Underground. Heroic accounts of cooperation, patriotic spirit, and supposed comfort have been published. Fewer sources speak of, first of all, the struggle to have the City of London permit the platforms of the stations as nightly quarters and, secondly, about the conditions. The trains were operating as usual, the sanitary facilities were the same, and the air was stale. But it was a safe place, and many people owed their lives to going "underground" at night during the Blitz.

Later in the war, the government constructed school shelters that could house hundreds of citizens. If one was lucky there was one nearby. Only 4 percent of Londoners could take advantage of the underground platforms; up to 9 percent could use other public shelters; and 27 percent used their Anderson Shelters. This left 60 percent on their own, downstairs or up.[30]

As the war continued and the Luftwaffe raids decreased, the need for civil defense slackened. Yet the government was still active in providing improved protection. As an example, many bombed houses east and around St. Paul's Cathedral were razed, their basements exposed, lined with concrete, and used as water reservoirs for future fire raids. Between 1939 and 1946, Britain spent over £1 billion on civil defense, a sizeable sum.[31]

As in Germany, Britain had a program for evacuating children from threatened areas. Children were sent to Canada and the United States. Parents must have suffered agonies while their children were en route in the U-boat infested Atlantic. Other children were sent to Wales and Scotland from where, as soon as the dangers subsided, they drifted back home.

The minimum civil defense preparation all major countries had was air-raid sirens to warn the citizens of the approach of enemy planes. These devices were mounted on roofs and controlled from one center for the entire area. In Britain and Germany a three-minute undulating (and ear splitting) sounding meant "alarm," take cover. When the danger was over another three-minute, equally penetrating steady sound meant "all clear." The sound of these sirens alone could instill enough terror to make one hurry for the shelter.

In Italy it frequently happened that the bombers were overhead before the alarm was sounded.[32] There was not enough money or determination on the part of the Italian government to provide defense for its civilians. Supposedly there was no need for it because when Italy joined the war in June 1940 Britain was all but defeated.

Similarly, Japan was very negligent in civil defense. At first, there was no enemy near enough to send bombers over the Japanese home islands. The situation in Japan was also quite different from other countries. Buildings, private as well as industrial, were and still are today of lighter construction than in Europe. It was not until 1944, after the loss of the Mariana Islands, that the need for civil defense was recognized.

The minister of home affairs was entrusted with the development of civil defense measures. There was no law providing funds and forcing individuals to create a system. It appeared to be all ad hoc, after a raid, when the need was obvious. Tokyo had no shelters.[33] There were no fire breaks and escape routes from the densely occupied quarters. The subway system offered no protection because it was not located deep enough. Most cities outside Tokyo were not considered to be in danger zones. Only after the first B-29 raids on Tokyo in October 1944 were fire breaks and escape routes established by razing whole lines of houses. By early 1945 about 10 percent of the residential homes of Tokyo had been torn down.[34]

The federal government and the city of Tokyo, in poorly defined lines of responsibility, organised civil defense groups with pumps, personal fire-resistant clothing, and a lot of information to combat fire storms.

All efforts on civil defense were looked upon by the all-powerful military with a critical eye—Japan would not need such measures as they were considered defeatist. It is not surprising that the fire raid of 9-10 March 1945 was so devastating. The people were neither physically nor mentally equipped to endure such an onslaught.

The only really successful measure of Japanese civil defense was the evacuation of anybody who was not absolutely necessary in the cities. In 1944 there were 7 million inhabitants in Tokyo. By August 1945, when the war ended, there were only 2.5 million.[35]

In summing up government organised civil defense measures, one comes to the conclusion that the German government had done the most for its citizens. Of course, as the bombing developed the need was the greatest there.

As part of civil defense, one must also mention the precautions individuals took which could be termed personal defense. We spread our more precious personal belongings, clothing, and food to places in the country and to what we thought were bombproof shelters in the city. Not all of them turned out to be. As an example three boxes containing about fifty pieces of antique fayence pottery, some of them four hundred years old, did not survive in a "considered safe" air-raid shelter next to the "Dom." My father's valuable and precious collection was lost. The loss became a bit of a mystery because years later, during reconstruction, no potsherds were found in the rubble. Had the boxes disappeared before the raid?

9

GAS IN AERIAL WARFARE

Dropping gas-filled bombs on civilians did not happen between 1914 and 1945. Douhet's theory of aerial warfare identified gas, after high explosives and incendiaries, as a means of knocking out the enemy's population. Gas bombs were to come last in an air raid for two reasons: first, to kill the inhabitants of the attacked city and second, to prevent outside help from arriving. Trenchard did not mention gas as a weapon to be carried into the enemy's hinterland in defense of the United Kingdom. Gas and chemical weapons were never used in the bombing campaigns of both world wars. Only the Regia Aeronautica stooped so low as to bombard enemy troops with gas, in the Abyssinian War in 1935.

In Article 23 of the 1899 Hague Convention, twenty-six major powers had agreed to outlaw the use of asphyxiating gases in warfare.

At the end of World War I, gas was established as a weapon in land warfare in the same manner as the bomber, the submarine, and the submerged sea mine; all outlawed or at least attempted to be outlawed by the major powers which had convened twice at Den Haag.

In 1925 Britain, Germany, the United States, and other governments signed a protocol at Geneva prohibiting chemical warfare and biological weapons. Germany ratified the protocol in 1929 and Britain in 1930. The United States never ratified it. It left the back door of gas warfare open for the United States. But all U.S. presidents after 1925 pledged that they would abide by it.

The concern of the governments at the time was biological

weapons. Gas as a tactical weapon was a known quantity from World War I. Even if used against civilians, as proposed by Douhet, the antidotes were scientifically available. Biological warfare, such as bacteria or simply poisoning water supplies of cities, was unknown, and its devastating effect was greatly feared.

After World War I there was little doubt that gas and biological warfare would be used in any future conflict. Douhet, in his treatise on aerial warfare, predicted in 1927 that it would only take eighty to one hundred tons of gas to eliminate London or Paris.[1]

Both sides of the past conflict experimented with gas. The German army, as stated in the Versailles Treaty, was not to have any capability of chemical warfare, but as with other provisions of the treaty, clandestinely worked on and developed methods to drop gas from the air. German research between 1925 and 1928 established that it would take thirty-four liters to poison a hectare from the air. Parameters were established as to what different heights, wind velocities, and other factors would do to the success of an aerial gas attack.[2] To ensure a supply in the event of a new war, Weimar Germany cooperated with the Soviet Union under the auspices of the Rapallo Treaty to build a poison gas factory at Samara.[3]

British experiments and industrial development of chemical weapons were not far behind the German effort. The RAF participated actively and funded the expenses with 7 percent from its annual budget. What exactly was done cannot be ascertained, because some files such as PRO: AIR 9/123 are still closed and will be until 2017. One wonders what there is still to be hidden. The attitude of the British military was that after the slaughter in the trenches in World War I, gas was a "humane" weapon because it had killed fewer soldiers than shells and bullets, and had been a good catalyst in attacking enemy positions.

From the records and publications available it would appear that Britain was ahead of Germany in research in gas and chemical/bacteriological warfare. In 1934 the Cabinet approached the Medical Research Council to work on biological weapons.[4] The scientists refused on moral grounds. By 1937 it was recognized that such weapons would be a two-edged sword, because they would contaminate the attacked areas for years and, because of the interdependence of the European countries in peace time, there was the danger of the bacteria coming home to the delivering country.

That both sides were serious about the threat of gas aerial warfare is manifested in the effort to provide all citizens with gas masks. We were never told against what types of gases the masks would protect us and what we should do in the event of a gas attack. Could one smell the lethal gas? When would one put the device on and when would one take it off? Was there to be a public warning like the sirens indicating enemy aircraft approaching? The planning was sketchy at best and the saving grace was that, fortunately, there was never a need.

The records reviewed also say nothing about how areas contaminated by chemical weapons would be decontaminated to make them livable again. Probably there was no money for that and the military did not think beyond the point of delivering their own gas onto the enemy. The civil authorities were similarly unconcerned.

When World War II broke out, both sides waited for the other to strike first because neither wanted to start such a horror. It is said that Hitler was against gas warfare because he had been poisoned in the trenches at the end of World War I.

Churchill considered using gas against German troops if they invaded the Isles.[5] To what degree that would have hurt the local population cannot be ascertained from the files. It would have been a tactical application. The use of gas anywhere was subject to Cabinet approval.[6] The type of gases contemplated were phosgene and tear gas contained in bombs up to 500 pounds. Blenheim, Lysander, and Battle squadrons were trained in early World War II to deliver gas attacks. About sixteen squadrons were involved, i.e. about 150 planes. About 120,000 bombs of 30 to 500 pounds were in stock as of 1 January 1941.

Further planning involved the poisoning of German crops, animals at pasture, and the defoliation of woods. Pellets containing bacteria were to be dropped. After a number of training accidents the scheme was cancelled.[7] It was also found that reducing German food supply would require a considerable number of bomber missions. A compound was available in 1942 which could, with up to three pounds, destroy an acre of crop, but it would take 7,000 sorties to destroy one sixth of one German crop year. There would also not be enough chemicals available to sustain the campaign.[8] More important for Churchill and his bomber leaders must have been the consideration that a campaign against German crops would reduce the area attacks and their expected impact on German morale.

As the war went on and the cruelty developed correspondingly, further means of poisoning enemy civilians and their countrysides were invented. Both sides, of course, always pretended that they would only employ their weapons if provoked. But like a modern-day accidental missile launching, the danger of chemical warfare actually happening was immense.

In a letter to Churchill dated 19 April 1943, Stalin proposed to warn Hitler of a powerful retaliatory attack if the Germans used gas in the front lines.[9] In March 1942 the Red Army had captured a German Ju-88 which, in their opinion, was equipped with tanks for gas delivery. The USSR requested from the British government supplies to retaliate. They were assured that in the next convoy there would be 1,000 tons of mustard gas and 1,000 tons of other agents for chemical attacks. Churchill stated that if the Wehrmacht used poison gas at the Eastern Front, Bomber Command would attack German military installations with gas bombs. But internally Churchill and Portal were concerned that the Russians were trying to inveigle the RAF into starting gas warfare. Any German actions would have to be verified beyond the slightest doubt to avoid serious consequences. The Ju-88 was in fact found to have extra fuel tanks not suitable for carrying gas.[10]

Agents, gases, and bacteria were developed which could poison large areas for up to five hundred years. A compound became available which would cause damage to the human spleen. If fifty kilograms of these germs were dropped on a city of 500,000 inhabitants, 60,000 would become sick and 24,000 would die. The city would have to be evacuated and then destroyed by conventional means. It would be a variation on the Douhet Doctrine. Gas would come first. Churchill ordered

500,000 of these 4-lb. bomblets from the United States, where there had been production facilities for this type of weapon for some time.[11]

The main British research and development effort seemed to have centered around anthrax. The island of Gruinard off the Scottish coast became a proving ground and is to this day still contaminated and uninhabitable.[12] Anthrax spores if inhaled would kill a person within one week. Cherwell, Churchill's scientific adviser, strongly recommended it in February 1944 as a weapon against the Germans.[13] That it was never used depended on short supplies and the moral qualms of starting a new form of warfare for which the public neither in the United Kingdom nor in the United States appeared to be prepared.

The official position of the British government was still that the enemy would have to start it. There were plans for how retaliation would be implemented. Operation Instruction No. 79 of 24 January 1945, superseding earlier plans, comprised two alternatives:

> Plan I: To fit into the existing bombing policy.
> Plan II: To make a maximum separate effort against German population centers.
> Gas weapons available were: 65-lb. Mustard gas bombs and 500-lb. Phosgene bombs.
> Plan I would employ 75% Mustard and 25% HE
> Plan II would employ 50% Mustard, 25% Phosgene, and 25% HE

Advance notice would be: Plan I, 48 hours; Plan II, 7 days; but only strictly after enemy gas action had been verified.[14] The operation instructions were updated when there was fear that Hitler, realizing that there was not the faintest hope for even a negotiated peace, would use gas and/or chemical warfare as the ultimate weapon.

German planning, research, and development appear harder to trace. It seems that most records were destroyed at the end of the war. British intelligence knew that the Germans did little in this field. There were fears that the V-1 flying bombs would carry a biological warhead containing botulinus toxin, eight ounces of which could kill the earth's population.[15]

There was an enormous relief when the first V-1 carried only high explosives.

There was a German army chemical warfare section. Professor Ferdinand Flury of Würzburg University was an advisory member and his laboratory and staff were studying the effect of gas on humans. Flury was a specialist in pharmacology and toxicology, and his main concern was the treatment of heart disease. When he was interrogated after the war he testified that the Wehrmacht gave up the idea of using gas six months after the Normandy invasion because they were aware of the superior capabilities and capacities of the Allies.[16]

In August 1943 Roosevelt issued a statement of Allied policy if the Axis Powers started to use gas or chemical weapons. He assured the world, the United States, and Allied powers that swift and merciless retaliation would be meted out to the Axis military forces and their peoples. He could confidently announce this, because the United States had a sizeable arsenal of such weapons and agents. The country was not bound by the 1925 Geneva Protocol and therefore there was no legal barrier to the development and manufacture of such weapons. As a precaution against surprise gas attacks in the European theater, mustard gas was shipped in a convoy aboard the *John Harvey* to Bari for possible use by the Fifteenth USAAF.

On 2 December 1943 between 7:30 and 7:50 P.M., 105 Ju-88 bombers attacked thirty ships anchored in the harbor of Bari. A total of seventeen ships were sunk including the *John Harvey* which had one hundred tons of 100-lb. mustard gas bombs on board together with other explosives. It exploded and the gas spewed into the water and the air.[17] The raid has been called the second worst air attack on Allied shipping after Pearl Harbor. The confusion was immense as could be expected after such a massive raid. Soldiers arriving at Allied field hospitals and Italians arriving at the city hospitals were treated for shock and the obvious wounds. But after a few days, many victims showed strange signs of skin blisters, and vomiting, and many of them died.

The port was under British administration and it refused to divulge bills of lading. American hospitals soon found out that the victims died from mustard gas and treated their other patients accordingly. The British refused to accept the fact of gas and treated their patients as normal air-raid victims. The Italians were kept completely in the dark and left to their own medicines. A total of 617 Allied soldiers were affected by the gas and 84 of them died. The exact Italian civilian losses were never established, but are estimated to be considerably higher.[18]

Did the Luftwaffe really drop gas bombs and start a new phase of warfare? Nobody at Bari knew for sure. Cooler heads prevailed and after a bomb casing was recovered from the harbor and positively identified as having contained mustard gas of U.S. origin, the mystery unfolded. The shipping into Bari of gas was kept secret and Churchill, in particular, forbade any mention of it to British troops and media. It was feared that world opinion, and especially the Germans, would make a propaganda campaign out of it.

Fortunately, aerial gas warfare in Europe was avoided. It would have been a mega-disaster because most countries were not equipped to deal with it, not even Britain or Germany, where gas masks of doubtful value had been issued to the people.

However there were plans by the U.S. War Department for use of biological weapons against Japan. General George Marshall, the U.S. army chief of staff, had ordered them in early 1944. The attacks on Japanese cities were not to be in retaliation of possible Japanese attacks—there could be no such attacks on any of the Allied homelands because of geography—rather this was to be a first-strike campaign.[19]

Fortunately cooler and more humane heads prevailed. Among them Admiral William Leahy, Roosevelt's military advisor, who convinced the president that such a step would be against all Christian principles.[20] Nevertheless the United States was prepared to fight a gas war. The Chemical Warfare Service (CWS) had received $1 billion. This seems a tremendous amount compared with the total war budget. In 1942 there were already 60,000 employees in this service.[21]

Though mankind was spared gas and chemical warfare in World War II, the belligerents were prepared for it. In the end there were the following stocks ready for use: United States, 135,000 tons; Germany, 70,000 tons; Britain, 40,000 tons; Japan, 7,500 tons.[22]

Considering these figures, the U.S. position is baffling. At the time it was not technically possible to deliver gas or chemicals onto American cities. That is, America had no need for these weapons to be ready for retaliation. Why then such stocks? Roosevelt's declaration of August 1943 condemning chemical warfare seemed to be nothing but a political gesture. At the time the Manhattan Project, the development of the atomic bomb, was well underway and what else but chemical warfare is the effect of lingering radiation after the blast of an atomic bomb?

But fortunately, gas was never used because both sides were afraid of it and feared the retaliation.

10

LOSS OF CULTURAL ASSETS

Würzburg, as most German cities, had a rich cultural heritage ranging from Celtic-times to modern art and artifact. By the morning of 17 March 1945 most had been destroyed. Bombs had blasted them to pieces or the fire storm had consumed them. A few miraculously survived the inferno and it is a pleasure to see and enjoy them today more than fifty years after their narrow escape. The chapel in the Residenz escaped destruction though the palace itself was gutted by fire with only the façades surviving. Fortunately no high explosives fell in its vicinity thereby leaving the façades with their ornamental beauty intact. Even more important, although fire ranged through the rooms and consumed the antique furnishings, made ceilings and floors collapse, the spacious staircase and the high ceilinged Emperor Hall with their world famous Tiepolo frescos were not destroyed. The roofs above them were gone, but the vaulted ceilings with the frescos survived.

Soon after the American army occupied Würzburg an officer of the U.S. Army "Commission to Save and Protect Art and Historical Monuments in the War Zone"(ACPS) organised the construction of temporary roofs over the frescos to save them from the effects of weather. In the chaos of the time this officer, John D. Skilton, did the impossible and brought together workmen and materials. He earned the gratitude of not only the locals but also of art aficionados the world over. He writes sparingly about this achievement in his memoirs, but the Würzburgers will always remember him.[1] It was the beginning of the restoration of the palace to its original splendour which took many years and millions of DM of the Bavarian State government. Today, the building, the rooms, halls, and the staircase appear so beautiful that the American historian Stephen A. Garrett, when he visited the palace, asked the guide how everything could be so immaculately preserved over the centuries. He could hardly believe the almost complete destruction and the success of the painstaking rebuilding.[2]

Another architectural treasure which survived the intense fire in the inner city is the Schönborn Chapel, a baroque structure attached to the transept of the romanesque cathedral. The cathedral itself, as most churches, was gutted by fire but the outer walls survived, although, in most cases they were badly damaged. During reconstruction of the cathedral the north wall collapsed a year after the raid and necessitated the modern look of the "Dom" in order to rebuild it at all.

On the hill, southwest of the city, the pilgrimage church called "Käppele" designed by Balthasar Neumann, the same architect who had built the Residenz, received a few incendiaries but the caretakers were able to extinguish them. The Käppele with all its baroque beauty still looks down on the city. Not so fortunate was the castle on the hill west of Würzburg. No high explosives had fallen in its precincts but incendiaries must have come down on it by the hundreds. The buildings and towers were gutted and again only the façades survived. Today it has been restored to its original beauty and no trace of the inferno of 16 March 1945 is visible.

As the city was 89 percent destroyed, all the houses in the inner core, including the palaces of the lesser nobilities of prince bishopric times, were destroyed. Countless treasures became smoking ruins. Few could be rebuilt to their original appearance. But reconstruction of the entire city has been complete for some years and not a single ruin is visible today. To me, the city looks more beautiful today than it did before the raid. The city council and the citizens did an unbelievable job in recreating a community which is today modern but deeply anchored in its past. It was all hard work, with little outside help. Würzburg was rebuilt without the publicity that surrounded such heavily damaged cities as Hamburg and Dresden, which received more absolute damage, but percentage-wise suffered much less.

The damage to buildings in Würzburg was immense, but just as bad were the losses of other cultural assets. The 400-year-old university with its libraries went up in flames, museums became piles of rubble, theaters and concert halls were destroyed, all elementary and high schools were burnt out, the city hall, a Renaissance building, became a shell, and worst of all many sculptures, paintings, and antiques disappeared. Many of the latter had been evacuated to safe places in the country, but since Würzburg was not expected to suffer a major raid, owners of such treasures were reluctant to let them out of sight. Some treasures even survived the immense heat but then disappeared. They were either stolen by fellow citizens or by the occupying American troops, who were at times quite free in taking along war booty, sometimes even taken during break-ins into private homes.[3] As an example, it is a mystery to this day what happened to a one-meter-tall Tilman Riemenschneider Madonna, a gothic wood carving, which miraculously had survived the fire. It was seen hanging on one of the pillars inside the Dom after the raid.[4]

Riemenschneider was next to Veit Stoss, the greatest German sculptor. Due to the foresight of owners and museum directors, most of his works in wood or stone survived. What did not survive were the busts, each about one meter tall, of the three Franconian/Irish apostles considered safe in the crypt of the Neumünster Church. Fire entered the crypt and consumed its treasures. Fortunately exact replicas were carved after the war.

As Würzburg was a very Catholic place, with many monasteries and a university, the institutions of church and higher learning suffered immeasurable damages. The university clinics on the outskirts were only lightly damaged and could attend to the thousands of wounded citizens. Most other university institutes were destroyed, although the historical place where Professor Röntgen discovered x-rays in 1895 escaped damage. What cultural assets in private homes were lost will never be known.

Würzburg, of course, was not alone in suffering cultural losses due to air raids. Bombing continued until late April 1945 a few days before VE Day. The last major area raid took place on 14-15 April when Potsdam, the city of Frederick the Great of Prussia, with all its palaces, the famous "Garnisonskirche," the archives, and much more became the target of RAF bombs.

But not only the RAF and the USAAF succeeded in destroying valuable treasures. The Luftwaffe, when it was still capable of dropping bombs, was equally effective. When the railway station of Cologne was attacked and some damage was sustained to the adjacent world famous cathedral, Göring in his blustering manner announced that: "If they bomb our cathedrals, we will bomb theirs." He promptly ordered a raid on Canterbury Cathedral. Other buildings of fame destroyed by the Luftwaffe were the London Guild Hall and the Coventry Cathedral, and raids were launched on historic Bath. Further damages in London were inflicted on the National Gallery, the Tate Gallery, and the British Museum. Buckingham Palace received damage and St. Paul's Cathedral was only saved because brave men extinguished the fires on the dome. These so-called Baedeker raids were purposely dispatched to cities with cultural assets. As the war progressed it became apparent that the military paid little attention to enemy treasures.

Since the Ministry of Economic Warfare (MEW) was able to prepare lists of the strategic installations in target cities, it should also have indicated the cultural assets before recommending a raid. It would have acted in accordance with the 1907 Hague Conventions and the 1923 Rules of Air Warfare.

The great fire at the Alexandria Library destroyed half a million documents and books and was considered for 2,000 years the biggest cultural loss in time of war. Twenty-five million German books were destroyed in the bombing raids in World War II.[5] The Würzburg University alone lost 550,000 volumes.

The military leaders, perhaps understandably so, did not consider the enemy's culture. On 26 November 1943 the Marquess of Salisbury questioned Sinclair in the British Parliament about Harris's pronouncement of bombing "until the heart of Nazi Germany ceases to beat." Sinclair defended Harris's statement confirming that there are terrible human and material losses.[6] Earlier in September, Lord Esher, chairman of the Society for the Protection of Ancient Buildings, had written Sinclair urging a more cautious approach in the bombing of museum towns and had enclosed a list of eight such cities which should not be bombed. After some discussion the air staff advised Sinclair that the ongoing campaign did not allow avoidance of such monuments, particularly, if there would be additional personal danger to the air crews—an understandable, but still regrettable statement.[7] A committee was set up under Harold McMillan for consultation by the War Office and the Air Ministry, but there are no records that there were any consultations.

In Germany it was not until May 1942 that the government decreed that art treasures must be removed or protected from bombs. Galleries were closed and their moveable exhibits stored in castles, vaults, and even individual homes in the countryside. Yet soon these places were not considered safe any longer and the treasures were shipped farther afield to salt mines and dry caves. By the time industry was being relocated underground, the art treasures were moved again to less suitable places and many suffered irreparable damage. Historical monuments that could not be moved were bricked up. The local party organizations decided what were historical monuments and, if metal-cast statues were considered not in line with party ideology, they were removed and melted down. From April 1943 onward photographs were made of all immoveable art works, historical buildings, paintings, etc. Most of these photographs survived the war and were used in the reconstruction and restoration.

The question of protecting art treasures from bomb damage became very acute after the Allies landed in Italy. Churchill and Roosevelt became involved. In December 1942 Churchill approved Portal's plan to bomb Palazzo Venezia, Mussolini's home and office. Churchill further approved the delivery of 4,000 tons of bombs per month on Italian cities. By August 1943 Roosevelt pleaded with Churchill to declare Rome an Open City. The Germans under Kesselring had withdrawn their troops from the center to indicate their concern for the Eternal City. Churchill's reply via the foreign secretary to Roosevelt's plea was "to continue to bomb Rome remorselessly."[8] The understandable military reasons were that Rome was a railway center.

Roosevelt's particular concern was damage to the Vatican. He proposed that bomber crews be so instructed and be provided with maps to avoid bombing the Holy See including the four churches in Rome, which per the Lateran Treaty are apostolic property. Air Marshal Tedder, the most cosmopolitan and intellectual of all RAF commanders, strongly favored caution in bombing Rome.[9] But George Marshall and Eisenhower considered only the military value of the marshalling yards and on 19 July 1943 at 11 A.M. USAAF B-17s unloaded. The yards were hit, but bombs being an inaccurate form of artillery also fell on some churches and their treasures. The outcry of the Catholic world was immediate and a second raid was cancelled.[10]

Rome was not the only place in Italy that suffered. Italy from Sicily to its northern borders was subjected to the sometimes senseless destruction of palaces, churches, and other ancient buildings. The most senseless was the destruction of the Abbey of Monte Cassino. The bombing was tactical, but added nothing to the advance of Allied troops. Over two hundred USAAF bombers completely flattened the sixth-century monastery. Fortunately a few weeks before a German staff officer had persuaded the abbot to evacuate all moveable treasures in German army trucks to the Vatican. A total of 80,000 books and 1,200 ancient manuscripts were delivered by 120 trucks into the hands of Vatican authorities.[11] Allied propaganda only reported the removal of the treasures, not the destination, and called it a typical Nazi art robbery.

Of course, the removal of cultural assets by occupying powers is a fact of warfare. Göring was not alone in this, although after the war his "acquisitions" received the most publicity. From antiquity to this day there is war booty in the hands of the victors but claimed by the vanquished. Many treasures are still in the British Museum, the Hermitage, or stored somewhere out of sight. In that category are works removed from Germany after the war by not only common soldiers of the Western Allies but by very senior officers.[12] The Russians sent in whole brigades to plunder East Germany. It is interesting to note that the Japanese are reported not to have touched the art treasures of the territories they occupied.[13]

Although it would appear that the leaders of World War II

cared little about their enemy's cultural assets and their preservation for mankind, there are some outstanding exceptions. The Luftwaffe did not bomb Leningrad's famous Hermitage, St. Isaac's Cathedral, St. Paul's Fortress, and other buildings, although Hitler had given orders to flatten the city. When in late 1944 Hitler wanted Paris "burning" the Luftwaffe "could not do it." Kesselring pulled German troops out of Rome and Florence to avoid these places being bombed and shelled.

The British effort to save enemy art treasures is not very pronounced because Churchill, Portal, et al, gave Harris a free hand in conducting the area campaign. Harris's statements during the war indicate that he did not waste any thoughts on the subject.

The most active in saving art treasures were Americans from the president down to museum directors and people of scholarly inclinations. In the autumn of 1942 William Bell Dinsmoor, the president of the Archeological Institute of America arranged that Roosevelt be made aware of the danger to these cultural assets.[14] Roosevelt reacted quickly and before long, in August 1943, he approved the founding of the American Commission for the Protection and Salvage of Artistic and Historic Monuments in War Areas, ACPS for short. It consisted of church leaders such as Cardinal Spellman, representatives of the Metropolitan Museum of Art, professors of Harvard, and many others. They prepared lists and atlases of the locations of art works, not only in Europe, but also in Asia including Japan, China, and Korea.[15] The information was passed on to the military who promised to use it and to instruct the soldiers accordingly.

Of particular interest are the efforts of Secretary of War Stimson and Assistant Secretary John McCloy. Kyoto, the beautiful Japanese temple town, was in first place as destination for the first atom bomb. It was bombed several times, because it had been ascertained that a number of cottage industries had been established in its precincts. When Stimson heard about the atom bomb plans he vetoed them. He had been to Kyoto in 1926, had an appreciation of Japanese history and culture, and, aside from his personal feelings, listed adverse world opinion if the ancient capital of Japan would be destroyed.[16] Kyoto was spared. A similar fate was experienced by Rothenburg ob der Tauber in southern Germany. Since medieval times it has been a walled city with houses, churches, towers, and fortifications built at that time. There was no industry because there was no room for it. Nor were there any infrastructure targets such as roads, railways, etc. in or around it. Nevertheless on 30 May 1944 the Eighth USAAF attacked the city outskirts and also caused considerable damage to the historical inner city. Assistant Secretary John McCloy flew to U.S. Army headquarters in Europe and ordered that Rothenburg be spared further raids.[17] The damage in Rothenburg was repaired and today it shines in its ancient splendor, the target of uncountable daily tourist buses. In closing the subject of damage and losses to cultural works one can only lament that Würzburg did not have such a protector in high places.

11

PSYCHOLOGICAL EFFECTS OF BOMBING

The psychological effect of area bombing as practiced by the RAF was not conceived and studied by qualified psychologists. Political, military, and scientific leaders thought and expected that area bombing would have an effect on the bombarded people. One must start the blame for failure with the scientists. What did Cherwell, Tizard, and the others know about human reactions to bombing? They were physicists or chemists or, like Zuckerman, a physician. The latter, although, did bring some scientific reasoning into the bombing. However, the majority of them had only their imagination to draw on for the recommendations they made to the military and politicians. Their recommendations cost millions of lives, untold sums of money, and, in the end, amounted to nothing.[1] There were no prior examples to draw on. Bombing in World War I had been on a small scale and could not provide any meaningful statistical data. The effects on Chinese morale after bombing by the Japanese just prior to World War II were not yet available.[2] The studies made by Zuckerman of the raids on Birmingham and Hull showed that in neither city had there been any evidence of panic.[3] Cherwell, however, in his minute to Churchill antedating Zuckerman's final report, maintains that there had been signs of strain at Hull.[4]

One would have thought that the Cabinet, prior to acting on Portal's famous November 1942 paper, would have sought expert advice. It was estimated that 6,000 bombers could destroy many enemy assets and could kill, as indicated, 900,000 of the enemy nation. But that still left about 99 million Germans with which to deal. To hope that a majority of them would force their government's hand, particularly under the well-known conditions of a dictatorship, borders on naiveté. A dead civilian was too dead to rebel and a dehoused civilian too busy to rearrange his life. For help, the dehoused person had only the government to turn to and would certainly not wish to destroy that last resort. British leaders might even be accused of carelessness when one considers what national effort had to go into the bomber campaign and that in the end it was the old-fashioned land campaign which sealed the fate of Germany.

It was against the warnings and input from people in influential positions that the campaign was started and continued. Vera Brittain, the prolific pacifist, published papers on the subject.[5] The bishop of Chichester raised his voice among many in Parliament in February 1944. As the insanity proceeded, Mr. Stokes, MP, tried to slow down the slaughter in early 1945. All in vain.

Normal human reaction to being hit is to hit back. The Germans did that in 1940 and in typical Germanic style with a vengeance. Their campaign, although painful for the people who were effected by it, was uncoordinated and more intended to cause physical damage. Mass intimidation of the British people was never intended.

The American approach to area bombing, as practiced on a grand scale by Bomber LeMay from March 1945 onward against Japan, also did not concern itself much with the psychological effects. The USAAF had a pragmatic approach. It was a campaign to get the biggest bang for the buck. Even the atomic bombs did nothing to raise the Japanese against their leaders.

Bombing did have some psychological effects but not on the scale the responsible leaders expected. It effected the bombers and the bombed.

The young men who delivered the deadly loads to their targets underwent unbelievable stress. They were exposed to fighters, flak, and searchlights and, once being found and targeted, had little chance to escape. Fear of collision with other aircraft over the target zone or at landing was also a big factor.

The well-known statistics of survival rates during a tour of duty had a terrifying impact.

Depending on the average loss rate of bombers during missions, the survival chances during the fifty obligatory operational flights for which Bomber Command air crews were signed on could be as low as 13 percent if the loss rate was 4 percent.[6] It was recognised that 4 percent would eventually lead to a decline of the force. An average of 5 percent would mean the end of a unit in short order.[7] Similar statistics were developed by the Americans which showed that, based on five missions flown per month and 6 percent combat losses, an airman had a 50 percent chance of survival at twelve missions and 25 percent at twenty-five missions.[8] No doubt these figures could not instill confidence. Most published personal accounts of air crews do not mention these facts and speak only of the glory of it all.

The selection of bomber crews did not include a testing by a qualified psychologist. The young men were trained, then given expensive weapons and only by experience over time was it assessed whether the men were psychologically capable of enduring the stress. It was not in the planning of the bomber campaign that human nature might suffer from flying and dropping bombs on the enemy. To staunch that oversight the RAF invented "Lack of Moral Fibre"(LMF); a catch-all phrase to deal with anything from obvious cowardice to nervous breakdown.

Little is written and said about LMF because the application of it was and is, today in particular, considered controversial.[9] Airmen were judged LMF if they frequently aborted their missions for any possible reason, if they did not get over the target but bombed at the fringes, if they dropped their bombs into the North Sea to improve the maneuverability of their plane, or if they openly refused to fly. An escape from the rigors of bombing missions was to land in neutral Sweden or Switzerland and be interned till the end of the war. The punishment of airmen for LMF was severe. Their flying badges could be removed on parade and they could be assigned to menial jobs such as cleaning toilets; all in front of their comrades. Officers were required to resign their commissions and lower ranks could be drafted to work in coal mines.[10]

The stigma of being found LMF was a burden on the conscience of all flying personnel. LMF occurred more frequently in Bomber Command than in the other RAF commands. To avoid hysteria the Air Ministry kept casualty figures secret, but looking around on the base would show what was happening.[11] Badly shot up planes returning with dead or wounded comrades on board or planes not returning at all put a strain on the crews. What made most members of Bomber Command not succumb to LMF was self-discipline expressed in doing one's duty, or with many the very fear of being declared LMF, but in most cases it was the daredevil attitude that it "cannot happen to me."[12]

Seemingly LMF was in all RAF personnels' mind, but only 0.2 percent of all air crew on the average were ever categorized as lacking moral fibre.[13] In Bomber Command one third of LMF occurred when the crews were still in the Operational Training Units, before they were exposed to the flak and nightfighters.[14]

No other air forces had procedures in place to deal with the psychological effects of flying and bombing. There are some accounts in literature telling how USAAF crews, under the stress of losses over Germany during daylight raids, complained. However, how these instances were handled is not reported. When by July 1944 there were 94 and 101 of Eighth USAAF bomber crews interned in Sweden and Switzerland respectively, rumors circulated that the crews had chosen an easy way out and enjoyed a comfortable life in the neutral countries. General Spaatz ordered an inquiry which dispelled most of the charges.[15]

As mentioned above, the psychological damage of bombing also effected the bombed. The German raids on London in World War I caused some mass reactions. Some people demonstrated for government action to protect them and their properties. They looted and rioted, they smashed the homes of naturalized Germans, and they insisted on retaliation against German cities.[16] But there are no reports of individual or mass hysteria. Similarly, bombing of German cities by the Independent Air Force caused apprehension but had no damaging psychological effects. The experiences of World War I gave no guidance for attacks on morale in World War II.

With the RAF so heavily committed to the area campaign and its psychological results one would have expected that there had been a thorough study of how and in what form the people would be driven to lose their senses and loyalties to their government. Basically one could expect three categories of victims:

> The people who were killed by bomb blasts, falling debris, asphyxiation, or any other multitude of causes.
> The people who were wounded and/or had lost all their belongings, but escaped the firestorms, time-delayed bombs, and falling façades.
> The people who were not bombed because their dwellings were outside the target areas.

Those in the first category were too dead to rebel. Their burnt or mangled bodies, often laid out in rows in public places for identification, caused shock among the survivors and gawkers. There are reports of outbursts of calls for revenge but mostly it was resignation. Nobody stayed too long near these decomposing bodies because the stench was unbearable.

The second category had their hands full looking after themselves and their wounds and salvaging their belongings from the ruins. They had no time to climb on the barricades.

The third category were glad they had escaped unscathed this time and were busy making more "personal defence" arrangements, i.e. distributing more of their chattels, and deciding to go to a safer air-raid shelter at the next alarm.

It is not clear from any of the consulted sources how the theoreticians from Douhet and Trenchard to Cherwell and Tizard expected the bombed civilians to behave. Did they expect that any of the second and third category people would get out of the shelters after an attack or days afterwards rally en masse and storm the government? Who would be the leaders, particularly since the Allies did not support any German opposition to the Nazi regime? Much is said in British and American literature about the Gestapo and police suppressing any incipient discontent. Little of such action if any is recorded in the files of the Bundesarchiv in Koblenz. There just was no mass hysteria in Germany after either small or massive air raids. People became stoic and went about reconstructing their lives. After the main raid on Würzburg one could certainly observe this attitude. People did not express feelings of hatred towards the RAF bombers or the German government. Many citizens also felt that after Warsaw, Rotterdam, the London Blitz, and Belgrade they got back what the Luftwaffe had meted out.

German propaganda was another thing. It tried to instill hatred against the bombers, and when the V-weapons started to fly, radio and newspapers announced that the hour of revenge had arrived.

There is evidence that there was hysteria in air-raid shelters which had all their escapes blocked. Heat, smoke and/or many other conditions had caused people to panic and scramble for the exits. There was no escape and the position of the bodies found, sometimes years later, showed that it was a struggle of individual against individual. Reports speak of bodies piled on top of each other with signs of physical violence.

In short the bombing offensive did not produce a large-scale mass hysteria or creeping paralysis. Some psychological changes could, however, be noted.

There was no general permanent damage to the civilian psyche, although the air raids did have short-term effects like fear and anxiety. There was some deterioration of the general behavior, such as an increase in alcoholism and smoking.[17] Finally, there was an increase in cardiac deaths, peptic ulcers, and increased menstrual problems among women.

There was also a phenomenon that occurred after air raids. The difference between "mine and yours" became blurred and many survivors helped themselves to goods from damaged dwellings of other people.[18] This syndrome developed so far that in the case of Würzburg farmers came into town with their horse-drawn wagons and removed goods which had been brought out of burning houses and were unattended while the owners were looking for transport.[19]

The least the perpetrators of the area raids might have expected was that the industrial workers would not come back to work. Here again, the assumption was based on undigested thoughts. The German industrial worker in general was glad to have a job after the Depression. They all remembered the time only too well when unemployment reached unbearable levels. There always has been a loyalty to the firm. But most important, the worker needed the pay envelope and proof that he worked in order to receive the ration cards for food and clothing. Men wanted to work and thereby stay with their families, because if they did not work, they were drafted into the armed forces. The scientists and planners had not evaluated these facts.

During the months of ever-increasing attacks and after the main raid on Würzburg, I experienced a number of psychological phenomena which are worth mentioning here, because not all of them have been mentioned in literature. In conversation with other survivors they appear to have been a common experience. During and immediately after the main raid I had a severe form of diarrhea. I was embarrassed. My father, who had been in the trenches in World War I, very understandingly explained to me that this was a normal experience for anybody exposed to bomb and shell bursts for the first time. I developed a sense of fatalism about being killed, but I had a tremendous anxiety about being buried alive in an air-raid shelter.

After the main raid and after it was clear that we had all survived but had been bombed out, I had a feeling of relief that after months of tension and worries it was finally over. We had touched bottom and except for our lives there was not much more to lose. Contrary to what is said by some psychologists, we were not demoralized to the extent of resignation and idleness. We went ahead and salvaged what there was to be salvaged, beginning the day after being dehoused. I was not afraid of time-delayed bombs, assuming instead an attitude of kismet. But they did go off for days after the raids.

The day after the main raid, despite my father's pleas, I went to the house we had lived in to salvage some of the precious things I had stored in the basement into which miraculously the fire had not penetrated. Soldiers were helping neighbors to recover their belongings and they were also getting ready to take my valuable violin and a basket of wine bottles from our locked wine cupboard, which had been pried open. I strapped these belongings onto my bicycle and left. A few hours later, across the street from the old apartment, a time-delayed bomb went off. Fortunately neighbors and soldiers were gone and nobody was hurt. This was my personal experience with looting and time-delayed bombs.

While walking through the burning city and collecting as much as we could carry from the various places we had stored goods, my father and I encountered several men who had drunk themselves senseless.

A lasting effect of the raids was a recurring nightmare. For about twenty years, with decreasing frequency, I would wake up at night bathed in sweat from a dream that I was crouched in a gutter not far away from our old home and the bombs were coming down around me.

My friend Fred S. had a high fever when the main raid started. After escaping his air-raid shelter and rushing through fires he had no more fever. He was fit enough to walk with his parents about ten kilometers to board a train taking them to relatives in southern Germany the next day.

In studying literature on what the Blitz did to civilians in Britain it is interesting to note that reactions there were the same as in Germany. People may have been temporarily shocked but there was no mass hysteria, little absenteeism from work, and no movement to force the government's actions. British morale did not crack. Less than 1.5 percent out of more than a thousand London shelter hospital patients showed signs of nervous problems.[20] Similar feelings of relief after it was all over, as experienced by me, are reported.[21] Calls for revenge against the German bombing came mostly from the unaffected and rural areas. The bombed citizens seemingly had no time to express an opinion. And it is said that these cries for revenge were exaggerated by the Beaverbrook Press.[22]

The attack on morale did not work, neither in Britain, Germany, nor Japan. There are claims that it worked in Italy but no hard facts could be found.[23]

Hitler had used the Luftwaffe as a psychological threat before the war to achieve his political ambitions. When he was coaxed by the fumbling RAF raids on Germany in 1940 to retaliate and start the Blitz, if there was an intent to affect British morale, he failed. Churchill said in 1917 that nothing he had learned would make him assume that the German people could be cowed into submission by bombing. By 1940 he had changed his mind and let the bombers loose on German morale. He also failed.

THE VICTIMS AND THEIR TREATMENT

When one speaks of victims of the aerial bombings one thinks of the unknown numbers of killed and wounded civilians. They include the victims of Britain, France, and Germany in World War I, the Ethiopians, Spaniards, and Chinese between the two world wars, and the masses of Europeans and Asians who suffered in World War II. However it was not only civilians who were killed and wounded. Many soldiers became victims. An airman shot down and falling into the hands of the enemy could end up in a POW camp, all in accordance with the Geneva Conventions. The other extreme was that he was lynched or shot by people of authority or hysterical civilians.

In World War I, Lord Fisher, the outspoken First Lord of the Admiralty, threatened to shoot any captured German bomber crew member who would come down over Britain. Sounder minds prevailed for fear of reprisals and all German airmen stranded in Britain were treated in accordance with the conventions. The same applied during World War II, when Luftwaffe crews were locked up in POW camps.

The suffering of Allied bomber crews started with the Doolittle raid on Japan in 1942. Eight U.S. flyers were caught in China and all were sentenced to death by a military court in Shanghai. Only three were executed (there is a terrible picture of a blindfolded kneeling flyer with a Japanese official poised to behead him). The other five were sentenced to life imprisonment by the "Emperor's Grace."[1] The Western community in

Japan, including the German embassy, were shocked by the executions. German reporters asked pointed questions at a press conference, but were given the advice to treat RAF flyers caught in Germany in the same manner to stop the raids of Bomber Command.

Some gauleiters and in particular Hildebrandt of Mecklenburg wanted the court-martialing of downed Allied bomber pilots in April 1942 following the Japanese example.[2] But no court-martial of Allied airmen ever took place in Germany.

No other U.S. flyers were executed in Japan later in the war, although the Japanese government had issued a law which called for severe penalties for enemy airmen who had bombed civilians.[3]

In 1942 the bombing war in Germany had not yet reached proportions to enrage the public and/or the government. It was not until the bomber offensive gained momentum that on 28 May 1944 Goebbels published an article in the *Völkische Beobachter* which called for reprisals against parachuted airmen. In 1940 he had warned the British not to do such a thing to German airmen. On 30 May 1944, Bormann instructed party offices to use lynch methods on shot-down air crews. The German population did not follow these suggestions and it was officially noted that up to that time their behavior was one of pity and compassion.[4]

On 3 September 1943, Hitler ordered the transfer of POW camps with Allied airmen into the centers of big cities.[5] It could not be done and there was apprehension that it might lead to reprisals against Luftwaffe POWs in British hands. Other government and party officials took it upon themselves to issue orders in their jurisdictions on the treatment of downed flyers. Himmler, as head of the German police, ordered that the police should not interfere when a civilian crowd or individuals were about to attack stranded airmen. The gauleiter of Baden-Alsace went further and ordered the shooting of all captured Allied air crew.[6] He was tried and executed by a French war tribunal after the war for these murders.

The worst incident of official crime against Allied airmen was the shooting by the Gestapo of fifty Allied air force POWs of the seventy-six who had tunneled out of Camp Stalag Luft III near Sagan on 24 March 1944. The official reason for their murder was that they had resisted recapture.[7]

As the bombing escalated not all German civilians maintained their benevolent attitude toward Allied air crews. In the Würzburg area the most shameful incident occurred on 18 March 1945, two days after the main RAF raid on the city. In Würzburg there was a commando unit, formed towards the end of 1943 on Himmler's instructions to arrest parachuted RAF air crews. During the raid over Würzburg on 16 March, Sergeant Donald G. Hughes's plane was shot down by a German nightfighter. Hughes bailed out and landed near Sommerhausen south of Würzburg. He hid for two days in nearby Eibelstadt when he was captured and transported by the local gendarme to the Sommerhausen jail. Two members of the Würzburg commando unit who had been bombed out during the raid and had relocated themselves with their families at Sommerhausen became aware of the captured airman and after 19:30 on 18 March killed him at the banks of the River Main. They dumped his body into the river. All civilians were chased away from the murder scene, although it is not clear from the report whether they were for or against the murder. After the war the two commando members were tried for war crimes. One was sentenced to death and shot and the other sentenced to twenty years in prison.[8] The other crew members of Hughes's plane were killed as their aircraft went down near Ochsenfurt farther south.

Other killings of Allied air crew occurred not far from Würzburg in 1944. Four USAAF airmen were killed by a commando at Ruppertshütten near Lohr am Main in full view of the civilian population. On 29 September 1944 another USAAF airman was killed by a commando near Bad Neustadt/Saale.[9] There were numerous other killings and lynchings of USAAF and RAF stranded flyers all over Germany. Most of them were dealt with after the war in trials which saw many of the perpetrators punished, many with the death penalty.

If one argues that the killing of shot-down air crew was an excusable reaction of enraged citizens, one has to take the position that one crime does not condone a second one. Bombing

and, particularly strafing civilians, irrespective of the interpretations of international law, is a crime. The men who did it,
although following orders as soldiers, were placed in an unten-
able position by their superiors. When they were in distress
they were on their own and at the mercy of their captors. The
captors had orders from their superiors to execute the prisoners. It left the executioners in conflict with humanitarian law
and they too paid a price for following orders.

Another aspect of victimizing the bombers is the obstruc-
tion of rescue operations. During the battle of Britain and the
London Blitz in 1940-41 the Luftwaffe had a number of obsolete twin-engine seaplanes operating from the French Channel
coast to pick up downed flyers and navy personnel, friend and
foe alike. They were clearly marked with red crosses on white
fields similar to the field ambulances of the fighting armies.
The German navy had sixty-four small vessels with similar
markings and for the same purpose. The German request
through the International Red Cross to respect these craft was
turned down by Britain.[10] Between June and December 1940,
the German rescue planes alone saved the lives of 197 souls, 78
of whom were enemy personnel.[11] As a sign of radicalization of
the war, already at this early stage, one can read in Churchill's
The Second World War that the War Cabinet ordered the shooting down or forcing down of all German sea rescue planes
clearly marked with the Red Cross insignia. The Germans
protested. Churchill's answer was that there was no provision
in the Conventions for this type of humane effort.[12] The pre-
tense was that these aircraft were also used for reconnaissance,
although one cannot imagine that they flew beyond the
English Channel coast in search of victims. It was not until 1949
that the gap in the Geneva Conventions was closed and rescue
aircraft were given the same status as field ambulances.[13]

By the end of World War II, after the Dresden raids, the
threat to captured flyers assumed unheard-of proportions.
Hitler had ordered the shooting of ten thousand Allied POW
airmen as a reprisal.[14] Ribbentrop dissuaded him and the Stalag
Luft III shootings remain the worst crime in this respect.

Long before World War II, most countries in Europe had
made motions to set up procedures to help the civilian victims

of an air raid. But only in Britain and Germany were measures in place when the war began. Even there, the authorities went through a steep learning curve when real action was required.

In Britain the Ministry of Health was responsible for treating the dead and the wounded. There had been planning before the war and calculations were made on the number of casualties to be expected. The Committee of Imperial Defence estimated in 1937 that there would be 1.8 million casualties, one third of them fatal, in the first two months of a new war. The figures were based on fifty casualties per ton of bombs, i.e. 36,000 tons of bombs were expected to be dropped or 600 tons per day.[15] The majority of the damage was expected in London. To cope with the imagined situation 2.8 million hospital beds were provided and £120 million foreseen as compensation for the victims. The actual events proved different. Nothing happened in the first months and only after the Blitz had begun were 13,596 Londoners killed and 18,378 wounded by the end of 1940.[16]

In the literature there is no mention of mass graves or problems with disposing of the dead in Britain. For the dehoused, new quarters were found and rescue efforts of people trapped in destroyed houses also went ahead. Churchill and his wife often visited the bombed areas the next day and were cheered.

None of the Nazi leaders ever showed their faces in the bombed cities of Germany; least of all Göring who had boasted that it would never happen. There are reports that Hitler, when he traveled in his private train through Germany, had the blinds pulled down to avoid the sight of the smashed cities.

The relief and help provided for the victims in Germany were legally the task of the Ministry of Aviation. In turn the ministry had delegated most duties to the police at the local level. Immediately after a raid, the search for people buried alive was started and many souls were rescued. The police organised work gangs, many of them from foreign labor and concentration camps, for the collection and burial of the dead. Unless relatives or friends took care of the victims, the bodies were interred in mass graves irrespective of whether they had been identified or not. There was a constant fear that epidemics might spread if the bodies were not buried quickly.

To avoid the demoralizing effect of bombing on the soldiers on the front lines, the Wehrmacht granted leaves to visit bombed hometowns. The leaves were short and often the soldier had to return to his unit before he could ascertain the fate of his family.

In Würzburg, where the main raid of 16 March 1945 killed about 5,000 citizens, about 3,000 were buried in four mass graves outside the main cemetery. Only about 1,300 of the 5,000 could be identified, the rest being burnt or mutilated beyond recognition. Immediately after the raid, the bodies were loaded like cordwood on trucks and, if not identifiable, dumped unceremoniously into the mass graves. Despite the chaos in the city the removal of the dead was completed in short order.

Similarly in Dresden, where to this day the actual number of victims has never been established, the disposal of the corpses was of the first order of urgency. The number was too big and the authorities decided to cremate the majority. Funeral pyres up to three meters high were built.

The treatment of the bombed out was in the hands of the Nazi Party. When in the beginning of the bomber offensive the police could not cope with the problem, Goebbels and Bormann took it upon themselves to push the party organization into the breach. It left the party in a non-legal position viz-a-viz Göring's Air Ministry, but no rivalries appeared to have developed, because the rescue and assistance measures worked. The bombed-out people could turn to the Party for help which, under Hitler also represented the government. There were no other organizations which had the means and the authority to provide any help. This meant that the gauleiters, the regional party leaders in their capacities as top civil servants of their districts, arranged for emergency relief like housing and food.

The first major relief action came after the raid on Lübeck on 28-29 March 1942, in which 341 people were killed; yet the industrial capacity of the city was reduced by only 0.3 percent. The Party took over the relief activities. The government lavishly distributed food and other goods to the dehoused people. As a result, several Party officials took advantage of this largesse and enriched themselves. They were tried and condemned to death. But Bormann insisted that the executions be stayed and the officials were reinstated. On the other hand, from then onward there were fast and strict court-martials against profiteers and looters. Many innocents were condemned based on trumped up or incomplete evidence.[17] The flying court-martials were initiated to keep the population in line. No official announcements were made of the verdicts, but the word spread around. The practices continued until the end of the war. The threat of legal action also helped to protect the chattels of people who were killed. The Party took control of them and added them to the goods to be distributed to the needy, such as food, suitcases of clothing, or even furniture.

In March 1945, after the raid on Würzburg, the dissolution of law and order had progressed so far that there were no punitive actions against looters. But the Party relief apparatus still functioned and within two days, dehoused people were advised where to turn for help. Victims of destroyed city districts were assigned to villages outside where they were billeted temporarily, which in most cases became housing for a long time. Soup kitchens were established in parks where for several weeks meals could be had for any comer at no cost and, above all, no surrender of ration stamps.[18] Within days many essential government offices were nominally reopened, although only until the fighting approached Würzburg when complete chaos returned. The most important of these offices was the one which issued to the dehoused citizens a paper which confirmed that they had lost their home. With this paper one could obtain, again through government organized institutions, help, ration cards, etc. As an example, the Luftwaffe had several motorized relief truck columns which were sent to bombed cities to provide food, clothing, and medication. The "Hilfszug Hermann Göring" was dispatched to Würzburg and provided such help for about a week.

Other organizations tried to get the bombed cities running again. The German railway had its own resources in materials, manpower, and mechanized tools to restart rail traffic. Even after heavy raids the railways were always operating again in short order. Postal services were slower to recover. Water and power came back depending on the damage inflicted on the systems.

As early as 1943, the German government had started a program of building emergency housing outside of the cities which needed them most to accommodate their citizens, who in turn were essential for keeping the cities functioning. These were twenty-square-meter detached houses on two-hundred-square-meter lots with a minimum of services and comfort and mostly of substandard quality. But they provided a roof over one's head, privacy, and a home not far away from where one previously lived. A total of 180,000 homes were built until June 1944 at which time the program stalled for lack of materials and manpower. The cost had been RM 300 million.[19] By 1960 these houses had either fallen apart or were razed for safety reasons.

When a bombed-out person or family had been accommodated in housing that had escaped the bombing and which was of reasonable construction and comfort, there was immediately after the war a new danger of being dehoused. The victorious Allies, particularly the Americans, had told us during the war through the Voice of America that their troops would not requisition private homes to house the occupying troops and their families. That turned out to be merely propaganda. Many houses and apartments, where bombed out families and the original owners were crammed into one room per family, had to be vacated with all furniture remaining in place. Notice was seldom more than fifteen minutes.

Compensation of victims or their dependents was spotty and slow in all countries affected by the bombing. The Japanese initiated a big effort to help the victims of the atomic bombs, but there was no help beyond immediate assistance for the victims of LeMay's B-29s.[20] There was no assistance or even recognition forthcoming for relatives of the 67,000 French civilians killed by Allied bombs.[21] Similarly, no support for the dependents of 15,000 Belgians, 5,000 Dutch, and 150 Luxemburgers killed by German bombs, V-weapons, and USAAF and RAF bombs.

To the best of my knowledge there are no local, national, or international organizations which represent the civilian victims. Governments and victims are not interested. They only want to forget because the war on the home front is a controversial subject. There were many heroes among the victims. But even the media showed scant interest.

In Germany there was some compensation for losses incurred during the war. In 1952 a law was passed by the Federal Republic intended to equalize the losses between the citizens. It meant that persons who had suffered little or no losses were taxed to compensate people who had been expelled from the eastern provinces of the Reich after the war and people who had lost everything in air raids. Any assets a dehoused persons might still have as the land of the destroyed home, investments, accounts receivable, etc. were assessed and 50 percent of the value became taxable. For many it became an additional hardship because they had to part with further belongings to pay the tax, which was due no later than 1978 including interest. By 1969 about DM 100 billion had been disbursed, about 70 percent to refugees from the East and 30 percent for bomb damages.[22] For my five cousins and I it meant receipt of the paltry sum of DM 200 each for the ruin of an apartment house our grandmother had owned. For my father it meant a substantial payment because he owned real estate. For the federal government it undoubtedly was a political stunt employing a substantial bureaucracy.

Today there are still victims of the bombing war. In 1994 three workers were killed when they drove sheet piling into an unexploded WWII bomb on a property in Berlin.[23] How many unexploded bombs still remain undiscovered as a deadly danger in the ground nobody knows.

13

STRATEGIC BOMBING AND
INTERNATIONAL LAW

If war is an inevitable fact of human life, there must be a return to the battlefield and civilians must be left unhurt. Civilians in war zones will always suffer, but civilians far removed from the action should not enter the planning of the military. It was the intention of the signatories of the conventions in the late nineteenth and early twentieth centuries to codify the security of populations and their assets.

When it came time to negotiate the terms and conditions of the conventions, the participating nations, despite all the humane clamor, had their own interests in mind and to protect. War itself was not to be outlawed. Only the conditions of warfare were to be regulated. It meant that a military advantage a nation enjoyed had to be upheld, so not to jeopardize the next conflict. As an example the position paper prepared by the British admiralty on the naval bombardment of coast towns for the 1907 Hague Convention, stresses that a naval power, such as Great Britain with the strongest navy in the world, could not be restricted attacking its enemies from the sea.[1] The paper especially mentions that a short and sharp bombardment of the coast of an uncivilized tribe would convey an unmistakable object lesson from the dominant race.

Many states were interested in outlawing naval blockades. Among them Germany which has always depended on feeding its population through overseas trade. Britain singularly refused to agree to give up its right for naval blockades during the Second Hague Conference in 1907. Germany in turn refused to have limitations attached to submarine warfare and the use of the contact mine. All powers objected to imposing limits on armaments in general.

But all participating nations agreed in 1907 on Article 25 of the Hague Land War Regulations which forbade the bombardment of inhabited areas by whatsoever means.

It is this article which is quoted by all scholars of bombing and, depending on the interpretation of it, whether it was outlawed or not. To this day the jurists argue this point. The road to bombing populated areas by aircraft passed the following milestones:

The First Den Haag Peace Convention of 1899 forbade the discharge of projectiles from airborne craft for a period of five years. The article was signed by all nations except Britain.

The agreement was extended to last until the planned Third Den Haag Convention, to be convened in 1914. The extension was signed by Britain but not by Germany during the Second Conference in October 1907. Since the Third Convention did not take place the agreement expired.

The outlawing of aerial warfare was defeated at the conference of l'Institut de Droit International in Madrid in 1911.

The raids on Britain and France by the Zeppelins and later the Gothas ignored Article 25 of the 1907 Land War Regulations.

The Den Haag Rules for Air Warfare were issued in 1923 but not signed by any government.

The Geneva Disarmament Conference from 1930 to 1934 dealt among many other aspects with the abolition of the bomber, but failed.

The proposals of Hitler in 1935 and 1938 to outlaw strategic bombing were not responded to.

The Chamberlain government announced in 1938 that Britain would adhere to the Rules of Air Warfare of 1923.

The bombardments of Warsaw and Rotterdam by the Luftwaffe in 1939 and 1940 respectively were carried out in accordance with the provisions of Article 25 of the 1907 Land War Regulations.

The raids on German cities by RAF Bomber Command from May 1940 onward ignored the provisions of Article 25.

The Blitz of the Luftwaffe against Britain, started in September 1940, was justified as per the Den Haag Conventions as a retaliation, but only to the point of equal destruction. As the Blitz went beyond tonnages dropped by Bomber Command, it became illegal.

The raid on Belgrade by the Luftwaffe in 1941 ignored the provisions of Article 25.

From the above listing one can deduct that it was the Germans who started strategic/area bombing in World War I. On a purely juridical assessment this can be said to be true. But from their point of view, the German supreme command and reluctantly the German government argued that the bombing was in retaliation for the British naval blockade, which they considered illegal. Strictly speaking, the blockade was not illegal. The Germans also countered with the U-boat campaign, which in the beginning was conducted in accordance with the provisions of the Conventions of Naval Warfare. In turn the British admiralty considered the submarine campaign completely illegal and, therefore, stepped up the blockade.

Further arguments proffered in favor of German bombardment were that any city to be protected under Article 25 had to have no military installations and defenses at all; not even any infrastructure that served to supply the armed forces.

Article 25 became unworkable and the Germans felt justified in bombing, which in turn caused the formation of the RAF Independent Air Force bombing German cities in retaliation.

In World War I the term "home front" became popular. It meant that whole nations were at war and not only the armed forces. If the term home front was meant as a psychological effect to make civilians feel important in the conduct of the war, it backfired. The hinterland now also became de facto a military front. To fight this front the bomber proved the ideal weapon. Once the home front was brought into the conduct of war, British/American military planners had a further incentive for bombing. International experts maintain that there are two schools of thought on warfare: The Continental one—army against army; and the U.S./UK one—people against people.[2]

The latter is based on historical developments that forced Britain to maintain its empire against indigenous people with armies much inferior in numbers to what the insurgents could muster. Fighting the enemy's people by whatever means compensated for the difference in strength.

Conversely one can interpret the Luftwaffe Service Order No.16 of March 1940 as an army against army school of thought, because it says in the introduction, paragraph 2, that the aerial attack is to be carried into enemy territory to target the enemy forces and reduce the will to resist of the enemy forces at its root.[3]

Bringing civilians into the war by stressing the home front was a self-defeating measure. It gave the enemy reason to attack this front. That these attacks were meant to be against military type targets was understood and could be condoned by the statutes of international law. That the attacks later included indiscriminate bombing of residential areas is the point where jurists still have different opinions.

There are opinions such as J. M. Spaight's, who was principal assistant secretary of the air ministry at the time, stating in 1944 that the bomber is the savior of civilization.[4] The timing and the historical facts must be considered in judging this extraordinary statement. The author refers to the tremendous losses of the British army in the battles of World War I and the deaths of Germans by starvation through the blockade.[5] What he did not know in 1944 was that the number of deaths by starvation in World War I was about the same as the number of deaths by bombing in World War II. Bombing indeed appeared a much less costly form of warfare for Britain, provided that Douhet and Trenchard could be proven correct in the end.

Area bombing as practiced indiscriminately from 1942 onward was not subject to Article 25 of the Rules of Land Warfare; such was the opinion of the air ministry. An opinion on that is proffered by Eberhard Spetzler, who during the war was a legal staff officer of the Luftwaffe. After the war, as a professor of law at the University of Göttingen, he pointed out:[6]

> Since there are separate rules for land and sea warfare and none was ever signed for aerial warfare, the Rules for Land Warfare cannot be applied to strategic bombing.
>
> Article 25 clearly states that it is meant to protect civilians

during the physical conquest of their land. Bombers do not occupy enemy territory, they only destroy it.

For a city to be protected by Article 25 it must not have any defenses. Fighters attacking bombers over their target must be considered defending the city.

As a legal expert, Spetzler points out that even if and when area bombing could be judged as contrary to international law, it became common international law, starting with World War I and raising few eyebrows in World War II, because all belligerents practiced it.

Had the Germans won the war, Arthur Harris would have expected to be tried as a war criminal. His countryman Spaight states that the bomber offensive could not be arraigned under international law.[7] Why then did Spaight write several books in defense of it?

Area bombing could have been forbidden by the League of Nations when civilians were bombed by the RAF and the French Air Force in Mesopotamia and Syria between the World Wars. These areas were de jure under the government of the League. A resolution by the League rejecting the British "people against people" interpretation of warfare in League territories would have made the Trenchard Doctrine unworkable.

Civilians were unprotected by international agreements until the end of World War II. In 1948 a Red Cross Convention gave protection to civilians. However, the arms race that started at that time, with intercontinental ballistic missiles still in place today, makes a mockery of that convention.

The Japanese are the only power that ever indicted active participants in bombing. The well-publicized trials of the captured flyers of the Doolittle raid in 1942 caused worldwide indignation, even in Japan's ally Germany. Before the trials Japan had passed legislation that made bombing civilians a crime. This was a unilateral move and legally speaking had no base for the indictment. Why Japan did not interpret Article 25 as applicable and based its prosecution on that is not explained.

Whether bomber crews expected to be protected by the Hague and Geneva Conventions when in distress is a moot point. Since there were no conventions regulating the bombing of civilians, how could the bombers expect to be protected by conventions that did not regulate their duties? There were no conventions about the treatment of stranded airmen.[8] This does not mean that the lynchings of Allied air crews can be condoned. Lynchings are illegal from any juridical point of view. The Allies conducted numerous trials after the war in Germany. The United States tried fifty-seven, Britain and Canada twenty-seven, and the USSR eight murders of Allied flyers.[9] However, the fairness of these trials is questioned when one considers that in the U.S. Zone of Occupation the defendant was at the mercy of U.S. military judges, prosecutors, and defence attorneys. Hearsay evidence was admissible, judgements of death sentences did not have to be unanimous, and there was no provision for appeal.[10]

J. M. Spaight considered strategic area bombing unassailable. Of all the crimes dealt with by the International War Crimes Tribunal at Nürnberg, that subject was studiously avoided. Neither the Luftwaffe as an organization, nor its top leaders were indicted for the killing of over 60,000 Britons in the Blitz, the Baedeker Raids, and the V-weapon bombardment. In the proceedings it was made clear that the court considered Warsaw, Rotterdam, and Coventry as raids in accordance with the conventions.[11] In later trials Kesselring and Sperrle were tried on other charges than area bombing of the British Isles. The Allies could have and should have done justice to the victims of their countrymen. The defense, by the rules established by the war crime courts, could not table evidence of similar crimes committed by the Allies against the Germans. This meant the tribunals could have had the defendants convicted on a very simple charge of mass murder, committed by disobeying international law.

This seemingly intentional oversight might have caused comments by the public and the media, but by the self-styled rules of the tribunals it would have been legally correct. Convicting the German bomber practitioners would have cast a shadow on the Allied bomber practitioners. Pronouncing the raids on Warsaw and Rotterdam legal made Churchill vulnerable for cancelling Chamberlain's orders and having the RAF start bombing German cities in May 1940.

In the conduct of area bombing there were clear infringements on the law. The killing of downed airmen without a proper trial was against any law, national or international. The transfer of Luftwaffe POWs from French to British custody at the time of the defeat of France in June 1940 was against the Hague Conventions. The intentional overflight of neutral countries by bomber formations on their way to targets in enemy territory and the bombing of targets in neutral countries was against international law.

The area bombing of enemy cities is only illegal since the Red Cross Convention on the Protection of Civilians in Wartime, signed in Stockholm in August 1948. The mass killings of civilians through aerial bombardment in World War II is still considered justified in the British and American camps, although there are many and loud voices condemning it. Most prominent is the British historian J. M. Spaight who already in 1924 stated that the Declaration of St. Petersburg of 1868 and The Hague Convention of 1899 are broad enough to prohibit the conduct of aerial warfare.[12]

14

CONCLUSION

W hy was Würzburg destroyed by Bomber Command in an area raid on 16 March 1945? The review of over three hundred pieces of relevant literature and countless documents in United Kingdom, Canadian, German, and American archives have not given me an answer.

Of course it was not Würzburg alone that was destroyed at a time when it was obvious that Germany was rapidly collapsing. The world's media continued to report how German territory was being occupied by the USSR from the east and Allied troops from the west. The increasing collapse of Germany came with the physical occupation of the land. The media did not report, except for the raid on Dresden in February 1945, on the progress of destruction of German cities and the at-one-time expected decisive impact of the bomber offensive. After Dresden, Churchill had even called for a reassessment of the bombing in his famous minute to the Chief of Staffs Committee on 28 March.

The bombing progressed as planned without consideration of the changed military situation. The destruction of German cities continued until the end of April. Seemingly once the military machine was moving it could not be stopped. It had a life of its own. There were now all the equipment and soldiers on hand. It must have been that aspect that made Harris decide to have Würzburg attacked, but there are no records of why No. 5 Group was instructed to strike that city.

Bomber Command, as all units of the RAF, kept Operational Records Books, which describe daily activities. The ORB of the headquarters of Bomber Command at High Wycombe does not contain minutes of meetings or abstracts of discussions in the morning meetings deciding which targets were to be attacked the following night. It would appear that Harris, who made the final decisions on all targets, and his staff played their cards very close to their chests. The ORB for 16 March 1945 reports on general issues pertaining to Bomber Command and nothing else.[1]

This leaves one to guess why Bomber Command chose Würzburg, which was so low on the list of recommended targets. Some of the answers seem to be: 1) The experimental raids of the weeks before the main raid had shown that the city could be easily located with the electronic aids available at the time;[2] 2) There were no defenses such as flak or searchlights as the experimental raids had also shown; 3) The city was still about 150 kilometers from the advancing armies and therefore there was no danger of hitting friendly troops. Since the bombing campaign was still in full swing Würzburg represented an easy and riskless target.

The timing of the attack is strange. If the city had been important for its few strategic installations or for increasing the demoralization of the German population, why did the bombers not come earlier? Was it expected that attacking 107,000 Würzburgers would cause, at that stage of the hostilities, a revolt against the Nazis? Würzburg might not have been destroyed had Harris followed the orders of 25 September 1944 to attack infrastructure targets. Since the few industrial and military installations were purposely not bombed, the attack on the residential areas was an area/morale raid.

The decision to attack rested with High Wycombe. Political and economic considerations could not have entered the process. Bomber Command has justified the raids on East German cities such as Dresden, Magdeburg, Leipzig, and others as political and military support operations for the advancing Russian armies. But Würzburg was too far away from that theater of war.

The raid did not help the advance of the U.S. Army either.

On the contrary, Kesselring, the German commander, had his troops fight one week in the Würzburg rubble. It was the longest battle for any German town including the battle of Berlin. There is little doubt that the troops would have been withdrawn earlier had the city been intact.

Can one blame Harris for selecting Würzburg? The answer is no because, as is evident, the bombing campaign, its concept, and its execution pursued its own mysterious logic. The bomber commanders can prove that they followed orders as soldiers; the Target Committee can prove that it had instructions from the chiefs of staff; the chiefs of staff cite guidance from the politicians of intermediate and high ranks all the way to Churchill and Roosevelt; and the politicians in turn hold up their hands and claim that they followed the recommendations of bomber commanders, scientific advisors, target committees, and chiefs of staff, who all promised a clean, quick, and efficient way to knock out the enemy. In short, one can blame them all as a group, but not individually. They can all hide behind each other's back. The subject of area attacks in World War II is so loaded with controversy that historians, academic and military alike, to this day are divided as to the ethics, necessity, success, and efficiency of it. Charles Messenger in his history of the bomber campaign mentions that such distinguished British historians as A. J. P. Taylor, Geoffrey Best, Michel Glover, and even Robert Saundby, Harris's second-in-command during the entire campaign, have condemned it or at least expressed doubts about the moral aspects of the bombing.[3]

The success of the bomber offensive can be assessed when one studies the British Bombing Survey. The survey, which has never been officially published, unequivocally states that the bombing was a failure.[4]

One must give Harris credit for not scheduling a second raid on Würzburg shortly after the first one as he had done on many occasions to increase the terror.

The RAF raid of 16-17 March spelled the end of Würzburg as a medieval historically grown city. The part the USAAF played in the demise of the city was small and actually accidental. The daylight attacks flown by the Eighth USAAF and the Ninth USTAAF were against legitimate infrastructure targets such as the marshalling yard, the gas works, the railway station, and military barracks. These targets were secondary choices, as primary assigned targets in other cities could not be bombed.

If the bomber offensives in Europe and the Far East were to have a political impact they failed. They did not change the governments of Britain, Germany, or Japan in two world wars. They did not impress the USSR leaders in WWII and many politicians have questioned the ethics of them ever since.

From the economic point of view they did have an impact. The cost of the bombing in Europe and the Far East in World War II shows staggering statistics. The United States produced 98,000 heavy bombers at a cost of $259,000 for a B-17, $304,000 for a B-24, and $894,000 for a B-29.[5] Britain constructed 28,000 bombers at an average cost of £150,000.[6] Germany manufactured 18,000 bombers at an average cost of RM 269,000, and Japan 15,000. The USSR produced 17,800.[7] The winner in the production of these aircraft was the United States. It was from the wartime effort of the U.S. aircraft industry that the United States established its leading postwar role as supplier of commercial airliners.

Another economic aspect of the bombing is that what had been destroyed would have to be rebuilt. The destruction of the German cities helped the U.S. export industry after WWII. The Marshall Plan provided the funds and, as is well known, the credits were all repaid.

From the military point of view, area bombing was not a success. It did not cause the collapse of the enemy war effort as promised by the bomber commanders. It could have done that had the campaigns been consistently executed. Though area bombing was to result in the defeat of enemy morale and cause the overthrow of the enemy political systems, that effort did not produce the desired result. What it did produce are appalling statistics of human losses.

These victims are the forgotten heroes of the fighting in the first half of the twentieth century. Aside from monuments in places where they are buried, there are no national memorials, no mentions on armistice days, or any recognition of their sacrifices. German bombs and V-weapons killed 60,595 British civilians.[8] The estimates of German civilians killed vary considerably. They range from 410,000, to 570,000, to 800,000.[9] In Japan the toll was considerably over 200,000 people killed by the fire raids (nobody knows the exact number) and 112,000 by the atomic bombs.[10] These "incidental losses," as Portal called them, cost the loss of 46,268 RAF bomber crew in action[11] and 161,000 of USAAF bomber crew in Europe and the Far East.[12]

The bomber commanders were proud of the results. Many wrote their memoirs, such as Harris and LeMay, after the war and claimed that without their efforts World War II could not have been won by the Allies. They were proud that they had done their duty. In Europe the USAAF even showed off the results to their ground crews who had serviced the bombers in Britain. Over 30,000 ground personnel were flown over Europe to see for themselves what bombing had done.[13]

Whether the bomber leaders were war criminals is a moot question. The British historian Spaight thinks it is the bombed and not the bombers who will be the judges of whether bombing is justified.[14] A telling aspect of how bombing has been judged is Churchill's treatment of the subject in his six volume The Second World War. He devotes a mere fourteen pages to the longest military campaign of the war, which consumed disproportional human, financial, and economic resources.

Würzburg was bombed because the bombing offensive had long ago become an end in itself, with its own momentum, its own purpose, devoid of tactical or strategic value, indifferent to the needless suffering and destruction it caused.

In summarizing the bombing between 1914 and 1945, one can say that the losses and destruction were unnecessary and do not represent a leaf of honor in the annals of mankind. They cannot be excused. The best one can do so many years after the wars is to analyze and assess them, dispatch them to history, and hope and pray that they will never happen again.

BIBLIOGRAPHY

Allen, George. *Images of the Spanish Civil War*. London: Unwin Publishers Ltd, 1986.

Allen, H. R. *The Legacy of Lord Trenchard*. London: Cassell, 1972.

Angelucci, E. and Matricardi, P. *World Aircraft*. New York: Rand McNally & Co., 1975.

Bekker, Cajus. *The Luftwaffe War Diaries*. London: Macdonald & Co. (Publishers) Ltd., 1967 (original German title: *Angriffshöhe 4,000*).

Bernstein, Barton J. "A Postwar Myth: 500,000 US Lives Saved," *Bulletin of Atomic Scientists*, Vol. 42, No. 6, June/July 1986.

Bernstein, Barton J. "Churchill's Secret Biological Weapons," *Bulletin of Atomic Scientists*, Vol. 43, No.1, January/February 1987.

Bernstein, Barton J. "Why We didn't Use Gas in World War II," *American Heritage, The Magazine of History*, Vol. 36, August/September 1965.

Best, Geoffrey. *Humanity in Warfare*. New York: Columbia University Press, 1980.

Bidinian, Larry J. *The Combined Allied Bombing Offensive against the German Civilian 1942-1945*. Lawrence, KS: Coronado Press, 1976.

Birkenhead, Earl of. *The Prof in Two Worlds*. London: Collins, 1961.

Blum, John Morton. *Roosevelt and Morgenthau*. Boston: Houghton and Mifflin, 1970.

Böhme, Hermann. *Entstehung und Grundlagen des Waffenstill-standes von 1940*. Stuttgart: Deutsche Verlagsanstalt, 1966.

Boog, Horst. *The Conduct of the Air War in the Second World War*. Providence, RI: Berg Publishers, Ltd., 1992.

Botting, Douglas. *In the Ruins of the Reich*. London: Grafton Books, 1985.

Boyd, Alexander. *The Soviet Air Force*. New York: Stein and Day, 1977.

Boyle, Andrew. *Trenchard*. London: Collins, 1962.

Bradley, Dermot. *Generalleutnant Walter Wever: Eine vorbildlche Persönlichkeit der Luftwaffe*. Europäische Wehrkunde, 1, 1979.

Brittain, Vera. "Massacre by Bombing," *Fellowship*, March 1944.

Brown, Eric. *Wings of the Luftwaffe*. Garden City, NY: Doubleday & Co. Inc.

Brown, Malcolm and Seaton, Shirley. *Christmas Truce*. New York: Hippocrene Books, 1984.

Brown, Shores and Macksay. *Guiness History of Air Warfare*. Middlesex: Guiness Superlatives Ltd., 1976.

Buelow, Hilmar von. *Die Luftrüstungen des Auslands, 1935/1936*. Jahrbuch der Deutschen Luftwaffe, 1937.

Carey, Otis. "The Sparing of Kyoto (Mr. Stimson's Pet City)," *Japan Quarterly*, October/December 1975, Vol. XXII, No. 4.

Carlson, Andrew R. *German Foreign Policy 1890-1914 and Colonial Policy to 1914*. Metuchen, NJ: Scarecrow Press Inc., 1970.

Carter, Kit C. and Mueller, Robert. *The Army Air Forces in World War II*. AFSHRC, 1973.

Cecil, Robert. *Hitler's War Machine*. London: Salamander Books Ltd., 1975.

Chronicle of Aviation. Liberty, MS: J.L. International Publishing Inc., 1992.

Churchill, W. S. *The Second World War*. Six volumes. Boston: Houghton and Mifflin Co., 1948-1954.

Clark, Ronald W. *Tizard*. Cambridge, MA: Massachusetts Institute of Technology Press.

Coffey, Thomas M. *Iron Eagle*. New York: Crown Publishers Inc., 1986.

Collier, Basil. *The Defence of the United Kingdom*. London: H.M.S.O., 1957.

Condon, Richard W. *The Winter War, Russia against Finland*. New York: Ballantine Books, 1972.

Connot, Robert E. *Justice at Nuremberg*. New York: Carroll and Graf Publishers, 1984.

Craven, Wesley Frank and Cate, James Lea. *The Army Air Forces in World War II*. The University of Chicago Press, 1948.

Czesany, Maximilian. *Alliierter Bombenterror: Der Luftkrieg gegen die Zivilbevölkerung Europas 1940-1945*. Berg am Starnbergersee: Druffel Verlag, 1986.

Czesany, Maximilian. *Nie wieder Krieg gegen die Zivilbevölkerng*. Graz, Austria: Selbstverlag, 1951.

Deutsches Weissbuch 1943, *Englands Alleinschuld am Bombenterror*. Zentralverlag der NSDAP.

Divine, David. *The Broken Wing*. London: Hutchinson & Co. Ltd., 1966.

Dokumente aus den Jahren 1945-1949. *Um ein antifaschistisch-demokratisches Deutschland*. Berlin: Staatsverlag der Deutschen Demokratischen Republik, 1968.

Domarus, Max. *Der Untergang des alten Würzburg*. Gerolzhofen: Verlag Franz Teutsch, 1978.

Douhet, Giulio. *Command of the Air*. London: Faber and Faber Ltd. 1943.

Dülk, Franz. *1883-1983: 100 Jahre Zeitungen im Hause Richter*. Würzburg: Mainpresse Richter Druck und Verlag, 1983.

Dunkhase, Heinrich. *Würzburg, 16. März 1945*. Volkach: Hart Druck, 1980;

Edoin, Hoito. *The Night Tokyo Burned*. New York: St. Martin's Press, 1987.

Eisgruber, Heinz. *So schossen wir nach Paris*. Berlin: Vorhut Verlag Otto Schlegel, 1934.

Emme Eugene M. *The Impact of Air Power*. Princeton, NJ: D. van Norstrand Co. Inc., 1959.

English, Allan D. *The Cream of the Crop*. Montreal: McGill University Press, 1996.

Eyermann, Karl-Heinz. *Der grosse Bluff*. Berlin (Ost): aus Geheimarchiven der Deutschen Luftfahrt, 1963.

Fehrenbach, T. M. *F. D. R.'s Undeclared War*. New York: David McKay Inc., 1967.

Fredette, Raymond H. *The First Battle of Britain*. London: Cassell & Co. Ltd., 1966.

Freeman, R. A. *The Mighty Eighth War Diary*. London: Jane's Publishing Co. Ltd., 1981.

Garlinski, Josef. *Hitler's Last Weapons*. London: Magnum Books, 1979.

Garrett, Stephen A. *Ethics and Airpower in World War II*. New York: St. Martin's Press, 1993.

Globe and Mail, Toronto, 4 June 1999.

Goss, Hilton Proctor. *Civilian Morale under Aerial Bombardment, 1914-1939*. Montgomery, AL: Maxwell Air Force Base, Documentary Research Division, Air Universities Libraries, 1940.

Greenhous, Harris, Johnston, and Rawling. *The Crucible of War*. Toronto: University of Toronto Press, 1994.

Grenfell, Russell. *Bedingungsloser Hass*. Tübingen: Verlag Fritz Schlichtenmayer, 1955 (original English title: *Unconditional Hatred*).

Groehler, Olaf. *Geschichte des Luftkriegs 1910 bis 1970*. Berlin: Militärverlag der Deutschen Demokratischen Republik, 1975.

Groehler, Olaf. *Bombenkrieg gegen Deutschland*. Berlin: Akademie Verlag, 1990.

Guillain, Robert. *I Saw Tokyo Burning*. Garden City, NY: Doubleday and Co. Inc., 1981.

Gundelach, Karl. *Der Alliierte Luftkrieg gegen die Deutsche Treibstoffversorgung*. Wehrwissenschaftliche Rundschau, 13, 1963, Heft 12.

Hampe, Erich. *Der Zivile Luftschutz im Zweiten Weltkrieg*. Frankfurt/Main: Bernard & Graefe Verlag, 1963.

Hansell Jr., Haywood S. *The Air Plan that Defeated Hitler*. Atlanta, GA, 1972.

Hansell Jr., Haywood S. *Strategic Air War against Japan*. Alabama: Maxwell Air Force Base, Air War College, Air Power Research Institute, 1980.

Harris, Arthur T. *Despatch on War Operations*. London: Frank Cass & Co. Ltd., 1995.

Harris, Arthur. *Bomber Offensive*. London: Collins, 1947.

Harrison, Thomas. *Living through the Blitz*. New York: Schocken Books.

Harvey, S. "The Italian War Effort and the Strategic Bombing of Italy," *History*, Vol. 70, No. 228, February 1985.

Heimann, Bernhard and Schunke, Joachim. *Eine geheime Denkschrift zur Luftkriegkonzeption Hitler-Deutschlands vom Mai 1933*. Zeitschrift für Militärgeschichte, 1964.

Helmreich, Jonathan E. "The Diplomacy of Apology: US Bombings of Switzerland during World War II," *Air University Review*, May/June 1977, Vol. XXVIII, No.4.

Hoch, Anton. *Der Luftangriff auf Freiburg am 10. Mai 1940*. Vierteljahresheft für Zeitgeschichte 4, 1956, Heft 3.

Hohn, Uta. *Die Zerstörung Deutscher Städte im Zweiten Weltkrieg*. Dortmund: Dortmunder Vertrieb für Bau-und Planungsliteratur, 1991.

Höppner, Ernst von. *Deutschlands Krieg in der Luft*. Leipzig, 1921.

Huldt, Bo and Böhme, Klaus-Richard. *Vårstormar, 1944-Krigsslutet skönjes*. Stockholm: Probus Förlag, 1995.

Huldt, Bo and Böhme, Klaus-Richard. *Horisonten klarnar: 1945-Krigsslut*. Stockholm: Probus Förlag, 1995.

Infield, Glenn B. *Disaster at Bari*. New York: Macmillan Co., 1971.

Irving, David. *The Destruction of Dresden*. Morley, Yorkshire: William Kimber and Co. Ltd., published by the Elmfield Press, 1974.

Irving, David. *Churchill's War*; Bullsbrook, Australia: Veritas Publishing Co. Pty. Ltd.

Irving, David. *Die Tragödie der Deutschen Luftwaffe*. Klagenfurt, Austria: Hans Kaiser Verlag, 1970.

Irving, David. *Von Guernica bis Vietnam*. Wilhelm Heine Verlag, 1982, (original English title: *From Guernica to Vietnam*).

Irving, David. *Hitler's War*. New York: The Viking Press.

Jablonski, Edward. *America in the Air War*. Alexandria, Virginia: Time-Life Books, 1982.

Jäckel, Eberhard. *Frankreich in Hitler's Europa: Die Deutsche Frankreichpolitik im Zweiten Weltkrieg*. Stuttgart: Deutsche Verlagsanstalt, 1966.

Jackson, Robert. *Air War over France*. Shepperton, Surrey: Ian Allen Ltd., 1974.

Janis, Irving L. *Air War and Emotional Stress*. Westport, CT: Greenwood Press, 1976.

Jones, Neville. *The Beginnings of Strategic Air Power*. London: Frank Cass & Co. Ltd., 1987.

Jonge, Alex de. *The Weimar Chronicle*. Meridian Books, 1979.

Killen, John. *A History of the Luftwaffe*. Toronto: Bantam Books, 1986.

Kilzer, Louis C. *Churchill's Deception*. New York: Simon and Schuster, 1994.

Koessler, Maximilian. *American War Crimes Trials in Europe*. Georgetown Law Journal, Vol. 39, 1950/1.

Kuehn, Volkmar. *Der Seenotdienst der Deutschen Luftwaffe 1939-1945*. Stuttgart: 1978.

Kurowski, Franz. *Das Massaker von Dresden*. Berg am Starnbergersee: Druffel Verlag, 1995.

Le Goyet, P. *Évolution de la doctrine de l'emploi de l'aviation entre 1919 et 1939*. Revue d'histoire de la deuxieme guerre mondiale, Nr. 73, 1969.

Leahy, William D. *I Was There*. New York: Whittlesey House, 1950.

LeMay, Curtis. *Mission with LeMay*. Garden City, NY: Doubleday Inc., 1965.

Levine, Isaac Don. *Mitchell Pioneer of Air Power*. New York: Duell Sloane and Pearce, 1943.

MacIsaac, David. *Strategic Bombing in World War Two*. New York and London: Garland Publishing Inc., 1976.

Macksey, Kenneth. *Kesselring, the Making of the Luftwaffe*. New York: David McKay Co. Inc., 1978.

Martin, B. *Deutschland und Japan im Zweiten Weltkrieg*. Göttingen, 1969.

Maser, Werner. *Der Wortbruch: Hitler, Stalin und der Zweite Weltkrieg*. München: Olzog Verlag, 1994.

Maurer, Harryman. *The End Is Not Yet*. New York: Robert M. McBride, 1941.

McCarthy, John. *Air Crew and Lack of Moral Fibre in the Second World War*. Australia: War and Society, September 1984.

McKee, Alexander. *Dresden 1945*. New York: Dutton, 1984.

McKee, Alexander. *Caen Anvil of Victory*. London: Souvernir Press, 1984.

Mee Jr., Charles L. *Meeting at Potsdam*. New York: M. Evans & Co., 1975.

Mee Jr., Charles L. *The End of Order, Versailles 1919*. New York: E.P. Dutton, 1980.

Messenger, Charles. *Bomber Harris and the Strategic Bombing Offensive: 1939-1945*. London: Arms and Armour Press, 1984.

Middlebrook, Martin. *The Battle of Hamburg*. Harmondsworth, Middlesex: Penguin Books, 1984.

Middlebrook, Martin. *The Nuremberg Raid*. Penguin Books, 1986.

Middlebrook, Martin and Everitt, Chris. *The Bomber Command War Diaries, an Operational Reference Book: 1939-1945*. Penguin Books, 1990.

Mierzejewski, A.C. *The Collapse of the German War Economy, 1944-1945, Allied Air Power and the German National Railway*. Chapel Hill and London: The University of North Carolina Press, 1988.

Miller, Russell. *The Soviet Air Force at War*. Chicago, IL: Time-Life Books, 1983.

Miller, Henry W. *The Paris Gun*. London: George G. Harap & Co. Ltd., 1930.

Omissi, David E. *Air Power and Colonial Control, the Royal Air Force 1919-1939*. Manchester: Manchester University Press, 1990.

Oppelt, Hans. *Würzburger Chronik des denkwürdigen Jahres 1945*. Würzburg: Verlag Schönigh, 1947.

Overy, R. J. *The Air War 1939-1945*. New York: Stein and Day, 1981.

Owen, Roderic. *Tedder*. London: Collins, 1952.

Peters, Ludwig. *Volkslexikon Drittes Reich, die Jahre 1933-1945*. Gräbert Verlag Tübingen, 1994.

Poolman, Kenneth. *Zeppelins over England*. London: Evans Brothers Ltd., 1960.

Preston, Paul. *Franco*. London: Fontana Press, 1995.

Reitberger, Heiner. *Das alte Würzburg*. Würzburg: Richter Druck und Verlags GmbH, 1977.

Rengger, Nicholas. *Treaties and Alliances of the World*. Longman Current Affairs, 1990.

Richards, Denis. *Portal of Hungerford*. London: Heinemann, 1977.

Rimell, R. *Zeppelin*. Canada Wings Inc., 1984.

Rockenmaier, Dieter. *Als vom Himmel Feuer fiel*. Würzburg: Echter Fränkische Gesellschaftsdruckerei und Verlag, 1995.

Rohden, Hans-Detlev Herhudt von. *Letzter Grosseinsatz Deutscher Bomber im Osten*. Wehrwissenschaftliche Rundschau, 1951, Heft 1.

Rumpf, Hans. *Deutsche und Englische Luftkriegsstrategie im Zweiten Weltkrieg*. Wehrkunde, 1955, Heft 10.

Rumpf, Hans. *Westdeutsche Zivilverluste*. Wehrwissenschaftliche Rundschau, 1953, Heft 10.

Russell, Lord of Liverpool. *The Scourge of the Swastika*. London: Cassell and Co. Ltd., 1954.

Saunders, Hilary St. George. *Royal Air Force 1939-1945*. London: HMSO, 1954, Volume III.

Saward, Dudley. *Bomber Harris*. London: Sphere Books Ltd, 1986.

Schaffer, Ronald. *Wings of Judgment*. Oxford: Oxford University Press, 1985.

Schnellpressenfabrik Koenig & Bauer AG, Würzburg. *Festschrift zum 150 jährigen Jubiläum, 1817-1967*. (Brochure for 150 year jubilee of the factory).

Schott, Herbert. *Mainfränkisches Jahrbuch 1992*. Volkach: Verlag Hartdruck.

Seaman, L. C. B. *From Vienna to Versailles*. London: Methuen & Co., 1985.

Segre, Claudio G. *Italo Balbo, A Fascist Life*. University of California Press, 1987.

Shores, C., Cull, B. and Malizia, M. *Guiness History of Air Warfare*. Middlesex: Guiness Superlatives Ltd., 1976.

Skilton, John D. *Defence de l'art Européen*. Paris: Les Éditions Internationales, 1948.

Spaight, J. M. *Bombing Vindicated*. London: Geoffrey Bles, 1944.

Spaight, J. M. *Air Power and War Rights*. London: Longmans, Green and Co., 1947.

Spaight, J. M. *Air Power and War Rights*. London: Longmans, Green and Co., 1924.

Spetzler, Eberhard. *Luftkrieg und Menschlichkeit*. Göttingen, 1956.

Statistisches Bundesamt, *Wiesbaden. Bevölkerung und Wirtschaft 1872 -1972*. Stuttgart: Verlag Kahlhammer, 1972.

Steinert, Marlis G. *Die 23 Tage der Regierung Dönitz*. Düsseldorf: Econ Verlag, 1967.

Stern, Vol. 45, 1994.

Studtrucker, Rudolf. *In stummer Klage*. Mainfränkisches Museum Würzburg, 1985.

Suworow, Victor. *Der Eisbrecher-Hitler in Stalins Kalkül*. Stuttgart: Cottasche Buchhandlung Nachfolger, 1989.

Süddeutsche Zeitung. München: No. 278, 3 June 1997.

Taylor, A. J. P. *The Origins of the Second World War*. Penguin Books, 1964.

Taylor, J. R. W. *History of Aviation*. New York: Crown Publishers Inc., 1972.

The Treaties of Peace 1919-1923. New York Carnegie Endowment for International Peace, 1924.

Thomas, Gordon and Witts, Max Morgan. *Guernica*. New York: Stein and Day, 1975.

Time Magazine, 7 August 1995.

Tripp, Miles. *The Eighth Passenger*. McMillan London Ltd., 1978.

Truelle, J. *La production aéronautique militaire Française*. Revue d'histoire de la deuxieme Guerre Mondiale, Vol. N. 73, 1969.

Ullrich, Volker. *Die nervöse Grossmacht*. Frankfurt: S. Fischer Verlag, 1997.

Verrier, Anthony. *The Bomber Offensive*. New York: Macmillan Company, 1968.

Vierteljahreshefte für Zeitgeschichte, July 1961, Vol. 3.

Völker, Karl-Heinz. *Dokumente und Dokumentarphotos zur Geschichte der Deutschen Luftwaffe*. Stuttgart: Deutsche Verlagsanstalt, 1968.

Völker, Karl-Heinz. *Die geheime Luftrüstung der Reichswehr und ihre Auswirkung auf den Flugzeugbestand der Luftwaffe bis zu Beginn des Zweiten Weltkrieges*. Wehrwissenschaftliche Rundschau 12, 1962.

Völker, Karl-Heinz. *Die Deutsche Heimatluftverteidigung im Zweiten Weltkrieg*. Wehrwissenschaftliche Rundschau, 1966, Heft 2.

Webster, Charles and Frankland, Noble. *The Strategic Air Offensive against Germany, 1939-1945*. London: H.M.S.O., 1961.

Weitz, John. *Joachim von Ribbentrop: Hitler's Diplomat*. London: Weidenfeld and Nicholson, 1992.

Weygand, Maxime. "How France is Defended," *International Affairs*, Vol. 18, 1939.

Whitehouse, Arch. *Heroes of the Sunlit Sky*. New York: Doubleday & Co. Inc., 1967.

Winterbotham, F. W. *The Ultra Secret*. Toronto: Fitzhenry & Whiteside Ltd., 1974.

Wyden, Peter. *La Guerra Apasionada*. Barcelona: Ediciones Martinez Roca, 1983, (original English title: *The Passionate War*).

Zank, Wolfgang. *Kaiserlicher Frieden*, Die Zeit No. 35, 3 September 1993.

Zuckerman, Solly. *From Apes to Warlords*. New York: Harper and Row Publishers Inc., 1979.

ENDNOTES

Preface

1. Geoffrey Best. *Humanity in Warfare* (New York: Columbia University Press, 1980), p. 283.
2. Ronald Schaffer, *Wings of Judgment* (Oxford: Oxford University Press, 1985), p. xiv.
3. Horst Boog, *The Conduct of the Air War in the Second World War* (Providence, RI: Berg Publishers Ltd., 1992), p. x.
4. Hoito Edoin, *The Night Tokyo Burned* (New York: St. Martin Press, 1987), p. vii.

Introduction

1. Dokumente aus den Jahren 1945-1949: Um ein antifaschistisch-demokratisches Deutschland (Berlin: Staatsverlag der Deutschen Demokratischen Republik, 1968), p. 107ff; Charles L. Mee, *Meeting at Potsdam* (New York: M. Evans & Co., 1975).
2. Ronald Schaffer, *Wings of Judgment*, p. 88; John Morton Blum, *Roosevelt and Morgenthau* (Boston: Houghton and Mifflin, 1970).
3. Dokumente aus den Jahren 1945–1949, p. 14ff.
4. Marlis G. Steinert, *Die 23 Tage der Regierung Dönitz* (Düsseldorf: Econ Verlag, 1967), p. 337.
5. Dokumente aus den Jahren 1945–1949, p. 43.

Chapter 1: Würzburg as Target

1. Martin Middlebrook, *The Battle of Hamburg* (Middlesex: Penguin Books, 1984); David Irving, *The Destruction of Dresden* (Yorkshire: William Kimber and Co. Ltd, published by Elmfield Press, 1974); Alexander McKee, *Dresden 1945* (New York: Dutton, 1984).
2. "Schnellpressenfabrik Koenig & Bauer AG: Festschrift zum 150 jährigen Jubiläum, 1817–1967," p. 56 (Brochure for 150 year jubilee of factory).

3. Wesley Frank Craven and James Lea Cate, *The Army Air Forces in World War II*, Vol. III (The University of Chicago Press, 1948), p. vi.
4. Public Records Office, London (PRO): FO 837/1314, pp. 742–745.
5. PRO: FO 837/1315.
6. PRO: AIR 42/17.
7. PRO: AIR 25/125.
8. Bayerisches Staatsarchiv (Würzburg: Collection Schäffer), folder 28.
9. Stadtarchiv Würzburg: XXXI Verwaltungsbericht der Stadt Würzburg (1943).
10. A. C. Mierzejewski, *The Collapse of the German War Economy, 1944-1945* (The University of North Carolina Press, 1988), p. 45.
11. PRO: AIR 8/428.
12. PRO: AIR 20/6110.
13. PRO: AIR 20/3724.
14. Hansard, House of Commons, Vol. 407, London, 1945.

Chapter 2: The Raids Begin

1. PRO: AIR 14/3408.
2. PRO: AIR 14/232.
3. R. A. Freeman, *The Mighty Eighth War Diary* (London: Jane's Publishing Co. Ltd., 1981).
4. AFSHRC, 525.332 and 525.3081; NA: RG 18, 8th Air Force, Box 814 for 21/7/1944.
5. NA: RG 18, 8th Air Force, Box 814.
6. PRO: AIR 14/3422.
7. Roger A. Freeman, *The Mighty Eighth War Diary*, p. 447.
8. AFSHRC, 520.322.
9. AFSHRC, 519.322-1.
10. AFSHRC, 525.3081 and 520.332.
11. Martin Middlebrook and Chris Everitt, *The Bomber Command War Diaries, an Operational Reference Book, 1939-1945* (*BCWD*) (Penguin Books, 1990), p. 682.
12. PRO: AIR 25/125, AIR 27/689.
13. PRO: AIR 24/310, Document B1593.
14. PRO: AIR 27/689.
15. Hans Oppelt, *Würzburger Chronik des denkwürdigen Jahres 1945* (Verlag Schönigh, 1947); Max Domarus, *Der Untergang des alten Würzburg* (Gerolzhofen: Verlag Franz Teutsch, 1978); Heinrich Dunkhase, *Würzburg, 16. März 1945*; (Volkach Hart Druck, 1980); Rudolf Studtrucker, *In stummer Klage* (Würzburg: Mainfränkisches Museum, 1985); Dieter Rockenmaier, *Als vom Himmel Feuer fiel* (Echter Fränkische Gesellschaftsdruckerei und Verlag, 1995).

16. *BCWD*, pp. 271, 664.
17. PRO: AIR 24/312, Report No. K4020 of 19/3/45 and 10/4/45
18. Imperial War Museum, London, copy at Stadtarchiv Würzburg.
19. PRO: AIR 24/311.
20. AFSHRC, 520.332.
21. R. A. Freeman, *The Mighty Eighth War Diary*, p. 470.
22. AFSHRC, 526.331A.
23. AFSHRC, 520.332.
24. AFSHRC, GP 322-SU-OP(Bomb).
25. AFSHRC, 534.332A.
26. AFSHRC, SQ-FI-527-HI.
27. C. Webster and N. Frankland, *The Strategic Air Offensive against Germany, 1939-45* (SOAG), (London: H.M.S.O., 1961), p. 486.

Chapter 3: The Road to Area Bombing

1. Eugene M. Emme, *Impact of Air Power* (Princeton, NJ: D. van Norstrand Co. Inc., 1959), p. 21ff.
2. Quote of Harris. Anthony Verrier, *The Bomber Offensive* (New York: Macmillan Company, 1968), p. 275.
3. Arthur Harris, *Bomber Offensive* (London: Collins, 1947), p. 176.
4. J. M. Spaight, *Bombing Vindicated* (London: Geoffrey Bles, 1944), p. 22.
5. AFSHRC, K239.0512-755, pp. 14, 17.
6. AFSHRC, K239.0512-627, p. 3.
7. Giulio Douhet, *Command of the Air* (London: Faber and Faber Ltd., 1943).
8. Andrew Boyle, *Trenchard* (London: Collins, 1962).
9. As displayed in the RAF Church St. Clement Danes in the City of London.
10. Isaac Don Levine, *Mitchell Pioneer of Air Power* (New York: Duell Sloane and Pearce, 1943).
11. Earl of Birkenhead, *The Prof in two Worlds* (London: Collins, 1961).
12. Stadtarchiv Darmstadt: Letter Dr. R. Anton, 1971.
13. Technische Hochschule Darmstadt Archivstelle: Personalverzeichnis der Grossherzoglich Hessischen THD, 1905-1908.
14. Humboldt Universitäts Archiv, Berlin: Philosophische Fakultät, Littr P, No.4, Vol. 290.
15. Birkenhead, *The Prof*, p. 245.
16. PRO: AIR 20/4770, this file also contains copies of the original Cherwell memo to Churchill and subsequent evaluations of the air staff.
17. Ronald W. Clark, *Tizard* (Cambridge, MA: Massachusetts Institute of Technology Press).

18. Solly Zuckerman, *From Apes to Warlords* (New York: Harper and Row Publishers Inc., 1979), p. 113ff.
19. Ibid., p. 242.
20. S. Harvey, "The Italian War Effort and the Strategic Bombing of Italy," *History*, Vol. 70, No. 228, February 1985, p. 41ff.
21. PRO: AIR 10/3866.
22. Raymond H. Fredette, *The First Battle of Britain* (London: Cassell & Co. Ltd., 1966), p. 31.
23. Dermot Bradley, *Generalleutnant Walter Wever: Eine vorbildliche Persönlichkeit der Luftwaffe* (Europäische Wehrkunde, 1, 1979), pp. 23–28.
24. Eugene M. Emme, *The Impact of Air Power*, p. 181ff.
25. Ibid, p. 184.
26. Karl-Heinz Völker, *Dokumente und Dokumentarphotos zur Geschichte der Deutschen Luftwaffe* (Stuttgart: Deutsche Verlagsanstalt 1968), p. 482.
27. Bernhard Heimann and Joachim Schunke, *Eine geheime Denkschrift zur Luftkriegkonzeption Hitler-Deutschlands vom Mai 1933* (Zeitschrift für Militärgeschichte, 1964).

Chapter 4: The Bomber Practitioners

1. Arthur Harris, *Bomber Offensive*, p. 242; Dudley Saward, *Bomber Harris* (London: Sphere Books Ltd., 1986), p. 373.
2. Andrew Boyle, *Trenchard*, p. 287.
3. Ibid., p. 244.
4. Ibid., p. 365.
5. Ibid., p. 508ff.
6. Ibid., p. 712.
7. Ibid., p. 468.
8. Ernst von Höppner: Deutschlands Krieg in der Luft, Leipzig, 1921.
9. Ibid., p. 152.
10. Andrew Boyle, *Trenchard*, p. 509.
11. Denis Richards, *Portal of Hungerford* (London: Heinemann, 1977), p. 87.
12. Ibid., p. 163.
13. Dudley Saward, *Bomber Harris*, p. 193.
14. My thanks once more to the gentleman, whose name I unfortunately cannot decipher from my notes.
15. Dudley Saward, *Bomber Harris*, p. 40.
16. Arthur Harris, *Bomber Offensive*, p. 28.

17. Ibid., p. 147.
18. Dudley Saward, *Bomber Harris*, p. 160.
19. Ibid., p. 130.
20. Charles Messenger, *Bomber Harris and the Strategic Bombing Offensive, 1939-1945* (London: Arms and Armour Press, 1984).
21. *The Strategic Air Offensive against Germany, 1939-1945 (SOAG).*
22. Charles Messenger, *Bomber Harris*, p. 55.
23. Ibid., p. 193.
24. Dudley Saward, *Bomber Harris*, p. 430 ff.
25. Charles Messenger, *Bomber Harris*, p. 197.
26. Arthur T. Harris, *Despatch on War Operations* (London: Frank Cass & Co. Ltd., 1995), "Editorial Preface."
27. Ronald Schaffer, *Wings of Judgment*, p. 62.
28. Ibid., p. 102.
29. Ibid., p. 14.
30. AFSHRC, 520-3233-40.
31. Thomas M. Coffey, *Iron Eagle* (New York: Crown Publishers Inc., 1986), p. 10.
32. *Time* Magazine, 7 August 1995, p. 35.
33. Thomas M. Coffey, *Iron Eagle*, p. 3.
34. Curtis E. LeMay, *Mission with LeMay* (Garden City, NY: Doubleday Inc., 1965), p. 565.
35. Ronald Schaffer, *Wings of Judgment*, p. 92.
36. Ibid., p. 12.
37. Ibid., p. 56.
38. Craven and Cate, *The Army Air Forces in World War II*, Vol. I; p. 443.
39. Ronald Schaffer, *Wings of Judgment*, p. 97.
40. Ibid., p. 252.
41. Dudley Saward, *Bomber Harris*, p. 209.
42. Ludwig Peters, *Volkslexikon Drittes Reich, die Jahre 1933 -1945* (Gräbert Verlag Tübingen, 1994).
43. Kenneth Macksey, *Kesselring, the Making of the Luftwaffe* (New York: David McKay Co.·Inc., 1978), p. 8.
44. Basil Collier, *The Defence of the United Kingdom* (London: H.M.S.O., 1957), p. 452.
45. Kenneth Macksey, *Kesselring, the Making of the Luftwaffe*, p. 80.
46. Hans Rumpf, *Deutsche und Englische Luftkriegsstrategie im Zweiten Weltkrieg* (Wehrkunde, 1955), Heft 10.
47. Anthony Verrier, *The Bomber Offensive*, p. 276.
48. Roderic Owen, *Tedder* (London: Collins, 1952), p. 277.
49. Ibid., p. 286.

Chapter 5: Bombing in World War I

1. Volker Ullrich, *Die nervöse Grossmacht*, (Frankfurt: S. Fischer Verlag, 1997), p. 21ff.
2. L. C. B. Seaman, *From Vienna to Versailles* (London: Methuen & Co., 1985), p. 41.
3. Volker Ullrich, *Die nervöse Grossmacht*, p. 193.
4. Ibid., p. 25.
5. Ibid., p. 135.
6. Statistisches Bundesamt, *Wiesbaden: Bevölkerung und Wirtschaft 1872-1972* (Stuttgart: Verlag Kahlhammer, 1972), p. 115.
7. Andrew R. Carlson, *German Foreign Policy 1890-1914, Colonial Policy to 1914* (Metuchen, NJ; Scarecrow Press Inc., 1970), p. 59.
8. Ibid., p. 60.
9. Maximilian Czesany, *Nie wieder Krieg gegen die Zivilbevölkerung*; (Graz, Austria: Selbstverlag, 1951), p. 54.
10. Andrew R. Carlson, *German Foreign Policy 1890-1914*, p. 110.
11. Ibid., p. 108.
12. Schnellpressenfabrik, *Festschrift*, p. 15.
13. L.C.B. Seaman, *From Vienna to Versailles*, p. 158.
14. Maximilian Czesany, *Alliierter Bombenterror* (Berg am Starnberger See: Druffel Verlag, 1986), p. 724.
15. Olaf Groehler, *Geschichte des Luftkriegs 1910 bis 1970* (Berlin: Militärverlag der Deutschen Demokratischen Republik, 1975), p. 85.
16. Charles L. Mee Jr, *The End of Order* (New York: E.P. Dutton, 1980), p. 260.
17. Nicholas Rengger, *Treaties and Alliances of the World* (Longman Current Affairs, 1990), p. 162.
18. *Vierteljahreshefte für Zeitgeschichte*, July 1961, Vol.3, p. 234ff.
19. Olaf Groehler, *Geschichte des Luftkriegs 1910 bis 1970*, p. 15.
20. Ibid., p. 18.
21. Ibid., p. 19.
22. Alexander Boyd, *The Soviet Air Force* (New York: Stein and Day, 1977), p. 1; Ernst v. Höppner, *Deutschlands Krieg in der Luft*, p. 4.
23. E. Angelucci and P. Matricardi, *World Aircraft* (New York: Rand McNally & Co., 1975); J. R. W Taylor, *History of Aviation* (New York: Crown Publishers, 1972).
24. BMA: RH 8 V.3594, p. 77; PRO: AIR 8/258; Olaf Groehler, *Geschichte des Luftkriegs*, p. 58.
25. *Chronicle of Aviation* (Liberty, MS: J.L. International Publishing Inc., 1992), p. 120.
26. R. H. Fredette, *The First Battle of Britain: 1917-1918*, p. 11.
27. Ernst v. Höppner, *Deutschlands Krieg in der Luft*, p. 21.

28. Malcolm Brown and Shirley Seaton, *Christmas Truce* (New York: Hippocrene Books, 1984).
29. Andrew Boyle, *Trenchard*, p. 208.
30. R. H. Fredette, *The First Battle of Britain*, p. 31.
31. J. M. Spaight, *Air Power and War Rights* (London: Longmans, Green and Co., 1947), p. 375.
32. Ibid., p. 222.
33. J. M. Spaight, *Air Power and War Rights* (London: Longmans, Green and Co., 1924), p. 45.
34. R. H. Fredette, *The First Battle of Britain*, p. 32.
35. Kenneth Poolman, *Zeppelins over England* (London: Evans Brothers Ltd., 1960).
36. R. H. Fredette, *The First Battle of Britain*.
37. J. M. Spaight, *Air Power and War Rights* (London, 1924), p. 41.
38. Arch. Whitehouse, *Heroes of the Sunlit Sky* (New York: Doubleday & Co. Inc., 1967), p. 234.
39. R. Rimell, *Zeppelin* (Canada: Wings Inc., 1984).
40. R. H. Fredette, *The First Battle of Britain*, p. 118.
41. Ernst v. Höppner, *Deutschlands Krieg in der Luft*, p. 57.
42. J. M. Spaight, *Air Power and War Rights* (London, 1924), p. 41.
43. Olaf Groehler, *Geschichte des Luftkriegs 1910 bis 1970*, p. 36.
44. J. M. Spaight, *Air Power and War Rights* (London; 1924). p. 200, quoting D. Vincent, *La bataille de l'air*, 1918, p. 49.
45. Giulio Douhet, *Command of the Air*, p. 24.
46. Russell Miller, *The Soviet Air Force at War* (Chicago, IL: Time-Life Books, 1983), p. 31.
47. J. M. Spaight, *Air Power and War Rights* (London, 1947), p. 232.
48. Thomas Harrison, *Living through the Blitz* (New York: Schocken Books), p. 18.
49. Heinz Eisgruber, *So schossen wir nach Paris* (Berlin: Vorhut Verlag Otto Schlegel, 1934).
50. Henry W. Miller, *The Paris Gun* (London: George G. Harrap and Co., 1930), p. 66.
51. Ibid., p. 123.
52. R. H. Fredette, *The First Battle of Britain*, p. 72.
53. Geoffrey Best, *Humanity in Warfare*, p. 270.
54. Andrew Boyle, *Trenchard*, p. 312.
55. Ernst v. Höppner, *Deutschlands Krieg in der Luft*, p. 152.
56. PRO: AIR 1/2104.
57. R. H. Fredette, *The First Battle of Britain*, p. 222.
58. Ibid., p. 220.
59. PRO: Parliamentary Papers 1919, Vol. LIII, p. 927 ff, report by Ernest H. Starlin; J. M. Spaight, *Bombing Vindicated, 1944*, p. 119.

Chapter 6: Between the World Wars

1. As quoted from other sources in: Spaight, *Bombing Vindicated*, (1944), p. 13.
2. Bayer Presse-Information: November 1994 and personal correspondence with Bayer, 9 January 1998.
3. Charles L. Mee, *The End of Order*, p. 261.
4. Ibid., p. 222.
5. Ibid., p. 260.
6. Alex de Jonge, *The Weimar Chronicle* (Meridian Books, 1979), p. 75ff.
7. W. S. Churchill, *The Second World War: Triumph and Tragedy* (Boston: Houghton and Mifflin Co., 1953), p. 753.
8. Karl-Heinz Eyermann, *Der grosse Bluff* (Berlin [Ost]: aus Geheimarchiven der Deutschen Luftfahrt, 1963), pp. 337, 339.
9. David Irving, *Churchill's War* (Australia: Veritas Publishing Co. Pty. Ltd.), p. 125.
10. *Süddeutsche Zeitung, München*, No. 278, 3 June 1997, p. 51.
11. John Weitz, *Joachim von Ribbentrop: Hitler's Diplomat* (London: Weidenfeld and Nicholson, 1992), p. 304.
12. *The Treaties of Peace 1919-1923* (New York: Carnegie Endowment of International Peace, 1924).
13. Maximilian Czesany, *Alliierter Bombenterror*, p. 68ff.
14. Ibid., p. 74.
15. J. M. Spaight, *Air Power and War Rights* (1947), p. 246.
16. Maximilian Czesany, *Alliierter Bombenterror*, p. 17.
17. Andrew Boyle, *Trenchard*, p. 339.
18. Russell Miller, *The Soviet Air Force at War*, p. 35.
19. Alexander Boyd, *The Soviet Air Force*, p. 3ff.
20. Hilton Proctor Goss, *Civilian Morale under Aerial Bombardment, 1914-1939* (Montgomery, AL: Maxwell Air Force Base, Documentary Research Division, Air Universities Libraries, 1940), p. 77.
21. Brown, Shores and Macksay, *Guiness History of Air Warfare* (Middlesex: Guiness Superlatives Ltd., 1976), p. 64.
22. Ibid., p. 63.
23. David E. Omissi, *Air Power and Colonial Control: The Royal Air Force 1919-1939* (Manchester: Manchester University Press, 1990), p. 11.
24. Andrew Boyle, *Trenchard*, p. 354.
25. Ibid., p. 369.
26. Ibid., p. 389.
27. Brown, Shores and Macksay, *Guiness History of Air Warfare*, p. 64.
28. PRO: CAB 23/55, Meeting 52 (1927).

29. Andrew Boyle, *Trenchard*, p. 570.
30. PRO: AIR 2/1385.
31. Russell Grenfell, *Bedingungsloser Hass* (Tübingen: Verlag Fritz Schlichtenmayer, 1955) (original English title: *Unconditional Hatred*), p. 201.
32. Andrew Boyle, *Trenchard*, p. 468.
33. Eugene M. Emme, *The Impact of Air Power*, p. 51ff.
34. J. M. Spaight, *Air Power and War Rights* (1947), p. 251.
35. David E. Omissi, *Air Power and Colonial Control*, p. 185ff.
36. Ibid., p. 195.
37. Ibid., pp. 199 and 200.
38. R. J. Overy, *The Air War 1939-1945* (New York: Stein & Day, 1981), p. 18.
39. Claudio G. Segre, *Italo Balbo: a Fascist Life* (University of California Press, 1987).
40. Brown, Shores and Macksay, *Guiness History of Air Warfare*, p. 74; David E. Omissi, *Air Power and Colonial Control*, p. 203.
41. Peter Wyden, *La Guerra Apasionada* (Barcelona: Ediciones Martinez Roca, 1983), p. 103 (original English title: *The Passionate War*).
42. Paul Preston, *Franco* (London: Fontana Press, 1995), p. 166.
43. Ibid., p. 157.
44. Russell Miller, *The Soviet Air Force at War*, p. 65.
45. Paul Preston, *Franco*, p. 203.
46. Ibid., p. 200ff.
47. Russell Miller, *The Soviet Air Force at War*, p. 65.
48. Olaf Groehler, *Geschichte des Luftkriegs*, p. 186ff.
49. Peter Wyden, *La Guerra Apasionada*, p. 144ff.
50. Alexander Boyd, *The Soviet Air Force*, p. 81.
51. Ibid., p. 79.
52. Olaf Groehler, *Geschichte des Luftkriegs*.
53. Paul Preston, *Franco*, pp. 237, 238.
54. BMA Freiburg: RL 35/38.
55. Paul Preston, *Franco*, p. 244.
56. Peter Wyden, *La Guerra Apasionada*, p. 340.
57. Paul Preston, *Franco*, p. 243.
58. David Irving, *Von Guernica bis Vietnam* (Wilhelm Heine Verlag, 1982), p. 38 (original English title: *From Guernica to Vietnam*).
59. Gordon Thomas and Max Morgan Witts, *Guernica*, (New York: Stein and Day, 1975), p. 288.
60. Peter Wyden, *La Guerra Apasionada*, p. 429ff.
61. George Allen, *Images of the Spanish Civil War* (London: Unwin Publishers Ltd., 1986), p. 152.
62. Paul Preston, *Franco*, p. 303.

63. BMA Freiburg: RL 35/22 and RL 35/7.
64. Olaf Groehler, *Geschichte des Luftkriegs*, p. 186ff.
65. Ibid., p. 186ff.
66. Harryman Maurer, *The End Is Not Yet* (New York: Robert M. McBride, 1941), p. 104ff.
67. J. M. Spaight, *Air Power and War Rights* (1947), p. 256.
68. Olaf Groehler, *Geschichte des Luftkriegs*, p. 509.
69. Hilton Proctor Goss, *Civilian Morale under Aerial Bombardment*, p. 138ff.
70. J. M. Spaight, *Air Power and War Rights* (1947), p. 256.
71. P. Le Goyet, "Évolution de la doctrine de l'emploi de l'aviation entre 1919 et 1939," *Revue d'histoire de la deuxieme guerre mondiale*, Nr. 73, 1969, p. 15.
72. Alexander Boyd, *The Soviet Air Force*, p. XIII.
73. Olaf Groehler, *Geschichte des Luftkriegs*, p. 122.
74. Greenhous et al, *The Crucible of War 1939-1945* (University of Toronto Press, 1994), p. 528.
75. Olaf Groehler, *Geschichte des Luftkriegs*, p. 120.
76. P. Le Goyet, *Évolution de la doctrine d'emploi de l'aviation*, p. 4ff.
77. J. R. W. Taylor, *History of Aviation*, p. 124.
78. Russell Miller, *The Soviet Air Force at War*, p. 53.
79. BMA Freiburg: RH8v.3620, p. 22.
80. Claudio G. Segre, *Italo Balbo: a Fascist Life*, p. 149.
81. Ibid., p. 155ff.
82. BMA Freiburg: RH8v.3594.
83. BMA Freiburg: RH8v.3594, p. 30.
84. BMA Freiburg: RH8v.3605.
85. Karl-Heinz Völker, *Dokumente und Dokumentarfotos zur Geschichte der Deutschen Luftwaffe*, p. 12ff.
86. Karl-Heinz Völker, *Die geheime Luftrüstung der Reichswehr und ihre Auswirkung auf den Flugzeugbestand der Luftwaffe bis zu Beginn des Zweiten Weltkrieges* (Wehrwissenschaftliche Rundschau 12, 1962), pp. 540–549.
87. Ludwig Peters, *Volkslexikon Drittes Reich, die Jahre 1933-1945 in Wort und Bild*.
88. Alexander Boyd, *The Soviet Air Force*, p. 24.
89. BMA Freiburg: RH8v.3621.
90. BMA Freiburg: RH8v.3680.
91. BMA Freiburg: RH8v.3610.
92. Karl-Heinz Völker, *Dokumente und Dokumentarfotos*, p. 12ff.
93. BMA Freiburg: RH8v.3601.
94. David Irving, *Die Tragödie der Deutschen Luftwaffe* (Klagenfurt, Austria: Hans Kaiser Verlag, 1970), p. 38.

95. Olaf Groehler, *Geschichte des Luftkriegs*, pp. 144, 145.

96. BMA Freiburg: RH8v.3601, p. 67.

97. Andrew Boyle, *Trenchard*, p. 708.

98. Ibid., p. 709.

99. Olaf Groehler, *Geschichte des Luftkriegs*, p. 205.

100. A. J. P. Taylor, *The Origins of the Second World War* (Penguin Books, 1964), p. 16.

101. R. J. Overy, *The Air War 1939-1945*, p. 19.

102. Olaf Groehler, *Geschichte des Luftkriegs*, p. 204.

103. Maximilian Czesany, *Alliierter Bombenterror*, p. 88.

104. W. S. Churchill, *The Second World War: The Gathering Storm*.

105. A. J. P. Taylor, *The Origins of the Second World War*, p. 17.

106. T. M. Fehrenbach, *F.D.R.'s Undeclared War* (New York: David McKay Inc., 1967), p. 2.

107. BMA Freiburg: RH12-1/121.

108. Hilmar v. Buelow, *Die Luftrüstungen des Auslands: 1935/1936* (Jahrbuch der Deutschen Luftwaffe, 1937), p. 87.

109. R. J. Overy, *The Air War 1939-1945*, p. 21.

110. Maximilian Czesany, *Alliierter Bombenterror*, p. 86.

111. David Irving, *Die Tragödie der Deutschen Luftwaffe*, p. 121.

112. A. J. P. Taylor, *The Origins of the Second World War*, p. 249.

113. Louis C. Kilzer, *Churchill's Deception* (New York: Simon and Schuster, 1994), p. 149.

Chapter 7: Bombing in World War II

1. Eugene M. Emme, *The Impact of Air Power*, p. 68.

2. J. M. Spaight, *Air Power and War Rights* (1947), p. 257ff.

3. Maxime Weygand, "How France is Defended," *International Affairs*, Vol. 18, 1939, p. 471.

4. Cajus Bekker, *The Luftwaffe War Diaries* (London: Macdonald & Co. Publishers Ltd., 1967), p. 58 (original German title: *Angriffshöhe 4,000*).

5. David Irving, *Hitler's War* (New York: The Viking Press), p. 27.

6. Alexander Boyd, *The Soviet Air Force*, p. 84ff.

7. Richard W. Condon, *The Winter War, Russia against Finland* (New York: Ballantine Books, 1972).

8. Ibid., p. 21.

9. Alexander Boyd, *The Soviet Air Force*, p. 90.

10. Maximilian Czesany, *Alliierter Bombenterror*, p. 520.

11. F. W. Winterbotham, *The Ultra Secret* (Toronto: Fitzhenry & Whiteside Ltd., 1974), p. 6; Maximilian Czesany, *Alliierter Bombenterror*, p. 106.

12. R. J. Overy, *The Air War 1939-1945*, p. 14.

13. Greenhous et al, *The Crucible of War*, p. 534.

14. Neville Jones, *The Beginnings of Strategic Air Power* (London: Frank Cass & Co.Ltd., 1987), p. 141.

15. K. H. Völker, *Die Deutsche Heimatluftverteidigung im Zweiten Weltkrieg* (Wehrwissenschaftliche Rundschau, 1966) Heft 2, p. 89.

16. BMA Freiburg: RL 2II/25.

17. Ibid.

18. Ibid.

19. R. J. Overy, *The Air War 1939-1945*, p. 14.

20. John Killen, *A History of the Luftwaffe* (Toronto: Bantam Books, 1986), p. 97.

21. BMA Freiburg: RL 2II/25.

22. BMA Freiburg: RL 2II/24.

23. PRO: CAB 66/4.

24. PRO: CAB 65/12.

25. PRO: CAB 65/12.

26. BMA Freiburg: RL 2II/25.

27. *BCWD*, p. 30.

28. PRO: FO 371/17751, File C7884/247/18.

29. Basil Collier, *The Defence of the United Kingdom*, pp. 26, 27.

30. R. J. Overy, *The Air War 1939-1945*, p. 27.

31. PRO: CAB 65/5 and CAB 65/11.

32. Cajus Bekker, *The Luftwaffe Diaries*, p. 112.

33. Greenhous et al, *The Crucible of War*, p. 533.

34. David Divine, *The Broken Wing* (London: Hutchinson & Co. Ltd., 1966), p. 237.

35. *BCWD*, p. 42.

36. R. J. Overy, *The Air War 1939-1945*, p. 36.

37. Robert Jackson, *Air War over France: May-June 1940* (Shepperton, Surrey: Ian Allan Ltd., 1974), p. 134.

38. Ibid., p. 135; J. Truelle, *La production aéronautique militaire Française 14 jusqu'en Juin 1940,* Vol. N. 73 (Revue d'histoire de la deuxieme Guerre Mondiale, 1969), p. 76ff.

39. J. M. Spaight, *Bombing Vindicated*, p. 46.

40. Anton Hoch, *Der Luftangriff auf Freiburg am 10 Mai 1940* (Vierteljahreshefte für Zeitgeschichte 4, 1956), Heft 3.

41. Robert Jackson, *Air War over France*, pp. 106, 107.

42. Private communication of author with BMW Works, Munich.

43. *BCWD*, p. 51ff.

44. Robert Jackson, *Air War over France*, p. 122ff.

45. Hermann Böhme, *Entstehung und Grundlagen des Waffenstillstandes von 1940* (Stuttgart: Deutsche Verlagsanstalt, 1966), p. 41.

46. Ibid., p. 46.

47. *Chronicle of Aviation*, p. 376.
48. Eberhard Jäckel, *Frankreich in Hitlers Europa: Die Deutsche Frankreichpolitik im Zweiten Weltkrieg* (Stuttgart : Deutsche Verlagsanstalt, 1966), p. 75.
49. Robert Jackson, *Air War over France*, Appendix 4.
50. Louis C. Kilzer, *Churchill's Deception*, p. 266ff.
51. R. J. Overy, *The Air War 1939-1945*, p. 39.
52. Karl-Heinz Eyermann, *Der grosse Bluff*, p. 290.
53. Basil Collier, *The Defence of the United Kingdom*, Appendices X, XII and XIV.
54. PRO: AIR 20/4704.
55. David Divine, *The Broken Wing*, p. 231.
56. R. J. Overy, *The Air War 1939-1945*, p. 23.
57. Ibid., p. 28.
58. Karl Gundelach, *Der Alliierte Luftkrieg gegen die Deutsche Treibstoffversorgung* (Wehrwissenschaftliche Rundschau, 13, Heft 12), pp. 686–706.
59. David Irving, *Churchill's War*, p. 336.
60. *Deutsches Weissbuch 1943, Englands Alleinschuld am Bombenterror* (Zentralverlag der NSDAP), p. 125.
61. Uta Hohn, *Die Zerstörung Deutscher Städte im Zweiten Weltkrieg* (Dortmund: Dortmunder Vertrieb für Bau-und Planungsliteratur, 1991), p. 223.
62. *BCWD*, p. 93.
63. Basil Collier, *The Defence of the United Kingdom*, Appendix XVII.
64. Cajus Bekker, *The Luftwaffe Diaries*, Appendix 6.
65. Basil Collier, *The Defence of the United Kingdom*, Appendix XXX.
66. Uta Hohn, *Die Zerstörung Deutscher Städte im Zweiten Weltkrieg*, p. 293.
67. David Irving, *Die Tragödie der Deutschen Luftwaffe*, p. 176.
68. *BCWD*, p. 111.
69. Basil Collier, *The Defence of the United Kingdom*, p. 261.
70. Ibid., Appendix XXVIII.
71. PRO: AIR 20/2565.
72. R. J. Overy, *The Air War 1939-1945*, p. 150.
73. Ibid., p. 150.
74. Ibid., p. 50.
75. C. Shores, B. Cull and N. Malizia, *Air War for Yugoslavia, Greece and Crete, 1940-1941* (London: Squadron Signal Publications, 1987), Ch. 1.
76. Ibid., Ch. 4.
77. Maximilian Czesany, *Alliierter Bombenterror*, p. 240ff.
78. W. S. Churchill, *The Grand Alliance*, p. 175.
79. Maximilian Czesany, *Alliierter Bombenterror*, p. 243.

80. Olaf Groehler, *Der Bombenkrieg gegen Deutschland* (Berlin: Akademie Verlag, 1990), p. 14.
81. C. Shores, B. Cull and N. Malizia, *Air War for Yugoslavia, Greece and Crete*, Ch. 4.
82. PRO: AIR 24/1670.
83. Wolfgang Zank, *Kaiserlicher Frieden*, Die Zeit No. 35, 3 September 1993.
84. Victor Suworow, *Der Eisbrecher-Hitler in Stalins Kalkül* (Stuttgart: Cottasche Buchhandlung Nachfolger, 1989).
85. Werner Maser, *Der Wortbruch: Hitler, Stalin und der Zweite Weltkrieg* (München: Olzog Verlag, 1994), p. 324ff.
86. Russell Miller, *The Soviet Air Force at War*, p. 80.
87. Werner Maser, *Der Wortbruch*, p. 137.
88. Alexander Boyd, *The Soviet Air Force*, p. 98.
89. Russell Miller, *The Soviet Air Force at War*, p. 87.
90. Olaf Groehler, *Geschichte des Luftkriegs*, p. 510.
91. Olaf Groehler, *Der Bombenkrieg gegen Deutschland*, p. 160ff.
92. Alexander Boyd, *The Soviet Air Force*, p. 128.
93. Ibid., p. 121.
94. Russell Miller, *The Soviet Air Force at War*, p. 111.
95. Ibid., p. 116.
96. Ibid., p. 93ff.
97. Ibid., p. 151.
98. Olaf Groehler, *Geschichte des Luftkriegs*, p. 391ff.
99. Hans-Detlev Herhudt v. Rohden, *Letzter Grosseinsatz Deutscher Bomber im Osten* (Wehrwissenschaftliche Rundschau, 1951), Heft 1, p. 21.
100. Eric Brown, *Wings of the Luftwaffe* (Garden City, NY: Doubleday & Co. Inc.), p. 49.
101. Maximilian Czesany, *Alliierter Bombenterror*, p. 230.
102. Curtis E. LeMay, *Mission with LeMay*, p. 358.
103. *BCWD*, p. 209.
104. *SOAG*, Vol. IV, p. 135.
105. *BCWD*, p. 180.
106. Craven and Cate, *The Army Air Forces in World War II*, Vol. I, p. 109.
107. Ibid., p. 104.
108. Olaf Groehler, *Geschichte des Luftkriegs 1910 bis 1970*, p. 494.
109. PRO: AIR 14/3526.
110. W. S. Churchill, *The Grand Alliance*, p. 492.
111. T. R. Fehrenbach, *F. D. R.'s Undeclared War*; p. 225.
112. Haywood S. Hansell, *The Air Plan that Defeated Hitler* (Atlanta, GA, 1972), p. 70.
113. R. J. Overy, *The Air War 1939-1945*, p. 15.

114. Anthony Verrier, *The Bomber Offensive*, p. 275.
115. Arthur T. Harris, *Despatch on War Operations*, p. 206, item 10.
116. *SOAG*, Vol. IV; p. 143.
117. *SOAG*, Vol. I; p. 324.
118. PRO: AIR 20/8146.
119. PRO: AIR 14/232.
120. PRO: CAB 120/300.
121. Ibid.
122. Ibid.
123. Ibid.
124. PRO: AIR 8/1015.
125. *BCWD*, p. 259ff.
126. Uta Hohn, *Die Zerstörung Deutscher Städte im Zweiten Weltkrieg*, table 16, p. 240.
127. PRO: AIR 20/4770.
128. Solly Zuckerman, *From Apes to Warlords*, p. 143.
129. Anthony Verrier, *The Bomber Offensive*, Appendix 3.
130. PRO: AIR 20/4770.
131. *SOAG*, Vol. I, p. 182.
132. Ronald W. Clark, *Tizard*, p. 310.
133. Ibid., p. 309.
134. PRO: AIR 20/4770.
135. Ibid.
136. PRO: AIR 8/1014.
137. PRO: AIR 20/4770.
138. Denis Richards, *Portal of Hungerford*, p. 167.
139. W. F. Craven and J. L. Cate, *The Army Air Forces in World War II*, Vol. II, p. 218.
140. Haywood S. Hansell, *The Air Plan that defeated Hitler*, Appendix IV.
141. *SOAG*, Vol. IV, p. 153.
142. Arthur Harris, *Bomber Offensive*, p. 147.
143. Ibid., p. 176.
144. H. R. Allen, *The Legacy of Lord Trenchard* (London: Cassell, 1972), p. 103.
145. Arthur Harris, *Bomber Offensive*, p. 177.
146. *BCWD*, p. 242.
147. Arthur Harris, *Bomber Offensive*, p. 141.
148. *SOAG*, Vol. IV, p. 152.
149. Anthony Verrier, *The Bomber Offensive: Harris Memo to Churchill, 28 June 1942*, p. 340.
150. Olaf Groehler, *Der Bombenkrieg gegen Deutschland*, p. 151.
151. Arthur Harris, *Despatch on War Operations*. p. 208.
152. Arthur Harris, *Bomber Offensive*, p. 101.

153. *BCWD*, p. 360.
154. *BCWD*, p. 407.
155. *BCWD*, p. 244.
156. *BCWD*, p. 409.
157. Examples are Martin Middlebrook, *The Battle of Hamburg*; Hans Brunswig, *Feuersturm über Hamburg*.
158. Josef Garlinski, *Hitler's Last Weapons* (London: Magnum Books, 1979), p. 90ff.
159. PRO: AIR 20/2565.
160. S. Harvey, "The Italian War Effort and Strategic Bombing of Italy," *History*, p. 36.
161. Ibid., p. 32 ff.
162. Olaf Groehler, *Geschichte des Luftkriegs*, p. 345.
163. Olaf Groehler, *Der Bombenkrieg gegen Deutschland*, p. 69.
164. PRO: AIR 14/2853.
165. S. Harvey, *The Italian War Effort and Strategic Bombing of Italy*, p. 32ff.
166. Larry J. Bidinian, *The Combined Allied Bombing Offensive against the German Civilian 1942-1945* (Lawrence, KS: Coronado Press, 1976), p. 9.
167. Olaf Groehler, *Geschichte des Luftkriegs*, p. 376.
168. Anthony Verrier, *The Bomber Offensive*, p. 330.
169. Ronald Schaffer, *Wings of Judgment*, p. 64.
170. Ibid., p. 66.
171. A. C. Mierzejewski, *The Collapse of the German War Economy*, p. 20.
172. Edward Jablonski, *America in the Air War* (Alexandria, VA: Time-Life Books, 1982).
173. Olaf Groehler, *Der Bombenkrieg gegen Deutschland*, p. 322.
174. W. F. Craven and J. L. Cate, *The Army Air Forces in World War II*, Vol. II, p. 667.
175. LC: Spaatz Papers, Box 215.
176. John Killen, *A History of the Luftwaffe*, p. 264ff.
177. A. C. Mierzejewski, *The Collapse of the German War Economy*, p. 20.
178. Olaf Groehler, *Der Bombenkrieg gegen Deutschland*, p. 188; the full details can be read in the *Bomber Command War Diaries*, pp. 446–484 and Martin Middlebrook's *The Berlin Raids* (Penguin Books, 1990).
179. *SOAG*, Vol. II, pp. 56, 190.
180. *BCWD*, p. 475.
181. Martin Middlebrook, *The Nuremberg Raid* (Penguin Books, 1986), p. 294.
182. *BCWD*, p. 488.
183. BA Koblenz: R 55/1357 Fiche 1.

184. Solly Zuckerman, *From Apes to Warlords*, Appendix 3, p. 406.

185. *BCWD*, p. 492.

186. Solly Zuckerman, *From Apes to Warlords*, p. 252.

187. Hilary St. George Saunders, *Royal Air Force 1939-1945* (London: HMSO, 1954), Vol. III, p. 88.

188. Alexander McKee, *Caen Anvil of Victory* (London: Souvenir Press, 1984), p. 287.

189. Maximilian Czesany, *Alliierter Bombenterror*, p. 545.

190. Alexander McKee, *Caen the Anvil of Victory*, p. 207.

191. Kit C. Carter and Robert Mueller, *The Army Air Forces in World War II*, (AFSHRC, 1973).

192. Josef Garlinski, *Hitler's Last Weapons*, Appendix III.

193. Ibid., p. 12.

194. Hilary St. George Saunders, *Royal Air Force 1939-1945*, Vol. III, p. 175.

195. PRO: PREM 3/89.

196. PRO: AIR 8/1225.

197. Dudley Saward, *Bomber Harris*, p. 339.

198. Hilary St. George Saunders, *Royal Air Force 1939-1945*, Vol. III, p. 85ff.

199. Maximilian Czesany, *Alliierter Bombenterror*, p. 527.

200. Ronald Schaffer, *Wings of Judgment*, p. 56.

201. Maximilian Czesany, *Alliierter Bombenterror*, p. 510.

202. Ibid., p. 626.

203. S. Harvey, *The Italian War Effort and Strategic Bombing of Italy*, p. 41ff.

204. Maximilian Czesany, *Alliierter Bombenterror*, p. 399.

205. Russell Miller, *The Soviet Air Force at War*, p. 152.

206. Hans Detlev Herhudt v. Rohden, *Letzter Grosseinsatz Deutscher Bomber im Osten*, p. 21ff.

207. Ronald Schaffer, *Wings of Judgment*, p. 62.

208. Ibid., p. 89.

209. Ibid., p. 84.

210. BA Koblenz: R 55 602, Fiche 4.

211. Arthur Harris, *Despatch on War Operations*, p. 200.

212. Dudley Saward, *Bomber Harris*, p. 360ff.

213. Solly Zuckerman, *From Apes to Warlords*, p. 355.

214. J. M. Spaight, *Air Power and War Rights* (1947), p. 280, quoting a Speer report of 19 January 1945.

215. Olaf Groehler, *Bombenkrieg gegen Deutschland*, p. 357.

216. Alfred C. Mierzejewski, *The Collapse of the German War Economy*, p. 210.

217. Olaf Groehler, *Geschichte des Luftkriegs*, p. 428.

218. Hilary St. George Saunders, *Royal Air Force 1939-1945*, Vol. III, p. 385.
219. *BCWD*, p. 641.
220. Hilary St. George Saunders, *Royal Air Force 1939-1945*, Vol. III, p. 388.
221. Olaf Groehler, *Bombenkrieg gegen Deutschland*, p. 227.
222. Hilary St. George Saunders, *Royal Air Force 1939-1945*, Vol. III, p. 388.
223. W. F. Craven and J. L. Cate, *The Army Air Forces in World War II*, Vol. III, p. 649.
224. Greenhous et al, *The Crucible of War 1939-1945*, p. 346.
225. PRO: AIR 20/4122.
226. Olaf Groehler, *Bombenkrieg gegen Deutschland*, p. 370.
227. LC: Spaatz Papers, Box 84.
228. Roger A. Freeman, *The Mighty Eighth War Diary*, p. 246.
229. J. M. Spaight, *Air Power and War Rights* (1947), p. 384.
230. Olaf Groehler, *Bombenkrieg gegen Deutschland*, p. 367.
231. Kit C. Carter and Robert Mueller, *The Army Air Forces in World War II*.
232. Bo Huldt and Klaus Richard Böhme, *Vårstormar, 1944—Krigsslutet skönjes* (Stockholm: Probus Förlag, 1995), p. 241.
233. Jonathan E. Helmreich, "The Diplomacy of Apology; US Bombings of Switzerland during World War II," *Air University Review*, May/June 1977, Vol. XXVIII, No. 4, p. 19.
234. *BCWD*, p. 22.
235. Jonathan E. Helmreich, "The Diplomacy of Apology."
236. Bo Huldt and Klaus-Richard Böhme, *Horisonten klarnar: 1945-Krigsslut* (Stockholm: Probus Förlag, 1995), p. 127.
237. Bo Huldt and Klaus-Richard Böhme, *Vårstormar*, p. 128.
238. Bo Huldt and Klaus-Richard Böhme, *Vårstormar and Horisonten klarnar*, pp. 154 and 133 respectively.
239. Bo Huldt and Klaus-Richard Böhme, *Horisonten klarnar*, p. 35.
240. PRO: AIR 24/309.
241. Craven and Cate, *The Army Air Forces in World War II*, Vol. III, p. 307.
242. Maximilian Czesany, *Alliierter Bombenterror*, p. 485.
243. Ibid., p. 494.
244. Herbert Schott, *Mainfränkisches Jahrbuch 1992* (Volkach: Verlag Hartdruck), p. 206.
245. PRO: AIR 20/3724.
246. Two of the most informative titles are: David Irving, *The Destruction of Dresden* and Franz Kurowski, *Das Massaker von Dresden* (Berg am Starnbergersee: Druffel Verlag, 1995).

247. Ibid. (Kurowski), p. 101.
248. *BCWD*, p. 663.
249. *BCWD*, p. 673.
250. PRO: AIR 14/3412.
251. PRO: AIR 16/572.
252. Maximilian Czesany, *Alliierter Bombenterror*, p. 186.
253. Roger A. Freeman, *The Mighty Eighth War Diary*, p. 340.
254. PRO: AIR 25/125.
255. Greenhous et al, *The Crucible of War*, p. 725.
256. PRO: AIR 20/4069.
257. T. R. Fehrenbach, *FDR's Undeclared War*, p. 279.
258. B. Martin, *Deutschland und Japan im Zweiten Weltkrieg* (Göttingen, 1969).
259. Hilary St. George Saunders, *Royal Air Force*, Vol. III, p. 411.
260. R. J. Overy, *The Air War 1939-1945*, p. 94.
261. AFSHRC, 118.04D.
262. NA: RG.165, file ABC, file 384.5, Japan 9/11/43.
263. Haywood S. Hansell, *Strategic Air War against Japan* (Montgomery, AL: Maxwell Air Force Base, Air War College, Air Power Research Institute, 1980), pp. 17–24.
264. R. J. Overy, *The Air War 1939–1945*, p. 96.
265. Ibid., p. 113.
266. Thomas M. Coffey, *Iron Eagle*, p. 147.
267. Barton J. Bernstein, "A Postwar Myth: 500,000 US Lives Saved," *Bulletin of Atomic Scientists*, Vol. 42, No. 6, June/July 1986, p. 38.
268. AFSHRC, 118.04D.
269. AFSHRC, 118.151-17.
270. Haywood S. Hansell, *Strategic Air War against Japan*, p. 49.
271. Ronald Schaffer, *Wings of Judgment*, p. 121.
272. Curtis E. LeMay, *Mission with LeMay*, p. 384.
273. Hoito Edoin, *The Night Tokyo Burned*, p. 204.
274. Ibid., p. 184.
275. R. J. Overy, *The Air War 1939–1945*, p. 99.
276. Hoito Edoin, *The Night Tokyo Burned*, p. 4.
277. Thomas M. Coffey, *Iron Eagle*, p. 150.
278. Ronald Schaffer, *Wings of Judgment*, p. 132.
279. Curtis E. LeMay, *Mission with LeMay*, p. 353.
280. Robert Guillain, *I Saw Tokyo Burning* (Garden City, NY: Doubleday and Co. Inc., 1981), report of a French national living during the war and the raid in Tokyo.
281. David MacIsaac, *Strategic Bombing in World War Two* (New York and London: Garland Publishing Inc., 1976), p. 101.
282. Charles L. Mee, *Meeting at Potsdam*, p. 252.

283. Larry J. Bidinian, *The Combined Allied Bombing Offensive against the German Civilian, 1942-1945.*
284. Otis Carey, "The Sparing of Kyoto (Mr. Stimson's Pet City)," *Japan Quarterly*, October/December 1975, Vol. XXII, No. 4.
285. Ronald Schaffer, *Wings of Judgment*, p. 148.
286. R. J. Overy, *The Air War 1939-1945*, p. 100.

Chapter 8: Military and Civil Defense

1. Dudley Saward, *Bomber Harris*, p. 16.
2. R. H. Fredette, *The First Battle of Britain*, p. 261.
3. Olaf Groehler, *Geschichte des Luftkriegs*, p. 82ff.
4. Robert Cecil, *Hitler's War Machine* (London: Salamander Books Ltd., 1975), p. 155.
5. Basil Collier, *The Defence of the United Kingdom*, p. I.
6. David Divine, *The Broken Wing*, p. 227.
7. Hilary St. George Saunders, *Royal Air Force 1939-1945*, Vol. III, Appendices VIII to X.
8. Earl of Birkenhead, *The Prof. in Two Worlds*, p. 176.
9. Erich Hampe, *Der Zivile Luftschutz im Zweiten Weltkrieg* (Frankfurt/Main: Bernard & Graefe Verlag, 1963), p. 96.
10. Ludwig Peters, *Volkslexikon Drittes Reich, die Jahre 1933-1945.*
11. Greenhous et al, *The Crucible of War*, p. 824.
12. Hoito Edoin, *The Night Tokyo Burned*, p. 26.
13. Olaf Groehler, *Geschichte des Luftkriegs*, p. 83.
14. Maximilian Czesany, *Alliierter Bombenterror*, p. 378.
15. K. H. Völker, *Die Deutsche Heimatluftverteidigung im Zweiten Weltkrieg*, p. 106.
16. David Irving, *Die Tragödie der Deutschen Luftwaffe*, p. 247.
17. Cajus Bekker, *The Luftwaffe Diaries*, p. 112.
18. BMA, Freiburg: RH12-4/v. 33.
19. Olaf Groehler, *Bombenkrieg gegen Deutschland*, p. 230.
20. Erich Hampe, *Der Zivile Luftschutz im Zweiten Weltkrieg*, p. 2ff.
21. Stadtarchiv Würzburg.
22. Olaf Groehler, *Bombenkrieg gegen Deutschland*, p. 247.
23. Ibid., p. 252.
24. AFSHRC, 187.2-52.
25. Tom Harrison, *Living through the Blitz*, p. 23.
26. Ibid., p. 24.
27. J. M. Spaight, *Bombing Vindicated*, p. 58.
28. Tom Harrison, *Living through the Blitz*, p. 36.
29. Ibid., p. 39.
30. Ibid., p. 112.
31. Ibid., p. 39.

32. S. Harvey, *The Italian War Effort and Strategic Bombing of Italy*, p. 32.
33. Robert Guillain, *I Saw Tokyo Burning*, p. 59.
34. Hoito Edoin, *The Night Tokyo Burned*, p. 27ff.
35. Ibid., p. 29.

Chapter 9: Gas in Aerial Warfare

1. Giulio Douhet, *The Command of the Air*, p. 147.
2. BMA Freiburg, RH8v.3618.
3. Werner Maser, *Der Wortbruch*, p. 8.
4. Barton J. Bernstein, "Churchill's Secret Biological Weapons," *Bulletin of Atomic Scientists*, Vol. 43, No. 1, January/February 1987, p. 47.
5. PRO: AIR 9/448.
6. PRO: AIR 9/441.
7. Olaf Groehler, *Der Bombenkrieg gegen Deutschland*, p. 332.
8. Barton J. Bernstein, *Churchill's Secret Biological Weapons*, p. 48.
9. PRO: CAB 120/292.
10. PRO: AIR 8/449.
11. Olaf Groehler, *Der Bombenkrieg gegen Deutschland*, p. 333.
12. Barton J. Bernstein, *Churchill's Secret Biological Weapons*, p. 47.
13. Ibid., p. 46.
14. PRO: AIR 24/306.
15. Barton J. Bernstein, *Churchill's Secret Biological Weapons*, p. 49.
16. AFSHRC: 119.0412-290, No. 293.
17. Glenn B. Infield, *Disaster at Bari* (New York: Macmillan Co., 1971).
18. Ibid., p. 209.
19. Ronald Schaffer, *Wings of Judgment*, p. 164.
20. William D. Leahy, *I Was There* (New York: Whittlesey House, 1950), p. 440.
21. Barton J. Bernstein, "Why We Didn't Use Gas in World War II," *American Heritage, The Magazine of History*, Vol. 36, August/September 1965, pp. 40-45.
22. Ibid., p. 44.

Chapter 10: Loss of Cultural Assets

1. John D. Skilton, *Défence de l'art Européen* (Paris: Les Éditions Internationales, 1948).
2. Stephen A. Garrett, *Ethics and Airpower in World War II* (New York: St. Martin's Press, 1993), p. IXff.

3. Stadtarchiv Würzburg, Wurfzettel Nos. 10 and 11 of May 1945
4. Heiner Reitberger, *Das alte Würzburg* (Würzburg: Richter Druck und Verlags GmbH, 1977), p. 75.
5. Erich Hampe, *Der zivile Luftschutz im Zweiten Weltkrieg*, p. 194.
6. Charles Messenger, *Bomber Harris and the Strategic Bombing Offensive 1939-1945*, p. 145.
7. Ibid.
8. PRO: AIR 20/2565.
9. Roderic Owen, *Tedder*, p. 226.
10. Ronald Schaffer, *Wings of Judgment*, p. 47.
11. Maximilian Czesany, *Alliierter Bombenterror*, p. 393.
12. Douglas Botting, *In the Ruins of the Reich* (London: Grafton Books, 1985), p. 281; Curtis E. LeMay, *Mission with LeMay*, p. 406.
13. NA: RG 331: *Report of the American Commission for the Protection and Salvage of Artistic and Historic Monuments in War Areas (ACPS)*, p. 158.
14. Ronald Schaffer, *Wings of Judgment*, p. 47.
15. NA: ACPS Report, RG 331, p. 33.
16. Otis Carey, *The Sparing of Kyoto (Mr. Stimson's Pet City)*.
17. Ronald Schaffer, *Wings of Judgment*, p. 47.

Chapter 11: Psychological Effects of Bombing

1. PRO: AIR 20/7639, Article 168.
2. Harryman Maurer, *The End Is Not Yet*, pp. 104, 111.
3. Solly Zuckerman, *From Apes to Warlords*, p. 143.
4. Ibid., p. 142.
5. Vera Brittain, "Massacre by Bombing," *Fellowship*, March 1944.
6. *BCWD*, p. 300.
7. Greenhous et al, *The Crucible of War*, p. 526.
8. Haywood A. Hansell Jr., *The Air Plan that Defeated Hitler*.
9. Allan D. English, *The Cream of the Crop* (Montreal: McGill University Press, 1996), p. 81.
10. Ibid., p. 85.
11. Ibid., p. 126.
12. Miles Tripp, *The Eighth Passenger* (McMillan London Ltd., 1978), p. 180.
13. Greenhous et al, *The Crucible of War*, p. 787.
14. John McCarthy, "Air Crew and Lack of Moral Fibre in the Second World War," *War and Society* (Australia), September 1984, p. 92.
15. Craven and Cate, *The Army Air Forces in World War II*, Vol. III, p. 307.

16. R. H. Fredette, *The First Battle of Britain*.
17. Larry J. Bidinian, *The Combined Allied Bombing Offensive against the German Civilian, 1942-1945*, p. 55ff.
18. Irving L. Janis, *Air War and Emotional Stress* (Westport, CT: Greenwood Press, 1976), p. 149.
19. Dieter W. Rockenmeier, *Als vom Himmel Feuer fiel*, p. 107.
20. Tom Harrison, *Living through the Blitz*, p. 308.
21. Ibid., p. 349.
22. Ibid., p. 316.
23. S. Harvey, *The Italian War Effort and Strategic Bombing of Italy*, pp. 32–45.

Chapter 12: The Victims and Their Treatment

1. Robert Guillain, *I Saw Tokyo Burning*, p. 62.
2. Olaf Groehler, *Der Bombenkrieg gegen Deutschland*, p. 266.
3. Ibid.
4. Olaf Groehler, *Geschichte des Luftkriegs*, p. 418.
5. Lord Russell of Liverpool, *The Scourge of the Swastika* (London: Cassell and Co. Ltd., 1954), p. 38.
6. Ibid., p. 40.
7. Olaf Groehler, *Bombenkrieg gegen Deutschland*, p.368.
8. Bayrisches Staatsarchiv, Würzburg: Sammlung Schäffer, Binder 28.
9. Ibid.
10. J. M Spaight, *Air Power and War Rights* (1947) p. 361.
11. Volkmar Kuehn, *Der Seenotdienst der Deutschen Luftwaffe 1939-1945* (Stuttgart: 1978), p. 198.
12. W. S. Churchill, *Their Finest Hour*, p. 322.
13. Maximilian Czesany, *Alliierter Bombenterror*, p. 20.
14. J. M. Spaight, *Air Power and War Rights* (1947), p. 375.
15. Tom Harrison, *Living through the Blitz*, p. 23.
16. Ibid., p. 97.
17. Olaf Groehler, *Der Bombenkrieg gegen Deutschland*, p. 44ff
18. Franz Dülk, *1883-1983: 100 Jahre Zeitungen im Hause Richter* (Würzburg: Mainpresse Richter Druck und Verlag, 1983), p. 58.
19. Olaf Groehler, *Der Bombenkrieg gegen Deutschland*, p. 260.
20. Hoito Edoin, *The Night Tokyo Burned*, p. 239.
21. *The Globe and Mail*, Toronto, 4 June 1994.
22. 20 Jahre Lastenausgleich: Ein Bericht des Bundesausgleichamtes, 1969.
23. *Der Stern*, Vol. 45, 1994, p. 244.

Chapter 13: Strategic Bombing and International Law

1. PRO: FO 881/9328.
2. H.R. Allen, *The Legacy of Lord Trenchard*, p. 54; Maximilian Czesany, *Nie wieder Krieg gegen die Zivilbevölkerung*, p. 34.
3. Karl-Heinz Völker, *Dokumente und Dokumentarfotos zur Geschichte der Deutschen Luftwaffe*, p. 467.
4. J. M. Spaight, *Bombing Vindicated*, p. 7.
5. Ibid., pp. 13, 14.
6. Eberhard Spetzler, *Luftkrieg und Menschlichkeit* (Göttingen, 1956).
7. J. M. Spaight, *Air Power and War Rights*, (1947), p. 280.
8. J. M. Spaight, *Bombing Vindicated*, p. 21.
9. Olaf Groehler, *Bombenkrieg gegen Deutschland*, p. 369.
10. Maximilian Koessler, "American War Crimes Trials in Europe," *Georgetown Law Journal*, Vol. 39, 1950/1, pp. 18–112.
11. Robert E. Connot, *Justice at Nuremberg* (New York: Carroll and Graf Publishers, 1984), p. 494.
12. J. M. Spaight, *Air Power and War Rights* (1924), p. 169.

Chapter 14: Conclusion

1. PRO: AIR 24/310.
2. PRO: AIR 14/3412 and 3422.
3. Charles Messenger, *Bomber Harris and the Strategic Bombing Offensive, 1939-1945*, p. 209ff.
4. PRO: AIR 10/3866, p. 67ff.
5. Olaf Groehler, *Geschichte des Luftkriegs*, p. 495ff.
6. H. R. Allen, *The Legacy of Lord Trenchard*, p. 117.
7. Olaf Groehler, *Geschichte des Luftkriegs*, p. 496.
8. Basil Collier, *The Defence of the United Kingdom*, Appendix L.
9. Uta Hohn, *Die Zerstörung Deutscher Städte im Zweiten Weltkrieg*, p. 51; Maximilian Czesany, *Alliierter Bombenterror*, p. 652; Hans Rumpf, *Westdeutsche Zivilverluste* (Wehrwissenschaftliche Rundschau, 1953), Heft 10.
10. Hoito Edoin, *The Night Tokyo Burned*, p. 238.
11. Charles Messenger, *Bomber Harris and the Strategic Bomber Offensive, 1939-1945*, p. 191.
12. Eugene M. Emme, *The Impact of Air Power*; p. 693.
13. Craven and Cate, *The Army Air Forces in World War II*, Vol. III, p. VI.
14. J. M. Spaight, *Air Power and War Rights* (1947), p. 230.

INDEX